SPENSER STUDIES

VIII

SPENSER STUDIES
A Renaissance Poetry Annual
VIII

EDITED BY

Patrick Cullen AND *Thomas P. Roche, Jr.*

AMS PRESS, INC.
NEW YORK, N.Y.

SPENSER STUDIES:
A RENAISSANCE POETRY ANNUAL

edited by Patrick Cullen and Thomas P. Roche, Jr.

is published annually by AMS Press, Inc. as a forum for Spenser scholarship and criticism and related Renaissance subjects. Manuscripts must be submitted *in duplicate* and be double-spaced, including notes, which should be grouped at the end and should be prepared according to the format used in this journal. All essay-length manuscripts should enclose an abstract of 100-175 words. They will be returned only if sufficient postage is enclosed (overseas contributors should enclose international reply coupons). One copy of each manuscript should be sent to Thomas P. Roche, Jr., Department of English, Princeton University, Princeton, N. J. 08544 and one copy to Patrick Cullen, 300 West 108th Street, Apt. 8 D, New York, N. Y. 10025.

ISSN 0195-9468
Volume VIII, ISBN 0-404-19208-4

Contents

The Shepheardes Calendar, Dialogue, and Periphrasis
ROLAND GREENE
1

The most immediate plot of *The Shepheardes Calender* concerns the recuperation of Colin Clout as the lyric voice of his society by the shepherds' collective
efforts. This generic plot entails a vision of lyric discourse as potentially
dialogic in several senses: within itself, between speakers in a culture, and
among its extramural contexts. Because it amounts to a critical statement
about the conditions of poetry in its time, the *Calender* has the discursive status
of a periphrasis. It does not exemplify the properties it urges for lyric, except
locally and intermittently (as in the elegy for Dido in "November"), but
surrenders some of its own efficacy in order to define the conditions of a
hypothetical discourse at odds with much of the poetry of its time. This essay
provides a brief reading of each eclogue in view of this generic plot, and offers
fresh interpretations of certain episodes—notably the fable in "Februarye,"
and the roundelay in "August"—as important to the work's periphrastic
polemic.

Spenser's "Twelve Private Morall Virtues"
ROBERT CUMMINGS
35

I propose a source in the *Corpus Hermeticum* for Spenser's characterisation and
disposition of the moral virtues in *The Faerie Queene*. To be more than trivial,
the analogy requires a reassessment of Arthur's role as Magnificence. The
second part of the paper accordingly attempts a more serious reading than is
customary of the relationship between Magnificence and Glory. The third
part offers a sketch of the six Books of *The Faerie Queene* using the Hermetic
terminology to gloss Spenser's.

Irony and the Pseudo-physical in *The Faerie Queene*
ANTHONY M. ESOLEN
61

Spenser's irony is often characterized by an inappropriate or irrelevant concentration upon the physical nature of an allegorical figure. Errour, dame
Nature and her sergeant Order, Munera the bribetaker of book five, and the
nude young ladies in the Bower of Bliss all provide examples of how Spenser
can produce irony by allowing his allegories to slide tantalizingly close to
physical reality. The result does not necessarily undermine Spenser's didactic
messages, however. Sometimes, as in the case of Nature, a too-physical
presentation of a character allows for greater provisionality and variety in
interpretation; at other times the irony arises from a Spenser's allegorical
affirmation of an action that would be impossible or immoral if performed in
our physical world. Such irony may serve any purpose, and must neither be
ignored nor taken as simply subversive of Spenser's philosophical or political
views.

Planting Words in the Soul: Spenser's Socratic Garden of Adonis
RICHARD T. NEUSE
79

The Garden of Adonis does not "solve" the problems of chastity, or of love,
posed by Book III. However, even as it subverts the idea of the mirror self and
the associated, Petrarchan idea of love as a form of image magic or bondage, it
serves to recast the idea of the self in such a way as to allow Britomart to
resolve the questions of love and chastity with which she is confronted in the
House of Busyrane. A major subtext of the Garden of Adonis is Plato's
Phaedrus, a dialogue about love and dialogue, in which, while discussing the
relative value of writing and speaking, Socrates makes a dismissive reference
to gardens of Adonis. Penetrating through the Socratic irony, Spenser "rehabilitates" these gardens and turns them into a myth of the human self or soul.
To the narcissistic and imprisoning mask/masque of selfhood that the society
of Book III takes for granted, the Garden of Adonis opposes a symbolic self
which has no fixed role or identity but instead defines and discovers itself in its
dialogical relation to other persons and to the world. During the absence of
the heroine from the narrative, the Garden represents and anticipates a crucial
moment in her spiritual evolution when she recognizes the radically symbolic
dimension of human destiny. It is by achieving this understanding that she is
able to free Amoret from the enchanter Busyrane at the climax of her quest in
Book III.

The Limitations of Friendship
MARK HEBERLE
101

Book IV has been characterized as relatively simple in its moral allegory, presenting a conventional virtue conventionally through a series of satisfying resolutions that satisfy the problematical, incomplete love quests of Book III. Like all of Spenser's books, however, the Legend of Friendship allegorizes the difficulty and imperfection of human ethical virtue rather than an achieved ideal. Spenser reminds us of the limitations of friendship through contrasting foreground and background narratives, through defining friendship as a relationship between men and women, and by establishing connections between friendship and justice, the virtue that extends his moral allegory. Friendship is fully realized only in episodes that are characterized as fictions, myths or stories that are completed within the book itself: Spenser's Squire's Tale, his analogue of the Amis and Amiloun story, and the epithalamion of the Thames and Medway. By contrast, friendships between recurrent male and female characters (Britomart and Artegall, Timias and Belphoebe, Scudamour and Amoret, Amoret and Arthur, Marinell and Florimell) are uneasy, unstable, or incomplete and represent the problem of reconciling virtue and desire in heterosexual love, Spenser's highest form of friendship. The internal and external threats to such friendship must be overcome by the rigorous exercise of justice, which both protects and politicizes love between men and women, as the relationship between Books IV and V indicates.

Home-Making in Ireland:
Virgil's Eclogue I and Book VI of
The Faerie Queene
JULIA LUPTON
119

In the *Faerie Queene*, Spenser pastoralizes the iron age Ireland of Book V into the golden world of Book VI through two interlocking versions of Virgil's Eclogue I. First, in Meliboe's tale of his trip to the city and home again, Spenser rewrites Virgil's story of exile into a narrative of return. Meliboe's construction of "home" out of distance from city and court parallels Spenser's two-fold position as a kind of exile from England and a home-making colonizer in Ireland. Second, in the story of Meliboe's murder at the hands of the Irish-like Brigants, this "lawlesse people" appears as the agent rather than the victim of dispossession; Spenser softens the tragic Virgilian fate of his character by restoring the pastoral lands to young Coridon. In both cases, Spenser resolves Virgil's painful structural contrast between "exile" and "home" into a redemptive narrative sequence of exile followed by return or repossession. In the "Argument" to Canto X, Virgilian dissonance momentarily returns, placing the poetic home-making of Mount Acidale beneath its "unheimlich" banner.

"The thing S. Paule ment by . . . the courteousness that he spake of": Religious Sources for Book VI of *The Faerie Queene*
MICHAEL TRAINER
147

The word "courtesy" is used repeatedly to name a religious virtue in texts well known to Elizabethans, most notably in sixteenth-century English translations of the Bible and of the writings of John Calvin. No critics have noticed that the word "courtesy" appears in these texts, possibly because the word essentially disappears from later, more familiar English translations. These texts provide straightforward sources that explain Spenser's use of a term that has seemed to most critics either unworthy of being in the company of "holiness" and "justice" or idiosyncratically redefined by Spenser. Moreover, they allow us to see that Book VI is based on the theology of grace that is at the center of Elizabethan Protestantism.

In sixteenth-century religious texts, courtesy is a virtue that characterizes the ideal Christian community. Since for Elizabethan Protestants the human will is utterly sinful, such a community can be built only by God's taking control and causing humans to have proper relationships. God does this through his "graces," parts of God placed inside humans, "heavenly seedes" implanted in human flesh. A courteous community grows from these seeds, in two steps: first, a group of sinners are gathered together through mutual recognition of the seeds of grace within them; second, once the community is formed, courtesy becomes the nurturing and sharing of the "fruits" that grow from those seeds of grace. Book VI is organized to show these two steps: in the first seven cantos and half of the eighth, Spenser shows knights and religious hermits and even the God of love recognizing the seeds of grace in despised persons, in savages and sinners, and thus bringing them into the community of the faithful; then, in Canto viii, Spenser turns to contrasting the ways three different communities (the Cannibals, the shepherds, and the Brigants) attempt to keep growing and share in the graces of those in their communities. Calidore's tale, running throughout the book, shows the essential difference between a secular or humanistic notion of courtesy and one based on Protestant concepts: Calidore is transformed from a person trying hard to make himself courteous into a person driven, rather against his will, to do what God intends him to do.

Although this episode of *The Faerie Queene* explicitly focuses on abuse of religion, very little consideration has previously been given to its religious implications. It is another of Spenser's many allegorized theological satires, we find, for numerous details of language and imagery have an allegorically satiric significance relating to doctrinal and other aspects of Elizabethan religious conditions. Study of the episode thus helps resolve the two fundamental current controversies about Book VI: whether it is more literal or more subtly allegorical than the preceding books, and whether Spenser's Courtesy, the titular virtue of Book VI, is secular or semi-theological. The Savages episode is indeed a complex allegory in which Courtesy has a religious application, in keeping with some medieval precedent. However, whereas religious satire in Books I to III of *The Faerie Queene* is mostly aimed at Roman Catholicism, Spenser turns to attack Protestant extremists, and especially Puritans in a broad sense, in this part of his final instalment. Hence the episode further reveals that Spenser's religious affinities were conservatively Protestant in at least his later career, for it constitutes a devastating, blackly comic rejection of the whole radical Reformation. In this way the episode is a significant expression of late Elizabethan attitudes toward nonconforming Protestants and their doctrines, besides being an unusually fine and intriguing example of both allegory and religious satire.

According to a critical "commonplace," Spenser in his late work becomes disillusioned with the humanist idealism informing his earlier poetry. Yet evidence from his last published peom, *Prothalamion*, may help us revise this view. The poem has a three-part structure: Part 1 (Stanza 1) shows the poet withdrawing from "Princes Court"; Part 2 (Stanzas 2–7) shows him "chanc-[ing] to espy" an idealized vision: a "Flocke of Nymphes" deck "two Swannes of goodly hewe" with "flowers" and "Garlands"; Part 3 (Stanzas 8–10) shows the swan procession entering "mery London," prompting him to celebrate the national ideal inspired by Essex's heroic service to Elizabeth. This peculiar three-part structure enacts the humanist ideal *The Faerie Queene* promotes: it presents a meta-allegory of the allegorical process in order to defend the poet's power to "fashion" virtuous readers. Part 1 traces the first stage: frustrated with court politics, the poet withdraws into pastoral *otium* to "ease" his "payne." Part 2 traces the second stage: through grace augmented by faith, the poet sees an imaginative vision in which he symbolically witnesses the virtuous effect of his own poetry, figured when the swans overcome their fear of marriage through inspiration from a "Lay" of wedded love sung by one of the Nymphs. Part 3 traces the third stage: inspired by the idealized vision, the poet and his readers (the swan-brides) return to actuality transformed, signaled when the "birdes" of the earlier stanzas suddenly become "brides" in the last stanza. In addition to the poem's structure, its strategy of imitation supports the humanist ideal. Allusions to the Ovidian myths of Leda and the swan, Apollo and Daphne, and Orpheus and Eurydice, and to the Virgilian myth of Venus and her swans show Spenser presenting himself as an Orphic poet serving a national ideal of wedded love. In *Prothalamion* an occasional poet does more than passively celebrate a double marriage: at the end of his career, a major poet responds to his frustration by offering a defense of allegorical love poetry in the national epic itself, and in so doing offers an *apologia* for the humanist program inspiring his peotry. *Prothalamion* functions as a defense of Spenser's career.

Spenser and Sidney at Leicester House

S. K. HENINGER, JR.

239

The Gaps and the Whites: Indeterminacy and Undecideability in the Sonnet Sequences of Sidney, Spenser, and Shakespeare

ROGER KUIN

251

The only way to write about gaps in the sonnet-sequences, and to "accomplish the plural of the text" (Barthes) is to engage oneself completely, and to dis-concert. Here, a performance of gaps attempts to make visible the undecideable, and simultaneously to question our discourse. Four kinds of gap are explored in (a) sequence: Ingarden's Gap, Iser's Gap, Derrida's Gap, and the White Gap. The sonnet-sequence is shown (not) to contain these: due perhaps to its unusual nature as a form carefully practiced but never theorized, its gaps *overflow*, in all directions. This (indefinite) article tries not to stem the flow but to cross it. The Duke of Portland's under-gardener, when a house-maid upset a vase of flowers five minutes before a dinner honoring the Queen of Rumania, arranged the blooms to follow the water-courses along the damask, and was complimented by Her Majesty.

The Duality of Romantic Spenserianism
GREG KUCICH
287

During the Romantic period, Spenser's influence and popularity reached a zenith that is unparalleled in the history of his reputation. The Romantics' enthusiasm for him has been disparaged by most twentieth-century Spenserian scholars because of its seemingly reductive and distortive celebration of his beauty to the utter exclusion of his thought. However, such a conventional idea of the Romantics' Spenser comes out of our limited focus on a small body of their most sensational responses to him, which are usually taken out of context and presented reductively as the Romantics' definitive notion of his art. A satisfactory examination of the full range of their Spenserianism—as it appeared in a voluminous amount of imitations, biographies, critical essays, casual discussions, and annotations of Spenser texts—has never been attempted. I wish to suggest, here, the important outlines such a project might take by showing how the Romantics learned to appreciate a dialectical cast of mind in Spenser, a "play of double senses," that anticipates some of our most innovative ways of approaching his peotics. By coming to recognize their tendency to find in his drama of contraries an empowering agency for their own poetics of modern experience, we may better understand the nature of his achievement and its relevance for post-Renaissance poets.

Forum
309

Index
349

Contents of Previous Volumes
361

ROLAND GREENE

The Shepheardes Calender,
Dialogue, and Periphrasis

DESPITE THE advances that have occurred in our working theories of lyric discourse since the New Critics, some questions remain continually unanswered—and are maybe all but unanswerable. One of these problems, raised years ago by the neo-Aristotelian critic Elder Olson in his essay called "The Lyric," has to do with how lyric becomes dialogic, or whether and when examples of dialogic interplay in lyric "overpass the bounds of lyric and become something else." Olson suggests that this generic shift happens "precisely when external circumstances and events cease to be mere *occasions* for individual action as purely individual action and become something prior; when the continuity of the external overrules the internal continuity of individual action and reaction; when, for example, the consequences of former actions or the working out of Nemesis or the changes of circumstance take priority over the individual."[1] In other words, as Olson sees it, lyric evaporates when individual action and reaction, utterance and response harden into a plot. Naturally, this is to provoke certain questions. What are the elements and prerogatives of a *lyric* plot? How have poets addressed the matter of dialogic lyric in practice?

In a body of critical work earlier than Olson's but more contemporary with the immediate colloquies of literary theory, M. M. Bakhtin has examined the question of when and how lyric becomes dialogic, and arrived at a similar conclusion, though from the standpoint of voice or perspective rather than that of plot. "The world of poetry," Bakhtin argues, "no matter how many contradictions and insoluble conflicts the poet develops within it, is always illuminated by one unitary and indisputable discourse. Contradictions, conflicts and doubts remain in the object, in thoughts, in living experiences—in short, in the

1

subject matter—but they do not enter into the language itself. In poetry, even discourse about doubts must be cast into a discourse that cannot be doubted."[2] And again: "The polysemy of the poetic symbol presupposes the unity of a voice with which it is identical, and it presupposes that such a voice is completely alone within its own discourse. As soon as another's voice, another's accent, the possibility of another's point of view breaks through this play of the symbol, the poetic plane is destroyed and the symbol is translated onto the plane of prose."[3] Of course where other genres are concerned, the limitations of Bakhtin's novel-centered theory are notorious. His ideas of lyric's capacities, for instance, take no account of the heterogeneous (and heterogeneric) examples of Western modernisms, while his sense of historically distant works seems to rely on an implicit, tightly-bounded canon of unambitious cases.

The *Shepheardes Calender* is an especially appropriate text through which to examine this type of question—a first-order generic problem with which lyric theory ought to be involved even as various critical strategies come and go—and to stretch the approaches of Bakhtin and Olson toward an answer. In the generic context of the lyric sequence established by Petrarch's *Rime sparse,* the *Calender* is the most prominent experiment with multivocal play in the sixteenth-century English lyric; something equivalent to its interrogation of generic borders will not be seen again until the twentieth century.[4] My interest now is not in using the *Calender* to examine Bakhtin's or Olson's ideas. Rather, I suggest that in *The Shepheardes Calender,* Spenser responds to the 1570s' version of what recent theorists still perceive as lyric's generic limitations. The *Calender* instigates against the monologic tendency of English poetry in its time, argues for dialogue; and its vision of dialogue involves not simply multivocal form such as Spenser adapts from his pastoral and satirical models, but an epistemology of composition, a politics of perspectives, and a fresh situation for the poet as an agent of collective cultural renewal.[5] "I can appropriate meaning to my own purposes only by ventriloquating others," and "My voice can mean, but only with others: at times in chorus, but at the best of times in a dialogue": with these factitious statements, Michael Holquist paraphrases the dialogic imperative in the theoretical work of Bakhtin, Roman Jakobson,

Jan Mukařovský, and others.[6] The words might as well be Spenser's. The *Calender* theorizes a kind of discourse that would be radically dialogic in these fashions, a hypothetical lyric speech that would span generational, ideological, and sectarian difference. Exactly because *The Shepheardes Calender* imagines such a discourse, it realizes for itself the job of a periphrasis: it does not—except intermittently, and with qualifications— exemplify the kind of discourse it argues for, but is a critical text describing absent conditions. Its implied understanding of lyric is cognate, in several ways, with Bakhtin's theory of the novel and other serio-comical literary genres. And while the hypothetical discourse itself is often abstract, the urge to achieve it is manifest everywhere, serving as something like the exoskeleton of the *Calender*, or the topical matter that pulls the fiction along from one eclogue to the next.

In these pages, I propose to recover at least the outline of that generic "plot" in *The Shepheardes Calender*, which has remained latent in the alternate plots proposed by A. C. Hamilton, Paul McLane, Harry Berger, Jr., and others.[7] Unlike most critical work on the *Calender*, which isolates the eclogues in order to develop particular ecclesiastical, political, or intellectual themes, this essay offers to do something highly preliminary: to read all of the eclogues for that exoskeletal continuity as a way of approaching an answer to the most fundamental questions we are likely to ask about the *Calender*. How does it work as a fiction? What are its manifest continuities from eclogue to eclogue—the protracted concerns, in other words, that would move an audience to hold out long enough to recover allegorical significances, and against which such significances must play?[8] The *Calender* has been read partially and quite deeply, sometimes by scholars who have returned to it over many years, but its criticism has proceeded as though on a tacit agreement that certain issues are to be left unaddressed—and like my original question out of lyric theory, are perhaps impossible to answer.[9] Here, then, in a clearing where two problems—one theoretical, the other interpretive—potentially intersect, it may be feasible, not to resolve anything, but to allow them to strike a fresh relation to each other.

What with the ironies of E. K.'s apparatus and the manifest organization of the *Calender*, recent critics have generally understood that the work is structured so as to generate versions of dialogue among its parts.[10] To summarize the extrafictional matter briefly—since it is beyond the scope of this paper, and has been superbly treated by others—I might say simply that everything around the fictional discourse locates the reader in a space where a type of dialogic exchange happens: between E. K.'s surmises and the poems of Immerito, between the crude woodcuts and the visually sophisticated redaction, even between rival ideas (in the "Generall Argument") of when the year ought to begin.[11] As for the fiction of the *Calender,* Patrick Cullen, and more recently Michael McCanles and Wolfgang Iser, have attended to what McCanles calls the eclogues' "continued refusal to rest conclusively in any one attitude and one perspective as irrevocably the right and true one."[12] Dialogically speaking, this is a partial, though certainly an accurate, observation of Spenser's practice in the eclogues. It might perhaps be inflected by an assimilation to what Bakhtin (through his recent translator, Caryl Emerson) calls "the serio-comical" genres of literature, where the "starting point for understanding, evaluating, and shaping reality, is the living *present,* often even the very day," and where there appears "a deliberate multi-styled and hetero-voiced" discursive practice. These genres, according to Bakhtin,

> reject the stylistic unity (or better, the single-styled nature) of the epic, the tragedy, high rhetoric, the lyric. Characteristic of these genres are a multi-toned narration, the mixing of high and low, serious and comic; they make wide use of inserted genres—letters, found manuscripts, retold dialogues, parodies on the high genres, parodically reinterpreted citations; in some of them we observe a mixing of prosaic and poetic speech, living dialects and jargons . . . are introduced, and various authorial masks make their appearance.[13]

Conceived in terms like these, Spenser's dialogism may well have begun from a young poet's apprehension of certain fatal limits in the poetry of his time, which would prompt his well-known critical reinterpretations of pastoral and other conventions and his implicit rejection of most contemporary lyric. It would naturally allow for what Iser has noticed as the series' most striking fictional property, the "telescoping of genres" that neutralize one another in particular eclogues; in as large a sense, it would tend toward the internal valorization of dialogue that characterizes the *Calender*.[14] However it might have originated, this sense of poetry's multivocal possibilities inevitably gives onto philosophical, political, and ethical positions as well: of the politics of the *Calender,* for instance, David Norbrook has recently argued that "throughout the sequence [Spenser contrasts] relationships based on power and subordination with those based on mutuality."[15] Even in local instances where, say, the political or ecclesiastical dimensions of a passage or an eclogue are seemingly uppermost, lyric's dialogic capacity to exchange perspectives—its articulation of a standpoint conceived as contemporaneous and internal to both the speaking and the auditing selves—is shown as an integral means to that mutuality. It is this unifying myth of lyric dialogue—which other critics have inevitably noticed, and remarked in their particular ways—that I am here concerned to trace and emphasize.

Perhaps as an extension more than a contradiction of the several critics who have interpreted the first eclogue, I believe that the inefficacy of Colin's song in "Januarye" is tied to a stilling of the necessary dialogue in the poetic process.[16] As Spenser introduces it here, the difficulty seems to be that Colin's art no longer transforms and transvalues his world, but is anticipated or mirrored by that world before it can be expressed. It is no matter simply that Colin is in love, as commentators sometimes assume, but that his account of love is dictated ("and now is come thy winters stormy state, / . . . All so my lustfull leafe is drye and sere" 23, 37) by external circumstances.[17] Spenser's reply to the aesthetic of Gascoigne, Googe, Turberville, and the *Mirror for Magistrates*—to the commonplace, stagnant by the late 1570s, that poetry properly reflects reality—is to insist on showing that relation gone awry in the case of a poet who has lost his referential priority to his world and has become, in fact, its object. If poetry mirrors reality, the implicit argument goes, reality may just as easily be seen as forestalling poetry. As Harry Berger has suggested, Colin's world here properly includes not only external nature but poetic convention as represented by "the countless poems in which such references and images" figure.[18] The pun at lines 19 and 20 is triple:

Thou barrein ground, whome winters wrath hath wasted,
Art made a myrrhour, to behold my plight:
1. You, ground, are made a mirror by an unspecified agent;
2. You, ground, are made a mirror by art;
3. You, ground, made a mirror of art.[19]

Though the latter alternative probably seems least natural in context, it comes closest to what we hear in memory—"art made a myrrhour," now an absolute phrase—when the first clause of 20 is carried forward as an imprecation, muttered under the poem's breath, to haunt much of the *Calender*. It is the condition described in this clause that the general context of "Januarye" argues strenuously against, the more so because it is the common property of mid-sixteenth-century aesthetic doctrine.[20]

What are the consequences of this lost authorial primacy? For Colin as subject, it means he feels himself turn from a person into a two-dimensional emblem without the possibility of development; for his governance of the sheep, it entails an abdication of leadership; for his rhetoric, it lets in paronomasia (29, 30, 61, 62) and other marks of what seems an obsessive, senseless circularity; and for his love life, it means a confusion as to whether his lack of success in getting through to Rosalind is the cause or the result of his poetic incapacity. Moreover, we are invited to understand Colin's stunted expression ultimately as a cultural blockage, like the miasma that might afflict a given society in a classical myth because some representative person has lost contact with the truth.[21] It is a pastoral fact that an insufficiency in a principal shepherd will be felt by his sheep and the other shepherds. For Spenser's purposes, this fact occasions the dialogic dimensions of both the problem and its eventual solution, for as everyone in the world of the *Calender* is affected by the contagious cultural danger of Colin's quiescence, so all the characters will contribute to his restoration. The fiction of the *Calender* tells of the struggle of a collective mind to reestablish an ideal.

It is important to emphasize how such eclogues as "Februarie," "March," and "Aprill" follow the expository task of "Januarye," for each of these opens onto the cultural extensions of Colin's paralysis. "Januarye" is shown to have social, political, and personal consequences even where Colin himself is not

in the picture. "Februarie," like the preceding eclogue, is Spenser's somewhat risky attempt at a deliberate failure, here associated with Thenot's insistence on sharing his old man's point of
view through a "tale." That word, in fact, occupies a central site
in the clash of paronomasias that occurs over the first hundred
lines of the eclogue. We see and hear young Cuddie speak up for
tailes over *tales,* for *lust* over *loss* or *lostness*—in both cases
comprehending the former word, as a complex of moral and
emotional meanings, much better than the latter—and we hear
old Thenot speak for the opposite standpoint. It is as though
this struggle is projected into "Februarie" from Colin's earlier
lapses into paronomasia, the general consequence of a particular, representative shepherd's frustration. We also recover the
respective psychic attitudes toward time that color these re-
flexes: Cuddie lives entirely in the present moment, of course,
so that tales of lostness have no value for him, while Thenot
compulsively looks out for the past and the future and lives as
lightly in the present as he can manage—or by Cuddie's values,
does not live at all. Thenot then proposes to communicate
through one of the very words that expose their differences:
"But shall I tel thee a tale of truth, / Which I cond of *Tityrus* in
my youth, / Keeping his sheepe on the hils of Kent?" (91–93).
How does a "tale" differ from lyric speech? As a vessel for
Thenot's viewpoint, this tale falls short not simply because it is
so obviously didactic but because it draws a different kind of
attention, and affords a different pleasure, than a poem does,
while the moral and emotional gulf between the young and old
shepherds here can be bridged only by something adapted to the
problem, a discourse that honors the shifts between *lust* and *lost*
as it spins out a context where they can cohabit.[22] The tale
shows Thenot's viewpoint *as* his viewpoint, rather than (pro-
visionally) as Cuddie's, a limitation which both speakers un-
consciously anticipate in the brief exchange before the tale is
spoken: to Thenot it is a tale of youth, since he heard it from
Tityrus when he was young, while to Cuddie it is colored as the
device of "that good old man." When Thenot absently replies
that it is indeed a tale of youth, their tendency to speak around
and past each other seems certain to continue indefinitely, part
of the eclogue's plan.

As for the announced model of the tale, "*Tityrus*" or Chaucer, it avails us to remember, in this fiction where frames are in

effect, the difference between the Chaucers inside and outside
the framing discourse of the *Canterbury Tales,* and to notice that
this Tityrus is introduced within Spenser's frame, which suggests perhaps the teller of "Sir Thopas" more than the author of
the *Tales* altogether or of *Troilus and Criseyde.* Thenot's tale
itself, which has always been allegorically difficult, belongs to
the honorable Renaissance genre of the badly-told or ineffectual
tale—stretching back to "Sir Thopas," and including, for instance, Sancho's ludicrous narrative in *Don Quixote* I.20—
where we are typically asked to observe a given character, who
works in an unsuitable genre, trying to articulate something
almost beyond speech. Here in the immediate context of
"Januarye," then, we are obliged to measure the distance between the failed narrative ("a long tale, and little worth" 240)
and other imaginable strategies of getting across the original
object of the exercise, the "truth." On the whole, this reading of
"Februarie" as an argumentative standoff between Cuddie and
Thenot does not differ substantially from that of, say, Patrick
Cullen, who insists that each perspective is fatally partial and in
need of the other's balance.[23] It assumes, perhaps, a rather more
dynamic idea than usual of the eclogue's aesthetic risks and
fictional stakes—for the poet as well as the unlucky community
of shepherds.

"March" represents an alternate show of consequences for
that community, in which a Thomalin can be in love without
knowing how to describe the sensation. He dwells on the
immaterial bits of his *innamoramento* story, and gives his present
situation in a comically matter-of-fact, non-Petrarchan register:

> A shaft in earnest snatched,
> And hit me running in the heele:
> For then I little smart did feele:
>   But soone it sore encreased.
> And now it rankleth more and more,
> And inwardly it festreth sore,
>   Ne wote I, how to cease it.
>   ("March" 96–102)

Concave where later eclogues are convex—that is, the months
in which a character innocent of amatory feeling quotes one of
Colin's lyrics, creating a surplus of lyric speech—"March" dis-

closes another consequence of Colin's incapacity. It is not exactly "Februarie's" principle that the shepherds in lacking a dialogic lyric model are out of conversation with each other, but that they may be unable to interrogate themselves as well. This poem, like "Februarie," largely succeeds as an inconclusive play of sounds and viewpoints. But we must recognize that both eclogues incorporate longing for a lyric speech that excludes these very poems, that while they may have "poeticall sinnewes" by comparison with much poetry of the time, they are not efficacious lyrics according to the measures they propose.

In other words, *The Shepheardes Calender* is more a statement about the conditions of contemporary poetics than a poem proper. It is a periphrasis around the conditions it proposes for the genre: here in the thick of a manifestly conversational poem, the idea of dialogic lyric is an enigma—something to be reached for, hypothesized, but seldom realized within the bounds of the *Calender* itself. Michael Riffaterre's notion of periphrasis as a semantic phenomenon in lyric has some application here, transposed out of semantics and into genre:

> The actualization of a word's descriptive system is not necessarily dependent on that word's physical presence in the sentence. On the contrary, that actualization can be even better observed if the sentence is literally the transformation of the word—if the sentence is a periphrasis. In fact, *periphrasis* is an extreme case of the overdetermination of grammatical relationships by semantic relationships: whether it is narative or descriptive, periphrasis simply develops and distributes a given throughout the syntagm. . . . [The] substitution functions as a riddle . . . [and] the riddle is perceived to exist because the reader finds himself faced with instances of ungrammaticality.[24]

In the context of the *Calender* one might even insist that periphrasis—the body of the series as we have it, with its *copie* and redundancies—follows from the overdetermination of formal and ideological elements by a generic imperative, a need to show certain discursive conditions as missing and missed.[25] It is conventional to think of the *Calender* as critically detached from its models: Berger calls it "a reading of the collective sources, the tradition, that fathered it, [that] thus provides a model of readership, or perhaps several models, for us to consider in our own readings."[26] But I would emphasize that it stands apart from that tradition's present as well, gesturing toward a poem of now or later that it cannot, or will not, be. We ought to consider how much of the polysemous substance of the *Calender* is such because it constitutes that periphrasis or detour, defining the qualities of an unavailable discourse rather than speaking of and for itself. And in any case, whether or not one goes as far as that, it is vitally important to discern where and how the *Calender* introduces expressive and interrogative ungrammaticalities, and to read these rigorously back into our historical predications about the particular eclogues and the whole.

Thenot and Hobbinol's dialogue in "Aprill" completes the triadic series begun in "Februarie," offering a quotation of Colin's lovely song that includes appeals for participation in the praising of Eliza:

> Ye dayntye Nymphs, that in this blessed Brooke
> doe bathe your brest,
> Forsake your watry bowres, and hether looke,
> at my request:
> And eke you Virgins, that on *Parnasse* dwell,
> Whence floweth *Helicon* the learned well,
> Helpe me to blaze
> Her worthy praise,
> Which in her sexe doth all excell.
>   ("April" 37–45)

It seems the quoted song is held together more by its mood—which is evenly imperative or hortatory, allowing a handful of sentences that neither implore nor command participation in the lay—than by its object.[27] E. K.'s insistence on the song's verisimilitude ("what is moste comely for the meannesse of a shepheards witte, or to conceiue, or to vtter") goes halfway toward suggesting that Eliza is the sort of convenient object to justify such strenuous participatory motions in lyric. In fact, as an ideal poetic mistress, she is exactly the right object to show the former conditions of Colin's song when "nature was completely poetized": expressive of his feeling, transformative of the world, transitive to other circumstances, and usable by his shepherd society.[28] The song, of course, sorts poorly with the present conditions of the shepherds' world—as one commentator remarks, it is ludicrous now for the lovesick Colin to be recalled celebrating virginity—but such is the best this crowd of nostalgic poetasters can manage.[29]

Hobbinol's prefatory remarks corroborate Colin's block as we saw it in the first eclogue: "once he made" this lay and "tuned it vnto the Waters fall," reconstituting the natural music of his setting into an artifact of his device, but "nowe fayre *Rosalind* hath bredde hys smart, / So now his frend is chaunged for a frenne" (35–36, 27–28). To lose that referential and expressive priority over the natural world (as Colin has now, for presumably the waters anticipate his song and he can merely echo it back to them) is not only to lapse into an emotional and moral chaos, where sounds disengage from meanings and friends might as well be (to quote E. K.'s gloss on "frenne") "forenne." It is to deprive the shepherds of mastery over their feelings, collective and individual—to threaten the cultural applicability of poetry at its stock—and thus to strike at the unity of that culture, especially when it is portrayed as naturally unanimous and songful. Under this miasma, the shepherds interact in the fashions that the representative episodes "Februarie" through "Aprill" give us: they reach out tentatively, they misconstrue each other and themselves, they quote longingly from the time when Colin's music worked. In the case of "Aprill," I believe, the emblem and its gloss tell us how to read the eclogue's main business, namely the quotation of an efficacious lyric. On hearing Hobbinol's appropriation of Colin, Thenot experiences a surplus of personal feeling for which no template is available except a half-banal classical tag (he "being otherwise vnhable, then by soddein silence, to expresse the worthinesse of his conceipt"). Whether Spenser means to call attention to the matter of substitution here—that is, Hobbinol's incomplete standing-in for Colin, and vice versa—by having E. K. erroneously substitute Hobbinol for Thenot in the gloss, must be an open question, while the more radical problem of whether text or gloss might be correct is properly moot: in this world everyone can stand in for nearly everyone else, which underscores the urgency of their having no master-poet on whom to depend. The stilling of Colin represents the "silence" of those songs by which the shepherds apprehended and shared their emotions, or by which those of different experience (say, Cuddie and Thenot) understood each other, while the successive eclogues through "Aprill" offer dialogue's gross form without the achievement of a properly dialogic discourse.

In this range of episodes, moreover, we see notions like that of Olson, with its assumption that lyric is necessarily "individual" and "internal," severely tested, as though by a poet who wanted to question and pry open these categories in the most uncompromising kind of practice. Some of the most distinctive and perplexing features of the *Calender,* in fact, can be explained in part as belonging to this experimental impulse. The frequent stand-ins for and quotations of one speaker by another, for instance, a chain of reported speeches leading to E. K.'s startling behind-the-scenes gloss in "October":

> I doubt whether by Cuddie be specified the authour selfe, or some other. For in the eyght Aeglogue the same person was brought in, singing a Cantion of Colins making, as he sayth. So that some doubt, that the persons be different.

What is this, from the standpoint of generic invention, but Spenser's undermining of the criterion of lyric individuality?[30] And the elaborate framing devices that have been so persuasively treated by McCanles and others: what are these, again from the vantage of lyric experiment, but a radical attempt to change our ideas of what is "inner" and "outer" in this world, setting the boundaries of the "inner" in such a place that they will circumscribe the collective mind of this pastoral community as it works off its miasma? Olson is therefore a spokesman in our own idiom for the kinds of generic restrictions that Spenser interrogates, while Bakhtin—making a more stringent account of lyric itself—affords a sight of the dialogic standard to which the poet proposes to hold lyric poems. It is useless to push for more, to say (for example) that the *Calender* is actually a fully dialogic lyric in the sense in which Bakhtin reserves that condition for the novel. Bakhtin's shrewdly constructed theory of the novel is in fact conceived more as a fiction than an argument: if we accept its opening premise, which erases the category of narrative so as to set epic and novel into action as competing, mutually illuminating entities, then everything else it tells us inevitably follows.[31] It is better, I think to propose that the *Calender,* instead of standing in some kind of exemplary relation to Bakhtin's theory, exists in parallel to it, says something equally specious but equally compelling in its alternative vision of lyric's power against the insufficiency or bankruptcy of other kinds of speech. The eclogues "Maye" through "August" belong to what might be called the middle episode in the plot of the *Calender.* In these segments the distinctions of sect, class, and occupation among the characters are more acutely drawn than before; the superficially dialogic form is put away in favor of speech-blocs that more vividly enclose their speakers' ideologies; and the poetry, accordingly, becomes more removable and removed from the experience of the community, even more a concrete object for public comment apart from its hypothetical purpose of culture-binding and communication. The ecclesiastical polemics of "Maye" and "Iulye," in fact, are not so much interruptions in the fiction as stipulations in the theory of the *Calender:* as sectarian difference in Spenser's world corresponded to class difference in Bakhtin's—served, in other words, as the empirical boundary with the keenest edges, and the greatest possibility of exposing discordant ideologies, after the phenomenological divide between individuals—so on this middle ground of the sequence, the incommunicability of passion and conviction is emphasized by association with the principal intellectual and spiritual parting of the age.[32] Both "Maye" and "Iulye" represent new parables of the dysphasic problem that has only expanded its dimensions since Colin's original, paradigmatic failure in "Januarye": as Berger has it, "[the] moral eclogues are mainly about the inadequacy of the artless to verbalize or clearly reflect on the problems of the great world . . . These eclogues argue the ethical function of poetic skill."[33]

In "Maye," the depreciation of dialogue as a medium of communication between well-articulated standpoints is especially evident. The speeches of Piers and Palinode are longer, more sententious and self-involved than those of, say, Cuddie and Thenot in "Februarie"; and their remarks to each other not only (as usual) miss the mark substantively and undo the potential efficacy of this dialogue, but call into question the premise of dialogue itself:

But of all burdens, that a man can beare,
Moste is, a fooles talke to beare and to heare.
I wene the Geaunt has not such a weight,
That beares on his shoulders the heauens height.
(Palinode 140–143)

Shepheard, I list none accordaunce make
With shepheard, that does the right way forsake.
(Piers 164–165)

Truly *Piers,* thou art beside thy wit,
Furthest fro the marke, weening it to hit . . .
(Palinode 306–307)

The main business of the eclogue, of course, is another tale "like
to that in Aesops fables," but this one, of the fox and the kid,
plainly builds on the inaptness of other failed exempla in the
Calender while it raises the stakes of such missed opportunities.
According to E. K., the fable of the fox and the kid represents
the dangers posed by "false and faithlesse Papistes" to "faythfull
and true Christians"; behind his comment is the Anglican idea
that that sect stands for the old and true church, while the
church of Rome represents a deviation from traditional values—
in other words, that the new is really old and the old new. But
Palinode obviously misses the lesson of the tale, at least as it
involves his own role as a "fond" shepherd who stands in for
Roman Catholics: he identifies with the kid, and even proposes
to lend the tale for use as a Sunday sermon by a high-church or
Catholic priest, "our sir Iohn" (308–310). The tale's failure
within the eclogue is a matter of worldmaking, having to do
with the fable's lack of a mooring to relatively stable structures
of identity and ideology in the world occupied avidly by Palinode and scornfully by Piers.[34] To say, as Piers does, "Ah
Palinodie, thou art a worldes childe" (73), is more than to
condemn the lusty shepherd as "worldly," it is to admit the
terms on which a fictional appeal to Palinode's erected wit may
succeed. Such a fiction must allow Palinode to mediate between
his world and the one it posits, locate him in a determinate role
within its world, and (in this case) enforce his self-identification
with the fox. How else will he recognize and fulfill the stated
purpose of Piers's anecdote?[35]

Shepheard, I list none accordaunce make
With shepheard, that does the right way forsake.
And of the twaine, if choice were to me,
Had leuer my foe, then my freend he be.
For what concord han light and darke sam?
Or what peace has the Lion with the Lambe?
Such faitors, when their false hearts bene hidde,
Will doe, as did the Foxe by the Kidde.
                                              (164–171)

As it happens, Piers's fable, practically free of ideological link-
ages to the real world, gives Palinode free play to select an
identity out of it, and he chooses the kid. Of course E. K.'s
commentary delicately suggests that even in the real world of
contemporary religious politics, competing individuals and
sects may appropriate roles for themselves as though out of
such unanchored fables: so both Anglicans and Roman Catholics claim the identity of the older church, everyone wanting to
be the kid. Piers' failed fable perhaps only exaggerates a problem of worldmaking that existed in Spenser's world itself. In
any case, Palinode's determination to use the fable in Catholic
settings indicates that the two positions will only grow farther
apart, as each standpoint accepts the role of kid while hardening
its wariness of its particular foxes; they cannot interpenetrate
and criticize each other as long as they cast themselves in these
self-flattering roles and rehearse this single, reinforcing anecdote.[36]

"Maye" participates, of course, in the commentary on the
epistemology of both poetry and religion that was begun in
"Januarye" with its notable censure of the mirror as a standard.
Just as Colin's expression was hindered by a too-exact relation
to its empirical models, blurring the issues of originality and
priority, so in "Maye" Piers means to show that the mirror is an
instrument of self-glorification that can easily give way to self-
loss. That lesson is clear enough. But the fable also enacts what
it denounces: just as the fox's reflectory trick leads to the disappearance of the subject, so the fable's easy admittance and
loose specification suffers both the teller and the auditor to see
themselves in it, illusorily, and thus to evade responsibility for
their relative positions. Palinode will never take account of his

and his fellows' correspondence with the fox, nor will Piers
have to answer for the complex attitude toward Christian love
implied in the kid's destiny. Once again art has been "made a
myrrhour," and again the capacity of subjects like Colin, Piers,
and Palinode to master their moral and aesthetic situations—to
see their way out of present circumstances, to criticize their own
standpoints—has been compromised. In that instant of its plot
where the fox "popt [the kid] in, and his basket did latch" (291),
"Maye" actually plays over the central dilemma of the *Calender,*
Colin's disappearance from the middle eclogues, and explains it
as a type of kidnapping by stale aesthetic and religious ideals. The
eclogue revivifies the broad-based social implications of the poet's
failure in the fact that everyone wishes to jump into the basket
after him, to identify with the silenced and stolen subject.

   "Iulye," as I have suggested, offers a still more schematic and
inconclusive encounter between standpoints: the idea itself is
now literalized by the sites, either high or low, on which
characters stand to maintain their convictions. One of the values
that "Maye" and "Iulye" implicitly hold in common, I think, is
their postulation of a kind of discourse that could exist in both
Piers's and Palinode's worlds, that could bring Morrell down
from his hill to join the shepherds, that could work across the
divides of age, sect, and ideology to reunify this culture. It still
seems certain that the hypothetical discourse in question, associated since "Januarye" with Colin's lost expression and defined
by its absence, would largely resemble what today we call lyric.
It is a discourse that lies just beyond the circumscription of the
Calender, the fondly remembered and eagerly anticipated dialogic speech-that-they-do-not-now-have. As its abeyance
seems more difficult in the tensions and irresolutions of these
middle episodes, this unrealized discourse becomes more capital
to these shepherds' thoughts: they come to hypostatize it as a
kind of place where certain properties may be realized. It is
invoked, one might say, as a pastoral within the general pastoral
landscape of the *Calender,* a particularly ideal "here." Hence
Hobbinol's bluffing seduction:

Hobbinol
Lo *Colin,* here the place, whose pleasaunt syte
From other shades hath weand my wandring mynde.
Tell me, what wants me here, to worke delyte? . . .

Colin

O happy *Hobbinol,* I blesse thy state,
That Paradise hast found, whych *Adam* lost.
Here wander may thy flock early or late,
Withouten dreade of Wolues to bene ytost:
Thy louely layes here mayst thou freely boste.
But I vnhappy man, whom cruell fate,
And angry gods pursue from coste to coste,
Can nowhere fynd, to shroude my lucklesse pate.
                                        ("Iune" 1–3, 9–16)

To attract a Palinode, a Cuddie, a Morrell "here" would be to
see them abandon their inaccessible positions and join a participatory enterprise; to entice Colin "here" would be to reinstall
the common voice of these shepherds and so to cancel the curse
of isolation and divergence. These middle eclogues, then,
gather a new imaginative force behind the idea of a dialogic
speech; it becomes the fiction within the fiction that central
speakers such as Hobbinol passionately believe in as they exert
themselves to turn their pastoral universe inside out, to claim
title to this once-and-future dialogic world as their home here
and now. The starkness of the middle episode's monologic
crisis, and the force of its characters' desires for something else,
clear a space for the reinvention of a dialogic lyric discourse
within the *Calender.*

An awareness of commonweal and role-playing in the *Calender* can lead us to a climax along the axis of continuity I have
been following: "August." For here Willy and Perigot, two
more or less *ad hoc* figures, perform an act of renewal that lays
bare the making of a dialogic lyric without exactly being one
itself. Their two voices start from a single point,

> *Perigot.* It fell vpon a holly eue,
> *Willye.*   hey ho hollidaye,
> *Perigot.* When holly fathers wont to shrieue:
> *Willye.*   now gynneth this roundelay.
>   (53–56)

pull apart, concretizing such lyric elements as irony, glossolalia,
and closure and exposing the cohabitation of alternate "seman-

tic and axiological belief systems" (in Bakhtin's abbreviated term, "languages") within this concrete poem,

> *Perigot.* All as the Sunnye beame so bright,
> *Willye.*   hey ho the Sunne beame,
> *Perigot.* Glaunceth from *Phoebus* face forthright,
> *Willye.*   so loue into thy hart did streame:
> *Perigot.* Or as the thonder cleaues the cloudes,
> *Willye.*   hey ho the Thonder,
> *Perigot.* Wherein the lightsome leuin shroudes,
> *Willye.*   so cleaues thy soule a sonder:
> *Perigot.* Or as Dame *Cynthias* siluer raye
> *Willye.*   hey ho the Moonelight,
> *Perigot.* Vpon the glyttering waue doth playe:
> *Willye.*   such play is a pitteous plight.
> *Perigot.* The glaunce into my heart did glide,
> *Willye.*   hey ho the glyder,
> *Perigot.* Therewith my soule was sharply gryde,
> *Willye.*   such woundes soon wexen wider.
> *Perigot.* Hasting to raunch the arrow out,
> *Willye.*   hey ho *Perigot.*
> *Perigot.* I left the head in my hart roote:
> *Willye.*   it was a desperate shot.
> *Perigot.* There it ranckleth ay more and more,
> *Willye.*   hey ho the arrowe,
> *Perigot.* Ne can I find salue for my sore:
> *Willye.*   loue is a cureless sorrowe.
>
>   (81–104)

then come together in the end ("our roundelay" 124). The participatory lyric is the second version of Colin's lay to Eliza in "Aprill," its two voices actually "help[ing] to blaze" where the earlier poem hollowly implored dialogic collaboration. As Cullen observes, "Willye's B-lines are for the most part a mock-earnest extension of an idea, image, or sentiment found in Perigot's preceding lines. . . . [frequently] carrying Perigot's lofty seriousness one step further to absurdity"—the absurdity or irony, I might add, that self-interrogating lyrics must find in themselves.[37] Willye speaks for the designed pleasures of form and sound as well as an ambivalence of attitude: he speaks the motions that surround and finish the poem ("now [it] endeth"

124), and sings out as quasi-verbal music what in a Colin-like lyric would be integrated with the sense or poured into a refrain. The roundelay is hardly what commentators often hear, a self-cancelling exchange that marks time until the more "weighty and tragic" sections of the eclogue and the Calender return.[38] Though decomposed and examined, it is a blueprint for what the shepherds have been awaiting since "Januarye," a fully dialogic lyric. Like most concrete poetry, it surrenders something of its own status as a lyric in order to expose the processes by which poems are made. It is therefore an aggravated version of the Calender itself, namely a critical poem that takes its stand apart from contemporary practice in order to disclose the unexamined limits of that practice.[39]

The concreteness of the Calender has often been a submerged theme in criticism: despite avowals of the work's materiality by readers as different as Jonathan Goldberg and John King, no one, as far as I know, has integrated that fact with a reading of the fiction.[40] Any reader ought to acknowledge the value of concreteness in what McCanles (following Michel Foucault) calls the "monumentality" of the Calender, but I would urge that we read it back into the "documentary" fiction as well, as part of the regenerative motion that leads away from the stasis of "Januarye." After "Maye," where the hypothetical dialogic poem begins to occupy the status of a supposed world within the larger universe of pastoral fiction, the materiality or concreteness of language flares out of prior hints—the paronomasias, the anagrammatic "Algrind" for "Grindal," the independent materiality of "art made a myrrhour" as an absolute phrase—and clears the epistemological ground for a fully realized material poem such as the roundelay to become, literally, that "here," qualifying the immediate relevance of "Januarye" and directing the way to a new efficacy.

Within the fiction, the roundelay's result is immediate: a sestina of Colin's, quoted by Cuddie, that is probably the first really successful quoted-and-inset lyric in the Calender. The sestina may be tuned to "a deeper pulse in the rhythm of things" than the preceding poem, but it is unmistakably enabled by the roundelay because it is built on a fresh awareness of how lyric becomes dialogic.[41] Its end-words, including "resound," "part," and "augment," indicate the sestina's obsessive concern with its own making. Like the lay to Eliza, it exerts a strong effort to pull completing voices out of itself, but the tone is different: less frantic over the poem's monologism, less vulnerable in its exhortations, more authoritative:

> Let all that sweete is, voyd: and all that may augment
> My doole, drawe neare. More meete to wayle my
>   woe,
> Bene the wild woddes my sorrowes to resound,
> Then bedde, or bowre, both which I fill with cryes,
> When I them see so waist, and fynd no part
> Of pleasure past.
>
>   (164–169)

Most crucial to the shepherd world's recuperation, the sestina enacts from its first line the poet's struggle for priority over his matter and his setting—for referential and figurative command—and, after the turn of line 169, demonstrates how such a poet may find his way out of the echo chamber:

> Here will I dwell apart
> In gastfull groue therefore, till my last sleepe
> Doe close mine eyes: so shall I not augment
> With sight of such a chaunge my restlesse woe:
> Helpe me, ye banefull byrds, whose shrieking
>   sound
> Ys signe of dreery death, my deadly cryes
> Most ruthfully to tune. And as my cryes
> (Which of my woe cannot bewray least part)
> You heare all night, when nature craueth sleepe,
> Increase, so let your yrksome yells augment.
> Thus all the night in plaints, the daye in woe
> I vowed haue to wayst, till safe and sound
> She home returne, whose voyces siluer sound
> To cheerefull songs can chaunge my cherelesse cryes.
>
>   (169–182)

In the verses preceding this passage, the matter of the speaker's "woe" is adduced almost by obligation or rote. The real topic of the sestina, we are sure, is that speaker's efficacy as an instigating collective voice. The emotional situation he describes in terms of his own experience fairly represents that of the shepherd society at large: that is, he laments that a mounting surplus of "woe" has gone unspent by his cries, and proposes to invert that eonomy while hearing the cries themselves "aug-ment[ed]," and a general woe dispelled, by a chorus of others. Accordingly, these lines propose a retreat into isolation and deprivation, where the speaker can begin to redress that lyric imbalance and to see his and the culture's stalemates break down. In retirement, where experience does not accumulate ("Were not better, to shunne the scortching heate?," Willye proposed before the concrete roundelay), poetry can perhaps regain authority. "August," then, may be construed as a bend in the process of the *Calender* ("How I admire ech turning of thy verse," Perigot says), its stand-in participants as achieving the most effective act of renewal to this point in the fiction. For Cuddie to "rehearse" the lay out of the repertory of Colin's extant material comes over as a momentary alignment—of a Colin-figure with an entirely apposite song—that allows all concerned to see the prospect of a way out.

"September" has generally been seen, in William Nelson's words, as "more obscure—or more confused—than the other eclogues of [the moral] group."[42] If this cloudy characterization is accurate, perhaps the eclogue confuses because it interjects new crisis into the ameliorating, post-"August" sequence. In its emphasis on matters of "plentye" and "penuree," it sets poten-tial limits around the sestina's interest in augmentation or in-crease. Such interest, it is suggested, can be misdirected, and this caution's relevance to poetry appears in the return of the pun of "Januarye" 20:

> Ah fon, now by thy losse art taught,
> That seeldome chaunge the better brought.
> Content who liues with tryed state,
> Neede feare no chaunge of frowning fate:
> But who will seeke for vnknowne gayne,
> Oft liues by losse, and leaues with payne.
>   (68–73)

But the more obvious crisis of "September" has to do with the return of the traveler Diggon Davie from a foreign place. What he has seen there of human vice has great pertinence to the shepherds' situation in his native setting, and he is eager to tell it. But how? In the two long speeches that begin with lines 73 and 104,

> Then playnely to speake of shepheards most what,
> Badde is the best (this english is flatt.)

we hear Diggon caught in utterances that are either too "dirke" or too "plaine." Once again an eclogue presupposes a kind of speech that both involves the speaker's perfect mastery over his figures and enables the auditor's understanding of his relation to larger, transpersonal realities; a subjective speech, variable as to the person that might fulfill the role of subject, that nonetheless treats the objective world in some of its political, moral, and economic complications. Here in "September," following on the other so-called moral eclogues, the *Calender* perhaps comes nearest to dramatizing the lack of a discourse that would respond to ideological difference as tractably as the novel does in Bakhtin's theory or the romance in Fredric Jameson's.[43] The need for such a speech in "September" is first observed in Diggon's difficulty at relating his traveler's tale in a morally comprehensible fashion. Try as he does, he finds that the confessional element ("I was so fonde") pulls apart from the indictment of others, making it impossible for Hobbinol to assess Diggon's conduct in its social context (68–73); that to his auditor's confusion, the "dirke" and the "plaine" are uncompromisingly separated out (102–103, 136); and that his cautionary account is so uninvolving that Hobbinol can stick on a quibble over literalness where the figurative meaning ought to be the urgent, immediate one:

> Fye on thee Diggon, and all thy foule leasing,
> Well is knowne that sith the Saxon king,
> Neuer was Woolfe seene many nor some,
> Nor in all Kent, nor in Christendome:
> But the fewer Woolues (the soth to sayne,)
> The more bene the Foxes that here remaine.
> (150–155)

Perhaps the most striking indication of the community's expressive default is Diggon's anecdote of Roffy, which— though unacknowledged as such by the characters of "September" and by Spenser's critics—amounts to a recapitulation of the shepherds' general trouble. Of course the parable is chiefly concerned with the issues of prelacy that have surfaced in earlier episodes of the *Calender,* and probably is meant to celebrate the watch kept over his faithful by Bishop John Young of Rochester.[44] But in counter-measure to the many contemporary poets who managed to implicate the political in the personal, the distant in the immediate, or the controversial in the consensual, Spenser has this anecdote retell Colin's complaint of "Januarye" from an episcopal standpoint, assimilating this work's self-defined generic plot—which started from the local, personal costs of incommunicability, and only gradually moved out to the cultural extensions of_that fact—into a wider, more polemical context. Roffy's difficulties with a wolf that mimics animal and human voices restate Colin's relation to his surroundings in "Januarye" and thereafter, where the "barrein ground" as mirror anticipates the poet's expression, cancelling, in effect, its referentiality and its necessity. Here in "September," Roffy's authority is tangled by this prefiguring imitation. His only (negligible) advantage is the dog, "Lowder," whose name of course suggests the limits of the shepherd's and poet's capacity to make himself heard over the din of anticipations. Climactically, Hobbinol's wide-eyed question ("If sike bene Wolues, as thou hast told, / How mought we Diggon, hem be-hold," 228–229) discloses a double blindness on the parts of this most representative shepherd and his society: not only is this the same question they have been unable to answer since "Januarye," but Hobbinol seems unable, even now, to recognize it as such. Pastoral history repeats itself—perhaps instructively for our redoubled apprehension of the issues at play, but unfortunately for the shepherds themselves and their elder statesman, who must have their predicament analyzed for them by the fortune-seeker Diggon, as remote and extraneous a character as the *Calender* ever shows.

The series from "October" to "December" brings us, at last, from the former eclogue's further stand-in explorations of the community's bane, to the latter's implied resolution of that long-running problem. "October," I believe, is about as ironic as "Februarie." Two shepherds rehearse a debate about the contemporary state of poetry that must have had an especially parodic ring in the later 1570s, when this topic was under serious, continual discussion by real poets. Neither speaker quite approaches a position that could be identified with that of the work itself. Cuddie is the less cogent, but he astutely sees both the material causes of national and epideictic poetry in patronage, and the indifference of present-day patrons; he remarks that Colin's poetry might be suited for "so large a flight" if he were not distracted by love. Piers, whom we know from "Maye" as a sane but hardly unanswerable critic, insists that what Cuddie sees as the site of blockage is really the source of Colin's power:

Pires
Ah fon, for loue does teach him climbe so hie,
And lyftes him vp out of the loathsome myre:
Such immortall mirrhor, as he doth admire,
Would rayse ones mynd aboue the starry skie.
And cause a caytiue corage to aspire,
For lofty loue doth loath a lowly eye.

Cuddie
All otherwise the state of Poet stands,
For lordly loue is such a Tyranne fell:
That where he rules, all power he doth expell.
The vaunted verse a vacant head demaundes,
Ne wont with crabbed care the Muses dwell.
Vnwisely weaues, that takes two webbes in hand.
(91–102)

Piers's eloquent burst is half-true. Colin's love does in fact account for his purpose and interest as a poet, but the question of efficacy still remains open: how can he gain a predicative power over love, which now lifts and teaches him? How can he become the subject to love as object? The incompleteness of Piers's position is thrown into view where he extols the "immortall mirrhor" of Colin's object, Beauty, for if anyone in the *Calender* should know the liabilities of mirror-gazing, it is the teller of "Maye's" fable of the fox and the kid. If Rosalind's beauty is a Platonic mirror, if Colin's art mirrors that, and if his landscape (as in "Januarye") reflects his emotions as well, one can understand something of the shepherd-poet's stranding in a house of mirrors. Cuddie's answer is more firmly grounded in the current reality of the shepherds' situation—that love has manifestly taken Colin's power—but proceeds to an equally ironic conclusion, that poetry ought to have chemical inspiration and is properly about nothing ("a vacant head demaundes") in the artist's life.

The work's own answer, I guess, emerges from the play of these perspectives. The *Calender* here holds to its announced departure from a poetics that would have fiction dependent on its external surroundings—that would lament the fact that there are no more Troys, knights, or jousts—as well as from the complementary view that would see it as the outpourings of a supercharged mind. The argument that "October" implicitly quits for us to occupy, and that is most consonant with the rest of the eclogues, is that poetry is produced out of a dialogic experience between poet and world: a relation neither strictly imitative, since that is no tribute to a beauty which is itself a mirror of higher perfections, nor utterly independent. Like the eclogues before it, "October" plays out a failure of dialogic exchange in order to introduce the conditions of such an exchange by their absence, their tantalization even within the evident form of dialogue. What separates "October" from the rest is that here dialogue's requisites are brought to light while the two shepherds and their readers are arguing the topic of poetry's origins, elements, and functions. Where the disparity between an implied poem, the material *Calender*, and an explicit debate over poetics is most stark, it should be quite clear that the entire work has been, and is, a periphrasis around a hypothetically dialogic discourse. The question from this eclogue that every reader hears in memory ("O pierlesse Poesye, where is then thy place?" [79]) contains its own answer, in the "place" occupied by the question itself: between interlocutors, or as though between interlocutors, in the space where alternate standpoints meet and criticize one another.[45]

As most commentators have assumed, Colin's elegy for Dido in "November" breaks through that periphrasis to achieve distinction against the background of the *Calender*; in the terms for efficacy implicitly prescribed across the other eclogues, it works. How? If the condition of "Januarie" was defined by a relation of posteriority or belatedness that intervened between the poet and his setting—that made his lyric speech redundant— "November" conserves that relation but puts it entirely under

Colin's control. His song is now not subsequent to something in the world, but is made subsequent to itself by Colin's regular turning back over his words. It finds an elegiac distance within itself. The result is of course to engage Colin's song with itself, to make it self-interrogating or dialogic, in exactly the way that "Januarye" was not, that "Aprill" tried to be, that "August" was dismantled to exemplify. The difference in the shepherd-poet's control might be measured in obviously congruent moments from the first and eleventh eclogues:

> I loue thilke lass (alas why do I loue?)
> And am forlorne (alas why am I lorne?)
> She deignes not my good will, but doth reproue,
> And of my rurall musick holdeth scorne.
>   ("Januarye" 61–64)

> Why do we longer liue, (ah why liue we so long)
> Whose better dayes death hath shut vp in woe?
> The fayrest floure our gyrlond all emong,
> Is faded quite and into dust egoe. . . .

> She while she was, (that was, a woful word to sayne)
> For beauties prayse and plesaunce had no pere:
> So well she couth the shepherds entertayne,
> With cakes and cracknells and such country chere.
>   ("November" 73–76, 93–96)

In the first instance, an accidental paronomasia gives onto shock and despair and the speech stops on its way—as though Colin becomes instantly aware of the materiality, and through it the referential unreliability, of his medium; but in the latter cases he examines, revises, and ironizes himself, always able to turn the materiality of his discourse to the deliberate purposes of his lament. What falls out as chiasmus in "Januarye" is disposed into epanorthosis (in the Greek, a "putting straight") in the song of Dido. E. K. sees an epanorthosis in both passages, which not only is wrong—for "Januarye" 61 and 62 do not correct themselves, they hear something new, a bigger and even more daunting question, in their own language—but misses the mutually convolving and unravelling effects of rhetoric, sense, and emotion. The paronomasia of "Januarye" exemplifies a poet-lover who is caught in "art made a mirror" and whose speech in turn reflects and supports his condition, while "November" represents escape from that deauthorizing, bottomless gaze. "November," in fact, marks a return of efficacy and deliberateness as certain as the difference between the two breakings of Colin's pipe, the one ("Januarye" 67–72) an act of passion, the other ("November" 71) a calculated histrionic gesture.

Why does Colin's efficacy return? Some of the answer is collective and cultural: the explorations of dialogic speech by pairs such as Cuddie and Thenot, the revivals and rehearsals of Colin's lyrics by surrogates, and the ritualized anatomy of lyric by Willy and Perigot all work to rediscover the values of an equivocal, self-examining discourse and to make a habitable climate for it. Colin's problems have always been everyone's, as I have said, and everyone can give something toward resolving them. The eclogue's logic sees Colin move in from the outskirts of the mourning community ("waile ye" / "waile we" 64–65) toward the subject-position, which he will not really occupy ("Als *Colin Cloute* she would not once disdayne" 101) but tries on, in effect, for an emotional fit. Likely important as a last-minute cause of Colin's renewed skill, however, is Thenot's rusticized offer of patronage. In its way this too is a version of dialogue between the poet and his setting, and Spenser is probably eager to see it not overlooked when we reconstitute the poet's best world and the conditions of a poetry disposed to engage with it. The enactment of exchange in patronage, in fact, materially embodies the paradigm of how art is *not* made a mirror. The gift incites or interrupts Colin's (overly) mimetic process and introduces fresh considerations for the poet to negotiate: "He must, on the one hand, be able to disengage from the work and think of it as a commodity. He must be able to reckon its value in terms of current fashions, know what the market will bear, demand fair value, and part with the work when someone pays the price. And he must, on the other hand, be able to forget all that and turn to serve his gifts on their own terms."[46] Thenot's patronage instigates Colin's first participation in a reciprocal process that actually produces a poem; its practical tit-for-tat seems a hard-headed, slightly ironic recognition that earlier visions in the *Calender* of poetry's origins gave less than the whole picture, and perhaps that the patronage of

Spenser's day is hardly as regenerating, as dialogically provoking, as this eclogue's stripped-down model.

The final eclogue is comforting in the breadth of its closural motions—it sums up the entire series and explains, for instance, what Colin was doing while offstage for most of the *Calender*— as well as unsettling in its dismissal of the eclogues that precede it. For if most of the *Calender* is a periphrasis on lyric's possibilities, "December" shows their attainment in an exquisitely fashioned song that is introduced by a perfunctory frame (1–6) but followed by nothing: with Spenser we presumably emerge out of the special retirement of the *Calender* to rejoin the literary process of the age, our assumptions about all the dimensions of lyric speech having been bracingly examined. Retrospectively, Colin's story has the moral and emotional mordancy of other contemporary (especially Ovidian and Petrarchan) myths of the artist's fate. Like other celebrated poet-figures, Colin must give up much of his happiness as a man in order to achieve, or reachieve, cogency as an artist; but unlike other such sixteenth-century antitypes whose myths are not coextensive with the works they inhabit, Colin's regaining of poetic power is closely linked with the seasonal rhythm of the *Calender*, so that his eventual mastery, shown here and now in the internal song of "December," is outweighed pathetically by his hastening end. But those readings that see the *Calender* as Colin's journey, or his artistic success or failure as central, miss the most prominent stroke of Spenser's periphrastic experiment: that Colin is not the protagonist of the *Calender,* but the instrument on which its continuing quarrel with lyric individuality and monologism is made to register. Spenser takes apart Colin's protagonism, and distributes his song, in order to realize his argument about lyric's process and place, its intrinsic and extramural dialogues. When he reassembles the shepherd-poet and gives him efficacy again, it is simply to close down the lyric plot of the *Calender*—to show, however fleetingly, the results of dialogue achieved—without allowing Colin any import in his own right as man or artist.[47]

The Shepheardes Calender, then, argues periphrastically for a fresh orientation for lyric discourse, offering models of how dialogue might enter and reconstitute lyric's relations with its culture, the transhistorical dynamic between specimens of the genre, and lyric utterances themselves. Probably coming into existence from Spenser's sensation of contemporary poetic crisis, the *Calender* shows an impasse in the world of poetry, and settles it with poetry—all the while gesturing away from itself, for it is neither the problem nor the solution, but a critical discourse about these things. If the foregoing account of the series as periphrastic polemic seems feasible, it remains to draw out its origins in Spenser's contemporary situation: to explain this concern with dialogue, in other words, not only as one more strategy of self-presentation but as correspondent to the Grindalian era, the rise of Ramism, the rule of the plain style, and the ascendancy of proto-novelistic fictional genres. As for the particular eclogues that have often been the sites of analysis conducted in the name of the entire *Calender,* I could wish to see Spenser's dialogic bent tested and defined there much more extensively than this essay can manage. His dialogism ought to be treated not as an inert fact or a frustrating given of the poem—its appearance as such in criticism perhaps confirms that we have lost sight of, or interest in, the work's manifest continuity—but as the engine of a purpose that encloses the ideological, thematic, and generic elements we usually identify. This essay is offered in token of one that might have been written long ago on the generic exoskeleton of the *Calender.* Belated, it seeks to "introduce" many particular interpretations that have actually influenced it greatly, and to clear the way for more acute and uncompromising discussions of Spenser's dialogic experiment.[48]

Harvard University

NOTES

1. Elder Olson, "The Lyric," in *On Value Judgments in the Arts and Other Essays* (Chicago, Ill.: University of Chicago Press, 1976), p. 217.
2. M. M. Bakhtin, "Discourse in the Novel," in *The Dialogic Imagination,* ed. Michael Holquist, trans. Caryl Emerson and Michael Holquist (Austin: University of Texas Press, 1981), p. 286.
3. Bakhtin, *Dialogic Imagination,* p. 328. Tzvetan Todorov, *Mikhail Bakhtin: The Dialogical Principle,* trans. Wlad Godzich, Theory and History of Literature, Vol. 13 (Minneapolis: University of Minnesota Press, 1984), pp. 60–74, summarizes and analyzes Bakhtin's dialogism in relation to genres and other literary typologies.

4. This is not to say, of course, that the *Calender* is the first lyric text in English that takes the form of dialogue; much more specifically, I would insist that it is the first fictional sequence in the language, in the manner of the *Rime sparse*, that achieves its fiction by apportioning its voice more or less evenly among several speakers. Since Spenser's aesthetic, religious, and political concerns in the *Calender* are so obviously English, the national character of the work's firstness is perhaps more relevant than is usual in discussions of the double reification called "the English Renaissance."

5. Spenser's classical models are discussed in the Variorum edition of the *Works*, eds. E. A. Greenlaw *et al.*, 10 vols. (Baltimore, Md.: Johns Hopkins University Press, 1932–57), VII, Pt. 1, pp. 589–609. John N. King, "Spenser's *Shepheardes Calender* and Protestant Pastoral Satire," in *Renaissance Genres*, ed. Barbara Kiefer Lewalski, Harvard English Studies Vol. 14 (Cambridge, Mass.: Harvard University Press, 1986), pp. 369–398, identifies a number of native sources.

6. Michael Holquist, "The Politics of Representation," in *Allegory and Representation*, ed. Stephen J. Greenblatt, Selected Papers from the English Institute N. S. no. 5 (Baltimore, Md.: The Johns Hopkins University Press, 1981), pp. 169, 165. Holquist's contextualizing discussion of dialogism (163–183) is excellent.

7. Since my purpose in this paper is partly to "interpret" previous criticism in light of the dialogic imperative of the *Calender*, in subsequent notes I will sometimes invite the reader to compare local observations by other critics that significantly complement, contextualize, or extend my own arguments. Among the treatments of the *Calender* that propose "plots" of one sort or another are A. C. Hamilton, "The Argument of Spenser's *Shepheardes Calender*," *ELH*, 23 (1956), 171–182, reprinted in *Spenser: A Collection of Critical Essays*, ed. Harry Berger, Jr. (Englewood Cliffs, N. J.: Prentice-Hall, 1968), pp. 30–39; Paul E. McLane, *Spenser's "Shepheardes Calender": A Study in Elizabethan Political Allegory* (Notre Dame, Ind.: University of Notre Dame Press, 1961), pp. 304–323; Patrick Cullen, *Spenser, Marvell, and Renaissance Pastoral* (Cambridge, Mass.: Harvard University Press, 1970), pp. 120–148; Wolfgang Iser, "Spenser's Arcadia: The Interrelation of Fiction and History," *Protocol of the Thirty-Eighth Colloquy: 13 April 1980*, The Center for Hermeneutical Studies in Hellenistic and Modern Culture, The Graduate Theological Union and the University of California, Berkeley; and the various essays of Harry Berger, Jr., cited below at note 9. My reading of the generic plot owes much to Paul Alpers, "Pastoral and the Domain of Lyric in Spenser's *Shepheardes Calender*," *Representations*, 12 (1985), 83–100.

8. Louis Adrian Montrose, " 'The perfecte paterne of a Poete': The Poetics of Courtship in *The Shepheardes Calender*," *Texas Studies in Literature and Language*, 21 (1979), 35, is typical of several other critics in his circumlocutory excision of this kind of basic fictional question: "Spenser's conspicuous concern with the creation and projection of a poetic persona and his thematic emphasis on erotic desire and social ambition proffered to readers a range of verbal strategies that could give formal expression to the complexity and ambivalence of an emergent generational consciousness." Montrose's adoption of E. K.'s division of the *Calender* into "ranckes" seems to mark the spot

at which the fundamental issues of fictional continuity disappear. It would be interesting to trace the irruption of that classification by E. K. into several critics' essays, perhaps as a cautionary example of how an element of the text supposedly under critical scrutiny has been taken more or less at face value and allowed to control the reading of the whole.

9. The work of Harry Berger, Jr. is the best example of this deliberate mining of the *Calender*; its results have been, of course, extraordinarily rich for students of the text. The pertinent essays are: "The Prospect of Imagination: Spenser and the Limits of Poetry," *Studies in English Literature*, 1 (1961), 93–120; "A Secret Discipline," in *Form and Convention in the Poetry of Edmund Spenser*, ed. William Nelson (New York: Columbia University Press, 1961), pp. 35–75; "Mode and Diction in the *Shepheardes Calender*," *Modern Philology*, 67 (1969), 140–149; "The Mirror Stage of Colin Clout: A New Reading of Spenser's *Januarye* Eclogue," *Helios*, 10 (1983), 139–160; "Orpheus, Pan, and the Poetics of Misogyny: Spenser's Critique of Pastoral Love and Art," *ELH*, 50 (1983), 27–60; and "The Aging Boy: Paradise and Parricide in Spenser's *Shepheardes Calender*," in *Poetic Traditions of the English Renaissance*, eds. Maynard Mack and George deF. Lord (New Haven, Conn.: Yale University Press, 1982), pp. 25–46. All of these essays have been reprinted in his *Revisionary Play: Studies in the Spenserian Dynamics* (Berkeley: University of California Press, 1988), but I cite them by their original publications.

10. Among the more suggestive treatments of the glosses are Michael McCanles, "The *Shepheardes Calender* as Document and Monument," *Studies in English Literature*, 22 (1982), 5–19; Theodore L. Steinberg, "E. K.'s *Shepheardes Calender* and Spenser's," *Modern Language Studies*, 3 (1973), 46–58; Jonathan Goldberg, *Voice Terminal Echo* (New York: Methuen, 1986), pp. 38–67; and of the envoys, David L. Miller, "Authorship, Anonymity, and *The Shepheardes Calender*," *Modern Language Quarterly*, 40 (1979), 219–227. Compare Lawrence Lipking, "The Marginal Gloss," *Critical Inquiry*, 3 (1977), 609–655.

11. Along with McCanles, the most exhaustive recent essays on the extrafictional matter of the *Calender* are by Ruth Samson Luborsky: "The Allusive Presentation of *The Shepheardes Calender*," *Spenser Studies* I, ed. Patrick Cullen and Thomas P. Roche, Jr. (Pittsburgh, Pa.: University of Pittsburgh Press, 1980), 29–67, and "The Illustrations to *The Shepheardes Calender*," *Spenser Studies* II, ed. Patrick Cullen and Thomas P. Roche, Jr. (Pittsburgh, Pa.: University of Pittsburgh Press, 1981), 3–53.

12. McCanles, 17. Compare Cullen, pp. 29–32, and Iser, p. 11.

13. M. M. Bakhtin, *Problems of Dostoevsky's Poetics,* ed. and trans. Caryl Emerson, Theory and History of Literature, Vol. 8 (Minneapolis: University of Minnesota Press, 1984), p. 108. A recent attempt to establish similarities between Bakhtin's novel-centered theory and a late sixteenth-century fiction is Ann Rosalind Jones, "Inside the Outsider: Nashe's *Unfortunate Traveller* and Bakhtin's Polyphonic Novel," *ELH*, 50 (1983), 61–81.

14. Iser, p. 10.

15. David Norbrook, *Poetry and Politics in the English Renaissance* (Boston: Routledge and Kegan Paul, 1984), p. 86.

16. For more or less complementary readings of "Januarye," see John W.

Moore, Jr., "Colin Breaks His Pipe: A Reading of the 'January' Eclogue," *English Literary Renaissance*, 5 (1975), 3–24; and Berger, "Mirror Stage."

17. All quotations of *The Shepheardes Calender* are from the one-volume Oxford edition of the *Poetical Works*, eds. J. C. Smith and E. de Selincourt (Oxford: Clarendon Press, 1912).

18. Berger, "Mirror Stage," 146. Compare his "Orpheus," 42.

19. Compare Berger, "Mirror Stage," 146.

20. Compare Montrose, 36–37, on the "tense relationship to literary and social patriarchy" and creative imitation that characterizes the generation of Spenser. I intend the present section of my argument to be congruent with this historical interpretation.

21. Robert Parker, *Miasma: Pollution and Purification in Early Greek Religion* (Oxford: Clarendon Press, 1983), pp. 1–17, introduces the theology and pathology of his key term, which implies the "defilement, the impairment of a thing's form or integrity" (p. 3) and a "contagious religious danger" (p. 5). Of course, I am treating Colin's miasma as a contagious cultural danger.

22. Compare Berger, "Mode and Diction," 144.

23. Cullen, pp. 37–38.

24. Michael Riffaterre, *Text Production*, trans. Terese Lyons (New York: Columbia University Press, 1983), pp. 50–51.

25. Berger, "Orpheus," 43–44, remarks cogently on the redundancies and *copie* in the *Calender*.

26. Berger, "Orpheus," 51.

27. Compare Nancy Jo Hoffman, *Spenser's Pastorals* (Baltimore, Md.: The Johns Hopkins University Press, 1977), pp. 100–102.

28. Berger, "The Aging Boy," pp. 39–40.

29. Jeffrey Knapp, "An Empire Nowhere: England and America, From *Utopia* to *The Tempest*," Ph.D. diss., University of California at Berkeley, 1988, p. 57.

30. Compare Goldberg, p. 63.

31. The fictional dimension of Bakhtin's theoretical works hardly ends here: see Holquist, "The Politics of Representation," pp. 169–174, on the authorial and ideological ventriloquism of Bakhtin's several major texts.

32. John N. King, "Was Spenser a Puritan?" *Spenser Studies* VI, ed. Patrick Cullen and Thomas P. Roche, Jr. (New York: AMS Press, 1985), 5, describes how the "religious schism" between "progressive" and "moderate" Protestants "cut across class lines" in Spenser's time.

33. Berger, "Secret Discipline," 46.

34. Nelson Goodman, *Ways of Worldmaking* (Indianapolis, Ind.: Hackett, 1978), accounts for fiction's moorings to extant structures: "Worldmaking as we know it always starts from worlds already on hand: the making is a remaking" (p. 6). On worldmaking in Spenser's poetry, see Berger, "Introduction," in *Spenser: A Collection of Critical Essays*, pp. 3–8.

35. Compare Miller, "Authorship," 234.

36. Compare Norbrook, p. 72.

37. Cullen, pp. 108–109.

38. Cullen, p. 111.

39. For present purposes, the most useful theoretical texts on concreteness in -

poetry, and on concrete poetry as a generic and historical phenomenon, are Pierre Garnier, *Spatialisme et poésie concrète* (Paris: Gallimard, 1968), especially pp. 69–82 in relation to "August"; Bob Cobbing and Peter Mayer, *Concerning Concrete Poetry* (London: Writers Forum, 1978); and because of its correspondence to McCanles' concerns, Rudolf Arnheim, "Visual Aspects of Concrete Poetry," in *Literary Criticism and Psychology*, ed, Joseph P. Strelka, Yearbook of Comparative Criticism Vol. 7 (University Park, Pa.: Pennsylvania State University Press, 1976), pp. 91–109.

40. A survey of the topic of concreteness in Spenser's critics might be assembled out of McCanles; the two essays by Luborsky; Berger, "Mirror Stage," 140, and "The Aging Boy," pp. 38–39; Goldberg, pp. 38–67; King, "Was Spenser a Puritan?," 15–16; and S. K. Heninger, Jr., "The Implications of Form for *The Shepheardes Calender*," *Studies in the Renaissance*, 9 (1962), 309–321.

41. McCanles, 17. Berger, "Orpheus," 41, qualifies the sestina eloquently.

42. William Nelson, *The Poetry of Edmund Spenser* (New York: Columbia University Press, 1963), pp. 47–48.

43. Fredric Jameson, "Magical Narratives: On the Dialectical Use of Genre Criticism," in *The Political Unconscious: Narrative as a Socially Symbolic Act* (Ithaca, N.Y.: Cornell University Press, 1981), pp. 103–150, describes romance as a sophisticated response to certain historical and ideological conditions. In this paragraph and throughout the essay, I am indebted to Jameson's chapter for helping me to recover and fill in (in ways Jameson would not recognize) Spenser's valorization of dialogic lyric.

44. McLane, pp. 158–174.

45. For complementary readings of "October," see Cullen, pp. 68–76, and Montrose, 44–49.

46. Lewis Hyde, *The Gift: Imagination and the Erotic Life of Property* (New York: Vintage, 1979), p. 276.

47. Compare Richard Helgerson's helpless note summarizing Moore's essay: Moore "suggests that the January eclogue and, more particularly, Colin's breaking of his pipe with which it ends 'introduces us to the issue which gives unity to the *Calender*'—the nature of Colin's poetic vocation and the question of his fitness for it. I agree and would further suggest that the series as a whole fails either to resolve the issue or to answer the question." *Self-Crowned Laureates* (Berkeley: University of California Press, 1983), pp. 69–70.

48. I would like to express my regard for the work done on *The Shepheardes Calender* by several students in English 124 at Harvard, 1987–88: Paul Donohoe, W. Caleb Crain, Esther Morgo, and Mark Laroche. Their papers provoked me to think about the matters set forth in this essay.

ROBERT CUMMINGS

Spenser's "Twelve Private Morall Virtues"

I labour to portraict in Arthure, before he was king, the image of
a brave knight perfected in the twelve private morall virtues, as
Aristotle hath devised, the which is the purpose of these first
twelve bookes.

S O WROTE Spenser to Ralegh, in a passage which has vexed
the commentators.[1] I want to indicate a source in the Hermetic
tracts for Spenser's scheme of moral virtues in *The Faerie
Queene*. The virtues that Hermes names are neither twelve nor
Aristotelian; but, quite patently, neither are those of *The Faerie
Queene*. And while it is clear that Spenser intended twelve
virtues, it is less clear that he ever intended we should take them
as Aristotelian. My proposal is that Spenser at some presumably
early stage in the poem's composition entertained the Hermetic
scheme as a kind of elementary moral programme.

I.

The thirteenth tract of the *Corpus Hermeticum,* sometimes
called "The Sermon on the Mount," expounds the mystery of
regeneration.[2] As Hermes explains it to his son and disciple Tat,
regeneration consists in the recovery of one's human birthright
as a child of God. This recovery is achieved by passing out of
oneself, as in a waking dream; and it begins with suppression of
the activity of the senses, by clearing oneself of the irrational—
and properly called demonic—torments of matter.[3] These torments are twelve: ignorance, sorrow, incontinence, lust, injustice, self-seeking (*pleonexia*), falsehood, envy, guile, wrath,
rashness, and malice. These uphold the rights of matter, and
imprisoning man in the body, condemn him to a life of sense
and unfulfillable desires. But the various torments can with

goodwill and God's mercy be expelled and replaced by a sequence of regenerative powers.

> It has come to us, the knowledge of God. By its coming, my son, ignorance is cast out. It has come to us, the knowledge of gladness. By its presence, my son, sorrow has fled to those who have place for it.

These powers are ten: the knowledge of God, the knowledge of gladness (*tēs charas*), continence (*egkrateia*), patience (*karteria*), justice, fellowship (*koinōnia*), truth, good, life, and light.[4] The symmetry of the torments and the regenerative powers is for complicated (and in this context irrelevant) reasons not complete; but it survives up to the advent of truth. With that, good follows close behind together with life and light to overcome the remainder. The virtuous decad triumphs over the vicious dodecad and brings with it the putting on of indestructiblity and immortality. "I have gone out of myself into a deathless body, and I am not now what I was before," says Hermes, "I have been begotten in Mind."[5]

The failure of Spenser's commentators to discover a definitively plausible model for Spenser's "twelve private morall virtues" suggests that there may be no conventional and properly public sense for the expression. That is, it is not in a category with formulae like the "four cardinal virtues," or the "seven deadly sins." What he writes was presumably intelligible in a private way to Ralegh to whom the letter is addressed, but probably not to the reading public for whom the letter was printed. Despite this, the oppositions important in the Hermetic account of regeneration are sustained with remarkable fidelity in Spenser's poem. In Hermes, the knowledge of God overcomes ignorance, the knowledge of gladness overcomes sorrow, continence overcomes incontinence, patience overcomes lust, justice overcomes injustice, fellowship overcomes self-seeking. The pattern and the substance of this are quite familiar to readers of Spenser: I shall proceed in Section III to a commentary on the resemblances. First, it is worth indicating that they are made possible by the special character of the poetic scheme. The particular apparatus of the Hermetic fiction (its use of educative dialogue, its charting the pupil's progress from ignorance to enlightenment), and its particular values (its obses-

sion with Mind, with the One) are unlikely to have moved
Spenser much. Yet a specifically *Christian* conception of excellence is imaginable in Hermetic terms where it is not, despite
the efforts of centuries of philosopher-theologians, in Aristotelian ones. Relevant biblical resonances already inform the
Hermetic passage.[6] Patrizi, who along with the rest of his
generation misreads Hermes's eclecticsm as confirming his inspiration of Plato and Aristotle and the rest, supposes the tracts
"as by far of more service and advantage to Christian folk,"
arguing it would be "more useful hereafter to read Hermetic
lore than Aristotelian, which to our shame flows unstopped in
the universities and monasteries."[7] Nor are the attractions of the
Hermetic account limited to its substance, easily translatable to
a Christian context. Spenser looks to fashion a gentleman by
schematising the operations of the virtues in a dynamic way.
His poetical enterprise is rhetorically quite distinct from the
philosophical or analytical one which might give an account of
what Bryskett calls the procedures "whereby vertues are to be
distinguished from vices."[8] This characteristic is essential in *The
Faerie Queene*. Holiness or temperance are not partial unfoldings
of magnificence, but enablings of it. The Hermetic scheme
likewise subordinates the enabling activity of various moral
virtues to an end which represents their perfection: only when
their activity is complete is the end realised. That is, it yields
precisely what is wanting in the schemes conventionally re-
sorted to by commentators on Spenser, an evolutionary account
of virtue that should be compatible with a rhetoric for fashioning gentlemen.[9]

II: MAGNIFICENCE AND GLORY

At the core of the analogy with Spenser is the Hermes's basic
concern with rebirth and the recovery of perfection. That it is
not exclusively Hermetic, but Christian too, makes it immediately appealing: "Except a man be borne againe, he cannot
see the kingdome of God" (John 3.3); and Paul advises the
Galatians that they are children "of whom I trauaile in birth
againe, vntil Christ be formed in you" (Galatians 4.19).[10] The
formation of the Christian gentleman is by regeneration. Spenser's story (though not the narration of it) begins with Arthur's

virtuous effort to recover a vision. Arthur dreams of Gloriana and loses her:

> From that day forth I cast in carefull mind,
> To seek her out with labour, and long tyne
>
> (I.ix.15)

This story adumbrates an account of the relationship between Magnificence and Glory. "In that Faery Queene I meane glory in my generall intention . . . So in the person of Prince Arthure I sette forth magnificicence in particular." Arthur's magnificence is fitness for an end, which is what Spenser means by talking of it as the "perfection" of other virtues.[11] The end is glory. The action begins in the dream of the Faery Queen—an image of transcendent glory, and it ends with the poet's prayer for rest in the company of the host that surrounds the ultimate reality of that glory: "O that great Sabbaoth God, graunt me that Sabbaoth's sight' (VII.viii.2). Potential magnificence is summoned by glory, and achieved magnificence (anticipated as the poet's and no longer Arthur's) meets it as peace. "Marke the vpright man," says the Psalmist (37.37), "and behold the iust: for the end of that man is peace." "Behold the perfect man," says the Authorised Version.[12] Beyond the Psalmist's meaning, "perfection" is in the specifically Christian context specifically rich: "If therefore perfection had bene by the Priesthood of the Leuites . . . what needed it furthermore?" (Hebrews 7.11). But the Son who replaces the law and the Levites is consecrated or (as the margin explains) perfected for ever (Hebrews 7.28). Perfection in this novel context is the theme of the Epistle to the Hebrews.

The poem's story implies that magnificence is not an aspect of glory (somehow "particular" against the more "general" glory), but rather what desires and quests for glory. And the laborious acquiring of magnificence represents the recovery of an original lost gift of glory. This squares with the Hermetic doctrine of regeneration, and also with the Christian one. The body is "sowen in dishonour," says Paul (1 Cor. 15.43) but it is "raised in glorie." We escape "the corruption that is the world through lust" because we are called, says Peter (2 Peter 1.3) "vnto glorie and vertue," or even (as Calvin renders it) "by glory and vertue."[13] We only have to obey the call. The first step is the recognition of it. We then fulfil our vocation and remedy our forgetfulness, says Peter, by following through a chain of recommendations to "ioyne moreouer vertue with your faith: and with vertue knowledge: And with knowledge, temperance: and with temperance, patience: and with patience, godlines: And with godlines, brotherlie kindenes: and with brotherlie kindenes loue" (5–7). And, he concludes, "he that hathe not these things, is blinde, and cannot see farre of, and hath forgotten that he was purged from his olde sinnes" (9).[14] The poetic advantages of the Hermetic scheme as against the Christian one are in its more energetic articulation and its fabrication of a dialectic of virtues and vices. Hermes makes a pattern of struggle and suffering and relief.

Spenser says that magnificence "is the perfection of all the rest" of the virtues. This definition does not suggest that the perfection of the virtues follows on their cultivation. Christ "being consecrate was made authour of eternall saluation vnto them that obey him" (Hebrews 5.9). Christ's perfection (which is how the Authorized Version renders the notion of "consecration") valorises ours. In obeying him, we can be presented "perfect in Christ Iesus" (Colossians 1.28). Writing to the Ephesians, Paul gives the promise that we shall attain "vnto a perfite man, and vnto the measure of the age the fulnesse of Christ" (Ephesians 4.12). The Geneva gloss notes that before "our perfit age, which we shall haue at length in another world" there is a "steadie going forward to perfection." In Spenser, our Christian regeneration begins in a visionary calling "to glorie." It is an analogue of what is ritually secured in baptism, which effects the result "that like as Christ was raised vp from the dead to the glory of the Father, so we also should walke in newness of life" (Romans 6.4).

Christ's Transfiguration echoes his Baptism. At the moment of his transfiguration, Christ is a symbol, says the *Glossa Ordinaria* (on Matthew 17.1), "of his own resurrection and of ours." Repeated in 2 Peter 1, this symbolical assurance of being "raised in glorie," is precisely the moment of Christ's *magnificence,* the only one explicitly so called in his earthly life.

with our eyes we saw his maiestie. For he receiued of God the Father honour and glorie, when there came suche a voyce to him from the excellent glorie, This is my beloued Sonne, in whom I am wel pleased.

(16–17)

So the Geneva version. Calvin's word (for the Greek *megaleiotēs*) is not *maiestas* but *magnificentia*, which here acquires a sense well beyond those charted so ably by Tuve and others.[15] We were "spectatores facti eius magnificentiae," says Peter in Calvin's version, "We became witnesses of his magnificence." And when Peter from among all the manifestations of Christ's favour, specifies in particular the "voice from the magnificent glory," we may thence conclude, says Calvin, "what were those signs of magnificence" which the evangelists relate: "nothing earthly," he says, "was seen there." We may further notice that this specification crucially renders Christ's magnificence an affirmation of divine love, for what the voice says is, "This is my beloued Sonne, in whom I am well pleased." The father is himself "glorie" and what he gives is "honour and glorie." By virtue of this gift the son is "magnificent," and to be magnificent in this sense is to be pleasing to God. God's love may be worked for: "Make you perfite in all good workes, to do his wil, working in you that which is pleasant in his sight" (Hebrews 13.21). But magnificence is in the first instance a gift. Tertullian asserts that in baptism there is a "promised magnificence," a "magnificentia quae in effectu promittitur"—that of resurrection.[16] Here in the Transfiguration, in the Father's repetition of the loving formula first spoken at the Baptism, it is effortlessly realised.

Arthur's quest is an *imitatio Christi*, and a number of critics have already disembarrassed glory and magnificence of their secular senses.[17] His final magnificence is supposed to follow on the recovery or more precisely the realisation of the vision which the Faerie Queene gratuitously afforded him, "For dearely sure her loue was to me bent" (I.ix.14). Arthur is called by Gloriana: his somehow inclusive magnificence, potentiated by the encounter with her—by her gift of herself, aims at glory and may win to it. Calvin tells us that the human will is not of itself capable of seeking after the right because it is set in its fallen perversity (*Institutes* II.iii.4). It is from this perversity that Arthur's vision releases him. The vision is a sign of the potential magnificence that permits the search.

Why does Peter offer the assurance of Christ's magnificence? To encourage our own achievement of it. Summoned by glory, with the knowledge of the possibility of our own magnificence, it is open to us to perfect our virtues. Summoned by Gloriana,

Arthur finally becomes magnificent by way of his "perfecting" the twelve virtues of the projected twelve books. His magnificence is demonstrated in doing great things, in "working his own perfection," which is the best that mortality can do, but its promise consists in partaking of the divine nature (2 Peter 1.4). Spenser's narrative mode requires that in the poem this perfection would have been effected chiefly by the elimination of the threatening dishonours of the world. Neither in its specification of particular virtues, nor in its explicitly additive arrangement of them is Peter's account identical with Spenser's. But it suggestively adumbrates an ideal of the Christian gentleman of which Spenser could have approved; and indeed it goes on to express it in terms of one of the more important of Spenser's subsidiary metaphors—the Garden of Virtue: "for if these things be in you, and abound, they make you that ye shall neither be barren nor unfruitful in the knowledge of our Lord Jesus Christ" (2 Peter 1.8).[18] The dynamic of ascent, at its most strenuous that of the race, is at its quietest that of growth. Arthur's dream of glory is the germ of a magnificent enterprise. Una apostrophises the absent Queen (I.ix.16):

O happy Queene of Faeries, that hast found
Mongst many, one that with his prowesse may
Defend thine honour, and they foes confound:
True Loues are often sown, but seldom grow on ground.

The enterprise is supposed to flower when he finally encounters glory.

III: Six Virtues

Except in Book III, Arthur first enters on the events of each of the Books of *The Faerie Queene* at Canto viii.[19] These Arthurian interventions, concluding in peculiarly uncompromised triumphs over various vices, are often construed as representing the operation of grace. On a cue from I.vii.29, Kouwenhoven beautifully compares Arthur with Malachi's "'Sunne of righteousness' . . . rising and setting in each sign of the zodiac to blaze the night sky into temporary invisibility in its perpetual revolutions."[20] But his comparison may mislead: Arthur in fact

concentrates rather than outshines the metaphorical light otherwise apparent in the various titular heroes. His interventions are
less contentiously understood as focussing the primary moral
concerns of the book. So taken, their approximation to the
moral concerns of the Hermetic scheme are striking. That the
advertised topics of the books of *The Faerie Queene*—Holiness,
Temperance, and so on—are not named consistently with Hermes's regenerative powers is an only accidental anomaly. The
moral force of the Arthurian episodes is substantially identical
with them. They focus and clarify what is thematically dis-
persed in each book, implicitly establishing heads of discussion.
This concentration is effectively represented in Arthur's victory
over opposed vices or demonic torments, so that the emphasis,
like the Hermetic one, is on the work of purging vices rather
than of incorporating virtues.[21] The titles and the titular heroes
of each book represent revisions—at their least thorough, only
alternative modulations—of the original moral force. The
relationship between the two is sometimes more obvious,
sometimes less, and may not appear to all readers consistently
convincing. But, the account of each book being necessarily
sketchy and essentially unsophisticated, I have avoided recourse
to overly elaborate persuasions. My illustrative quotations from
the Fathers are taken mainly from two collections of devotional
and theological commonplaces, one of them probably familiar
to Spenser.[22]

1: Holiness

The context outlined above comfortably accommodates the
priority of Spenser's Holiness.[23] Hermes's account of regeneration begins with the knowledge of God supplanting ignorance.
Holiness is not identical with the knowledge of God. But in
Spenser the chief condition of Holiness is faith: "Above all,
taking the shield of faith, wherewith ye shall be able to quench
all the fiery darts of the wicked," says St. Paul in the passage of
Ephesians to which Spenser's Letter directs us (6.16). "Add
faith unto your force," cries Una (I.i.19); and Fidelia is the
eldest of Caelia's daughters, "able with her words to kill / And
raise againe to life the hart, that she did thrill" (I.x.19). We
should not understand here simply a pious predisposition.
Gregory says that "piety is unavailing if it lacks the discernment

of knowledge."[24] Faith, says Clement of Alexandria, is "the perfection of doctrine," and religion is "learning in pursuit of the knowledge of truth."[25] And truth has a specialised sense here. Man might have gone far towards perfect knowledge, says Calvin (*Institutes,* I.ii.1), guided by the "primal and simple knowledge to which the order of Nature would have led us if Adam had remained upright."[26] But the deficiencies of "primal and simple knowledge" in fallen man make it unreliable, and in any case sufficient only for the revelation of God the Creator. The knowledge of God the Redeemer is the achievement of learned faith, the acknowledgment of what is revealed. For this reason Fidelia carries a book "Wherein darke things were writ, hard to be vnderstood" (I.x.13; echoing the warning against ignorance of 2 Peter 3.16), and she directs the "schoolehouse" where Redcrosse tastes "heauenly learning" (I.x.18).

All things that "perteine vnto life and godlines" begin in what Peter calls the "knowledge of God" (2 Peter 1.2–3).[27] Holiness is the subject of the first Book of *The Faerie Queene,* not because Holiness is a greater virtue than the rest, but simply because it is prior. Augustine writes in words which are luminously appropriate: "Tu iam prius quaerebas magnificentiam: prius dilige sanctitatem; cum sanctificatus fueris, eris et magnificus" (You looked first for magnificence. First love holiness. When you have been made holy, you shall be magnificent.)[28] Perfection is achieved only if we start out from the right place. When Guyon is advised that his race is to be like Redcrosse's (II.i.32), he is in effect reminded that the zeal of the virtuous without holiness is like a runner off course, "for the more strenuously anyone runs who is off the path, the farther he gets from his goal."[29] Only in the context of holiness does the exercise of secondary virtues become salvific.

Orgoglio's defeat by Arthur dramatises the recognition of God. Orgoglio himself embodies pride and lust, but he is a foster child of Ignaro (viii.31), who acts as porter in his castle.[30] His pride is, as St. Bernard's words suggest pride must be, sustained by ignorance. Nohrnberg persuasively reads Orgoglio as a parody or false image of Christ.[31] It is precisely his defeat which makes room for Redcrosse's recognition of the true Christ; and he is overcome precisely by the unveiling or revelation of Arthur's diamond shield (itself identifiable with Christ, as Brooks-Davies indicates).[32] Una, taken as Truth,

leads Arthur to the fight (viii. Arg); and Arthur's victory exposes the deficiencies of untruth, concluding in a revelation of the
true nature of Duessa: "Such is the face of falshood . . . when
her borrowed light / Is laid away, and counterfesaunce
knowne" (viii.49).

St. Bernard on the Canticles writes that "real knowledge of
God and of oneself is necessary for our salvation, because from
self-knowledge arises the fear of God, and from the knowledge
of God arises love of him; on the other hand from ignorance of
oneself arises pride, and from ignorance of God arises despair".[33] A preoccupation with ignorance and revelation everywhere informs Book I. Everywhere the various manifestations
of deception and doubt and dark are set against the possibilities
of truth and light. Redcrosse's career opens in an encounter
with Error in her labyrinth: "Unless we look straight towards
God," writes Calvin (*Institutes,* III.ii.2), "we shall wander
through endless labyrinths." Redcrosse does indeed wander,
and continues in the company of "fair falshood" (ii.Argument).
Una's adventures bring her quickly into the company of Abes-
sa, the daughter of Corceca, who herself shadows unregenerate
insipience of heart (Romans 1.21), and she proceeds to the
Satyrs whom she teaches "Trew sacred lore" (vi.30). The
"many fauours" which Redcrosse obtains from Contemplation,
after his long education in the House of Holiness, consist princi-
pally in information about God as Redeemer (x.57) and about
his own origin and destiny (x.65–66). That is, the knowledge of
God and of himself, much as prescribed by St. Bernard, is the
summit of Redcrosse's spiritual achievement, the reward of his
holy ambitions to overcome pride and despair, and what makes
possible his recovery of Eden from the Dragon. It was only in
unwitting and largely unavailing "remembrance of his dying
Lord" (I.i.2) that he had earlier carried his "glorious badge" on
his breast and shield.

2: Temperance

In Hermes the knowledge of gladness supplants sorrow.
Guyon is rather too stern to be an obvious exemplar of gladness, but Spenser's modulation of the Hermetic emphasis is less
exceptional than may at first appear.[34] "Joy does not make away
with modesty," says Justin, "nor Modesty with feeling joy;

but each is kept safe by the other."[35] Phaedria's immodest mirth is not what sustains Guyon, nor indeed Arthur. "Believe me," says Seneca, "true joy is a serious business"—a *res severa*.[36] The severe and tempered joys of the Stoic sustain the balance of the good life. "Better to temper joy than restrain sorrow," writes Seneca in another place, which may be Guyon's motto, instructed by the Palmer's commentary on the case of Phedon (II.iv.35). Arthur however achieves more than the mere restraint of sorrow. His defeat, in Canto viii, of the alternative torments represented in Cymochles and Pyrochles is only preliminary to his disposal of Maleger in canto xi, which "end of that Carles dayes, and his own paines did make" (II.xi.46). Among Maleger's meanings is certainly Sorrow. Hamilton (on II.xi.23) quotes the definition of *aeger* from Cooper's *Thesaurus:* "sicke, sorowfull, pensiffe, or heavie." Maleger's elaborate iconography includes the detail that his bodily humour is cold and dry (xi.22), which specifically establishes the pattern of natural melancholy.[37] Arthur's victory destroys what Justin calls the inebriating power of spiritual perturbation or sorrow.[38] The mimicry of baptism, whereby he drowns Maleger, mortifies the "strong affections" applied against the fort of reason (the Book of Common Prayer's "evil and corrupt affections" in the Order for Baptism), and so effects a knowledge of gladness. Baptism is "of repentance for the remission of sins" (Luke 3.3.), affording proleptically the satisfaction of penitence. Hooker says (*Ecclesiastical Polity*, VI.iii.4), speaking of David, that "the comforts of grace in remitting sin carry him which sorrowed rapt as it were into heaven with joy and gladness."[39] Beside this, Arthur's comforts of "balme and wine and costly spicery" (II.xi.49) may seem feeble; but they are not less assured.

Calvin (*Institutes*, III.iii.3) quarrels with those who "understand vivification as the happiness that the mind receives after its perturbation and fear have been quieted." Spenser may not have. Guyon's achievement of unperturbedness of soul releases the Spring: "But *Verdant* (so he hight) he soone vntyde" (II.xii.82). On the other hand its benefits seem not to be for him at all. The only grace actually offered Guyon is Mammon's, which is false (vii.18, 32, 33, 50). The availability of any sort of gladness is sadly limited, and probably clearest in the Bower of Bliss's parody of it. To be sure, a well-tempered alternative to mere "courtly bliss" as the joyful Belphoebe calls it (iii.40), is fully present in the House of Alma. Alma is the soul of man, but her name signifies also that she is "full of grace," so that "even heaven rejoyced her sweete face to see" (ix.18). But Guyon is entertained there by Shamefastnesse. Everywhere he tempers joy, but his active mission is rather to restrain sorrows: lying at the other pole of distemperature, these are always more threateningly available. They may generate other malign impulses, or be generated by them: Phedon's rage is a consequence of grief (iii.31), Pyrochles's grief is a consequence of rage (vi.44–45). These are figures of excess. More typically, sorrow is embodied in figures characterized by temperamental errors of deficiency: the couple Elissa "discontent for want of merth" and Huddibras "more like a Malcontent" (ii.35–37), Cymochles characterised by "drowzie dreriment" (vi.27), Verdant lying in post-coital *tristitia* (xii.80). Guyon begins his career confronting the "image of mortalitie" (i.57), more sorrowful than instructive (i.14–15); he ends it with Grille repining (xii.86). Yet Guyon's progress, culminating in the release of Verdant, is itself comparable with the action of baptismal water, metaphorically described in the wanderings of the River Gihon.[40]

3: Chastity

In Hermes, Continence supplants Incontinence; or, since the distinction between continence and temperance was weak, it can be put as a victory of Temperance over Intemperance.[41] The relationship with Spenser's chastity is in either case problematic. This is not so much because the obvious form of the opposition is preempted in Book II, but that Book III, if it treated the specifically sexual modulation of temperance, might be committed to a view of sexuality to which Spenser was actually hostile. He would have rejected the identification of continence and chastity so complacently suggested in the arrangement of the Flores Doctorum where they constitute the same topic. Arthur's impetus towards glory being erotic, he can hardly be concerned to "contain," and for this reason he achieves no victory on behalf of egkrateia over akrasia. No doubt this results in a loss of thematic focus.[42] Had the scheme of Book III conformed to that of the previous two, Arthur should have rescued Britomart from an allegorically labelled antagonist in Canto viii. Instead, Florimell is the victim and Proteus the rescuer; the antagonist is a lecherous fisherman. The commentators properly find this troublesome.[43] Since the scheme is disrupted by Spenser's betrayal of narrative norms that operate even in Book IV, the problem is not likely to be owing simply to a shift to a more open and romantic method. Rather, Spenser's moral sense seems to have been intractable in terms of the opposition between virtue and vice which the narrative normally accommodates or enforces.

The Faerie Queene III.viii represents quite literally an act of containment. Such containment is entirely appropriate. We can interpret Verdant, released by Guyon at the end of Book II, as blossoming acratically into Florimell at the opening of Book III. She is beautiful, but her uncontrolled career is dreadful as a comet's (III.i.16); she loves Marinell beyond hope of attaining him (v.9–10); she is vulnerable to irrational fears (vii.1); she stirs into raging lust the "frozen spright" of the old fisherman (viii.23). And Proteus is not so improbable a rescuer as some critics pretend: Sannazaro had already cast him as a protector of threatened virginity.[44] Florimell's adventures with the fisherman, and her imprisonment, are modelled on incidents in the Orlando Furioso, viii. There, Angelica is rescued from the impotent attentions of a friar by marauding Ebudans in search of sacrificial flesh for the vengeful Proteus's orc. Spenser has drastically rewritten his sequence. Whereas in Ariosto the Ebudans' motives are unambiguously malign, Spenser has transferred to his Proteus the merely amorous motives which had once upon a time moved Ariosto's. The commentators apparently find it hard to forgive even these. Nohrnberg is an exception calling him "matter in its infinite receptivity of form, especially generable form" so that his detention of Florimell is precisely what permits the maturation of informed matter.[45] But this can be stated more strongly. Proteus in effect restates the benign mutability of the Garden of Adonis, where Genius admits the unfleshed "naked babes," and having clothed them "with sinfull mire," sends them "forth to liue in mortall state" (vi.32). Florimell remains "In bands of loue, and in sad thraldomes chayne" (IV.xi.1) until, matura viro, she is released for Marinell (another marine hero) in the following book. "If they cannot absteine [egkrateomai], let them marie" (1 Corinthians. 7.9), writes St. Paul. In the one book Florimell is contained, in the next she is freed to marry.

Elsewhere in the book, continence is mainly generalised to

temperance. Like Arthur, and indeed like Florimell, Britomart's vocation is to marriage, which might conventionally— following Paul—be strictly alternative to continence. To be sure, Britomart is specifically not incontinent, a word used for Malecasta and for Hellenore, to whom she is opposed (III.i.48), III.ix.1). But even if Glauce's extravagant words at III.ii.46 ("But if the passion mayster thy fraile might . . . Then I auow to thee, by wrong or right / To compasse thy desire"), never quite achieve relevance, sexual restraint is not what characterises her, more the sense of a proper mix. The mix is metaphorically expressed in the union of Cupid and Psyche at III.vi.50, or in the "faire Hermaphrodite" at 1590 (III.xii.46). Already at III.i.12 the reconciliation of Guyon and Britomart is achieved by "goodly temperance, and affection chaste," and their riding forth together itself emblematises the proper mix of those virtues. Throughout the Book this concern is sustained. In Belphoebe, rival virtues make "a perfect complement" (III.v.55), a perfect complementarity mysteriously extended in her twinning with Amoret. In Britomart herself, Fowler finds Minerva and Venus united; Roche finds the notion of *concordia discors* "everywhere implicit" in her image.[46]

4: Friendship

Continence, the word Everard gives (following the "continentia" of Ficino or Flussas) for the fourth of the regenerative agencies is not the happiest rendering of *karteria*. But it is certainly the sense that counts for most in Arthur's crucial intervention in Book IV. A simple opposition of continence and concupiscence (the Hermetic *epithumia*) is shadowed in Arthur's fight with Corflambo (viii.41–49). In the Book of Friendship— which can be accounted precisely continent love (x.26–28), Arthur's eros can rest a space. In these terms, the continuity with Book III is pressed in a contrast: in Book III, Arthur's allegiance to chastity ideally obliges his tempering eros, in Book IV his allegiance to friendship requires his containing it.

Extending the sense of the conflict summarised in Arthur's struggle with Corflambo, oppositions of continence and concupiscence are frequent in Book IV. But the positive sense of the Hermetic *karteria*—as patient endurance, or constancy— should be pressed more firmly than the early translators have allowed.[47] Even without taking advantage of the uncertain demarcations between virtues, we can say that it amounts to what in Latin is called *fortitudo*: "It is the strength—the *fortitudo*—of the just to overcome the flesh and oppose their own desires."[48] So, for example, Florimell's "constant mind" is immoveable in the face of Proteus's blandishments (xi.2), and undecaying (rather than simply contained) love is celebrated by the friends in the Temple gardens (x.27). Such constancy represents an assertion of the will against circumstances; and for this reason Plato makes courage a form of it. The boldness which Britomart is mysteriously enjoined to practise (III.xi.50), and which enables Scudamour to win Amoret (IV.x.54) are variants of it. It is obedience to a tempered ideal of it—"Be not too bold" (III.xi.54)—which enables Britomart to rescue her in the previous book, and it is his failure to observe that ideal that loses her to Scudamour.[49] Patience is the preferred form of it: Florimell's "unworthie paine" is advertised as the leading topic of the book (IV.i.1), Scudamour suffers in the House of Care (v.7–46); awaiting his reconciliation with Belphoebe, Timias makes "in his wonted wise / His doole" (viii.3). These cases are helpless in themselves. But elsewhere patience is commendable either for itself or for what it may achieve: taking refuge in the House of Sclaunder, Arthur endures "all with patience mild" (viii.28), which is a form of courage; and it is by courageous endurance (though not by boldness) that Marinell effects the liberation of Florimell (xii.17ff). The lovers whose reunion the book most clearly celebrates are models of two varieties of long-suffering. "Loue suffreth long," writes St. Paul (I Corinthians 13.4); and Cyprian identifies patience with what sustains the charity that is the "the bond of brotherhood, the ground of peace, what secures unity."[50] In sum, it enables the friendship which Book IV advertises as its topic.

5: Justice

Spenser's Justice translates the Hermetic *dikaiosunē*.[51] But since Arthur shares the triumph with Artegall, his particular role, is, as Dunseath puts it, "somewhat muted."[52] As his name suggests, Artegall is Arthur's equal. Arthur defeats the Souldan in V.viii.42; but it is Artegall who drives his wife Adicia (precisely Hermes's *adikia*) to beastly lunacy (viii.48–49). The significance of this division of labour is not fully clear. Book V as a whole variously sophisticates an elementary opposition between Justice and Injustice. Two problems attend this opposition. First, since justice is to an uncommon degree conventionally co-extensive with virtue in general, it is difficult to determine what might be exclusively apt to it. The apparent equivalence of Arthur and Artegall makes this point. Secondly, the pattern of justice is historically manifested, with the result that the allegories of Book V are historically contingent.[53] This alone may force the division of labour. Arthur overcomes what is conventionally read as the Spanish manifestation of injustice (the Souldan connotes Philip II), and Artegall overcomes its Irish manifestation. The different histories of English relations with Spain and Ireland may suggest a more general point. Artegall extends the rule of law and set limits to lawlessness, banishing Adicia beyond the pale to the "wyld wood" (viii.48). Arthur on the other hand enables a more radical operation of justice. We may want to call it equity, since Arthur is motivated immediately on behalf of the wronged and equitable Samient, and more distantly on behalf of Mercilla.[54] Since he actually enforces nothing, we may in a different perspective identify Arthur's action with the justice of God. In any case, the Souldan's punishment works itself out in the providential mechanism of history ("Deus flavit," says the Armada medal): Arthur exposes his shield—"Like lightening flash, that hath the gazer burned" (viii.38)—and, magically, the Souldan destroys himself.

6: Courtesy

"Be courteous," we are instructed by 1 Peter 3.8.[55] The significance of Spenser's Courtesy is vexed, since it cannot mean as little as the primitive sense strictly warrants.[56] Hermes's *koinōnia* (fellowship or communion), represents a more satisfactory generalisation of the elementary notion than those customarily adduced. At issue in Arthur's struggle in Canto viii is the opposition of the principles of sharing, "friendly offices that bind" (x.23), and self-seeking.[57] Mirabella "list not die for any louers doole", viii.21, and is content to "loue her owne delight" (vii.30); even in her exercise of something like virtue, Mirabella looks to her own well-being—she spares Disdain

because her survival depends on him (viii.17). Such egregious
self-seeking is allied to pride, and Hermes's word *pleonexia* may
indeed signify arrogance. Arthur's defeat of Disdain supplies an
easy and precise equivalence to the Hermetic opposition. As in
Book V, Arthur's role here too is curiously muted, but with a
significance easily guessed. He "assents" (viii.7) to Enias's attempted rescue of Timias, and having defeated Disdain, he
"accords" (viii.18) with Mirabella's desire to spare both him and
Scorn. Finally, he yields to her decision and he permits that she
choose her own bondage (viii.29). Behaviour so exemplarily
courteous could hardly be other than muted.

Communion is necessarily better exhibited in the behaviour
of the group than in that of the hero. It is grounded in Justice,
because as Hooker puts it (*Ecclesiastical Polity*, I.x.6), "The
greatest part of men are such as prefer their own private good
before all things," so they are constrained and encouraged by
public laws to prefer public goods to their own. At the core of
social or civil or "courtly" grace is the surrender of one's privi-
leges" hence the importance of giving and taking implicit in the
vision of the Graces on Acidale (x.23).[58] Near the heart of
Spenser's conception of courtesy is the notion of generosity as
practised in the group. The crudest opposition is in obvious
ways exemplified in the greed of the Cannibals and the Brigands. More subtly and more relevantly opposed is advantage-
seeking behaviour at the expense of the group: Coridon for
example prefers his own life to Pastorella's, (x.35), the captain
of the Brigands prefers his own pleasure to his fellows' benefit
(xi.12–21). The Book as a whole concerns itself with different
kinds of social order, and the frustration of its achievement by
self-seeking. Meliboe, eagerly misunderstood by Calidore, opposes the life of the shepherds to the life of the court (ix.25).
Donald Cheney relevantly associates pastoral, characteristic of
Book VI, with a "vision of human communion."[59] The life of
the shepherds is vulnerable, certainly; but it is vulnerable only
accidentally (whether to Coridon's jealousy of the depredations
of the Brigands) and not, as that of earthly courts is, essentially.[60]

That the shepherds are traditionally, and in this book particularly, custodians of poetry makes them especially suitable as
models of communion. Patrizi translates Hermes's *koinōnia* as
"Communicatio," and good speech has special importance in

the book: Calidore is characterised by "gracious speach" (i.2), and Calepine is named for it.[61] Society, Hooker argues (*Ecclesiastical Polity*, I.x.12): affords "the good of mutual participation," which is guaranteed only by the efficacy of human communication in speech. "Evil speakings corrupt good manners," says Paul (1 Corinthians 15.33). The book's heroes therefore avoid them: and the Blatant Beast epitomises them.

When, in Bryskett's symposium, Spenser is faced with the invitation to unlock the "goodly cabinet, in which [the] excellent treasure of virtues lieth locked up," he declines to give a lecture, and reminds his audience that the completed *Faerie Queene* should in some sort answer the request.[62] But he adds: "though perhaps not so effectually as you could desire." Any speculative scheme, even were it near the heart of Spenser's intention, would be poetically supplementary. The necessary priority of strictly poetical schemes—for example those based on Arthur's traditional twelve battles, or the twelve labours of Hercules, or the zodiac—make it unsurprising that the philosophical programme should be hard to recognise.[63] The elementary Hermetic scheme was only usable by Spenser because it matched closely his conception of *The Faerie Queene*'s narrative and imaginative possibilities. It is unlikely that any strictly philosophical scheme could have stimulated Spenser imaginatively. If there is a Hermetic matrix in his poem, it is not here, but (as Fletcher indicates) in the broader resources of "pagan mystery."[64] We have attended here to the force of the Hermetic scheme to articulate a Christian mystery.

University of Glasgow

NOTES

1. Spenserian quotations are from A. C. Hamilton's edition of *The Faerie Queene* (London: Longman, 1977). V. B. Hulbert's attempt to square the Aristotelian scheme of virtues with a duodecimal one are noticed in *Variorum Spenser*, I, 353–356. See also Robert Ellrodt, *Neoplatonism in the Poetry of Spenser* (Geneva: Droz, 1960), p. 110, Josephine W. Bennett, *The Evolution of "The Faerie Queene"* (Chicago: University of Chicago Press, 1942), pp. 229–230, Alastair Fowler, *Spenser and the Numbers of Time* (London: Routledge and Kegan Paul, 1964), pp. 51–52. Frances Yates, *The Occult Philosophy* (London: Routledge and Kegan Paul, 1979), pp. 101 ff. describes Francesco Giorgi's attempt to hermeticise the Aristotelian virtues by relating them to planetary

spheres, a scheme she relates only obscurely to a duodecimal (presumably zodiacal) one. See also Rosemond Tuve, "Spenser and the *Zodiake of Life*," reprinted in *Essays: Spenser, Herbert, Milton*, ed. Thomas P. Roche, Jr. (Princeton, N.J.: Princeton University Press, 1970), pp. 64–82. John Erskine Hankins's *Source and Meaning in Spenser's Allegory* (Oxford: Clarendon Press, 1971), pp. 2ff. developes from Bennett the suggestion that Spenser might have found in Francesco Piccolomini's *Universa Philosophia de Moribus* (1583) an influential revision of the Aristotelian scheme which raises the number of Aristotle's virtues from eleven to twelve, and which (more importantly) might include holiness. The notion that Spenser developed the scheme of cardinal virtues, deriving his twelve from the original four (as Bryskett explicitly does) is elaborately treated by Rosemond Tuve, *Allegorical Imagery: Some Medieval Books and Their Posterity* (Princeton, N.J.: Princeton University Press, 1966), pp. 62ff., and Appendix; and see Ronald Arthur Horton, *The Unity of "The Faerie Queene"* (Athens: University of Georgia Press, 1978), pp. 41ff. See also Gerald Morgan, "Spenser's Conception of Courtesy and the Design of the *Faerie Qeene*," *Review of English Studies*81, N. S. 32 (1981), 17–36, citing Dante's *Convivio* 4.17–4.8; and J. C. Bryce, *Times Literary Supplement*, August 10, 1933, on Aegedius Columna Romanus. The view that Spenser never intended to attribute to Aristotle a scheme of twelve virtues, and that his syntax is conventionally misread, is advanced by Jerry Leath Mills, "Spenser's Letter to Raleigh and the Averroistic *Poetics*," *English Literary Notes*, 14 (1976–7), 246–249, and followed by Jan Karel Kouwenhoven, *Apparent Narrative as Thematic Metaphor: The Organization of "The Faerie Queene"* (Oxford: Clarendon Press, 1983), pp. 13–14.

2. I rely on the standard modern edition, the *Corpus Hermeticum*81, edited by A. D. Nock and translated by A.-J. Festugière (Paris: Collection Budé, 1945). Three early versions are invoked in this paper. Ficino's was published first by Lefèvre d'Etaples (Paris, 1494) and reprinted with the *editio princeps* of the Greek text by Adrien Turnèbe, as *Mercurii Trismegisti Poemander* (Paris, 1554); François de Foix (Franciscus Flussas) gives another (along with a new Greek text) in *Mercurii Trismegisti Pimandras* (Bordeaux, 1574); Francesco Patrizi has one in *De Intellectu et Intellectibus* (Ferrara, 1591). The earliest English version, *The Divine Pymander*, by one Dr. Everard (1650) is of interest.

3. The Greek terms are *agnoia* (*ignorantia* in all Latin versions), countered by *gnōsis tou theou* (*Dei notitia* in the Latin, except in Patrizi, who has *Dei cognitio*); *lupē* (called *tristitia* by Ficino, *moeror* by Flussas, *dolor* by Patrizi) overcome by *gnōsis charas* (*gaudii cognitio* in all Latin versions); *akrasia* (*intemperantia* in Flussas and Patrizi, *inconstantia* in Ficino [=*incontinentia*?]), overcome by *egkrateia* (*temperantia* in all Latin versions); *epithumia* (*cupiditas* in Ficino and Flussas, *concupiscentia* in Patrizi) overcome by *karteria* (*continentia* in all Latin versions); *adikia* (*injustitia* in all Latin versions) overcome by *dikaiosune* (*iustitia* in all Latin versions); *pleonexia* (*avaritia* in Flussas and Patrizi, *luxuries* in Ficino) overcome by *koinōnia* (*communio*, but *communicatio* in Patrizi); *apatē* (*suadela* in de Foix, *deceptio* otherwise) overcome by *aletheia* (*veritas* in all Latin version); *phthonos* (*invidia* in all Latin versions) overcome by *agathon* (*bonum*); *dolos* (*dolus, fraus* in Ficino) overcome by *zōē* (*vita* in all Latin versions); *orgē* (*ira* in all Latin versions) overcome by *phōs* (*lux* in all Latin versions); *propeteia* (*temeritas* in all Latin versions); *kakia* (*pravitas* in Flussas, de Foix, otherwise *malitia*). Nock II, p. 24, note 57, compares the torments with the insatiable

appetites of the revenging demon of *Corpus Hermeticum*, I.23. C. H. Dodd *The Interpretation of the Fourth Gospel* (Cambrige: Cambridge University Press, 1953), p. 46, explains the breakdown in the symmetry of torments and powers in terms of a contradiction between an original planetary scheme and a revised zodiacal one. James Nohrnberg, *The Analogy of "The Faerie Queene"* (Princeton, N.J.: Princeton University Press, 1976), p. 783, gives mythographical and Hermetic references for planetary schemes.
4. Nock, II, p. 215, note 56, records that six is ordinarily the generative number. On the use of the Decad of virtues, of which the first seven may be planetary, see his note 57. The planetary symbolism of *The Faerie Queene* is not of specifically Hermetic inspiration: see Alastair Fowler, *Spenser and the Numbers of Time* (London: Routledge and Kegan Paul, 1964). Frances Yates, *Occult Philosophy*, p. 96, suggests that Spenser's *Hymns* recall the pattern of Hermetic ascent.
5. *Corpus Hermeticum*, XIII.3 and 13–14. A. Bartlett Giamatti, *Play of Double Senses* (Englewood Cliffs, N. J.: Prentice-Hall, 1977), p. 77, notes how the Books of *The Faerie Queene* terminate in images (however they are qualified) of restoration, redemption, and betrothal.
6. Dodd, *The Interpretation of the Fourth Gospel*, pp. 50–51, specifies the Joannine resonance of details. Nock's notes *passim* indicate biblical parallels.
7. Patrizi, Preface to *De Intellectu*, sig. B3.
8. Ludowick Bryskett, *A Discourse of Civill Life* (1606), p. 25.
9. Nohrnberg, *Analogy*, pp. 39–40, adduces the metaphor of the "clock," relevant not only for its circularity but for the movement of the hand towards the hour. Kouwenhoven, *Apparent Narrative*, p. 20, suggestively discounts the necessity of an evolutionary account: "the resurrection life is 'nothing but' the consummation in Eternity of God's *full* identification with Man in Time, through Christ. In Time, therefore, God's glory exists, paradoxically, 'already—not yet'."
10. All biblical quotations are from the Geneva version.
11. Kouwenhoven, *Apparent Narrative*, pp. 16ff, establishes the context of my own account. Some secular account of magnificence include an emphasis on desire. See Hugh MacLachlan, " 'In the person of Prince Arthur': Spenser's Magnificence and the Ciceronian Tradition," *University of Toronto Quarterly*, 46 (1976–7), 125–146, quoting R. G. Knight, *A Characterisme of the Four Cardinall Vertues* (1630): "*Magnificence*, is seen in the Meditation and pursuit of great and high Acts, with an honourable desire of glory." And Plutarch's *Life of Caesar* (58) describes how "Caesar's many successes, however, did not divert *his natural spirit of enterprise (to phusei megalourgon autou)* and ambition to the enjoyment of what he had laboriously achieved, but served as fuel and incentive for future achievements, and begat in him plans for greater deeds and a *passion for fresh glory (kaines erota doxes)*, as though he had used up what he already had." But Arthur's desire for glory is precisely not ambitious— though parodies of it are; it is on the contrary essentially transcendental. A good general account of magnificence is in William O. Harris, *Skelton's "Magnyfycence" and the Cardinal Virtue Tradition* (Chapel Hill: University of North Carolina Press, 1965).
12. Geneva's "vpright" translates the Hebrew *thum* (as in *Urim* and *Thummim*, "lights and perfections" in Exodus 28.30). *Cf.* Nock, II, p.214, note 51, on being *aklinēs* as being characterized by the stasis of the perfected and regenerate soul.

13. Calvin, *Commentary* on 2 Peter 1.3. I use the edition in the *Corpus Reformatorum*, 82 (Brunswick, 1895), cols. 441ff.

14. There are similar lists of virtues in Romans, 1.29–31, Galatians 5.19–21, 22–23, Mark 7.21–22. See B. L. Easton, "New Testament Ethical Lists," *Journal of Biblical Literature*, 51 (1932), 1–12. The emphasis on recovery of original virtue is important. Calvin explains (commenting on 2 Peter 1.9) that we are already purged by Christ's blood. On 2 Peter 1.4 he invokes the Manichean dream "that we are a part of God and that having run the race of life we shall revert to our original." *Cf.* the peroration to Mamertinus's panegyric for Maximian (3.19.2), in *Panégyriques Latins*, ed. E. Galletier, I (Paris: Collection Budé, 1949), p. 66: piety and felicity are not acquired virtues but come to being at birth. *Cf.* Calvin, *Institutes*, II.iii.4. I use the edition of John T. McNeill, 2 vols. (Philadelphia, Pa.: Westminster Press, 1960)

15. Tuve, *Allegorical Imagery*, pp. 57–60, following *Somme le roi*, identifies magnificence with the perseverance that enables perfection. See also Margaret Greaves *The Blazon of Honour* (London: Methuen, 1964). Thomistic values are attached to magnificence by Michael F. Moloney, "St. Thomas and Spenser's Virtue of Magnificence," *Journal of English and Germanic Philology*, 52 (1953), 58–62, and more recently by Gerald Morgan, "Spenser's Conception of Courtesy." See also Douglas D. Waters, "Prince Arthur as Christian Magnanimity in Booke One of *The Faerie Queene*," *Studies in English Literature*, 9 (1969), 53–62. The Stoic tradition is outlined in MacLachlan, *art. cit.* (note 13).

16. *De Baptismo* 2, in *Patrologia Latina*, I, col. 1309.

17. On Arthur as Christ see A. C. Hamilton, *The Structure of Allegory in "The Faerie Queene"* (Oxford: Clarendon Press, 1961), p. 77. On Orgoglio as Antichrist see Nohrnberg, *Analogy*, pp. 270ff.

18. A suggestive account of the Garden of Virtues is in Zailig Pollock, *The Sacred Nursery of Virtue: The Pastoral Book of Courtesy and the Unity of "The Faerie Queene"* (London: Norwood Editions, 1977); see also Horton, *Unity*, pp. 33ff and Tuve, *Allegory*, pp. 108ff. Carol V. Kaske, "Spenser's Pluralistic Universe: The View from the Mount of Contemplation," in Richard C. Frushell and Bernard J. Vondersmith, *Contemporary Thought on Edmund Spenser* (Carbondale and Edwardsville: Southern Illinois University Press, 1975), p. 230, compares the movement of the poem to tree-rings.

19. Janet Spens, *Spenser's "Faerie Queene": An Interpretation* (London: Edward Arnold, 1934), p. 32, argues on this basis that Spenser originally designed his books of eight cantos. Alastair Fowler, *Spenser and the Numbers of Time*, pp. 53–54, takes Spenser to be influenced by the medieval use of eight as the number of regeneration. In Hermetic texts it signifies "mind" opposed to "sense:" see *Corpus Hermeticum* XIII.15, I.26.

20. Kouwenhoven, *Apparent Narrative*, p. 47. In Jonson's *Masque of Beauty* Perfectio appears garbed in a Zodiac. T. K. Dunseath, *Spenser's Allegory of Justice in Book Five of "The Faerie Queene"* (Princeton, N. J.: Princeton University Press, 1968), p. 189, makes the point that Arthur "enacts" the virtues of each Book.

21. This is the usual view, explicit in S. K. Heninger, Jr., in Frushell and Vondersmith, p. 90. Tuve, *Allegory*, p. 89, working with the gardening metaphor, makes the procedure one of elimination.

22. The identification of literary and moral commonplaces was no doubt encouraged by the educational habits of grammar school and university: see

T. W. Baldwin, *William Shakespere's Small Latin and Lesse Greeke* (Urbana: University of Illinois Press, 1944), II, pp. 288–354, on the uses of "themes." The patristic commonplaces I adduce are from Thomas Hibernicus's (Palmeranus's) *Flores Doctorum* (n.p., 1601) much printed previously, and Francis Rous's *Mella Patrum* (London, 1650)

23. Holiness is the virtue most clearly related to the goal of perfection. Moral virtues are supplementary. *Cf.* Petrarch's "Of his own Ignorance," in *The Renaissance Philosophy of Man*, ed. Ernst Cassirer *et al.* (Chicago, Ill.: University of Chicago Press, 1948), p. 105: "For though our ultimate goal does not lie in virtue where the philosophers locate it, it is through the virtues that the direct way leads to the place where it does lie." But without supplementary virtue, Faith's powers may be irrelevant in the moral world: grown to "perfection of all heauenly grace," Redcrosse abhors the world and "mortall life gan loath, as thing forlore" (I.x.21). Hamilton, *Structure*, pp. 128–129, takes Books II–VI as unfolding a pattern already available in Book I. The antagonisms between different conceptions of the good life are examined by Carol V. Kaske, "Spenser's Pluralistic Universe: The View from the Mount of Contemplation (*F.Q.* I.x)," in Frushell and Vondersmith, pp. 121–149. See also Gerald Morgan, "Holiness as the First of Spenser's Aristotelian Moral Virtues," *Modern Language Review*, 81 (1986), 817–837; and "Spenser's Conception of Courtesy." Virgil K. Whitaker, "The Theological Structure of the *Faerie Queene* I," *ELH*, 19 (1952), 151–164 specifies the Calvinist bias. Anthea Hume, *Edmund Spenser: Protestant Poet* (Cambridge: Cambridge University Press, 1984), pp. 59–71, lucidly expounds the issues.

24. *Flores Doctorum*, p. 772, *s.v. Pietas;* also relevant are entries under *Sapientia* and *Scientia.* On faith as knowledge see also Calvin, *Institutes*, III.ii.2, and his gloss of "agnitio Dei" on his Commentary on 2 Peter 1. This bias reappears outside the strictly theological tradition, as in Bruno: "with the speculative intellect one first sees the beautiful and good, then the will desires it, and next the industrious intellect pursues and seeks it" (*Giordano Bruno's The Heroic Furies*, trans. Paul E. Memmo (Chapel Hill: University of North Carolina Press, 1964), p. 238. But Hooker, *Ecclestiastical Polity*, I.vii.7, explains that it is the disposition of the will to know that makes possible the secondary Christian revelation. I use *The Works of Richard Hooker*, 2 vols. (Oxford, 1850); the Folger Library Edition is as yet incomplete. And Spenser himself may give priority to a disposition of the will when he makes Humility the Porter for Dame Celia (I.x.5). Aristotle makes a distinction of moral and intellectual virtues in *Nicomachean Ethics*, VI.1–3.

25. See *Mella Patrum*, p. 164 and p. 166.

26. *Cf.* Calvin, *Institutes*, III.xiv.4, recalling Augustine.

27. On this originally Hebraic formula see J. N. D. Kelly, *A Commentary on the Epistles of Peter and of Jude* (London: Adam and Charles Black, 1969), pp. 298–299.

28. Augustine, *Enarrationes in Psalmos* (on Vulgate Psalm 95.6), *Patrologia Latina*, 37, col. 1232. On his use of the formula "Dilige, et quod vis fac," see Peter Brown, *Augustine of Hippo* (London: Faber, 1967), p. 209.

29. Spenser invokes the metaphor of the race at *Faerie Queene*, II.i.32; *cf.* Hebrews 12.1, and 1 Corinthians 9.24–27.

30. On personifications of ignorance Hamilton cites Wilhelm Fueger, *Deutsche Vierteljahrsschrift*, 45 (1971), 252–301.

31. Nohrnberg, *Analogy*, p. 274, treats Orgoglio as a false Christ.

32. Douglas Brooks-Davies, *Spenser's Faerie Queene: A Critical Commentary on Books I and II* (Manchester: Manchester University Press, 1977), pp. 76–78.

33. *Flores Doctorum*, p. 471, *s.v. Ignorantia*; also relevant are entries under *Doctrina* and *Error*. Calvin opens the *Istitutes* with a commentary on the relationship between knowledge of God and that of the self.

34. A witty account of Guyon's gloominess is given by K. W. Gransden, "Allegory and Personality in Spenser's Heroes," *Essays in Criticism*, 20, (1970), 298–310. On the principles of temperance see the headnote to Book II in Hamilton's edition. See also Gerald Morgan, "The Idea of Temperance in the Second Book of *The Faerie Queene*," *Review of English Studies*, N. S. 37 (1986), 11–39.

35. *Mella Patrum*, p. 65

36. Seneca, *Epistola Morales*, 23.4, and *De Vita Beata*, 25.3. Calvin, *Institutes*, III.viii.8–9, qualifies the Stoic position.

37. Burton, *The Anatomy of Melancholy*, I.ii.1 (5); see also I.i.3 (3). Nohrnberg, *Analogy*, p. 317 specifies acedia as the form of the melancholy. See also J. L. Mills "Prudence, History, and the Prince in *The Faerie Queene*, Book II," *Huntington Library Quarterly*, 41 (1978), 83–101.

38. *Flores Doctorum*, p. 994, *s.v. Tristitia*.

39. Cf. Calvin, *Institutes*, III.xiii.5.

40. Alastair Fowler, "The Image of Mortality: *The Faerie Queene*, II.i–ii," *Huntington Library Quarterly*, 24 (1961), 91–110, and "The River Guyon," *Modern Language Notes*, 75 (1960), 289–292. Nohrnberg, *Analogy*, p. 496 argues that Guyon acts in a Bacchic frenzy.

41. Aristotle, *Nichomachean Ethics*, 8.2 asserts the temperate man (the *sōphrōn*) does not have excessive or bad desires. The continent man (the *egkratēs*), on the other hand contains a tendency to *akrasia* (*Nicomachean Ethics*, VII.1). The Aristotelian antonym of *sōphrosunē* is *thēriotēs (ibid.)*.

42. Anthea Hume, *Edmund Spenser*, p. 109, complains of the lack of thematic focus.

43. But Paul Alpers, *The Poetry of "The Faerie Queene"* (Princeton, N. J.: Princeton University Press, 1967), pp. 30–11, treats the anomalous intervention of Proteus as a kind of parody of Cymoent's rescue of Marinell.

44. Sannazaro, *Eclogae*, 4, lines 46–58, casts Proteus as the saviour of the nymph Neris in a geographical allegory. As "Shepheard of the seas" (viii.30) Proteus may be confusingly identified with Ralegh as "shepheard of the Ocean" (*Colin Clouts Come Home Again*, line 66).

45. Nohrnberg, *Analogy*, p. 586, and see generally pp. 580ff. On similar lines, Thomas P. Roche, Jr., *The Kindly Flame: A Study of the Third and Fourth Books of Spenser's "Faerie Queene"* (Princeton, N. J.: Princeton University Press, 1968), p. 160, casts him as "man's body independent of but not opposed to his soul." On the mythography see A. Bartlett Giamatti, "Proteus Unbound: Some Versions of the Sea God in the Renaissance," reprinted in *Exile and Change in Renaissance Literature* (New Haven and London: Yale University Press, 1984), pp. 115–150. Angus Fletcher, *The Prophetic Moment: An Essay on Spenser* (Chicago, Ill.: University of Chicago Press, 1971), p. 94, says that Spenser "gives Proteus his familiar role of villain." Giamatti, *Play of Double Sense*, p. 123, calls him the "essence of formlessness, of deformation as the only formative principle," but his remarks on Florimell's horror of loss of form are suggestive in the context I outline.

46. Fowler, *Numbers of Time*, pp. 122–155; and Roche, *Kindly Flame*, p. 56.

47. Aristotle, *Nicomachean Ethics*, VII.7.4, emphasises the restraining sense; Plato, *Laches*, 192b gives the more positive sense. Stephanus's Dictionary, *s.v. karteria*, gives *Tolerantia, Patientia*.

48. *Flores Doctorum*, p. 399, *s.v. Fortitudo*. See Rudolph Wittkower, "Patience and Chance: The Story of a Political Emblem," reprinted in *Allegory and the Migration of Symbols* (London: Thames and Hudson, 1977), pp. 107–112.

49. A. Kent Hieatt, "Scudamour's Practise of *Maistrye* upon Amoret," *PMLA*, 77 (1962), 509–510.

50. Rouse, *Mella Patrum*, p. 933. See Roche, *Kindly Flame*, pp. 77–78.

51. The character of Spenser's sophistication of the elementary notion is lucidly discussed by James E. Phillips, "Renaissance Concepts of Justice and the Structure of *The Faerie Queene* Book V," *Huntington Library Quarterly*, 33 (1970), 103–20.

52. Dunseath, *Spenser's Allegory of Justice*, p. 190.

53. Fletcher, *Prophetic Moment*, p. 282, remarks the historical emphasis of equity. Spenser's turn to history is treated in Michael O'Connell, *Mirror and Veil: The Historical Dimension of Spenser's "Faerie Queene"* (Chapel Hill: University of North Carolina Press, 1977). On the identification of the Souldan and Philip II, see René Graziani, "Philip II's 'Impresa' and Spenser's Souldan," *Journal of the Warburg and Courtauld Institutes*, 27 (1964), 322–324.

54. Fletcher, *Prophetic Moment*, p. 209, suggests she represents "a quality of 'samience,' a *homonoia* or universal likemindedness." Hamilton's edition (on viii.23) offers an etymology from *sam*, meaning "together."

55. This translates *tapeinophrones*, given in the Vulgate as *humiles*. Beza translates *comes* [*sic*], explained by the Junius-Tremellius gloss as "commendat . . . quaecumque ad pacem et mutuam conjunctionem fovendam spectant."

56. But see Humphrey Tonkin, *Spenser's Courteous Pastoral* (Oxford: Clarendon Press, 1972), pp. 239 ff., 290 ff., who redefines Spenserian courtesy as "social harmony." Over-generalisation weakens its force: Dorothy W. Culp, "Courtesy and Moral Virtue," *Studies in English Literature*, 11 (1971), 37–51 relates it to Cicero's moral virtue, Gerald Morgan, "Courtesy and Design," p. 18, calls generosity its specific inner sense.

57. Jerome, cited *Flores Doctorum*, p. 162, *s.v. Communitas*, writes: "Pride quickly comes on men living alone, who sleep when they will and are busy when they will; but you living in society do not do as you will." Communities disintegrate where this kind of pride is given the rein. In Thucidydes, *History*, 3.82, it is the *pleonexia* of the opposed parties that creates civil war. In Herodotus, 7.149 it is the *pleonexia* of the Spartans that makes them refuse accommodation with Athens, even in the face of a Persian invasion. Nohrnberg, *Analogy*, p. 660, writes of the sense of Book VI as "of a variety of separate individuals, set apart from one another." It is against this separation that the superior spirit of community might be supposed to work.

58. Donald Cheney, *Spenser's Image of Nature* (New Haven and London: Yale University Press, 1966), pp. 229–30, and see Mark Archer, "The Meaning of Spenser's 'Grace' and 'Courtesy': Book Six of *The Faerie Queene*," *Studies in English Literature*, 27 (1987), 17–34.

59. Cheney, *Spenser's Image*, p. 74.

60. Discussing Book I, John N. Wall, "The English Reformation and the Recovery of Christian Community in Spenser's *The Faerie Queene*," *Studies in*

Philology, 80 (1983), 142–162 describes another relevant "pastoral" context.
61. Nohrnberg, *Analogy*, p. 676 calls Book VI "a romance analogy for 'ciuill conuersation'," and see pp. 681 ff. Tonkin *Courteous Pastoral*, pp. 213 ff. treats the role of poetry in the Book. See also Robin Wells *Spenser's Faerie Queene and the Cult of Elizabeth* (London: Croom Helm, 1983) pp. 135–136. On the etymology of Calepine Hamilton's edition (on iii.27) cites Parker; Tonkin, p. 66 wittily derives the names of Calepine and Mirabella from the names of dictionaries. "Language is the chief bond of society," says Calvin (on Psalm 81.5).
62. Ludowick Bryskett, *A Discourse of Civill Life* (1606), pp. 25–28.
63. Nohrnberg, *Analogy*, pp. 35ff. discusses a variety of duodecimal schemes. Spenser may have viewed some of them ironically: at III.x.31 Trompart affects the look of a "doughtie Doucepere."
64. Fletcher, *Prophetic Moment*, p. 127.

ANTHONY M. ESOLEN

Irony and the Pseudo-physical in *The Faerie Queene*

EVEN A devout Spenserian will admit that we do not read *The Faerie Queene* for laughs. Hazlitt, who loves the enchantment of Faery Land, and would not dream of taking its allegory quite seriously, still finds only one jest in the poem;[1] most critics since have found few others. But according to William Nelson, Spenser did sense the faint ridiculousness of reworking the old fantastical tales of knights and dragons and distressed damsels. Nelson cites a host of examples of burlesque, "pseudo-documentation," and "what must be deliberate bathos" in *The Faerie Queene*, and hints that Spenser's method of allegory forces him sometimes to verge on self-parody.[2] If we adopt Nelson's premise, that Spenser may have had fun toying with that ostensibly straitlaced allegory of his, we may be able to identify the muted but fanciful irony which is such a source of pleasure in *The Faerie Queene*.

Spenserian irony is everywhere in the poem, but it requires a sensitive ear for what is allegorically inappropriate or too appropriate. Consider Error, the tremendous dragon of the first book (I. i. 11–26). When we meet her she is an awesome presence lurking in darkness, as evil as our imaginations can make her out to be.[3] During her battle with Redcross, however, that evil suddenly becomes material and even comical. Wounded, she vomits forth a river of ink and paper; then, as if to highlight the grotesquerie, our hero decapitates her, whereupon a horde of eyeless spawn (who hide in her mouth whenever they sense danger) gorge themselves upon her neck until they burst. To call the scene ironic is to risk using a word whose definition, if it has one at all,[4] is meaninglessly vague. And yet when Error's black vomit reveals itself as books and papers, we sense, in the anticlimax, the sort of self-conscious incongruity that is the hallmark of irony. Error, as romance monster, possesses the requisite monstrous features, with her snaky tail and poisonous dugs; Error, as heresy, spews forth her books and hates the light. But the two natures of this creature do not quite meld into one seamless whole, nor are they meant to. Our pleasure derives, as all Spenserians insist, from reading both Errors simulatneously, but—and here the critics miss the mark[5]—not because Error the monster provides us with a smooth transition into Error the heresy. For even when Spenser begs us to shift our attention from the hulking dragon to its allegorical significance, his Errors are like the incongruous homonyms that flash on and off in a pun.[6] "God helpe the man so wrapt in Errours endlesse traine" (I. i. 18. 9), Spenser says, as Redcross is held fast by the monster's winding tail; "Such vgly monstrous shapes elswhere may no man reed" (21. 9), he says, comparing Error's abortive brood, and, by implication, the pamphleteers spawned by one original false teaching, to the half-formed creatures believed to be cast up by the Nile. In short, one Error is unaware of the other's existence. Sometimes they "shade imperceptibly" into each other, to use Freeman's phrase;[7] sometimes, as above, they fit together glaringly well, and sometimes Spenser seems to forget that he is an allegorist at all, as when he feigns indignation over the ingratitude of the monster's children (25).

No matter how it is defined, irony thrives upon a sense of friction between incongruous states of knowledge. Spenser's allegory is ideal for irony, for he constantly has the opportunity to highlight the incongruity between his world of allegorical signs and the worlds of significance they point to, while, as a modest man and a teller of old-fashioned romances, he can pretend to know less than he does about the process, referring to his allegories as if they were mere chronicles and treating his characters as if they were physical beings. This irony is justified, first of all, by the pleasure it gives. We enjoy irony, and our interpretation of Spenser's allegory ought to respect that enjoyment. Granted, Spenser's irony is often didactic. When we behold characters mistaking the significance of their actions—Duessa mounting her apocalyptic beast (I. viii. 6ff.), hopeful of a victory which we, who have read her story in another place (Rev. 17), know to be impossible—we are urged by the staged ignorance to think about what we are lucky to have known already. Such irony is virtually unmistakeable, and seems to require a response from the intellect. When Spenser compares the teeming worms that issue from Error's body to a cloud of gnats whose "tender wings" trouble the "gentle Shepheard in sweete euen-tide" (I. i. 23), he wishes us to understand that false doctrines are no more hurtful to the man of faith than a few gnats are to the pastor tending his flock. The image of the shepherd is, of course, motivated by Scripture (John 10), and is intellectually appropriate, since doctrinal error concerns pastors most of all. But it is the disjunction between the bland hillside and the battle which seizes our attention. That incongruity, made all the more noticeable by its presentation in a stanza-long conceit, arrests the action and entices us to stand above both the knight and the shepherd in our comprehensive understanding of what they signify. Still, if we insist that every shred of Spenserian irony must have some point or other, we may miss the fun Spenser has in lavishing Error with all that alliterative blood and guts—in other words, we may take too seriously his revelling in the physicality of a creature whose allegorical nature he pretends to forget. And, in fact, that single jest of Hazlitt's was just such a deliberate overphysicalization of an allegorical emblem: the cuckold Malbecco escapes notice by the herd of satyrs thanks to his "faire hornes on hight" (III. x. 47. 4).

Spenserian irony flourishes when we respect the fun of Spenser's fiction, the put-on naïveté of his narrative voice. As Paul Alpers says, Spenser's "manner of address" is "self-effacing . . . ; it makes sense only as a rhetorical instrument, appealing to the reader's feelings and awarenesses."[8] Spenser uses, disingenuously, the "wrong" or inappropriate symbols, says disparaging things about himself, has his good characters do what appear to be wrong deeds, partly in order to manipulate our responses[9]—as that unexpected pastoral simile leads us to reevaluate the power of Error—and partly for the sheer delight and effectiveness of irony itself, for, as Wayne Booth points out, irony often establishes a more intimate communion between author and reader than does straight narration.[10] Those purposes are not contradictory, and do not undermine Spenser's message.

For instance, when Spenser attempts to describe "dame Nature" on Arlo Hill, he pretends not to know her gender, not to know why she wears a veil, and not to be able to think of any proper comparison for her radiance. The ironic modesty helps

to teach us what Nature represents, and to prevent the scene
from acquiring too tragic an air:

> Then forth issewed (great goddesse) great dame *Nature,*
> With goodly port and gracious Maiesty;
> Being far greater and more tall of stature
> Then any of the gods or Powers on hie:
> Yet certes by her face and physnomy,
> Whether she man or woman inly were,
> That could not any creature well descry:
> For, with a veile that wimpled euery where,
> Her head and face was hid, that mote to none appeare.

> That some doe say was so by skill deuized,
> To hide the terror of her vncouth hew,
> From mortall eyes that should be sore agrized;
> For that her face did like a Lion shew,
> That eye of wight could not indure to view:
> But others tell that it so beautious was,
> And round about such beames of splendor threw,
> That it the Sunne a thousand times did pass,
> Ne could be seene, but like an image in a glass.

> That well may seemen true: for, well I weene
> That this same day, when she on *Arlo* sat,
> Her garment was so bright and wondrous sheene,
> That my fraile wit cannot deuize to what
> It to compare, nor finde like stuffe to that,
> As those three sacred Saints, though else most wise,
> Yet on mount *Thabor* quite their wits forgat,
> When they their glorious Lord in strange disguise
> Transfigur'd sawe; his garments so did daze their eyes.
>   (VII. vii. 5–7)

Notice how Spenser seems progressively to contradict himself,
as if he were attempting to teach us, indirectly through a profes-
sion of ignorance, that Nature's deity is inscrutable, paradoxical, unsearchable in her ways. At first she is great "dame"
Nature, taller than all the gods on high (although her presence
among classical gods, and those gods' meeting atop a hill in
Ireland, are surprising); then she is either man or woman (or,
we infer, neither or both); she wears a veil to hide the terror of

her face, or to hide its unparalleled beauty. Spenser's either-or statements are good examples of his subtle irony, since clearly he causes us to consider Nature from each point of view: she is both terrifying and unspeakably beautiful. Roche refers us[11] to the famous passage, 2 Cor. 3: 12–18, in which Paul constrasts the veil which prevents the hearts of the Jews from apprehending God, with the Holy Spirit's lifting of the veil so that we, after a life of seeing God as through a glass darkly, "revelata facie gloriam Domini speculantes, in eandem imaginem transformamur a claritate in claritatem" (18). The careful reader will apply Paul's lesson to Mutability's foolish and blasphemous desire "to see that mortall eyes have never seene" (vi. 32. 3). "Others tell," "may seemen true," "I weene," "my fraile wit"— the modest disclaimers allow Spenser to set up a daring equation between God himself—or Christ, the wisdom of God, through whom all things are made[12]—and Nature. Yet the same disclaimers, along with the gently comic handling of those poor apostles who, "though else most wise," "quite their wits forgat" (7. 7), remind us that Nature *is* only "great dame Nature," the lovely lady of the Mutability Cantos. For even in Spenser's impossible description of Nature's face, now that of a man, a woman, a terrible lion, we feel a shiver of delight which is not reducible to our understanding of why Nature's face theologically should be what Spenser says it is. That delight arises because of the incongruity between the homeliness of a hill packed with gods and units of time and theological principles and animals, all of which we are encouraged to imagine physically (think of old Mole decking himself with flowers as if he had fallen in love with a new nymph, vii. 11, or Nature's Sergeant Order, ushering everyone to his proper seat [4], and the profundity of the metaphysical truth which Spenser is trying to illustrate through their means. Spenser's ironic self-effacement and self-contradiction help us to interpret the figure of Nature, to keep in mind the provisionality of our interpretation, and to anchor us in the comedy of that unlikely meeting.

But in order to enjoy irony we must allow ourselves to play its game, and that may involve refraining from interpreting certain words or actions as we normally would interpret them. In the fifth book of *The Faerie Queene*, Talus, that sign of relentless justice, searches for Munera ("rewards"), the daughter of the tyrant Pollente ("possessing great power") who has

made himself rich by waylaying travellers, and whom Artegall
has recently slain. Talus finds her under a heap of gold. Her
execution shows how far off the track we can stray, and how
much humor we can miss, if we assume that the more weighty
or ambivalent or even humane the interpretation, the more
valid it is, and the richer the poem:

> Thence he her drew
> By the faire lockes, and fowly did array,
> Withouten pitty of her goodly hew,
> That *Artegall* him selfe her seemelesse plight did rew.

> Yet for no pitty would he change the course
> Of Iustice, which in *Talus* hand did lye;
> Who rudely hayld her forth without remorse,
> Still holding vp her suppliant hands on hye,
> And kneeling at his feete submissiuely.
> But he her suppliant hands, those hands of gold,
> And eke her feete, those feete of siluer trye,
> Which sought vnrighteousnesse, and iustice sold,
> Chopt off, and nayld on high, that all might them behold.

> Her selfe then tooke he by the sclender wast,
> In vaine loud crying, and into the flood
> Ouer the Castle wall adowne her cast,
> And there her drowned in the durty mud:
> But the streame washt away her guilty blood.
> Thereafter all that mucky pelfe he tooke,
> The spoile of peoples euill gotten good,
> The which her sire had scrap't by hooke and crooke,
> And burning all to ashes, powr'd it downe the brooke.

> And lastly all that Castle quite he raced,
> Even from the sole of his foundation,
> And all the hewen stones thereof defaced,
> That there mote be no hope of reparation,
> Nor memory thereof to any nation.
> All which when *Talus* throughly had perfourmed,
> Sir *Artegall* vndid the euill fashion,
> And wicked customes of that Bridge refourmed.
> Which done, vnto his former iourney he retourned.
>
> (V. ii. 25–28)

And everyone lives happily ever after. The morals: never take bribes. Justice pursued with impartiality would terrify many in power.

But if we solve Spenser's text by applying a one-to-one correspondence of character to moral principle, and often quite simple moral principle at that, how does the poetry remain interesting? Munera represents bribetaking and extortion, Talus represents *lex talionis,* the law of retribution in kind: an eye for an eye. The equations are clear. Judith Dundas notes that Spenser's poetry is sometimes formulaic, failing to inspirit its allegorical figures with life; there seems sometimes to be nothing for the critic to do but label the figures and move on.[13] What else can we do with Munera, "whereas she hidden lay / Vnder an heape of gold" (V. ii. 25. 5–6)? Surely it was no stroke of genius for Spenser to have Bribetaking lie there. We all know how wealth suborns the law. Spenser's vision cannot or should not be so embarrassingly plain.

At such an impasse, the reader may turn to a part of *The Faerie Queene* which is more ambivalent, more prone to the types of interpretation we are fond of, or to try to discover an irony or undermining which Spenser may not have acknowledged. Or we may dismiss the poetry as bad, as do even the best critics, most of whom cannot stomach Talus' actions. "Spenser was the instrument of a detestable policy in Ireland, and in the fifth book the wickedness he had shared begins to corrupt his imagination." "We can agree that here, as elsewhere in Book Five, there are personal reasons for the failure of Spenser's poetry." "Talus is his instrument for administering right in an alien world. . . . His task is simply destructive—he routs, he lays waste, he 'thresht out falshood, and did truth unfould.' The result is a willed sadism that would have been imaginable earlier only if the tyrant had been Busirane."[14] If we assume, with such criticism, that Spenser is too politically or sexually repressive to be anything but cruel in this scene, we leave the stage open for a good deal of irony, all of it directed against our poet who, lacking a Freudian grammar, happens in this case to understand less about himself that we do. Munera, one might say, is an abstraction until she appears in person. As soon as Spenser presents her he must fall from his realm of ideas into our world of uncertainty, where justice, if it were pure, would not be just. Once clothed with a body, Munera can, as a beautiful woman, claim our pity. Talus then is not Justice only but a man "vnmou'd with praiers, or with piteous thought" (23. 2). He is harsh, masculine, rigidly following what is abstractly right, rather than what is humane. When he draws her forth "by the faire lockes" (25. 7), even Artegall, the knight of justice, feels pity for her; unfortunately, Artegall is not yet united with his beloved Britomart, and so he is still too weak, too male, to let that pity sway his decision. Instead Talus chops off Munera's hands and feet—a gratuitous and gruesome act—and, rather than show mercy to a suppliant, and a woman, takes her "by the sclender wast, / In vaine loud crying" (27. 1–2). Why "sclender" wasit, if not that Talus, or Spenser, feels a strange glee in his righteous indignation? In any case Munera now is victim instead of victimizer.

So the analysis might continue. But what if Spenser were in control of his imagery, and not under the pressure of a divided soul? He does, after all, wish to teach, and it is often in the interest of a teacher to be clear. Suppose, then, that the puzzle were already solved for us, and we knew perfectly well what Munera was supposed to be, and we were always expected to remember it. Can there not be irony anyway—an irony which is neither simply didactic nor simply subversive of Spenser's ideal of justice?

Such questions help expose the tonal error of much Spenserian criticism. For there is often a bright humor, not despair at the impossibility of the task, in Spenser's channeling of the inexhaustible ideal into what seems physical. Kouwenhoeven, despite an eager willingness to assume that "the poem's meaning is given," understands that at least some of the pleasure of Spenser's allegory arises not through our attempts to figure out what it means, but through our appreciation of how it means: "The point of a riddle is not its solution but the transfiguration into intelligibility of the riddle itself."[15] Perhaps we should say, "not its solution *only*"; in any case, the solution of a riddle, like the correct interpretation of a bit of blatant irony, may be obvious, and yet the riddle may be clever and pleasurable, as the irony may be very funny. "The kingdom of God is like a mustard seed," says Christ. "The kingdom of God is like a woman who kneaded yeast into three measures of flour" (Luke 13: 18–21). Even after they have been explicated appropriately and plausibly, Christ's parables retain their beauty and their irony. Not that Christ subverts his own intentions, poking fun at the Father and His kingdom by comparing them to such humble things. The very lesson of the Incarnation was that God does descend into immediate involvement with everyday life. The greatness of God, rather, is given—Christ expects that it will not come under suspicion—and so the irony of his parables rests in his audacity to compare the Lord with something which he assumes his listeners will find unlikely, or even objectionable (see Luke's version of the parable of the talents, 19: 11–27), and then, in his somewhat simplistic explications, to make the message of those parables appear plausible. The Church Fathers made the parables even more parabolical by riddling in turn upon them: if the kingdom of God is a mustard seed, says Augustine, then the leaves of that tree are Holy Writ and the birds who build in that tree are the saints. We should remember that there is a pleasure, of which Renaissance poets were perhaps more keenly aware than we, in devising elaborate metaphors in order to clarify what, if delivered in plain language, might be perfectly obvious.

In Spenser the evil of Munera/Bribetaking is given, not under question. It would have been too clumsy for Spenser to intend that we read Munera as a full human being, and then to write her into his poem so briefly, with no effect on the story line or on any of the other characters.[16] She lacks also those touches of humanity—motive, personality, life history—with which Dante, for example, can color a few lines of poetry in order to create what we will consider a deeply human being. Furthermore, if we have read so far into Spenser's poem, we will have met other quasi-characters who are little more than paper allegories of some virtue or vice, but who say or do the apparently inappropriate thing and make the poem far more interesting because of it. Despair, for example (I. ix. 38–47), surprises us by speaking like a mild church-divine, administering the consolations of death; what he says about sin and the weariness of life might be accepted by a Christian as profoundly and hauntingly true. And yet a reader as wise as Una (53) understands that Despair omits from the equation the divine mercy that has conquered death and redeemed sin. Scudamour's "rape" of Amoret is recounted as a church-robbing (IV. x. 53) and a kidnapping (57); but the violence is gently humorous, since, what with Spenser's lush and sensual description of the

Temple of Venus, of the lovers who inhabit it and the allegorical figures like Concord who facilitate courtship and true love, we guess that Venus is willing to have her temple "robbed" and that Amoret is at least timidly willing to be stolen away. The whole scene is an elaborate and mock-heroic simile for courtship itself, and is pleasant in its contrast between the exotic Faery Land event and the everyday falling in love that it describes. Consider how much less effective, and less ingenious, it would have been if Despair were simply a raving suicide, or if Scudamour had fed Amoret a plausible line or two.

Finally, and a bit circularly, we must not read too much into Munera, because Spenser's humor depends upon the incongruity between what is moral in his world, and what would be moral in ours. It is humorous, in an odd way, that Talus should nail Munera's hands and feet on high. There is nothing morally profound in his act. It is simply poetic justice against extortion's hands by which she takes bribes and her feet which she allows suppliants to kiss. They are not actual hands and feet, nor do they represent actual hands and feet. We understand that. But despite themselves they must call up in our minds images of hands and feet, and metal ones, no less. Spenser is disingenuous, seems not to understand how close he appears— although he is really not close at all—to undermining what he wants to say. A tension exists between what he assumes we will understand from the beginning as an allegorical equation (Munera signifies extortion), and his presentation of that allegory with unnecessary or even pleasantly dangerous physical detail. Spenser has the confidence to allow Munera to remind us of the traditional woman in distress, whom true knights are supposed to help. "Slender wast" is a daringly incongruous and irrelevant stroke. We are forced to picture the absurd: a woman with hands and feet chopped off, thrown over the castle wall with hardly a shudder of remorse from the perpetrators; yet these are good characters, and we cannot doubt it. All intrusions of the physical into our minds may be seen as Spenser's emphasis, again through the incongruity between Munera's world and our physical world of men and women, of the validity of his allegory, as if extortion were so much the greater evil in that Artegall and Talus ignore so many "reasons" to show pity. One may explain Munera's beauty allegorically by saying that corruption is always whitewashed on the outside. But even that explanation, while perfectly believable, does not show why Spenser chose to flirt with Munera so openly. Indeed any rational or allegorical interpretation of the scene that ignores its irony is bound to appear either trivial or too deadly serious. For example, although it is true that Artegall will have to wait to have his justice tempered by Britomart's equity, we have no cause in this scene for calling his actions unjust. As for Talus, Hough is astute to see in him an ideal judicial system, speedy, efficient, certain, impartial, impervious to appeal: "Spenser shows great insight and discretion precisely in making Talus an insentient robot, not a human being".[17] The law is controlled by human beings; Artegall is the one to whom the convicted must plead for mercy. Human beings may bend, but law in itself must remain inflexible; any student of jurisprudence knows this to be so, and yet how oddly appropriate and inappropriate is Spenser's incorporation of this truth into the juggernaut Talus! Perhaps, if we learn to appreciate Spenser's irony for its own sake, we can understand why Hazlitt—with neither bloodthirstiness nor sangfroid—called Talus one of the two finest achievements of the last three books of *The Faerie Queene*.[18]

Our judgement of what an author probably means is not divorced from what we believe would be good or beautiful or in a thousand other ways worthwhile for him to mean. Our interpretations, we feel, should be most probable and should make the work appear in its best light; but critics often give the impression that the only worthwhile thing an author can do is to espouse some ideology, say, Christianity, or to attack it, or to forge a definite political or theological position of his own, or to undermine the conditions for significance itself. Yet an author may consider it worthwhile to entertain us with music, pageantry, humor, paradox, irony, or any of the thousand things which entertain most people. Broadly speaking, the pleasure derived from them is part of the meaning of the text, and criticism should not drown it out.

With Spenser we need to keep such pleasures in mind even when asking what he means by an encounter of allegorical figures. Take, for instance, Guyon's adventures at the Bower of Bliss (II. xii.). Faced with the task of describing a place which we will recognize at once as false and wicked, but also as tempting, Spenser uses some fairly plain irony to let us in on the joke. The Bower is "a place pickt out by choice of best aliue, / That natures worke by art can imitate" (xii. 42. 2–3); that sounds fine, unless we wonder why anyone would desire the imitation when the reality is at hand. Its gate imprisons the Bower's guests as well as it keeps away "those vnruly beasts"— which beasts we do not know, since the unruliest of creatures are inside—"yet was the fence thereof but weake and thin" (43. 2–3). Although the gate is made "of substaunce light" (8) only "wisedomes powre, and temperaunces might, / By which the mightiest things efforced bin" (6–7) can prevail against it. The fence, in other words, has no power for defense but the foolishness of those whom intemperance imprisons. The gate also bears a carving of "the famous history / Of Iason and Medaea" (44. 3–4), which Spenser describes rather matter-of-factly, compressing Medea's slaughter of her brother and then of her children into one innocent phrase: "her furious louing fit" (44.5). The appropriateness of the myth to the gate is plain to those readers learned enough to see through Spenser's understatement. Similar ironies abound, and Guyon understands that what we see in the Bower of Bliss is not what we get: Genius, robed in a "looser garment" "not fit for speedy pace, or manly exercize" (46. 7, 9) is not, as Spenser baldly states, the true god Genius to whom is encharged the "generation of all / That liues" (47. 3–4), but a Comus-like god of drunkenness. Likewise the meadow which Guyon and his friend the Palmer enter is compared with "Eden selfe, if ought with Eden mote compaire" (52. 9). And again we have the irony of Spenser pretending not to know what he wishes to teach us: all the dubious imagery of the preceding stanzas leads us to answer Spenser's implied question in the negative. No such garden can equal the beauty of Eden, although it may, perhaps, compare with Eden in the unhappy consequences that issue from it; nor is it far-fetched to say that the sin of Adam and Eve was that of intemperance, since they wished to surpass the bounds of humanity and become as gods. Even the name "Acrasia," by the way, possesses an ironic pair of meanings: commentators gloss it as the Greek "akrasía," "one who is powerless or not in command of himself"; but this meaning can be extended to apply to bodily incontinence, as evident in the Matthew's usage of the plural "akrasías" (23: 25) to describe the contents of that well-polished cup to which Christ so trenchantly compares the scribes and Pharisees.

Guyon marches through the garden, which is, critical fervor to the contrary,[19] a veritable roadside wax-museum of lifelike effects, what with its "painted flowers" (58. 5), its golden berries that almost snap the branches they hang from (55. 1–6), its metal ivy (61), its jasper pond-bottom (62. 8), and so on, all put together in such a way that the seams and rivets remain invisible. Finally there appear "two naked Damzelles" (63. 6), damsels of flesh and blood, to tempt Guyon and to test our ability to read Spenser. The passage merits quotation in full:

> Sometimes the one would lift the other quight
>   Aboue the waters, and then downe againe
>   Her plong, as ouer maistered by might,
>   Where both awhile would couered remaine,
>   And each the other from to rise restraine;
>   The whiles their snowy limbes, as through a vele,
>   So through the Christall waues appeared plaine:
>   Then suddeinly both would themselues vnhele,
> And th'amarous sweet spoiles to greedy eyes reuele.

> As that faire Starre, the messenger of morne,
>   His deawy face out of the sea doth reare:
>   Or as the *Cyprian* goddesse, newly borne
>   Of th'Oceans fruitfull froth, did first appeare:
>   Such seemed they, and so their yellow heare
>   Christalline humour dropped downe apace.
>   Whom such when *Guyon* saw, he drew him neare,
>   And somewhat gan relent his earnest pace,
> His stubborne brest gan secret pleasaunce to embrace.

> The wanton Maidens him espying, stood
>   Gazing a while at his vnwonted guise;
>   Then th'one her selfe low ducked in the flood,
>   Abasht, that her a straunger did avise:
>   But th'other rather higher did arise,
>   And her two lilly paps aloft displayed,

And all, that might his melting hart entise
To her delights, she vnto him bewrayed:
The rest hid vnderneath, him more desirous made.

With that, the other likewise vp arose,
  And her faire lockes, which formerly were bownd
  Vp in one knot, she low adowne did lose:
  Which flowing long and thick, her cloth'd arownd,
  And th'yuorie in golden mantle gownd:
  So that faire spectacle from him was reft,
  Yet that, which reft it, no lesse faire was fownd:
  So hid in lockes and waues from lookers theft,
Nought but her louely face she for his looking left.

Withall she laughed, and she blusht withall,
  That blushing to her laughter gave more grace,
  And laughter to her blushing, as did fall:
  Now when they spide the knight to slacke his pace,
  Them to behold, and in his sparkling face
  The secret signes of kindled lust appeare,
  Their wanton meriments they did encreace,
  And to him beckned, to approch more neare,
And shewd him many sights, that courage cold could reare.

On which when gazing him the Palmer saw,
  He much rebukt those wandring eyes of his,
  And counseld well, him forward thence did draw.
                                    (64–69. 1–3)

Guyon is understandably stunned by this, and has to be jolted
out of his stupor by his faithful Christian companion. The
situation is obviously and trivially ironic: the knight of temperance does not know how intemperate he can be. The spirit is
willing but the flesh is weak, especially when the flesh is tempted by that most delightful of pastimes, sexual play. We could go
further, if we wished, and say that no man, according to Spenser, is temperate unless God grants it to him, with God's grace
here personified by the Palmer.

But that would be to explain the passage away, while its
humor rests on the fact that the women are beautiful and are
quite lusciously described. The reader must fall into the same
trap with Guyon—indeed in three lines we are tugged abruptly

away from the scene in order to get on with business. One might say, validly enough, that Spenser has planned it this way so that we might see our own sin with greater clarity. How could we and Guyon, after all, in a place we "know" is wicked, allow ourselves to be won over so easily? No doubt—yet the ladies are still beautiful, we enjoy watching them, and Spenser does not bother to unmask the ugliness beneath them, as he does to Duessa in Book One. Physical creation is beautiful, and the human body is most beautiful of all, the explanation might continue; that is why we lust for it. Again, no doubt this is true; yet Spenser indulges himself, and we indulge ourselves even as we watch, from our comfortable moral positions, Guyon's confusion—even as we watch our own confusion. A tension remains between what we discern as morally true, and the lascivious beauty of the women; this tension is not resolved by the explanation that Spenser wished us to become entangled in the same sin. Of course he did. Nor will it do to say that Spenser was of the devil's party although he knew it not, nor, more subtly, that the price Spenser paid for his civilization was the thorough and violent repression of perfectly natural instincts.[20] Such explanations rely upon an image of Spenser divided against himself; yet the Garden of Adonis and the Temple of Venus show us that Spenser was no prude. We never fully reject the beauty of the women, nor do we deny the evil of intemperance; nor do we deny that our own failure to make a wholehearted decision in this case tells us something about our moral weakness; nor do we fail to enjoy the women even when our moral weakness is clear. We are not with the Palmer only (that would be humorless), nor with Guyon (that would be mindless, here), nor with the more tolerant Christian side of Spenser, nor with some crazy compromise among the three. The tension of unresolved contrarieties, or the play of different levels of knowledge of moral vulnerability, is humorous, an outstanding artistic achievement. It requires neither a stodgily conservative interpretation to seal it off, nor a stodgily radical interpretation which would question Spenser's own commitment to the virtue of temperance. To understand the confident playfulness with which Spenser likes to present his ideas sensually, all we need is a sense of humor, a liking for allegory, and a respect for Spenser's quiet intelligence; but without these three things, critics will continue to assign dire and dreadful consequences to incongruities which Spenser surely was aware of, and without which his poem would have been stiff as cardboard and not a whit more orthodox.

Furman University

NOTES

1. William Hazlitt, *Lectures on the English Poets and the Spirit of the Age* (London: J. M. Dent and Sons, 1963), p. 42. First included in Everyman's Library, 1910. All references to Spenser are from Edmund Spenser, *The Faerie Queene*, ed. Thomas P. Roche, Jr. (New York: Penguin, 1978).

2. See pages 88 and 91, respectively, in William Nelson, "Spenser *ludens*", pp. 83–100 in *A Theatre for Spenserians,* eds. Judith M. Kennedy and James A. Reither (Toronto: University of Toronto Press, 1969).

3. Rosemary Freeman, "*The Faerie Queene*": *A Companion for Readers* (Berkeley: University of California Press, 1970), 66.

4. In *Anatomy of Criticism* (Princeton, N.J.: Princeton University Press, 1957), Northrop Frye writes that "the literary structure is ironic because 'what it says' is almost always different in kind or degree from 'what it means' " (p. 81); Geoffrey Hartman, in *Saving the Text* (Baltimore, Md.: Johns Hopkins University Press, 1981), will go so far as to assert that irony is "coextensive with literariness" (p. 167). But if we admit that everything literary is ironic in some way—and, given the playfulness of common speech and the artificiality of language itself, there is no reason why we should not include under irony all but the driest statements of fact—then the word "irony" shall cease to mean much of anything. Modern studies of irony, including even D. C. Muecke's *Compass of Irony* (London: Methuen, 1969), my favorite book on the subject, are also hampered by the assumption that irony has some essential connection to philosophies espousing doubt and skepticism. Therefore it is no wonder that Muecke (pp. 124–125) considered irony foreign to Spenser, inasmuch as Spenser conceived of the universe as a closed and orderly system. By contrast, in *A Rhetoric of Irony* (Chicago, Ill.: University of Chicago Press, 1974), Wayne Booth will admit of an irony that can go hand in hand with faith, for any good discussion of God or God's kingdom must involve a self-conscious clash of planes of knowledge, since the artist knows that he can only pretend to speak about what is finally Unspeakable. Such irony would be "always meaningful and exhilarating" (p. 269). Both Muecke and Booth treat irony as a rhetorical device which involves two or more planes of meaning or consciousness in conflict with each other, necessitating some sort of rejection by the reader of the more foolish, innocent, wicked, or unenlightened meanings; my discussion of Spenserian irony owes much to their analyses.

5. Note, for instance, the subtle prejudice against allegory exhibited by Kathleen Williams in *Spenser's World of Glass* (Berkeley: University of California Press, 1966): "The virtues do not define the books which they name or the knights by whom they are defended; the books and actions of the knights

define the virtues, by working them out through the narrative in human terms" (p. xix). Or by Freeman: "He wrote excellently when the didactic Palmer and the learned Natalis Comes and Cesare Ripa were out of the scene. Can we not act rightly apart from that haunting undesired presence of the dark conceit which Spenser insisted had rights of access?" (p. 10). Or by Judith Dundas, who praises those figures in Spenser which are more than mere emblems: "Instead of being subordinated to didactic purpose, they have become art, in which the ordinary didactic yields to the pursuit of an imaginative beauty which can teach more effectively by swaying the hearts of the readers" (page x in *The Spider and the Bee: The Artistry of Spenser's "Faerie Queene"*, Urbana: University of Illinois Press, 1985). Such criticism is salutary and frees us, as Dundas puts it, from looking upon meaning as "an extractable residue from poetry." Unfortunately, the critics also assume that an allegory cannot work unless the literal sense provides natural symbols for the allegorical sense. But natural symbols do not exist; only conventional ones do, conventional symbols that are accepted by an audience as working in a natural way. These natural symbols exist along with other conventional symbols that work in other ways. My point is that Spenser's allegory can "naturally" arise from the text, or can arise from it by means of any number of systems of symbols and meanings, while at times playing one method of signification against another.

6. For Maureen Quilligan, allegories are narratives spun out of obsessive punning. Her definition seems too exclusive, yet I admit that to read Spenser one must play along with prolonged and often bathetic puns. See *The Language of Allegory* (Ithaca, N.Y.: Cornell University Press, 1979).

7. Freeman, *Companion*, p. 61.

8. Paul Alpers, *The Poetry of "The Faerie Queene"* (Princeton, N.J.: Princeton University Press, 1967), p. 9.

9. Alpers, *Poetry,* p. 33.

10. Wayne Booth, *A Rhetoric of Irony*, pp. 27–31.

11. *The Faerie Queene*, p. 1237.

12. Compare Nature with the similar figure of Sapience in Spenser's *Hymne in Honour of Heauenlie Beautie*. Both derive, ultimately, from the books of Proverbs and Wisdom. In some of the most Platonic passages in Scripture, Sapientia is described as God's consort: "Da mihi sedium tuarum assistricem sapientiam" (Wis. 9: 4); she is the light and mirror reflecting the glory of God: "Candor est enim lucis aeternae, et speculum sine macula Dei maiestatis, et imago bonitatis illius" (Wis. 7: 6); she was with God in the beginning when all things were made (Wis. 9: 9, Prov. 8: 23); and it is she who rules the world with perpetual reason, "disponit omnia suaviter" (Wis. 8: 1). In traditional exegesis she was often interpreted as the Word of John's gospel, and in fact the structure of Spenser's *Fowre Hymnes* encourages a tentative identification of Sapience with the glorified Christ, whose earthly life is the subject of the *Hymne in Honour of Heauenlie Loue*. See Robert Ellrodt, *Neoplatonism in the Poetry of Spenser* (Geneva: Librairie E. Droz, 1960), for a thorough discussion of the proposed sources, both biblical and neoplatonic, for Nature and Sapience.

13. Dundas, *The Spider and the Bee,* p. 25.

14. C. S. Lewis, *The Allegory of Love* (Oxford: Clarendon Press, 1958; first"

published 1936), p. 349; Alpers, *Poetry*, p. 301; Roger Sale, *Reading Spenser: The Faerie Queene* (New York: Penguin, 1978), pp. 168–169.

15. See pages 28 and 11, respectively, in J. K. Kouwenhoeven, *Apparent Narrative as Thematic Metaphor* (Cambridge: Cambridge University Press, 1983).

16. In "Murdering Peasants: Status, Genre, and the Representation of Rebellion (*Representations*, 1 [1983, 1–29], Stephen Greenblatt compares Sidney's "taut, cruel laughter" (p. 15) in describing the revolt of the peasants against their king Basilius (*Arcadia*, book II., ch. 25) with Spenser's in putting down the egalitarian giant of Book Five (ii. 30–54). The argument is well taken, but ignores the difference between the types of writing that Spenser and Sidney engage in. For the cruel irony visited upon Sidney's peasants is that they, who live in a world populated by human beings, should suddenly find themselves reduced, metamorphosed, as in Ovid, into emblematic representations of poetic justice taken upon members of their particular occupations. With Spenser the irony works in the opposite direction, as mere emblems assume human features. Sidney's humor is disturbing because throughout the Arcadia we have been encouraged to read his various characters as thinking human beings whose allegorical significance, intimated in names such as Pyrocles and Gynecia, arise out of their actions *as* human beings.

17. Graham Hough, *A Preface to "The Faerie Queene"* (New York: Norton, 1962), p. 196.

18. Hazlitt, *Lectures*, p. 43.

19. According to Greenblatt in *Renaissance Self-Fashioning: From More to Shakespeare* (Chicago, Ill.: University of Chicago Press, 1980), "Acrasia's realm is lavishly described in just those terms which the defenders of poetry in the Renaissance reserved for the imagination's noblest achievements" (p. 189). Perhaps; or perhaps the description is ironic, and the garden meant to be viewed as neither natural nor particularly artistic. Lewis, pp. 324–333, discusses the differences between the tacky Bower of Bliss and the sexually healthier Garden of Adonis.

20. Greenblatt, *Self-Fashioning*, p. 173.

RICHARD T. NEUSE

Planting Words in the Soul:
Spenser's Socratic Garden
of Adonis

*W*ITH THE exception of *Orlando Furioso, The Faerie Queene* probably has no rivals among Renaissance epics in the multiplicity of
its plot lines and the variety of its textual surfaces. And the
deeper we penetrate into Faeryland, the more labyrinthine its
terrain seems to become. In the first two books of *The Faerie
Queene* we still have the thread of the hero's quest to guide us,
but by the time we get to Book III this thread appears only
intermittently and we are no longer sure where it is leading us.
Not only does the heroine vanish from the book for almost five
cantos (from 4.18 to 9.12), to be replaced by other characters
and their parallel or intersecting stories; there is also the recurrent sense that conventional plot development is being displaced
or suspended by way of passages whose function seems more
discursive than narrative.

One such instance is the Garden of Adonis in Canto 6, which
has traditionally been regarded as a kind of philosophical interlude and as such has received an enormous amount of commentary since the turn of the century, much of it concerned
with identifying the particular system of thought on which it
might be based.[1] Significant and illuminating as much of this
commentary has been, I agree with more recent commentators
that it would be a mistake to consider a passage like this in
isolation from the rest of the book or *The Faerie Queene* as a
whole. I will begin, accordingly, by looking at the Garden in
conjunction with certain other passages in Book III set off from
the various narrative strands through their apparently digressive
and self-contained character. The tapestry in Malecasta's castle
in Canto 1, and Merlin's—or Venus'—mirror in Canto 3, are

79

two examples. In the context of passages like these, the Garden becomes, I think, identifiable as part of a complex "argument" that is being carried on in Book III, or, to put the matter somewhat differently, as a stage in a large-scale symbolic plot which constitutes a kind of commentary on the other, more distinctly narrative plots unfolding in the course of the book and beyond it in following books.

There are obvious links among the passages I have cited. Malecasta's tapestry features the story of Venus and Adonis— along with Cupid and Psyche the major *mythic* subtext of Book III—whose *triste* conclusion when Venus turns Adonis into a flower (3.38), is itself transformed into a happy ending in the Garden. By both form and content the tapestry suggests the dominance, even tyranny, of the visible in Castle Ioyeous: it serves Malecasta, whose chief knight is Gardante, the "looker," as a visual guide or model for falling in love, and much of Venus' erotic satisfaction derives from the use of "her two crafty spyes" (36). The same emphasis on the modality of the visible and on the connection between falling in love and seeing is to be found in Canto 3 with Merlin's mirror. When Britomart looks into the mirror and sees first herself and then the male image with which she falls in love, we are reminded of the "mirrour perilous" or fountain of Narcissus in the *Romance of the Rose* (1. 1601 in Chaucer's trans.), by looking into which the dreamer falls in love. Britomart, too, comes to fear that by pining for a mere image in the mirror she has fallen prey to a fate like Narcissus' (2.44). The mirror, in other words, brings out the narcissism that is already implicit in the eye-centered love psychology of Malecasta's tapestry.

Merlin's mirror is of course more than an icon of erotic psychology, but at this point in Book III it directs the focus on the visual image as both object of desire and emblem of self-hood. The simile applied to it in stanza 20 develops both ideas by allowing us a view (from) *inside* the mirror, as if it were a person's mind into which we could enter[2].

Who wonders not, that reades so wonderous worke?
But who does wonder, that has red the Towre,
Wherein th'Ægyptian Phao long did lurke,
From all mens vew, that none might her discoure,
Yet she might all men vew out of her bowre?

Great Ptolomæe it for his lemans sake
Ybuilded all of glasse, by Magicke powre,
And also it impregnable did make;
Yet when his love was false, he with a peaze it brake.

Phao, whose name means "light"[3] and thus represents the very condition of visibility, is at once the desired image entering into and locked away in her lover's mirror-tower (with which he feels free to deal as he sees fit); *and* she is the one who while looking out into the world remains herself unseen. The latter I take as a complex comment on the way in which the image serves to conceal the person, since the image others see will generally be no more than a reflection of their own desires or prejudices. The image is the mask behind which "lurks" a human being.

Britomart "lurking" in her impregnable suit of armor, hidden "[f]rom all mens vew" and yet able to look out on the hostile world of men, is a wonderfully incongruous version of Phao in her tower. The incongruity is of course deliberate. From the start she has an ironic sense of social masks *as* masks which will eventually enable her to break their quasi-magical power to imprison the soul. Her experience with Malecasta, to return to that episode once more, points up the tragicomic consequences of believing, as Malecasta does, that mask or image is the self. For Malecasta, as we have said, the tapestry on her wall functions as a kind of mirror and tells a story which must be interpreted quite literally as a truth about men and women: a woman must ensnare the man she loves because men are interested in deadly games but never in love. Venus and Adonis are Malecasta's "role models," and in her compulsion to act the part of Venus she is "evilly chaste" [*male casta*], that is, doomed to the negative chastity of staying true to the role in which she has cast herself.

By the end of Book III, Britomart finds herself in another house with elaborate tapestries, whose message is the same as Malecasta's except that it now represents the male perspective. Here Britomart is the silent spectator, as she was in her father's "closet" (2.22) with the mirror, but now she is no longer under the spell of images, and so she is able to liberate Amoret from the masque/mask in which the enchanter Busirane kept her captive. But before she can perform this act of disenchantment

or demystification, Britomart, like the heroes of the earlier
books, must come to terms with herself, and for her this includes her disappearance from—or perhaps into—the social
scene. It is during this eclipse, which to her may well seem like a
shipwreck of the self (see esp. 4.9), that her ideas about self and
love undergo a change.

The Garden of Adonis is, I suggest, the crucial passage marking this change. In the absence of Britomart from the stage of
narrative action, it constitutes, as I said earlier, part of a symbolic commentary on that and the various other narrative strands
of the book. The absence of a direct link between the Britomart
story and the Garden of Adonis, therefore, should not disturb
us, especially since, as I hope to show, the Garden represents an
experience or sense of the self and of the world in which various
antinomies like conscious and unconscious meet, so that it
would be wrong to speak of it in terms of a rational decision or
choice that a person might make. The Garden, it would be truer
to say, is an event that happens to one but in which one also
participates.

As we have already seen, one index of change signalled by the
Garden is its revised denouement of the Venus and Adonis story
depicted on Malecasta's tapestry. Another is its rejection of the
narcissism implicit in Britomart's love version in Merlin's mirror. Among the flowers growing at the exact center of its sacred
grove there is

Foolish Narcisse, that likes the watry shore.

(6.45)

This Narcissus is doomed to pine for what is not: the Garden of
Adonis is surely unique among earthly paradises in having *no
water whatever,* stream, pool, or fountain. It thus marks the
Garden as the antithesis of the eye- and ego-centered realm
epitomized by Malecasta's murals and Merlin's mirror, for
water, with its reflecting surfaces, produces what Gaston
Bachelard has called a "natural narcissism": "Pour une fleur,
naître près des ondes, c'est vraiment se vouer au narcissisme
naturel, au narcissisme humide, humble, tranquille."[4]

With its liking for the watery shore, the foolish Narcissus of
the Garden recalls Britomart in Canto 4, "sitting downe upon

the rocky shore" and gazing at the waves (26). She, too, might want, in Bachelard's phrase, to "narcisse herself,"[5] that is, to cling to the image she saw in her father's mirror before the other one appeared and caused the fateful intervention of Cupid (2.26). But the new sense of self—and, we should add, of love—of which the Garden allegorically acts as both sign and theory, cannot be identified by an image in a mirror or in the mind; it is a self-in-time, invisible, intangible, manifest only in and through an activity, preeminently, I suggest, that of dialogue.

The model for this dialogic notion of the self and of love is Plato's *Phaedrus,* a dialogue whose main outlines it will be necessary to recall briefly at this point. It begins in an idyllic landscape outside Athens with three speeches about love and concludes with a discussion between Phaedrus and Socrates about rhetoric, writing, and "living" speech as the sowing or planting of seeds in another person's soul. As in Book III, the idea of love in the *Phaedrus* changes radically midway through the dialogue: the first two speeches, one delivered by Phaedrus, the other by Socrates, consider love an irrational affliction and social inconvenience; the third speech is Socrates' "recantation," in which he remembers that love is after all a god, the son of Aphrodite, and therefore cannot be bad, as the previous two speeches have implied. He redefines it as a form of divine, inspired madness and links it with a myth of the soul. The soul is winged *and* composed of a charioteer and a chariot drawn by two winged horses, and there is a continual procession of souls, human and divine, orbiting the universe. In the course of every revolution, these souls, so long as their chariots are well man-aged—which is not a problem for the souls of the gods—obtain a vision of absolute Reality by which they are nourished. Love occurs when in the course of its earthly existence the soul is reminded somehow of what it saw during its extraterrestrial orbit in the meadow of Reality. The *memory* that is aroused quickens the growth of the soul's wings and leads to the restlessness, the sweet affliction that is known as love among mortals.

In his speech, Socrates singles out beauty as the source of the madness of love (249), but of course his discussion of the various forms of inspired madness has already made it clear that they are all essentially erotic. Indeed, as the dialogue between

Socrates and Phaedrus continues, we come to realize that it is itself intended as an instance of the love the two interlocutors are seeking to define. Here, then, a further, subtle change in the idea of love occurs, from a visually to a verbally centred one, paralleling that suggested for Book III.[6] Every dialogue of two persons, that is to say, in their attempt to "recollect" a truth about their existence, shares in this inspired madness, a point that seems to be reinforced by the concluding discussion about rhetoric as the art of influencing souls (261), and about the comparative merits of writing and speaking as alternative ways of practising rhetoric (274ff.). On this last point, the palm is given to speaking as the most effective way of planting and sowing words in a congenial soul (276). The imagery here is somewhat mixed, but I think the implication is clear that in the earnest dialogue between two congenial "souls" the words function as a way of recalling a vision of Reality which inspires the divine madness called love.

It seems equally clear, finally, that Socrates' image of the soul-as-garden implies the idea mentioned earlier, of the soul "in process," that is to say, not as a fixed entity but precisely as that which exists in and through the dialogical relation. And it is this idea, I shall argue, that is implicit in the Garden of Adonis as a garden of speech as well as of the self. That this idea of the Garden is already fully adumbrated in the *Phaedrus* is evident from the already-mentioned distinction that Socrates makes between the spoken and the written word, describing the latter as a bastard child unable to give an account of itself, the former as its legitimate brother able to fend for itself. Switching metaphors, Socrates asks:

Would a sensible husbandman, who has seeds which he cares for and which he wishes to bear fruit, plant them with serious purpose in the heat of summer in some garden of Adonis [el's 'Aδώνιδος κήπους], and delight in seeing them appear in beauty in eight days, or would he do that sort of thing, when he did it at all, only in play and amusement? Would he not, when he was in earnest, follow the rules of husbandry, plant his seeds in fitting ground, and be pleased when those which he had sowed reached their perfection in the eighth month?

PHÆDRUS: Yes, Socrates, he would, as you say, act in

that way when in earnest and in the other way only for amusement.

SOCRATES: And shall we suppose that he who has knowledge of the just and the good and beautiful has less sense about his seeds than the husbandman?

PHÆDRUS: By no means.

SOCRATES: Then he will not, when in earnest, write them in ink, sowing them through a pen with words which cannot defend themselves by argument. . . . No. The gardens of letters he will, it seems, plant for amusement. . . . but in my opinion serious discourse about [the just and the good and beautiful] is far nobler when one employs the dialectic method and plants and sows in fitting soil intelligent words which are able to help themselves and him who planted them, which are not fruitless, but yield seed from which there spring up in other minds words capable of continuing the process for ever. . . . IV (*Phædrus* 276B–277A, *LCL,* pp. 567–571)

This passage, together with Socrates' account of the invention of writing by the Egyptian God Theuth that precedes it (274), forms the basis of a fascinating essay by Jacques Derrida on the privileging of speech over writing in the Western tradition, as symptomatic of that tradition's dichotomous way of thinking, opposing presence and absence, life and death, truth and error, mind and matter, and so forth, and always with the idea that the second term is the undesirable negation of the first.[7] It would be an exaggeration to claim that Spenser's Garden of Adonis anticipates much of Derrida's argument, but I trust it is already clear that, far from implying a devaluation of writing as secondary to, or a mere imitation of, speech, the Garden treats speaking and writing as absolutely coordinate activities and language, and symbolism generally, in thoroughly "Derridean" fashion as a dialectic of absence and presence.

This last point is evident with respect to the figure of Adonis, who in one of his allegorical significations is identified as the logos principle at the basis of language itself. From the beginning of his known history, Adonis is celebrated as the absent— and presumed dead—god. In the ancient sacred drama of the annual Adonis festival or Adonia,[8] he was the fertility god whose death was ritually mourned until grief changed to exultation at his anticipated resurrection. This pattern of loss and eventual recovery formed the basis of the ancient Greek pastoral elegy, if we are to trust the evidence of poems like Bion's *Lament for Adonis* and Theocritus' *Idyll* XV.

Like the ancient elegy, the Garden bearing "Venus lost lovers name" (6.29) turns grief to joy, absence and loss into a presence of sorts, a *symbolic* presence whose paradoxical character is underscored by its allusion to another feature of the ancient Adonia, the so-called "gardens of Adonis," urns of rapidly blossoming and withering flowers that the worshipers placed around his shrine.[9]

The mere naming of the Garden initially suffices Venus as a compensation for her loss. But this naming seems to evolve into a shadowy figure hidden, at first, among the flowers at the center of the Garden and then gradually resurrected to full life:

> There wont faire Venus often to enjoy
>> Her deare Adonis joyous company,
>> And reape sweet pleasure of the wanton boy;
>> There yet, some say, in secret he does ly,
>> Lapped in flowres and pretious spycery,
>> By her hid from the world, and from the skill
>> Of Stygian Gods, which doe her love envy;
>> But she her selfe, when that she will,
> Possesseth him, and of his sweetnesse takes her fill.

> And sooth it seems they say: for he may not
>> For ever die, and ever buried bee
>> In balefull night, where all things are forgot;
>> All be he subject to mortalitie,
>> Yet is eterne in mutabilitie,
>> And by succession made perpetuall,
>> Transformed oft, and chaunged diverslie:
>> For him the Father of all formes they call;
> Therefore needs mote he live, that living gives to all.

> There now he liveth in eternall blis,
>> Joying his goddesse, and of her enjoyd:
>> Ne feareth he henceforth that foe of his,
>> Which with his cruell tuske him deadly cloyd:
>> For that wild Bore, the which him once annoyd,
>> She firmely hath emprisond for ay,

That her sweet love his malice mote avoyd.
In a strong rocky Cave, which is they say,
Hewen underneath that Mount, that none him lose may.

There now he lives in everlasting joy,
    With many of the Gods in company,
    Which thither haunt, and with the winged boy
    Sporting himselfe. . . .

(6.46–49)

This passage illustrates Spenser's recurrent mimesis of ritual language. The incantatory repetition of phrases, words, sounds: *There . . . There yet . . . There now . . . There now; . . . enioy, . . . company, . . . boy* (46, 1,2,3,); *. . . ioy, . . . company, . . . boy* (49, 1,2,3), and the reiterated formula *. . . some say . . . they say . . . they call . . . they say* create a kind of impersonal authority as well as "the forms of things unknown" out of "airy nothing."[10]

There is Adonis, created or recreated out of "airy nothing." I have already identified him as a principle basic to language, and the passage quoted would seem to bear out this idea. Adonis is simultaneously subject to the baleful night—and boar—of death and oblivion, and the means of triumphing over it. He lives on by becoming "the Father of all formes . . . that living gives to all." To be that Father means to be continually ready to die, to accept an unstable identity that is tantamount to nonidentity, to have an existence that is divided from itself, its only reality being the act of transformation, of succession from one phase or stage to another. This paradoxical Adonis, the reader will already have noticed, bears a startling resemblance to certain modern ideas about the nature of language which posit, not a stable structure of terms with fixed, clearcut meanings, but rather an open-ended system of differences. As Saussure, the originator of this theory, has written,

in language there are only differences. Even more important: a difference generally implies positive terms between which the difference is set up; but in language there are only differences *without positive terms.* Whether we take the signified or the signifier, language has neither ideas nor sounds that existed before the linguistic system, but only conceptual and phonic differences that have issued from the system. The idea of phonic substance that a sign contains is of less importance than the other signs that surround it.[11]

Adonis, then, would be the principle of differentiality that allows the system to be a signifying system, for which Derrida has coined the term *différance*, "combining the two senses of the French verb *différer*—'to differ' and 'to defer or postpone'—into a noun designating active non-self-presence both in space and time."[12] Derrida refers to *différance* as "the systematic play of differences" and says that it "is thus no longer simply a concept, but rather the possibility of conceptuality, of a conceptual process and system in general.[13]

Perhaps it was with a premonition of Derridean *différance* that Venus imprisoned the boar under the mount where Adonis lies. In so doing she secures their physical separation "for ay," but her action also serves as a reminder that *symbolically* the two belong together: in the symbol and in the symbolic system, boy and boar, hunter and hunted, passive victim and destructive beast coincide. This is true in a twofold sense. First, the symbol replaces, causes the absence of, the thing symbolized, or, in Lacan's dramatically apt formulation, "the symbol manifests itself first of all as the murder of the thing."[14] Second, every symbol or linguistic sign exists within a chain or system of symbols and therefore must constantly "die" so that the others may explain, amplify, specify, but in any case displace it. As the boar's victim and double, Adonis seems the perfect emblem of this (dual) process of symbolic substitution, the process by which he "is eterne in mutabilitie, | And by succession made perpetuall, | Transformed oft, and chaunged diverslie."

There is no question that Spenser had a profound feeling for this "systematic play of differences" and its associated process of endless substitution and repetition with variation. It could be called a central principle of *The Faerie Queene*'s poetics. Venus looking for Cupid "substitutes" for Britomart looking for Artegall, Florimell looking for Marinell, Amoret looking for Scudamour, and so forth. Adonis may be said to substitute for Artegall, for Marinell, for all those who are absent or lost, and in this vast game of appearances and disappearances nothing is ever totally lost but always returns in different or the same and yet different form.

By the end of our passage cited earlier, Adonis is sporting with Cupid; he has become a full-fledged member of Book III's cast of characters, a reminder that he is not just a linguistic principle or mark but also a symbolic self. He is thus in a sense his own son, who shares with the father, we need to remind ourselves, an evanescent, non-self-present selfhood. His destiny is tied to language: at once the product as well as the producer of speech, he constantly spends himself, succumbs to the boar of absence and loss; but like speech, he can constantly recuperate himself by the ability to generate endless combinations of words and sentences. This is the new self, "eterne in mutabilitie," that during her own disappearance from the surface narrative, I suggested earlier (above, p. 80), Britomart discovers, just as the reader, according to the poet, can become aware of the beneficent Genius within,

> that celestiall powre, to whom the care
> Of life, and generation of all
> That lives, pertaines in charge particulare,
> Who wondrous things concerning our welfare,
> And straunge phantomes doth let us oft forsee,
> And oft of secret ill bids us beware:
> That is our Selfe, whom though we do not see,
> Yet each doth in him selfe it well perceive to bee.
>
> (2.12.47)

Both Genius and Adonis combine individual and collective; each is a "self," invisible and indefinable, yet known indirectly, symbolically, Genius by intuitions, premonitions, the phantom images of dreams (let us say), Adonis by the Garden that bears his name.

The Garden, then, is Adonis writ large, an unfolding of his paradoxical nature in space, or rather in a variety of heterogeneous spaces. It, too, is "collective" in the sense of being a supra-individual garden of language; and as a garden of the individual soul it is itself an instance of the symbolic forms it generates. For Adonis and the Garden individual and collective coexist in a dialectical relation that is, we might say, like that of speech and language.

Let us return to the Garden's heterogeneous spaces. These do not cancel each other out but by their juxtaposition suggest that far from being a unified system, language is a many-layered structure "where there is a constant interchange and circulation of elements, where none of the elements is absolutely definable and where everything is caught up and traced through by everything else."[15] The first space, then, is that of "the first seminary | Of all things that are borne to live and die, | According to their kinds" (30). The wording suggests a vast, impersonal process obeying its own organic laws and serving the urge to define and classify things, for "[i]t is the world of words that creates the world of things—the things originally confused in the *hic et nunc* of the all in the process of coming-into-being— by giving its concrete being to their essence, and its ubiquity to what has always been."[16] Perhaps it is in that sense that it is the *first* seminary, because the idea that we are here at some absolute point of origin is certainly belied by the rest of the Garden. In the very next stanza the seemingly boundless seminary is found to be contained within an elaborately walled garden, and in this homely, *constructed* space there are now thousands of naked babes demanding to be clothed by a porter who is also called Genius:

> Such as him list, such as eternall fate
> Ordained hath, he clothes with sinfull mire,
> And sendeth forth to live in mortall state,
> Till they againe returne backe by the hinder gate.
> (32)

This Genius also exercises a degree of control over the babes that have somewhat disconcertingly evolved from the flowers and the weeds of the previous stanza, and the babes—recalling perhaps the child helpless among strangers to which Socrates compares the written word in the *Phædrus* (see p. 82 above)— have, doubtless, a human face and a certain volition of their own. However, once back in the Garden they also return to vegetation, as they "planted be againe; | And grow afresh" (33).

In the next stanza we return to the fully organic image of the seminary garden, which is now presented as a completely autonomous system except that it *remembers* the divine speech at the creation, which set it all in motion:

Ne needs there Gardiner to set or sow,
To plant or prune: for of their owne accord
All things as they created were, doe grow,
And yet remember well the mightie word,
Which first was spoken by th'Almightie lord,
That bad them to increase and multiply:
Ne doe they need with water of the ford,
Or of the clouds to moysten their roots dry;
For in themselves enternall moisture they imply.
                                                    (34)

Here is a paradigm of language as a perfect fit for the world of
created things, and the last three lines with their submerged pun
on the idea of "radical moisture"[17] provide a sense of the system's conceptual closure.

The following stanza, however, belies the idea of a closed
system:

Infinite shapes of creatures there are bred,
    And uncouth formes, which none yet ever knew,
    And every sort is in a sundry bed
Set by it selfe, and ranckt in comely rew:
. . . .
    And all the fruitfull spawne of fishes hew
    In endlesse rancks along enraunged were,
That seem'd the Ocean could not containe them there.
                                                    (35)

True, the ordering and classifying impulse, whatever its source,
is in full sway, but the first two lines of the stanza, echoing
Phantastes' chamber,

        in the which were *writ*
    Infinite shapes of things dispersed thin;
    Some such as in the world were never yit,
        Ne can devized be of mortall wit.
                            (2.9.50; my italics),

show the system is open to novelty and the world of imagination.

This openness prepares for the next "space" in the Garden, which is startlingly different from the previous ones in abandoning the idea of organic growth altogether and also constituting itself as a new beginning, a disclosure of a new and different origin:

> in the wide wombe of the world there lyes
> In hatefull darkenesse and in deepe horrore,
>   An huge eternall Chaos, which supplyes
> The substances of natures fruitfull progenyes.
>
> All things from thence doe their *first* being fetch,
>   And borrow matter, whereof they are made,
>   Which when as forme and feature it does ketch,
>   Becomes a bodie, and doth then invade
>   The state of life, out of the griesly shade.
>   That substance is eterne, and bideth so,
>   Ne when the life decayes, and forme does fade,
>   Doth it consume, and into nothing go,
> But chaunged is, and often altred to and fro.
>
> The substance is not chaunged, nor altered,
>   But th'only forme and outward fashion;
>   For every substance is conditioned
>   To change her hew, and sundry formes to don,
>   Meet for her temper and complexion:
>   For formes are variable and decay,
>   By course of kind, and by occasion;
>   And that faire flowre of beautie fades away,
> As doth the lilly fresh before the sunny ray.
>
>   (36–38; my italics)

These stanzas anticipate the revival of Adonis from "balefull night, where all things are forgot" (47), which we examined earlier. Both passages have the same conceptual terminology which envisions the symbolic process as one of ceaseless transformation, internal differentiation,[18] and controlled violence, where even *forme* and *feature* become like suits of armor in the battle for existence of all against all (37).

I said that the last stanzas quoted are like a new beginning— "All things from thence doe their *first* being fetch" (37; my italics)—but in fact I think it is more like the culminating stage in the Garden's exploration of language. Here, "in the wide wombe of the world," is what Lacan calls the Real: the realm of the unknown, of the chaos of unanalyzed sensations, or primitive terrors aroused by the wholly other, before it has been transformed by language into the order of the Symbolic.[19] This "huge eternall Chaos," then, is the ultimate matter of ground from and in response to which language takes its multifarious forms. The entire metaphorics of the Garden suggests that language also desires a return to the world-womb, Chaos, the Real, to be reunited with it, but its pathos is that it is forever cut off from its origin, which it can only recapture in its own (translated) terms.

This is illustrated, rather than explained, by one of those dissonant redundancies in which the Garden—and *The Faerie Queene* as a whole—abounds. I am referring to the elegiac stanzas (39–40) on the great enemy of all "[t]hat in the Gardin of Adonis springs": wicked Time with his death-dealing scythe *and* flaggy wings, who causes even "great mother Venus" to lament. These stanzas follow hard on the ones we have just examined dealing with the Chaos that supplies the Garden with its substance(s). There, Time both as the orderly measure of change and as the agent of disorder, discontinuity, disruption, dissolution—"By course of kind, and by occasion" (38)—was recognized as an integral element in the transformation of the originary chaos into a world of words. Yet in spite of that recognition, the poet, in company with the gods, now laments that Time is the great "troubler" of happiness in the Garden (41). In so doing, he demonstrates the ineluctable tendency of language to create its own reality and its own categories, like "*wicked Time*," quite at odds with its own interpretation of the Real, as summed up in the banal observation that "all that lives, is subject to that law: | All things decay in time, and to their end do draw" (40).

But of course it has been evident from the start that language has a self-proliferating dynamism and exuberance—Adonis, after all, is or was a god of fertility!—quite in excess of the practical and sciential demands of the Real. So if, as I implied earlier, there is in language a nostalgia for the Real, a desire to become part of the order of things, there is the contrary impulse to revel in its own fecundity and lack of external constraints. And this, it seems to me, is precisely what is realized, or perhaps I should say enacted, in the concluding stanzas of the Garden. Derrida's definition of language as "the systematic play of differences" was cited above (p. 86) with the emphasis on differences. We must now shift the emphasis to *play* because it is that which predominates in the finale. We have already observed Adonis playing with Cupid, who has laid aside his "sad darts" (49). Next—or are we dealing with a *ménage à trois?*—we find Psyche, too, in the Garden, playing with Cupid, having been reconciled to him,

> After long troubles and unmeet upbrayes,
> With which his mother Venus her revyld,
> And eke himselfe her cruelly exyld:
> But now in stedfast love and happy state
> She with him lives and hath him borne a chyld,
> Pleasure, that doth both gods and men aggrate,
> Pleasure, the daughter of Cupid and Psyche late.
> (50)

If *play* is the pleasurable activity which has no goal outside itself, Adonis' playing is different from Psyche's, since hers is sexual and hence involves the (possible) motive of reproduction. But since the offspring is so emphatically named Pleasure, "that doth both gods and men aggrate," it could also be said that this play, too, is for its own sake. Furthermore, Adonis and Psyche are after all (as I have been arguing) variant versions of the same thing: the self or soul. And it is now clear that their stories are in different ways the "untold" or hidden story of Britomart's love quest, which the poet *playfully* brings to an anticipated happy conclusion in the Garden—in sharp contrast to Merlin's prophecy, according to which Britomart will give birth to a son at the very moment that Artegall is treacherously killed (3.28).

The poet's play with the figures in the Garden, we may think, is another form of free play, an illustration of the imagination's penchant for wish-fulfilment and of the self-referential aspect of language, its capacity for ignoring what, following Lacan, we have called the Real. But here we must distinguish between play as purely self-pleasing, recognizing no rules other than the player's own whims and impulses, and controlled play which does recognize certain rules and may achieve certain "serious" goals without losing its character as play. The Garden, I have tried to show, is precisely Spenser's theoretical and practical demonstration that such a form of play is possible for the poet who has trust in the resources of language.

An important model for this idea of controlled play is, I suggest, the Platonic dialogue. The suggestion may strike the reader as somewhat paradoxical in Spenser's case, since his Garden of Adonis could be considered a counterargument to Socrates' in the *Phaedrus*, where, as we saw, his reference to the gardens of Adonis is intended to devalue at once writing and play as examples of frivolous horticulture. Rather than a counterargument, however, I believe Canto 6 represents an extended gloss on the *Phaedrus*, with full recognition of the Platonic irony that has Socrates condemn written speech as unfitted for serious dialogue—in a written dialogue!

As I already indicated much earlier, Spenser's Garden is indeed dialogic, but this must now be understood in a sense that goes beyond the idea of an earnest conversation between two or more partners, as something which antecedes or underlies such a conversation, as in Lacan's observation that "speech always subjectively includes its own reply,"[20] or Bakhtin's "dialogism" as a dialectic without resolution.[21] The clearest indication of its dialogic character is the Garden's doubleness, starting with the fact that it is

> girt in with two walles on either side;
>
> . . . .
>
> And double gates it had, which opened wide,
> By which both in and out men moten pas;
> Th'one faire and fresh, the other old and dride:
> Old Genius the porter of them was,
> Old Genius, the which a double nature has.
>
> He letteth in, he letteth out to wend,
> All that to come into the world desire. . . .
>
> (31–32)

This porter, like Adonis, may be thought to embody in his "double nature" the various dualities and antinomies that we found in the Garden at large. The porter of the Bower of Bliss was also called Genius, we recall, but as the "foe of life" (2.12.48) he was split off from his opposite, the Genius charged with "the care | Of life" (47). Our Old Genius would seem to antecede this split, or else to recombine and reintegrate the two Geniuses into his double nature; it is their dialectical interplay that makes the symbolic life of the Garden possible.

As porter, then, Genius is a *mediating* figure in the Garden's dialectic of presence and absence, being and nonbeing. He mediates between inner and outer, self and world, soul and body, language and speech, precisely by suggesting that these traditional pairs are *not* opposites but aspects of one nature. The double gates over which Genius presides recall the two gates of the Castle of Alma in Book II, the front one "doubly disparted" (2.9.23) evidently referring to both mouth and ears at once, and provided with a porter, doubtless the tongue (25). The Garden's *double* gates through which Genius lets the babes[22] in and out, symbolize something analogous to the anatomical details of the Castle and once again as aspects of *one* reality: not literal mouth, tongue and ears but their functional or conceptual counterparts that are presupposed in their simultaneity by the dialogic situation itself.

Let me briefly recapitulate the argument of this essay. The Garden of Adonis does not "solve" the problems of chastity, or of love, posed by Book III—if indeed there is a solution to such problems. What it does do, however, is to subvert the idea of the mirror self and the associated, Petrarchan idea of love as a form of image magic or bondage, that the society at large of Book III seems to take for granted. To this narcissistic and imprisoning mask/masque of love, the Garden of Adonis opposes a symbolic self which has no fixed role or identity but instead defines and discovers itself in its dialogical relation to other persons and to the world. In the absence of the heroine from the narrative of Book III, then, the Garden represents and anticipates a crucial moment in her spiritual evolution when she recognizes the radically symbolic dimension of human destiny. It is by achieving this understanding that she is able to free Amoret from the enchanter Busirane at the climax of her quest in Book III.

University of Rhode Island

NOTES

1. The most complete and wide-ranging discussion of the Garden along these lines to appear in recent years is undoubtedly that of James Nohrnberg, *The Analogy of "The Faerie Queene"* (Princeton, N.J.: Princeton University Press, 1976), "Seminarium Mundi: The Pregnancy and Primavera of the World," pp. 519–568. Excellent commentaries on the Garden have appeared in recent decades, to which I am obviously indebted. Since I do not stop to acknowledge specific debts in the course of this essay, I will just mention, from a long list, the names of those whose work on the subject I have found especially illuminating: Paul J. Alpers, Harry Berger, Jr., John E. Hankins, Isabel G. MacCaffrey, Judith C. Ramsay, and Humphrey Tonkin. The edition of *The Faerie Queene* I have used in this essay is that of J. C. Smith (Oxford: Clarendon, 1909).

2. It goes without saying that Merlin's mirror alludes to the traditional image of the mind as a mirror, which goes back to Plato (*cf. Republic* X.596), and has an intellectual scope and psychological depth that eventually come into full play as Britomart's story unfolds in this and the next two books. Like Plato's, Merlin's looking glass is objectively boundless but subjectively limited:

> It vertue had, to shew in perfect sight,
> What ever thing was in the world contaynd,
> Betwixt the lowest earth and heavens hight,
> So that it to the looker appertaynd.
>
> (2.19)

For Britomart's father, King Ryence, it is a mirror for magistrates, "That treasons could bewray, and foes convince (2.21), and it is also a visual model of the world, for it "round and hollow shaped was, | Like to the world it selfe, and seem'd a world of glas" (2.19).

3. From Gk φάος, Attic pŵs Her name also links her with Pharos, the lighthouse in the harbor of Alexandria, which became a generic name for "lighthouse." "Phao lilly white" (4.11.49) is one of two names Spenser invented for his catalogue of Nereus' daughters. Elsewhere I discuss the idea that the Ptolemy of the simile alludes also to the Alexandrian astonomer and geographer (2nd cent. A.D.) and that the entire passage dealing with Merlin's mirror is concerned with world models like the Ptolemaic and the "erotics of scientific discovery." Ptolemy and "th'Ægyptian Phao" may also connect with the Egyptian myth about the origin of writing that Socrates tells in the *Phaedrus* (on which see below). The Egyptian god Theuth, who is credited with the invention, is also the god of astronomy (*Phaedrus* 274).

4. For a flower to be born near water means truly to dedicate itself to a natural narcissism, to a narcissism that is humid, humble, and tranquil. Gaston Bachelard, *L'Eau et les rêves: Essai sur l'imagination de la matière* (Paris: José Corti, 1964), p. 38. As Bachelard's wording suggests, it is possible that Spenser intended this Narcissus to intimate an epistemologically naive perspective whose liking for water is actually a yearning for a nonsymbolic,

sensory reality. That would be another, more important, reason for the absence of water from the Garden. Incidentally, that Spenser meant the reader to recognize a void or absence at the very center of the Garden might well be indicated by the missing line in Stanza 45.

5. *Cf.* again Bachelard: "Le narcissisme généralisé transforme tous les êtres en fleurs et il donne à toutes les fleurs la conscience de leur beauté. Toutes les fleurs se *narcisent* et l'eau est pour elles l'instrument merveilleux du narcissisme" (p. 37).

6. However, the truth glimpsed by souls in the meadow of Reality is in fact not strictly visible, being "without shape or color, intangible, visible only to reason, the soul's pilot" (*Phaedrus* 247; trans. W. C. Helmbold and W. G. Rabinowitz in the Library of Liberal Arts series [Indianapolis, Ind.: Bobbs-Merrill, 1956], p. 30). For the notion that the Platonic dialogue typically "exhibits a form of inquiry which embraces the whole, making the whole, in this sense, an instrument of itself" (p. 206), see Ronald Hathaway, "Explaining the Unity of the Platonic Dialogue," *Philosophy and Literature*, 8 (1984), 195–206. On the unresolved question whether Spenser had first-hand knowledge of Plato's writings, I am proceeding on the assumption that John E. Hankins is correct in arguing that Spenser probably read at least some of the dialogues in Ficino's Latin translation. See his *Source and Meaning in Spenser's Allegory: A Study of "The Faerie Queene"* (Oxford: Clarendon Press, 1971), p. 236f. A discussion of the *Phaedrus* that I have found especially useful is Ronna Burger, *Plato's "Phaedrus": A Defense of a Philosophic Art of Writing* (Tuscaloosa: University of Alabama Press, 1980).

7. "Plato's Pharmacy" in *Dissemination,* trans. Barbara Johnson, (Chicago, Ill.: University of Chicago Press, 1981), pp. 61–171. Barbara Johnson, in her "Translator's Introduction," pp. vii–xxxiii, has a very useful summary of some of the central themes of Derrida's philosophy.

8. See the brief, helpful discussion in Renato Poggioli, *The Oaten Flute: Essays on Pastoral Poetry and the Pastoral Ideal* (Cambridge, Mass.: Harvard University Press, 1975), p. 66f. Bion's *Lament for Adonis* is the primary document in this connection.

9. These gardens of Adonis are mentioned in another ancient pastoral elegy, Theocritus' *Idyll* XV, "The Women at the Adonis Festival." They are twice referred to in the plural elsewhere in *The Faerie Queene*: 2.10.71 and 3.6.arg., and in *Colin Clout's Come Home Again*, 1. 804.

10. I am of course adapting Theseus' famous speech at the beginning of Act V of *A Midsummer Night's Dream* in the edition of Irving Ribner and G. L. Kittredge, *The Complete Works of Shakespeare* (Waltham, Mass. and Toronto: Xerox College Publishing, 1971).

11. Ferdinand de Saussure, *Course in General Linguistics*, trans. Wade Baskin (New York: Philosophical Library, 1959), p. 117; quoted from Jacques Derrida, "Différance," pp. 10–11 in *Margins of Philosophy*, trans. Alan Bass (Chicago, Ill.: University of Chicago Press, 1982).

12. I am quoting from Barbara Johnson's succinct definition in a translator's note on p. 5 of *Dissemination* (see above, n. 7).

13. "Différance," p. 11.

14. *Écrits: A Selection,* tr. Alan Sheridan (New York and London: W. W. Norton, 1977), p. 104. In this connection a citation from Rodolphe Gasché's

excellent commentary on Derrida, *The Tain of the Mirror: Derrida and the Philosophy of Reflection* (Cambridge, Mass. and London, England: Harvard University Press, 1986) seems appropriate:

Everything, hence, begins with representation; the possibility of reproduction, representation, and citation must be inscribed in any entity, sign, or act of speech in order for an entity, sign, or speech act to be possible in its singularity in the first place. If Derrida calls the inscription of these possibilities the death from which life with its limitations and finitude springs forth, then this is not merely a metaphorical manner of speaking. This is a meaning of death prior to the proper meaning of what we commonly understand by death and, *mutatis mutandis,* as the condition of iterability without which no unit could be exchanged, transmitted, represented, referred to, reproduced, remembered, and so on. (p. 214)

15. I am quoting from Terry Eagleton's discussion of post-structuralist language theory in *Literary Theory: An Introduction* (Oxford: Basil Blackwell, 1983), p. 129.

16. Lacan, *Écrits: A Selection,* p. 65.

17. A technical term of natural philosophy in the sixteenth century. See *O.E.D. s.v. radical* 1. See my remarks about the absence of water in the Garden in note 4 above.

18. In the present passage, I believe, Spenser deliberately fudges the technical distinction between (1) sustance and (2) substances, which in Aristotelian philosophical usage mean quite distinct things: (1) undifferentiated prime matter; (2) individual entities composed of form and matter. Poetically, in other words, he splits open (differentiates) what conceptually is undifferentiated. Elsewhere in Canto 6 Spenser sets homonyms against each other with, I believe, similar effect; for instance, the "weeds" that in Stanza 30 bud and blossom in the seminary, and the "fleshly *weedes*" with which the naked babes are clothed by Genius. In the Garden, finally, (almost) everything becomes metaphoric, but every metaphor is subsequently reinvested with concreteness.

19. *Cf.* Malcolm Bowie on Lacan's notion of the Real as "the primordial chaos upon which language operates . . . ; the Real is given its structure by the human power to name"; *Freud, Proust and Lacan: Theory as Fiction* (Cambridge: Cambridge University Press, 1987), p. 116.

20. *Écrits,* p. 85.

21. See Mikhail Bakhtin, *Problems of Dostoevsky's Poetics,* ed. and tr. Caryl Emerson (Minneapolis: University of Minnesota Press, 1984); and see esp. p. 93 of Derrida's discussion of the Egyptian Theuth/Thoth, the inventor of writing (see above, p. 83). That entire discussion is of direct relevance to the view of the Garden I have argued for in this essay.

22. These babes raise numerous interesting interpretive possibilities which I will leave untouched except to mention that the cycles of babes leaving and entering the garden—"So like a wheele around they runne from old to new"

(33)—may well point to cyclical linguistic change, parts of the language falling into disuse, being "recycled" in the Garden, and then reappearing in usage "with other hew" (33). E. K.'s "Epistle" to *The Shepheardes Calender* shows that our author thought of himself from the start as a kind of assistant to the Genius of the Garden with respect to exercising some control over the processes of archaization and renewal in English.

MARK HEBERLE

The Limitations of Friendship

MOST COMMENTARY on the Legend of Friendship has pointed out its comic resolutions: the frustrated heroic lovers of Book III, after additional conflict in Book IV, fulfill their desires.[1] Britomart is betrothed to Artegall and Florimell to Marinell, Scudamour recovers Amoret, Timias receives Belphoebe's grace. Within the book itself, each couple's story comically resolves an initial situation that is potentially tragic: the nearly mortal struggle of Artegall and Britomart, Marinell's lovesick grief and Florimell's imprisonment, Scudamour's jealous anxiety concerning Amoret and Britomart, Belphoebe's vengeful anger at Timias and the latter's own self-banishment. The book itself moves from discord to harmony, from the Ate of Canto 1 to the Concord of Canto 10, who makes Hate shake hands with Love and is the mother of the titular virtue.[2] Finally, friendship itself incorporates and transcends chastity (just as the latter incorporates and transcends temperance),[3] for the individual subjects of Book III become couples in Book IV.[4]

Despite these resolutions of "lovers' deare debate," A. C. Hamilton has pointed out that Book IV has long seemed the least interesting to most readers of the poem.[5] Our difficulty may stem from a sense that closure is at once too easy and yet unsatisfying, that Spenser's friendship may be edifying but is certainly dull, a "Renaissance commonplace" less imaginatively engaging than the virtues of the first three books,[6] each of them valuable yet incomplete or limited by fallen human nature: holiness, which radically exposes the dependence of "fleshly might" upon supernatural grace; temperance, that pedestrian virtue which can bind Acrasia but not eliminate her; and chastity, which includes and transcends temperance but can only be fulfilled in the relationships that friendship establishes. Friendship is also a complex and problematical virtue, however, and Book IV suggests its limitations through contrasting foreground and background narratives, redefining the virtue itself, and establishing relationships between friendship and the virtue of Book V.

I

The titular virtue of Book IV is most fully realized by figures, intruded into the poem in self-consciously fictional episodes, whose lives as characters end with the book in which they first appear. They contrast markedly in all these respects with Red Cross and Guyon, as well as with the heroic lovers of Book III, whose relationships are continued in Book IV. The heading to the book identifies two heroes, but, as Jonathan Goldberg notes, "Telamond" is simply a name on a title page, apparently replaced by the character Triamond within the action of the book.[7] The other hero, Cambel, is himself a character in another book, Chaucer's Squire's Tale. With their sisters, Canacee and Cambina, the titular heroes are part of a marriage quaternio that we first encounter traveling together in Canto 2, a perfect icon of concord that combines three interchangeable pairs: two brothers and two sisters; two married couples; and two pairs of friends.[8]

This quartet effortlessly equalizes the three kinds of affection—kinship, love, and friendship—identified in the introduction to Canto 9. That opening stanza asserts that friendship transcends eros, which itself "quenches" natural affection with "Cupid's greater flame" (9.2), and the narrator assures us that we will find this lesson "approved plaine" in the "storie" of Amyas and Placidas that he is continuing from Canto 8. Ultimately, Arthur's reconcilement of Poeana with Placidas enables him "to shut up all in friendly love" (9.5), establishing another quaternio of friends and lovers, one in which friendship transcends erotic love and kinship.

In the first marriage quaternio, kinship, love, and friendship are equalized and balanced, while in the second they are developmentally and hierarchically ordered, but in either case a double marriage provides the triple resolution of these love relationships. The fluvial epithalamion in Canto 11 celebrates another marriage. Moreover, Spenser's catalogue here goes beyond the union of bride and groom; the ordering of his art harnesses the energy of nature and creates a grand whole combining myth, history, contemporary empire-building, England, and Ireland.[9]

Although these three episodes culminate in concord, harmony, and marriage, they are also formally separated from the rest of Book IV. Each is introduced by a reference to past events, the first by the narrator (2.32), the second by the complementary explanations of Aemylia and Placidas (7.15, 8.50), the third by the narrator's address to "the noursling of Dame Memorie," who will unroll "records of antiquitie" (11.10.2,4). These episodes are additionally highlighted by their obvious fictiveness. The first is literally a lost story recovered from oblivion, introduced by an invocation to Chaucer, its begetter. The story itself, like Chaucer's, is highly artificial, filled with the magical props of medieval romance. A second retrospective narrative must be introduced to insert Triamond and his brothers into the retold Squire's Tale itself.

An invocation also introduces the epithalamion, which floods every stanza with traces of innumerable stories attached to Spenser's marine genealogy. The canto ends by giving names to things, the fundamental act of human language, poetry in its most primitive form, as the narrator lists the fifty daughters of Nereus.[10] If the whole episode is Spenser's earlier "Epithalamion Thamesis," its self-proclaiming fictiveness is even more striking.[11] Like the Cambell-Canacee story, it is a poem within a poem.

The Amyas-Placidas narrative has no invocation, but it too calls attention to itself as a story through the names of its characters: Aemylia initially identifies her beloved as a "squire of low degree," the title of a fifteenth-century English romance; "Amyas" and "Aemylia" echo *Amis and Amiloun,* the old French tale of exemplary friendship, whose heroes resemble Spenser's in their remarkable interchangeability.[12] Even more strikingly fictional is the formal close of the episode, so like a folk tale: the couples lived happily ever after, the narrator assures us, and Poeana, formerly both shrewish and lustful, became a model wife.

Arthur's intervention in this episode perfects friendship, but his own quest continues after the end of this story:

Thus when the Prince had perfectly compylde
These paires of friends in peace and settled rest,
Him selfe, whose minde did trauell as with chylde,
Of his old loue, conceau'd in secret brest,
Resolued to pursue his former quest;
And taking leaue of all, with him did beare
Faire *Amoret,* whom Fortune by bequest
Had left in his protection whileare,
Exchanged out of one into an other feare.

(9.17)

Arthur's search for Gloriana is still unsatisfied, and he has lost
Timias to shame and disgrace; Amoret, still separated from
Scudamour, does not recognize Arthur as her deliverer from
male lust, but as the same threat in another form, and she sees
herself as fortune's plaything. Amoret's anxiety and Arthur's
frustration contrast markedly with the happiness of the four
lovers and friends whom the Prince has just reconciled in endless harmony.

The other perfected friendship is also separated from the
subsequent action of the poem. Immediately after Canto 3
concludes Spenser's retrospective narrative, the heroes of that
tale are challenged by the characters in the narrative foreground,
the discordant quartet of Blandamour, Paridell, Duessa, and
Ate, whose falseness and malice so dominate the early cantos of
Book IV. Although Cambina's "persuasions myld" pacify these
hostile antitypes "for the present (4.5), the idealized foursome
soon finds itself caught up in Satyrane's confusing and uncertain
tournament. While Spenser's Squire's Tale had moved from
potentially tragic conflict to the comic triple resolution provided almost magically by Cambina's nepenthe, the tournament of Florimell's girdle moves from chivalric ideals to unresolved conflicts and degenerates into chaotic disorder and quar-
reling, its presiding genius not Cambina but Ate.

Finally, the grand epithalamion of Thames and Medway
gives way to the situation of Florimell and Marinell, both out of
place and unsatisfied in the palace of Proteus; indeed, Marinell
"being bred / Of mortall sire," is not even a spectator of the
vision in Canto 11. And although the final stanza of the book
restores Spenser's two lovers to each other, it does not record a
triumphant comic resolution:

Right so himselfe did *Marinell* upreare,
    When he in place his dearest loue did spy;
    And though his limbs could not his bodie beare,
    Ne former strength returne so suddenly,
    Yet chearefull signes he shewed outwardly
    Ne lesse was she in secret hart affected,
    But that she masked it with modestie,
    For feare she should of lightnesse be detected:
Which to another place I leaue to be perfected.

The weakened Marinell may only express his love indirectly, Florimell seems nervously to mask her inner feelings, and the poet defers the resolution of their story to another book.

In sum, the Spenserian Squire's Tale, the Amyas-Placidas episode, and the Thames-Medway pageant celebrate full resolutions of human relationships culminating in marriage. But their self-evident artifice distances these episodes from the ongoing narrative. Characters like Cambina, Placidas, Thames and Medway seem to enter the poem from a golden, fictive world that makes the rest of Faeryland seem fallen. Thus, Book IV, like the first three, presents a contrast between perfectly realized ideals of its titular virtue and the imperfect approximations of it possible in fallen experience, the world in which Arthur, Britomart, Scudamour, and Spenser's other heroes must pursue their quests—the world in which the reader lives.

The frustration, disappointment, and disorder following closure of the three perfected fictions strikingly emphasize this contrast between ideals and reality. But so does the foreground narrative itself: Britomart and Artegall are betrothed, but left unmarried, as he leaves her to pursue his own quest; Arthur's rescue of Aemylia and Amoret exposes all of them to "Sclaunder." Most significantly, the two apparently full reconciliations, Timias-Belphoebe and Scudamour-Amoret, are themselves separated from the ongoing narrative and limited in their resolutions.

The first of these ultimately reconciles squire and lady, but only by withdrawing them into Belphoebe's *locus amoenus*, an earthly paradise that paradoxically preserves its natural perfection by separating itself from nature. Deep within the forest, it is not part of the forest, but represents unfallen nature in the midst of the confused, fallen world outside its charmed circle.

This place is exactly analogous to the emblematic rose of virginity in Book III, which shuts up its leaves in stormy weather (III.5.51.4–7). Although friendship is re-established between the knight and his "dearest dred" (8.17.1), Spenser juxtaposes within a single stanza (8.18) Timias' complaisant security and Arthur's continued quest, his wandering in the world of Faeryland outside Belphoebe's golden world, friendless and alone:

> In which he long time afterwards did lead
>   An happie life with grace and good accord,
>   Fearlesse of fortunes chaunge or enuies dread,
>   And eke all mindlesse of his owne deare Lord
>   The noble Prince, who neuer heard one word
>   Of tydings, what did him betide
>   Or what good fortune did to him afford,
>   But through the endelesse world did wander wide,
> Him seeking euermore, yet no where him descride.
>
> (8.18)

Arthur wanders through a world without endings, friendless and alone, his quests both for Gloriana and his friend unresolved; conversely, Timias enjoys his mistress' "grace," a happy ending that removes him from fortune and the ongoing narrative.

But this resolution itself is also limited, particularly in comparison with the three retrospective fictions separated from the foreground action. Timias' service to Belphoebe involves oblivion of his service to Arthur. There can be no marriage, of course. And this reconciliation is possible only because Timias and Belphoebe have both deserted the wounded Amoret, who was the cause of their initial separation. Timias seems to love Amoret,[13] and she is Belphoebe's sister, so that the friendship of Timias and Belphoebe depends upon excluding two of the three kinds of affection reconciled in the Spenserian squire's tale, kinship and love.

Thus, Timias and Belphoebe realize the titular virtue only by denying other human relationships and removing themselves from the continuing narrative. Scudamour's realization of friendship is even more limited. Like the three episodes of idealized friendship, the Temple of Venus is a self-consciously fictional retrospective that ends happily for its hero and is separated from the ongoing narrative. But as Berger and Hieatt have noted, Scudamour's courtship of Amoret is marked by an aggressiveness and will to mastery that initiates their relationship but also undermines it.[14] This templar vision represents courtship only from Scudamour's perspective: Amoret is seen as an object of male desire ("this peerlesse beauties spoile"— 10.3.3), and the whole episode, presented as a conquest of female modesty, ends with her leaving the Temple reluctantly. This one-sided narration contrasts with the dual openings of the Amyas-Aemylia story, one representing her viewpoint, the other his, each a mirror of the other, so that male and female desire are equalized and complemented. Also, the entire Temple episode represents not the fulfillment of love that we see in the three exemplary fictions but its beginning. Finally, while Timias' friendship had to exclude love, Scudamour's love seems to threaten friendship; indeed, both lovers and friends walk in the garden outside the Temple (10.26), but the two groups are separated, being placed "farre away" from the other both literally and according to the "ground" of their desire.

These flat notes in Scudamour's rhapsody to his courtship point to the difficulties of the relationship it celebrates. The double sequel to the Temple of Venus episode further complicates the triumph celebrated in it. Scudamour's comments at the beginning of Canto 10 upon the frustrations of love (they outnumber its satisfactions a hundredfold) are the record of his subsequent relationship with Amoret. Book IV opens by noting the separation of the lovers on their wedding day and their resulting unhappiness through Amoret's imprisonment by Busyrane. The Temple of Venus episode suggests that this separation actually began with their mutual subjection to erotic desire itself, which fueled Scudamour's aggressiveness and Amoret's fear and hesitation. As Hieatt has noted, Scudamour cannot rescue Amoret from Busyrane because the torturer represents a part of his own nature.[15] Amoret's own sexual anxiety is epitomized in a comment that could apply equally well to Busyrane or Scudamour: "Ah who can loue the worker of her smart?" (III.12.31.7)

Thus, the dramatic sequel to the Temple of Venus episode, detailed at the beginning of Book IV and the end of Book III, frustrates its seemingly happy resolution. The formal close of

Scudamour's account in IV.10 suggests its limitations in another way. The poet ends the canto with the end of Scudamour's narrative: "So ended he his tale, where I this canto end." The explicit reference to the Temple episode as Scudamour's story and the narrator's enclosing it within his own formal structure doubly emphasize its fictiveness. Nor is there a final dramatic resolution after Scudamour finishes his incomplete tale. There is no mutual embrace like that of the original ending of Book III, and scarcely a sign of mutual recognition before or after Scudamour's story.

The meeting of Britomart and Arthur, together here in the text for the only time in the poem, is also curious. They speak in adjacent stanzas (9.37–38), but they do not speak directly to each other. Indeed, although Cantos 9 and 10 seem to bring together a quartet of heroic lovers, nothing is made of this potential resolution. Instead, Spenser turns to Florimell's imprisonment at the beginning of Canto 11. Scudamour, like the silent Amoret, virtually disappears from the poem after his last words, while Britomart and Arthur next appear separately and alone in Book V without reference to this understated "meeting." In short, the text nearly eliminates any sense of closure or resolution in the coming together of these four heroes. Here again, the contrast with the marriage quaternios is striking.

II

Thus, although Book IV celebrates friendship, these contrasts between foreground and background suggest that it may be fully realized only in stories. The problems of friendship derive from the poet's conception of the virtue, which is even more than normally syncretic, and complex enough to seem original. Spenser's friendship comprises three distinct aspects. As a force of nature, Lucretian and Pythagorean, friendship reconciles opposites: male and female, hate and love, kinship and *eros*.[16] This form of desire, which energizes sexuality, is celebrated openly in the Temple of Venus and implicitly in the marriage of rivers. As an ethical choice, Aristotelian and Ciceronian, friendship attracts those who are like each other in virtue. This "band of vertuous mind" (9.1.8—see also 2.29.6–9) is identified in Book III (1.12.8) as the "golden chaine of concord" that unites Britomart, Artegall, and Guyon—and, indeed, all of Spenser's virtuous exemplars. As a social relationship, friendship unites virtuous men and women in marriage, joining those who are unalike in nature yet equal in virtue. This third conception, a Christian domestication of classical friendship, appears in Renaissance dialogues like Tilney's *Flower of Friendship*.[17] It combines Lucretian and Aristotelian components of friendship and, by establishing the family, extends the end of virtuous actions beyond individual integrity or individual desire into history and community.

This culminating form of friendship, which reconciles *eros* and virtue, is completely realized only in the intrusive fictions, as we have seen. In those marriages, however, friendship is simplified: erotic desire is satisfied without moral conflicts or hesitations, as it can be in stories. But in the narrative foreground, the fallen world of human experience, desire is morally problematical. The only fully satisfied couple are the withdrawn Timias and Belphoebe, whose friendship finally excludes sexuality altogether. Elsewhere, relations between men and women are marked by aggression or suspicion, and the boundaries between friendship and sexual desire are confusing.

The problems attendant upon the erotic component of friendship for Spenser's heroic lovers are evident in the many fictional situations involving frustration, conflict, and disguise throughout the Book. Scudamour's stay at the House of Care (5.32–46) and his attack upon Britomart (6.7–10) are obvious examples of the former. Disguises symbolize the ways in which men and women are transformed by desire into new identities that either protect their own integrity, satisfy culturally sanctioned roles for the lover, or do both. Britomart's disguise in her *Venus Armata* role[18] and Artegall's disguise as the "Salvage Knight" are literal examples, while Timias in his ragged derangement and silence and Scudamour's identity as "*Cupid*'s man" (10.54.7), the victorious possessor of the shield of love that gives him his name, are figurative disguises, roles determined for these characters by the power of *eros*.[19] That such anxieties, conflicts, and transformed identities are integral to virtuous desire is also suggested by its counterfeit, the parodic fulfillment of love and friendship by Braggadochio and the false Florimell. These two are joined effortlessly and inevitably at the end of Satyrane's tournament as the factitious Florimell chooses Braggadochio, his worthlessness a perfect complement to her own. Lacking both virtue and desire, Braggadochio and the snowy Florimell are empty shells—once their disguises are removed (in Book V), there is nothing left of them (Florimell literally melts away, V.3.24). On the other hand, the disguises and role-playing of Spenser's heroic lovers, as well as their anxieties and conflicts, are the effects of a virtuous desire that is real but inexpressible and problematical within Book IV.

Unlike their antitypes, who are attracted by utility and plea-sure, the lower forms of friendship for Aristotle,[20] the heroic lovers of Book IV are attracted by the virtue of their beloved. For ultimately, friendship is a desire for the beautiful and good in human nature. But Spenser's heroes distrust this very desire, which is the efficient cause of their affection, but not its final cause.[21] The uncertain moral status of desire is present through-out Book IV: in Amoret's capture by Lust, Timias' inability to rescue her, Belphoebe's anger at both of them, Florimell's ner-vous bashfulness, and even the conflict of Britomart and Arte-gall. As a result, friendship between men and women is ex-tremely difficult to achieve or recognize. The book opens with Amoret, now dependent upon the disguised Britomart, but feeling more fear than gratitude toward her rescuer. Only after Britomart reveals her sexual identity can the two women, each suffering from desire, become friends. Timias cannot save Amoret from Lust, and his intervention brings about his own implication in her disgrace. When Arthur rescues Amoret and Aemylia, all are immediately subjected to the poisonous malignity of "Sclaunder" (scandal and slander), the public, so-cial form assumed by the psychological traumata that have accompanied the separation of Timias and Belphoebe: shame in the former, moral outrage in the latter.

Such misunderstandings, which implicitly deny dis-interested, virtuous affection between men and women, are shared by the "Stoicke censours" of the Proem, who deprecate erotic love as vanity and folly. Here Spenser turns away from such critics to his sovereign, "the queen of love," establishing a relationship between himself and one who by reading and approving the book will both sanction and exemplify its virtue.[22] Like the other friendships between men and women in the book, this relationship between poet and Queen is left incomplete, but it escapes the moral censorship that taints affection between the sexes—within the book itself and within society. Indeed, even readers are advised not to censure Aemylia and Amoret for "conversing" overnight with Arthur (IV.8.29.5). Since they find it almost impossible to read this pun innocently, they become dramatically aware of the corruption of language and their own viewpoints concerning friendship between the sexes.[23]

III

In correcting those who would take "Sclaunder's" part, Spenser distances the friendship of Arthur and Amoret-Aemylia by placing it in a past of "simple truth" and "blameless chastitie," when virtue was held in awe, while "loyall loue had royall regiment / And each vnto his lust did make a law" (8.30). The narrative foreground dissolves here for four stanzas into another retrospective ideal that contrasts with the devaluation and abuse of love in the world of our experience, after "faire grew foule, and foule grew faire in sight" (32.5).[24] The entire passage suggests that friendship as Spenser conceives it, the movement of *eros* toward virtue, is misunderstood or denied by contemporary society. These stanzas also anticipate the Proem to Book V, which decries society's general corruption: virtue is called vice and vice, virtue; "right now is wrong, and wrong that was is right" (4.4).

Aristotle relates friendship significantly to justice when he opens his discussion of the former in the *Nicomachean Ethics*:

When people are friends, they have no need of justice, but when they are just, they need friendship in addition. In fact, the just in the fullest sense is regarded as constituting an element of friendship.[25]

For Aristotle, therefore, friendship is more inclusive than justice: he treats the latter as the highest of the social virtues in Book Five of the *Ethics*, but friendship is handled later in the treatise as the happiness that is available to the wholly virtuous human being. By reversing the order of treatment of these two virtues, *The Faerie Queene* suggests that friendship is incomplete without justice.

For Spenser, friendship is ultimately the love of one virtuous soul for another. It is the first of the social virtues that he treats, because it establishes the fundamental relationships out of which civil society arises, marriage and love of the good. For true friendship to flourish, however, virtue and vice must be identified; the art of making such discriminating judgements is justice. But as we have noted, such discrimination is difficult in Book IV, even for Spenser's heroic lovers. In providing a capacity for differentiating virtue from vice, justice may enable friendship to be completely realized, doing away with the hesitations, conflicts, and role-playing that inhibit virtuous affection between men and women and the corrupted understanding of love by society in general.

Artegall's departure from the middle of the book suggests another way in which justice is necessary to the fulfillment of friendship. His quest as the exemplar of justice is mentioned in the middle of Book IV, and he leaves Britomart in order to pursue it:

> Tho when they had long time there taken rest,
> Sir *Artegall,* who all this while was bound
> Vpon an hard aduenture yet in quest,
> Fit time for him thence to depart it found,
> To follow that, which he did long propound;
> And vnto her his congee came to take.
> But her therewith full sore displeasd he found,
> And loth to leaue her late betrothed make,
> Her dearest loue full loth so shortly to forsake.
>
> (IV.6.42)

This stanza makes Artegall's falling in love appear to be both a diversion and a preparation for his proper responsibilities, which have preceded the betrothal to Britomart, and must be completed before their love and friendship may be fulfilled in marriage. The deeper implication is that although friendship is the greatest human happiness, it may be threatened by vicious forces of the larger fallen society that encloses such lovers. True friendship would establish a community of the virtuous, but friends must exist within a fallen social order whose representatives in Book IV include Ate, Discord, and the antitypes of friendship that populate the first half of the book. Justice attempts to reform that larger world, which constantly threatens lovers of virtue and virtuous lovers—indeed, Merlin has already revealed to Britomart that she will lose Artegall "to practise criminall / Of secret foes" (III.3.28.8–9).

Thus, justice seems necessary to the fulfillment of friendship in two ways. This helps to explain why the Legend of Justice follows the Legend of Friendship appropriately, despite the absence of an initial narrative link like those connecting the earlier books. Numerous details in both books suggest that perfected friendship is possible only as a consequence of justice. Here are the most obvious.

In Book IV itself, Arthur must overthrow the "tortious powre" of Corflambo and redistribute his "hoorded treasure" as a marriage dowry for Poeana before the second marriage quaternio may live happily ever after (9.12.2,4). The otherwise smooth flow of the epithalamion is broken (11.22) in an exhortation for the effeminate Britons to extend Elizabeth's empire to the Amazon, a charge that curiously anticipates the Radigund episode in Book V. As Goldberg points out, "the land [Guiana] is a woman to be purchased by spoil," but her conquest would also permit the poet to amplify his wedding ceremony by including the Amazon and her domains among the celebrants. As with the rescue of Irena in Book V, we may assume that this extension of Elizabeth's empire would exemplify political justice for Spenser. Florimell's restoration depends upon Neptune's justice, the assertion of his "high prerogative" to dispose of waifs of the sea (12.31.6). In Book V, the marriage of Florimell and Marinell, put off to "another place" at the end of Book IV, depends upon Artegall's justice, which exposes the False Florimell, restores the cestus to the real Florimell, and baffles Braggadochio in Canto 3. Artegall's intervention thus makes this episode the antitype of Satyrane's chaotic tournament in Book IV: justice finally expels false beauty and reveals the true. Indeed, Book V provides final solutions to several problems of the earlier books, none more startling than the sentence carried out against the false friends and lovers of Book IV, for Blandamour, Paridell, and Duessa are all executed.

In Book V itself, private affections involve political action. For example, Artegall's fall to Radigund mirrors his fall to Britomart in Book IV, but the result is not friendship but injustice. In rescuing him, Britomart acts not only as his lover but also as a justiciary. Conversely, the problematic courtship of Burbon and Flourdelis (one of Spenser's more tendentious episodes) reflects the lack of a just settlement of French civil religion. Finally, the friendship of Arthur and Artegall, whose similarity in names may recall pairs like Amis–Amiloun, Amyas–Aemylia, Amyas–Placidas, expresses itself through complementary imperial missions for the sake of those oddly indistinguishable twins, Mercilla and Gloriana.

IV

This study of friendship suggests that Spenser's moral allegory is more complex and more interesting than has generally been noted, the virtue itself more problematical. At the heart of Spenser's examination and celebration of human excellence is a fundamental awareness of man's fallen condition, a situation which places a moral imperative upon poetry (as well as upon all human learning) best defined by Sidney: "to lead and draw us to as high a perfection as our degenerate souls, made worse by their clayey lodgings, can be capable of."[26] In presenting his "speaking pictures" of the virtues, Spenser reminds us of what our souls are capable, but also of the limitations of human virtue. These limits are examined within individual books; they are also implied in the overall structure of the poem, which makes each book and each virtue a temporary resolution that requires what follows to correct, complete, or transcend it. Completely perfected virtue is always deferred, as Arthur's quest suggests, and the work as a whole anticipates its own incompleteness.

In Book IV, Spenser's contrasting foreground and background narratives make us aware of the unperfected nature of friendship in its fullest form, love between the sexes. As elsewhere in *The Faerie Queene*, episodes that flaunt their fictiveness remind us that the perfected virtue realized within them is an imaginative ideal, while the rest of the narrative demonstrates the difficulty of achieving such final resolutions. As Sidney notes, "our erected wit maketh us know what perfection is, and yet our infected will keepeth us from reaching unto it."[27]

Friendship is the culmination of Spenser's individual virtues but also the foundation of the social virtues. Book IV not only celebrates its effects, but also questions whether it can be fully realized in fallen experience, where sexual distrust and confusion of virtue and vice characterize human relationships and reflect society's corrupted viewpoint. As a result, justice seems necessary to allow a fuller realization of the earlier virtue. But although justice addresses the moral and social problems that hinder the fulfillment of friendship, it too has its limitations, as the transition to Book VI makes clear. In that book, friendship is realized in a form perhaps more appropriate to the fallen world so insistently represented in Book V, for courtesy is an extension of friendship to good and bad alike that allows them to realize the worst or the best in their nature.

University of Hawaii at Manoa

NOTES

1. I derive the term "heroic lover" from Mark Rose, *Heroic Love: Studies in Sidney and Spenser* (Cambridge, Mass.: Harvard University Press, 1968). He identifies fidelity as the characteristic of the heroic lover (p. 110). The first three couples exemplify such fidelity, and Timias' derangement in Book IV measures how deeply even the suspicion of infidelity affects him. While Belphoebe's allegorical role prevents her from being a lover herself, her "heroic mind" (III.5.55.5) incorporates chastity and courtesy and Spenser presents her as an exemplar for heroic lovers among his women readers (III.5.53).

2. As Jonathan Goldberg notes, "Ate" is a visual pun on "Hate." See *Endlesse Worke: Spenser and the Structures of Discourse* (Baltimore, Md.: Johns Hopkins University Press, 1981), p. 97. She is also the classical goddess of discord, of course (*Iliad*, XIX.91–94). Spenser's elaborate description of Ate and her dwelling, as well as her dramatic role in Book IV, make this dual identification plausible.

3. Maurice Evans notes that while Guyon binds Acrasia, he also preserves her safely—*Spenser's Anatomy of Heroism: A Commentary on "The Faerie Queene"* (Cambridge: Cambridge University Press, 1970), p. viii. A. C. Hamilton observes that the erotic love represented by Acrasia is freed and virtuously fulfilled in Books III and IV—Edmund Spenser, *The Faerie Queene* (London: Longman, 1977), p. 299: William Nelson points out that it is Britomart's task in Book III to combine chastity and affection, not to repress the latter, as Guyon must do—*The Poetry of Edmund Spenser: A Study* (New York: Columbia University Press, 1963), p. 228. While Guyon's final purpose is to fetter Acrasia, Britomart's is to liberate Amoret.

4. That the middle books are a unified whole, Book IV the resolution of

Book III, is the persuasive argument of Thomas P. Roche, Jr.'s *The Kindly Flame: A Study of the Third and Fourth Books of Spenser's "Faerie Queene"* (Princeton, N. J.: Princeton University Press, 1964). This common viewpoint is implicit in the structural organization of two important global studies of the poem, Isabel MacCaffrey's *Spenser's Allegory: The Anatomy of Imagination* (Princeton, N. J.: Princeton University Press, 1976) pp. 231–340 and James Nohrnberg's *The Analogy of "The Faerie Queene"* (Princeton, N. J.: Princeton University Press, 1976) pp. 427–651.

5. Despite Alastair Fowler's attempt to demonstrate a carefully wrought numerological structure, many commentators have noted the apparent narrative weaknesses of Book IV, as Graham Hough notes. See *Spenser and the Numbers of Time* (London: Routledge & Kegan Paul, 1964), p. 156 and *A Preface to "The Faerie Queene"* (London: Duckworth, 1962) p. 180. MacCaffrey refers to an "enfeeblement of structural forms" in the Book (p. 336). Hamilton's comment introduces Book IV in his edition of *FQ* (p. 423). All quotations from the poem will be taken from this edition, and my spelling of characters' names is based on Hamilton's list (pp. 19–21).

6. The phrase comes from Charles G. Smith's study of Book IV, *Spenser's Theory of Friendship* (Baltimore, Md.: Johns Hopkins University Press, 1935), p. 15. Another comprehensive earlier study of friendship as a virtue is Laurens J. Mills, *One Soul in Bodies Twain: Friendship in Tudor Literature and Stuart Drama* (Bloomington, Ind.: Principia Press, 1937). Both works view Spenser's friendship as a conventional conception, largely drawn from classical and medieval sources and rather easy to define and characterize. A recent study of Book IV, relating Spenser's friendship to his praise of Elizabeth, is Robin Headlam Wells, *Spenser's "Faerie Queene" and the Cult of Elizabeth* (London: Croom Helm, 1983). Like earlier critics, he sees the moral allegory of the Book as relatively uncomplicated: "friendship, like temperance, is not in itself a problematic virtue" (p. 92). Goldberg's is the first full-length study of Book IV; his deconstruction of the text demonstrates its complexity as narrative. Although his work provides a corrective to criticism that simplifies the book or dismisses its apparent confusions as narrative defects, he is unconcerned with the moral allegory, Spenser's anatomizing friendship through exemplars (the index, for example, includes no references to any of the characters in the book). I share his view of Book IV as open-ended and incomplete in its details, but I argue below that such irresolution is integral to Spenser's analysis of the titular virtue, which is more complex and problematic than earlier writers have considered it.

7. *Endlesse Worke*, p. 5. For a discussion of the etymological implications of the title page character ("perfect world"), see Roche, pp. 16–17.

8. I borrow the term "marriage quaternio" from Nohrnberg, who borrows it from Jung. Book IV is filled with groups of four, which is both numerologically and philosophically fitting: the importance of the Pythagorean tetrad in Renaissance cosmology is examined by S. K. Heninger, Jr., "Some Renaissance Versions of the Pythagorean Tetrad," *Studies in the Renaissance*, 8 (1961), 7–35; Fowler asserts that Spenser uses the tetrad as a narrative device throughout Book IV (p. 24). Since my focus is the moral allegory of Book IV, I use terms such as "quaternio," "quartet," or "foursome," appropriate to fictional characters, rather than "tetrad," which seems more appropriate to what Michael Murrin calls the "philosophical" levels of Renaissance allegory, in-

cluding cosmological allegory. See *The Veil of Allegory: Some Notes Toward a Theory of Allegorical Rhetoric in the English Renaissance* (Chicago, Ill.: University of Chicago Press, 1969) p. 119.

9. The union of England and Ireland is suggested by A. M. Buchan, "The Political Allegory of Book IV of *The Faerie Queene*," *ELH*, 11 (1944), 237–248; the political allegory is further defined by Fowler (pp. 172–175); Goldberg (pp. 135–144) suggests that the marriage represents and fantasizes the social realities of Elizabeth's court.

10. The entire pageant symbolizes the poetic imagination at work, according to A. Bartlett Giamatti, *Play of Double Senses: Spenser's "Faerie Queene"* (Englewood Cliffs, N. J.: Prentice-Hall, 1975), p. 131.

11. Hough suggests that Canto XI represents some version of that earlier poem, if not the poem itself (189–190). The "Epithalamion" is listed among Spenser's "lost" works in the first letter to Harvey (1580).

12. There are no surviving manuscripts of "The Squyr of Lowe Degree," but a printed version was published *ca.* 1560, and there are frequent references to it by Elizabethan writers. See *A Manual of the Writings in Middle English 1050–1500*, gen. ed. J. Burke Severs (New Haven: Connecticut Academy of Arts & Sciences, 1967), I, 157. English versions of the French romance survive in four manuscripts dating from the mid-thirteenth century to 1500. MacEdward Leach edited the English romance, *Amys and Amylion,* for the *Early English Text Society* (London, Oxford University Press, 1937).

13. As Goldberg notes (p. 55), Belphoebe sees Timias' attentions to Amoret as lustful; yet the narrative itself is ambiguous as Roche has noted (*Kindly Flame*, pp. 137–138). As I point out below, the distinction between "love" and "lust" is difficult to define, even for the lover, and Spenser represents this in Belphoebe's flight and Timias' shame, both of which seem to be unhealthily exaggerated.

14. Harry Berger, Jr., "Busirane and the War Between the Sexes: An Interpretation of *The Faerie Queene* III.xi–xii," *ELH*, 38 (1971), 99. A. Kent Hieatt, "Scudamour's Practice of 'Maistrye' upon Amoret," *PMLA*, 77 (1962), 510.

15. A. Kent Hieatt, *Chaucer, Spenser, Milton: Mythopoeic Continuities and Transformations* (Montreal: McGill-Queen's University Press, 1975), p. 130.

16. The lover's hymn in the Temple of Venus (10.44–47) paraphrases Lucretius' address to *alma Venus* at the beginning of *De Rerum Natura* (1–20). Wells examines the union of opposites as a cosmic principle (*Cult of Elizabeth*, pp. 93–96), noting various examples of the Pythagorean tetrad from Plato and Ovid to Du Bartas.

17. Discussed briefly by Rose, pp. 24–25. Valerie Wayne's critical edition is forthcoming from Cornell University Press.

18. On Britomart as a *Venus armata* figure, balancing feminine and masculine characteristics, see Kathleen Williams, *Spenser's World of Glass: A Reading of "The Faerie Queene"* (Berkeley: University of California Press, 1973), p. 91.

19. Goldberg points out that by winning the shield Scudamour becomes "Cupid's man, a generic type." (p. 65). In his reading, Scudamour becomes absorbed into a textual identity; but this is also the role, involving a change of identity, that centuries of literary and cultural tradition have made "natural" for male lovers.

20. *Nicomachean Ethics*, VIII.34

21. As Rose notes (p. 34), although marriage was romanticized and morally elevated by Elizabethan Protestants, the erotic desire that led to marriage was still ethically suspect. The moral status of love is a problem apparent in much of Spenser's poetry, most signally in the dedication of Four Hymns. The Palmer includes love, "a monster fell," along with wrath, jealousy, and grief as an enemy of reason (F. Q. II.35.1–4). Although Glauce makes an easy discrimination between "filthy lust" and love in comforting the heartsick Britomart (III.2.40), the distinction between them in experience is difficult to make, as the careless Amoret's capture by Lust suggests.

22. Pace Goldberg's questioning it (p. 125), the traditional view that Spenser is referring to Burghley (and other official critics) is cogent, and it strengthens the rhetorical effect I have suggested Spenser is making in turning from society to the Queen herself. For a recent restatement of this identification, see Maureen Quilligan, Milton's Spenser: The Politics of Reading (Ithaca, N. Y.: Cornell University Press), p. 200. Quilligan notes that Spenser's rhetoric here dismisses a male reader and then reconstitutes both male and female in the person of the Queen.

23. "Conversation" can mean "sexual intimacy" (O.E.D. 3), as it often does in Shakespeare. Curiously enough, however, the usage here suggests the opposite meaning as well, Milton's "conversation" as a spiritual intimacy that would realize Spenser's most complete form of friendship.

24. Spenser's use of antiquity as a moral standard against which to criticize the present is examined by Ronald Arthur Horton, The Unity of "The Faerie Queene" (Athens: University of Georgia Press, 1978), pp. 33–36. Insofar as such ideals are "historical" at all, we might place them in the aevum, a time intermediate between temporality and eternity. For an outline of this concept in Aquinas, with application to the Gardens of Adonis, see Frank Kermode, The Sense of an Ending: Studies in the Theory of Fiction (London, Oxford University Press, 1967), pp. 70–79. Kermode discusses aeviternity as fictional time (p. 71), a perspective used to define Spenser's fairyland in general by Michael Murrin, The Allegorical Epic: Essays in its Rise and Decline (Chicago, Ill.: University of Chicago Press, 1980), pp. 146–147.

25. Aristotle, Nicomachean Ethics, trans. Martin Ostwald (Indianapolis, Ind.: Bobbs-Merrill, 1962), p. 215.

26. Sir Philip Sidney, An Apology for Poetry or The Defence of Poesy, ed. Geoffrey Shepherd (London: Nelson, 1965), p. 104.

27. Sidney, p. 101. Besides the "stories" of Book IV, such ideals include the numerous mythopoeic passages in the poem, discursive statements by the narrator, and proverbial expressions throughout The Faerie Queene, all of which are removed in some sense from fallen experience as we know it. On the role that discursive statements and proverbs play in reminding the reader of the gap between ideals and experience, see MacCaffrey pp. 51–52.

JULIA REINHARD LUPTON

Home-Making in Ireland:
Virgil's Eclogue I and Book VI
of *The Faerie Queene*

B OOK VI of *The Faerie Queene* stands in bright relief against the
disturbing greys of Book V's stone and iron, a welcome allevia-
tion facilitated by pastoral as the genre of idealization and escape. A major subtext of Book VI's pastoral world, however, is
Virgil's Eclogue I, a poem which places an inherently con-
flicted, troubled relation between history and art at the
threshold of the Latin pastoral tradition. In *The Faerie Queene*,
Spenser adapts Virgil's Eclogue I in order to represent English
life in Ireland along the two finally inseparable axes of the
personal and the political. First, Eclogue I is used to redefine
"exile"—distance from the national center—as "home." In
Book VI, the shepherd Meliboee's painfully acquired happiness
far from city and court may help conceptualize and reconcile
Spenser's two-fold position as a kind of exile from England and
a home-making pioneer in Ireland. Second, Eclogue I trans-
mutes the brutal Irish politics of Book V into the golden world
of Book VI. This is achieved by converting the Irish from the
displaced to the dispossessing, and by softening Meliboee's
tragic fate at the hands of the Irish-like Brigants with the
restoration of pastoral lands to young Coridon. In both cases,
Spenser resolves Virgil's painful structural contrast between
"exile" and "home" into a redemptive narrative sequence of
migration or dispossession followed by return or repossession.
    This essay should help reconcile the views of Spenser as
alienated from England and the court with opposing representations of his career in Ireland as successful and satisfying: Spenser's revisions of Eclogue I accommodate the positions of both
exile and home-maker.[1] At the same time, I hope to enrich
what it means to relate life and work, poetic and political careers
by stressing the role of genre and subtext in laying down

119

specific narrative patterns and historical concerns for Spenser. The pastoral tradition offers poets autobiographical, political and poetic schemes which can be actively chosen and manipulated, but which in turn act upon their "author" and resist revision. Finally Annabel Patterson has written that Eclogue I's varied reception is an index of assumptions about culture and politics: "As each new set of readers has struggled, ever since, to meet the demand made on them by this subtle text, their own aesthetic or societal premises have been strikingly manifest."[2] This essay reaffirms the doubly "historical" importance of Eclogue I as the founding poem of Latin and Renaissance pastoral: significant in the history of the genre, and significant in its institutionalization of historical themes within pastoral.

1. "IAM SUMMA PROCUL": INVENTING HOME IN ECLOGUE I

Virgil's Eclogue I contrasts the experiences of Tityrus and Meliboeus, the first blessedly allowed to remain in his pastoral home, the second forced to leave, both at the will of a godly ruler and patron in the city. Since the fourth century commentary of Servius, the poem has been read as referring to Octavian's reclamation and distribution of farmlands to his soldiers after the battle of Philippi in 42 B.C. and to Virgil's own exemption from that policy.[3] The dialogue between the two shepherds alternately celebrates the pastimes of Tityrus, "Fortunate senex," and reveals the limits (geographical, temporal, psychological, poetic) of that life as Meliboeus prepares to cross its borders:

> impius haec tam culta noualia miles habebit,
> barbarus has segetes. en quo discordia ciuis
> produxit miseros: his nos conseuimus agros!

> [Some godless veteran will own this fallow tilth,
> These cornfields a barbarian. Look where strife has led
> Rome's wretched citizens: we have sown fields for these!]
> (70–72)[4]

The poem ends in the poignantly temporary respite of Tityrus' hospitality:

Tityrus: Hic tamen hanc mecum poteras
   requiescere noctem
fronde super uiridi: sunt nobis mitia poma,
castaneae molles et pressi copia lactis,
et iam summa procul uillarum culmina
   fumant
maioresque cadunt altis de montibus
   umbrae.

[However, for tonight you could rest here with me
Upon green leafage: I can offer you ripe fruit
And mealy chestnuts and abundance of milk cheese.
Far off the roof-tops of the farms already smoke
And down from the high mountains taller shadows fall.
                                                    (79–83)

In Panofsky's famous formulation, these lines " 'discovered' the
evening" in their task of resolving the poem's governing dissonance; this "discovery" at once canonizes and anatomizes the
twilight returns to fold and cottage which conclude so many
Renaissance pastorals.[5]
    Following Panofsky's example, I would say that this final
conciliatory image also invents home. Home, the paradigmatic
object of nostalgia, is a category of experience only fashioned in
the alienated, desiring distance from it; it is an imaginary place
of origianl plenitude envisioned only in memory, from which
every mature person is an exile. In this sense, the poem's final
image would be an ideal to be recreated in pastoral art, while
renounced in life. At the same time, however, "home" indicates
the later household, the second nature, built with another and
designed in the compensatory image of the first, ideal one.[6]
Tityrus dwells in a house, not a green shade; he lives by the
labor, technology and architecture of civilization. Thus the
closing image represents at once the childhood idyll from which
all (Meliboeus, the readers) are banished, and a second, provisional home of adulthood imperfectly and laboriously built in
its image.
    Virgil locates this pastoral home in what would become the
Roman empire, whose "god" has given one man leisure and
exiled the other. Historical conditions do much to establish the

specific shape of a domestic ideal and its realization, as well as the degree of correspondence between the two. Mental and material labor (writing a poem, building a family) helps restore the losses inflicted by the inseparable dramas of psyche and history (familial conflicts and their painfully renunciatory resolutions; economic dispossession).[7] Yet such resolutions tend to cover up, reinforce or reproduce the situation they strive to ameliorate, and often work at the expense of others. Home, the stage of Freud's family romance and Marx's division of labor, is both the putative origin and the ideological answer to central crises in Western culture.

Thus in Eclogue I, it is hard not to feel that Tityrus' happiness depends upon Meliboeus' privation; this sense of disparity is crucial to Eclogue I's poetic effect. The poem's contrastive form at once serves to glorify the sovereign's will as the emergent condition of life, and at the same time reveals the costs of Tityrus' carefree pleasure and the tragic consequences of divine *imperium*. Paul Alpers writes that the poem "holds potential conflicts in suspension."[8] The word "suspension" provocatively describes the poem's use of pastoral dialogue to juxtapose the shepherds' fates and the closing image's recapitulation of the tension it resolves. Within that final emblem, the shadows of approaching evening and the smoking rooftops, metonymies for civilization and its discontents, severely limit the offered asylum. The phrase "iam summa procul," "already highest in the distance," distills the suspended immanence of Meliboeus' departure and the approaching evening. At the eclogue's close, home is a figure simultaneously of lost plenitude, of laborious compromise, and of another's impending displacement. More generally, the pastoral genre, in this brilliant commencement of the Latin tradition, is instituted as performing the necessary yet often violent cultural work of finding a home in an economy political as well as domestic.

Freud finds in the word *unheimlich* (uncanny; literally, unhomey) its opposite, *heimlich* (homely, homey, familiar). He argues that the uncanny stems from the return of the repressed, the sudden reappearance of an ambivalent desire initially repudiated because of its conflict with opposed psychical interests or levels of development. Repression, and the *unheimlich* return of the repressed, thus involve relations of opposition both within an initial scenario (ambivalence), and across time. The return of Eclogue I throughout literary history often produces Virgilian dissonances not fully controlled or desired by the texts (including their Virgilian "original") which host them. The social, psychic and literary contradictions inherent in the construction of pastoral homes (*Heim*) condition the *unheimlich* aspects of their later returns. What returns may be specific displacements and contradictions (for example, that possessors are often, if unwillfully, dispossessors), or displacement and contradiction as *structures* capable of organizing—and disorganizing—Eclogue I's scenario around new historical circumstances. Renaissance repetitions of Eclogue I often serve to affirm cultural values while revealing their limits, costs and genesis. Indeed, the image of home is frequently lodged in a pastoral story which transforms exile into home-coming, a revision which at once tempers the Virgilian model, and presents it as, and in, a pattern of return.

2. "EACH HATH HIS FORTUNE IN HIS BREST": EXILE AS RETURN

Renaissance poets recast Virgils' poem of exile into a story of return by grafting Meliboeus' dispossession onto Tityrus' trip to the city and then changing the final image of hospitality from a way-station on the journey out of pastoral into the scene of a country homecoming.[9] Spenser follows this design in the Virgilian-named Meliboee's story to Calidore in Book VI, Canto ix of *The Faerie Queene*. Firmly located within a marital household of maturity, Meliboee praises pastoral contentment: "That having small, yet doe I not complaine / Of want, ne wish for more it to augment" (VI.ix.20).[10] Meliboee expresses his satisfaction not with an Edenic state of pastoral plenty, but with the meager fruits of a painfully won adulthood. The shepherd had left the country for the city as a prodigal son, "When pride of youth forth pricked my desire" (VI.ix.24); only later, returning disappointed and disillusioned, could he find happiness in his own garden. Meliboee remembers the genesis of "home" out of its abandonment:

> After I had ten yeares my selfe excluded
> From native home, and spent my youth in vaine,
> I gan my follies to my selfe to plaine,

And this sweet peace, whose lacke did then appeare.
Tho backe returning to my sheepe againe,
I from thenceforth have learn'd to love more deare
This lowly quiet life, which I inherite here.

(VI.ix.25)

The phrase "my selfe excluded / From native home" rewrites
the Virgilian Meliboeus' enforced exile into a self-imposed
migration in search of better pastures. The word "lacke" operates oddly between its grammatical attachment to the pastoral
world ("this sweet peace, whose lacke did then appeare"), and
its more commonsensical attribution to the city as the place
from which country virtues become visible. Pastoral's work of
home-making is to adjust expectations to reality by redefining
an initial "lack" (poverty as desire) into "enough" (poverty as
absence of desire).

Meliboee generalizes this lesson in the dicta, "each hath his
fortune in his brest" (VI.ix.29), and "It is the mynd, that
maketh good or ill" (VI.ix.30). The mind appears as the agent
of home-making, in the Stoic tradition of the exile's consolation, whose arguments include the praise of povety and contemplation, and the cosmopolitan doctrine of home
everywhere.[11] What Meliboee has, at cost, learned to do, is to
call "exile"—absence from the center, from the court—"home."
This work of accommodation occurs through and within the
restructuring of Eclogue I: a scenario of immanent departure
becomes a story of return when the poet combines Meliboeus
and Tityrus into one shepherd and temporalizes Virgil's suspended opposites into a happier narrative sequence of exile
followed by home-coming.

Meliboee's praise of poverty to his guest Calidore takes place
within the household of maturity:

There he was welcom'd of that honest syre,
And of his aged Beldame homely well;
Who him besought himselfe to disattyre,
And rest himselfe, till supper time befell.

(VI.ix.17)

Spenser has literally gone inside Virgil's closing image and
"disattyred" it. The word "homely" evokes the related virtues

of hospitality and domesticity, while the shadows of evening falling at the end of Virgil's poem are benignly revised and incorporated in the phrase "till supper time befell."[12] The presence of the "aged Beldame" and their foundling daughter renovates the playfully erotic (and homoerotic) pastoral of Virgil into a solidly familial scene. The story of self-imposed exile unfolded in this domestic setting narrates the manufacture of "home" out of the departure and return to it.

Within the scene of hospitality, Calidore strives to apply the shepherd's narrative to his present lapse in chivalric duty:

> Yet to occasion meanes, to worke his mind,
>   And to insinuate his harts desire,
>   He thus replyde; Now surely syre, I find,
>   That all this worlds gay showes, which we admire,
>   Be but vaine shadowes to this safe retyre . . .
>   (VI.ix.27)

Spenser represents Calidore's response as patently manipulative and self-serving, designed "to insinuate his harts desire," and Meliboee gently corrects him in the stanzas which follow (29, 30). The dialogue between the two men displays the pastoral of return as a narrative resource drawn upon by disparate home-making motives, whether by a prodigal shepherd finding his way home, or an errant knight seeking to justify his desire for love and rest. In this manner, the scene of hospitality serves to stage the interpretive transmission and manipulation of Eclogue I as a praise of pastoral poverty and a story of return.

Meliboee's pattern of return also governs the "September" eclogue of the *Shepheardes Calender* and *Colin Clouts Come Home Again*. In the earlier poem, Meliboeus' dispossession becomes Diggon Davies' prodigal poverty as he comes back "wasted" and deflocked from his unfortunate sojourn in the city. Set in the barren landscape of autumn, the poem concludes with an overt imitation of Eclogue I:

> But if to my cotage thou wilt resort,
> So as I can, I wil thee comfort:
> There mayst thou ligge in a vetchy bed,
> Til fayrer Fortune shewe forthe her head.
>   (254–7)

As in Meliboee's tale, the initial departure "in hope of better" (l. 60) indicates an original inadequacy; the state of pastoral contentment can be achieved only *after* an experience of lack within pastoral, followed by a later urban exposure to desire out of control. Diggon's Ovidian emblem, from the Narcissus myth, expresses the poem's pastoral concern wth the economics of desire: "*Inopem me copia fecit.*" Plenty impoverishes by creating demands whose successful harnessing is hinted at but by no means assured by the poem's closing scene of hospitality. The social and linguistic valences of *copia,* a term whch represents an alternate ideal of pastoral plenty as well as the luxury of Spenserian poetics, are disciplined and delimited by the poem's dominant concern with religious satire and its proprieties.

Both "September" and Meliobee's tale, by converting exile into return, resolve Virgil's difficult structural contrast between dispossession and preservation of land into a temporal sequence of departure from pastoral and a relieving return to it. *Colin Clouts Come Home Again* is, as its title evokes, also a pastoral of return. Yet in this poem, unlike the other two Spenserian examples, the conflation of Tityrus' trip to the city and Meliboeus' exile lies in a much rawer, more visible state. The landscape is a thinly disguised Ireland, which appears alternately as the "home" of the title in relation to England's corrupt court (ll. 660–794), and as a "desart" exile far from bounteous England (ll. 91, 180–3). As Nancy Jo Hoffman has argued, the passage negatively describing the bounty of England clearly resonates with the dangerous, devastated land depicted in Spenser's *View of the Present State of Ireland*:[13]

> No wayling there nor wretchednesse is heard,
> No bloodie issues nor no leprosies,
> No griesly famine, nor no raging sweard,
> No nightly bodrags, nor no hue and cries:
> The shepheards there abroad may safely lie,
> On hills and downes, withouten dread or daunger:
> No ravenous wolves the good mans hope destroy,
> Nor outlawes fell affray the forest raunger.
>
> (314–319)

Hoffman sees *Colin Clout* as in effect two unsuccessfully combined poems, a conventional poem of return and a second story of Spenser's actual journey to England and frustrations there and in Ireland.[14] Hoffman fruitfully insists on the importance of the Irish context to *Colin Clout*, but she too quickly opposes the "nonliterary facts of the quality of life in Ireland and England" to "the 'facts' of pastoral convention."[15] I would argue instead that *Colin Clout* leaves unfinished the metamorphosis of a pastoral of return out of Virgil's eclogue of exile. Virgil's inaugural pastoral poem already bears within it what Hoffman calls "the clash of literary pastoral with social conditions."[16] Eclogue I presents the social and the literary *as* disparity or clash; *Colin Clout* preserves this clash by maintaining the tension between staying and leaving home.

"September" exhibits Spenser's early attention to Eclogue I as a staging of domestic and social economies of desire. *Colin Clout*, presented and usually read as self-consciously auto-biographical, "agreeing with the truth in circumstance and matter," reveals the pertinence of Spenser's experiences in Ireland to his continued interest in Eclogue I.[17] Critics are divided over the nature of Spenser's political career: was he disappointed by the reception of *The Faerie Queene* and by his appointment in Ireland? or did he find confirmation of his value to the Queen in a prestigious, responsible Irish post? *Colin Clout,* in its conflicting representations of Ireland as home and as desert, offers material for both positions. Meliboee's narrative, teaching the powers of the mind to find the home proper to it, similarly underscores the possible co-existence of both positive and negative versions of Spenser's political career. Finally, Calidore's attempt to appropriate this narrative in order to justify his pastoral delay acts out the gravitation of the pastoral of return towards apologetic home-making projects.

During the period when *Colin Clout* and *The Faerie Queene* were written, Spenser was living in Ireland as an administrator for the Crown, first under Lord Grey in the early 1580s, and then under officials in the province of Munster.[18] As Nancy Jo Hoffman characterizes his position, "If in Elizabeth's court Spenser was a powerless man, in Ireland he represented the crown and its power in a nation engaged in resistance to colonization."[19] This double role accords with the work of accommodation represented in, and perhaps performed by, the eclogue of return in Spenser's poetry. As if echoing Meliboee's "each hath his fortune in his brest," Spenser dubbed Kilcolman,

his estate in Ireland, "Hap Hazard."[20] Spenser's twentieth-
century biographer Alexander Judson finds a parallel to Spenser's situation in the case of his friend Ludowick Bryskett, a
man of Genoese parentage, English birth and education, and
Irish career. Bryskett wrote,

> being fully resolved to esteem the coarse and hard,
> temperate fare of a plowman void of all indignities far
> sweeter than the dainty dishes of princes' court, where
> (with humility and duty I speak) I think it is easy for a man
> to fill his belly, and to be puffed up with vanities and never
> accomplished hopes and expectations, but very hard for an
> honest man to purchase the due reward of his service.[21]

The point here is not the accuracy of Judson's parallel (which is
unprovable) but rather Bryskett's use of language conventional
to the overlapping discourses of Horatian retirement, the
georgic praise of labor, and the pastoral of return, all contrasting city and country, public and private, in the service of
making oneself at home in a rigorous land.

Regardless of Spenser's "actual" experiences, *Colin Clout*
illustrates the way in which individual biographies crystalize
out of conventional narratives, not simply in reception, but also
in an author's choice of certain motifs to represent "the truth in
circumstance and matter" to a readership, and to him- or herself. Meliboee's more generalized tale shows Spenser's continued concern with Virgil's poem as a resource able, through
revision, to represent both exile and its consolations; this
"resourcefulness" is dramatized in the dialogue between Meliboee and Calidore. Spenser's repeated return to the pastoral of
return (as well as to other scenarios of disappointment, exile and
desertion) throughout his career recommends Eclogue I as a
crucial generative scenario for Spenser's *oeuvre*, a fiction which
probably found confirmation if not impetus from his political
experiences.[22]

The Meliboee of Book VI implies that the idyll of Tityrus is
simply the mental transformation of his fellow shepherd's exile:
"each hath his fortune in his brest" (VI.ix.29). Meliboee stresses
the individual's autonomy over against material conditions, in
order to accommodate himself to those very conditions. Fortune, however, is outside as well as in. Meliboee's later murder

and dispossession, echoing the fate of his Virgilian namesake, reveals the insufficiency of Stoic self-sufficiency, while *Colin Clout*'s incomplete rehabilitation of exile suggests the mind's inability to remake itself fully in the image of an ungiving reality. In each case, mental home-making appears as coming up aginst material limits: in Meliboee's tragic fate, in Calidore's dramatized interpretive failure to appropriate the shepherd's narrative, and in *Colin Clout*'s doubling of Ireland as desert and home. The poems' representation of the pastoral ideal at its limits is itself true to the Virgilian text elaborated in each. Yet, in the conflation of Meliboeus and Tityrus into a single character making home out of exile, the losses which the domestic economy regulates, or fails to regulate, appear personal rather than social; there is little sense that Meliboee or Colin adjusts to marginalization at the expense of others. The "return" of Virgilian dissonance within both poems' narratives of return stems in part from the broader implications of Spenser's Irish home economics. Spenser's poetic revisions paralleled a physical one, with effects reaching beyond—and created by—his own fences.

3. "AN ENDLESSE TRACE": EXILE AS COLONIZATION

By the end of the 1580s, Spenser was administratively involved in a very real home-making enterprise, for himself and an anticipated 8,400 English settlers. The projected Munster plantation would resettle a county devastated by war and famine with English-born landowners and tenants.[23] As in so many other English projects in Ireland, the plantation effectively translated Irish land tenure into English form, and, in this case, into English hands.[24] By replacing Irish "tannistry," a system of brief corporate land tenure suited to a nomadic, military society, with the English system of inherited territorial land, the settlers were in effect creating "home" in the modern English sense of private property. Spenser's *View* presents the conversion of Irish into English tenure, "to reduce things into order of English law," as crucial to the stabilization of the political and economic crises there.[25] With longer leases,

First by the handsomeness of his house, [the tenant farmer] shall take great comfort of his life, more safe dwelling, and

> a delight to keep his said house neat and cleanly, which
> now, being as they commonly are rather swinesteads than
> houses, is the chiefest cause of his so beastly manner of life
> . . . and to all these other commodities he shall find in
> short time a greater added, that is his own wealth and
> riches increased and wonderfully enlarged by keeping his
> cattle in enclosures.
>
> (*View*, 82–83)

Here, Spenser appeals explicitly to the civilizing effects of a
settled, permanent, "neat and cleanly" home on properly enclosed land. This creation of property and its values in Ireland
mirrored a similar process in England, as commons were progressively enclosed and copyhold (with its customary rents)
changed into leases suited to a money economy. In both
countries, one tool of translation was the new science of surveying, since the charting of the land was a necessary step in
changing it into real estate.[26] Spenser's title *View of . . . Ireland*
shares in this authoritative measuring of land for the purposes of
defining—and redefining—ownership; the first meaning of
"view" in the *O.E.D.* is "A formal inspection of survey or
lands, tenements or ground, for some special purpose."

The ground of the Munster plantation had been literally
cleared by the Desmond uprising of 1579–83, suppressed in part
by organized famine.[27] The most notorious passage from the
View offers the devastated landscape of Munster as proof that
Spenser's planned "reform" of Ireland through the military and
later legal eradication of Irish society would be brief and not "so
great a trouble":

> Although there should none of them fall by the sword, nor
> be slain by the soldier, yet thus kept from manurance, and
> their cattle running abroad by this hard restraint, they
> would quickly consume themselves and devour one an-
> other. The proof whereof I saw sufficiently ensampled in
> those late wars in Munster, for notwithstanding that the
> same was a most rich and plentiful country . . . yet ere one
> year and half they were brought to such wretchedness, as
> that any stony heart would have rued the same . . . in short
> space there were none almost left and a most populous and
> plentiful country suddenly left void of man or beast.[28]
>
> (104)

Spenser not only described the earlier desertion of Munster, but counseled the further removal of inhabitants at its borders:

> but also all those subjects which border upon those parts are either to be removed and drawn away or likewise to be spoiled, that the enemy may find no succour thereby, for what the soldier spares the rebel will surely spoil.
>
> (105)

The *View* counsels a program of organized famine, massacre, and land transfer, followed by the translation of Irish law and custom into England—a plan of imperial dispossession which rivals, if not overgoes, the military actions pictured in Virgil's Eclogue I.

Spenser made his home on the cleared land of the Munster plantation. His role as administrator of a program appealing, in one government prospectus, to " 'the younger houses of gentlemen,' " eventually led to his legal acquisition of Kilcolman, nicknamed "Hap Hazard," in 1590.[29] Making fortune his home, Spenser was caught in law suits throughout his tenure with an Anglo-Irish lord claiming ownership; Spenser eventually forfeited two ploughlands. Similar suits plagued most of the English undertakers in Munster, since the translation of Gaelic law into English, and the attendant dispossession of the Anglo-Irish, did not pass uncontested. Spenser was thus continually aware of the recent, constructed and willful quality of his home.

How, then, to address Book VI from the point of the *View*? While some critics represent the "Book of Courtesy" as a withdrawal from history after the iron world of Justice, others suggest the continuity of themes between the two.[30] At the beginning of Book VI, Calidore tells Artegall, "But where ye ended have, now I begin / To tread an endlesse trace" (VI.i.6). This "endlesse trace," I argue, passes through Ireland. Artegall's public relations are proclaimed a failure as he returns from his brutal Irish heroics wounded by the Blatant Beast of slander. Courtesy is a public virtue which reinflects but does not sever *The Faerie Queene*'s sovereign alliance of beauty and power, refigured in the *View* as the halter and the sword (93–95). If Books V and VI are views of Ireland, Artegall executes Irenus' violent reformation through cutting off, while Book VI presents the milder uses of courtesy, "friendly offices that bynde" (VI.x.23). Spenser's search for a pastoral Ireland in Book VI, far from signalling an escape from politics, in part strives to represent England's colonial activities in a milder light. The crucial tool in this program is Virgil's Eclogue I, which aids in pastoralizing the Elizabethan resettlement of Ireland, and also uncannily returns as one of the contradictions founding Spenser's new home.

Meliboee's name clearly recalls the exiled shepherd of Virgil's Eclogue I. While this allusion points in part to Spenser's conscious fusion of one shepherd's trip to Rome with the other shepherd's exile, it also anticipates Meliboee's later dispossession and murder at the hands of the Brigants.[31] "It fortuned" while Calidore was hunting,

> A lawlesse people, *Brigants* hight of yore,
> That never usde to live by plough nor spade,
> But fed on spoile and booty, which they made
> Upon their neighbours, which did nigh them border,
> The dwelling of these shepheards did invade,
> And spoyld their houses, and them selves did murder:
> And drove away their flocks, with other much disorder.
>
> (VI.x.39)

The Brigants emerge from the Ireland of the *View* as that race of nomadic outlaws living by "spoile and booty" rather than the domesticating "plough [and] spade." Destroying the "houses" of shepherds, the Brigants themselves appear homeless; these cave-dwellers pillage at the border, a marginal habitation which evokes the Ireland of Spenser's *View*, a country everywhere described as border, both in relation to England, and in its internal map of Pale (literally a fence), palatines, and plantations.[32] Borders, inscribed by the home-making activities of law, surveying and enclosure, tend to displace inhabitants in the act of demarcation, whether in the specific Irish case of Spenser's Kilcolman and its ousted lord, or in the enclosure movement in Elizabethan England, at the time linked to the rise of vagrancy.[33]

The Brigants are defined as the transgressive agents of dispossession by the very borders that exclude them, those lines of property which define "the dwelling" of shepherds and flocks in Elizabethan Ireland and England—and place Meliboee in the role of Virgilian dispossessed. As a "lawlesse people," the Brigants can be either a barbaric, uncivilized tribe existing before law, or "outlaws" who have fallen out of the social order, like the Anglo-Irish turned savage by Gaelic milk and language in Spenser's *View*.[34] In the Ireland of both the *View* and Book V, rocky barbarism, whether uncivilized savagery or the terrible intransigence of decadent backsliding, demands equally rigorous reform by the sword. In Book VI, the Brigants live at the borders of a culture for which they are both pre-historic memory and decadent after-image; their cave-dwelling indicates an undomesticated existence, while their dealings with the "Marchants" place them in a post-pastoral world of exchange founded on the continual displacement of property.

That the Brigants themselves might be victims of displacement is a possibility actively excluded by the poem, whose task rather is to place the Brigants outside the law, to "outlaw" them. The "legal fiction" of Ireland as an outlaw province without rights was an innovation of Elizabethan policy, which switched from a legal to an extra-legal definition of Ireland by redefining the inferiority of the Irish as natural rather than social. Spenser's *View* played a role in the transformation.[35] In *The Faerie Queene*, Virgil's eclogue helps "outlaw" the Brigants by casting them as the robbers of English literary shepherds. Eclogue I's displacement returns both as a specific content attached by Spenser to Meliboee, and as a mechanism of inflection allowing the poet to reposition the roles of possessor, dispossessor, and dispossessed. In this way, the eclogue of exile can be refigured as a defense of colonization.

Throughout the episode, sheep-farming operates precariously between the Irish context, where it was associated with the dangerously nomadic lifestyle of the Irish clans, "never usde to live by plough nor spade"; the English escalation of the sheep industry through enclosure, with its attendant social problems; and the conventions of literary pastoral. When the Brigants appear asleep with their pilfered sheep, they resemble the Irishmen whom Spenser urges must be converted from wandering drovers to home-steading farmers, "for this keeping of cows is of itself a very idle life and a fit nursery for a thief" (*View*, 157). When Calidore and Coridon disguise themselves to the Brigants as "poore heardgroomes, the which whylere / Had from their maisters fled, and now sought hyre elsewhere" (VI.xi.39), they resemble the growing vagrant population in

England seen by many Elizabethans as uprooted by enclosure. In both cases, historical sheep-farming appears in conjunction with two kinds of homelessness threatening to Tudor order: the wandering military tribes of Ireland, and the riotous vagabonds of England.

These evocations are controlled and deployed in part through Eclogue I, insofar as Virgil's poem offers a literary model for the juxtaposition of the "real" and the ideal, the historical and the conventional, and for pastoral as a genre about displacement. Rather than implying a failure or betrayal of pastoral, this felt disparity between literary and historical pastoralism is in keeping with, and indeed institutionalized by, Virgil's poem. Here as elsewhere, Spenser uses this disparity to keep in line possessor and dispossessor in his pastoralized Ireland. Yet these moments, presenting actual sheep-farming in conjuction with dangerous homelessness may also represent a return of Virgilian and historical contradiction within Spenser's governing apologetic purposes. This return is *unheimlich*: un-homey, or even homeless. In Spenser's text, displacement is a shifty machine whose capacity to transpose positions can run away with itself; thus the Brigants and the men disguised as their friends can appear momentarily as victims as well as agents of dispossession.

Artegall, clearly masking Lord Grey, the infamous militant governor for whom Spenser had worked as secretary, sends Talus in Book V "to search out those, that usd to rob and steale," but, like his historical counterpart, he is recalled prematurely to Faerie Court dimmed by "envies cloud" (V.xii.26–27). The thieving, Irish-like Brigants may remain from Talus' truncated mission. Calidore, swatting at the Brigants like flies—a simile earlier attached to Talus (V.ii.53)—slashes through the bodies with a reaper's efficiency: "And all that nere him came, did hew and slay, / Till he had strowd with bodies all the way" (VI.xi.48–49). This momentary condensation of Talus behind Calidore signals Spenser's continued concern with Ireland and his effort to pastoralize Talus' specifically counterpastoral wolfish scattering of men like sheep (V.iv.44, V.vi.30).

The Ireland of Book V and the *View* also echoes in the Brigants' mutiny against their captain, which ends in the slaughter of the shepherd prisoners, including old Meliboee,

"Least they should joyne against the weaker side" (VI.xi.18). This preventative massacre recalls the notorious slaughter at Smerwick in 1580, where Lord Grey denied the Spanish papal soldiers mercy (and was accused of breaking his word) lest, "being saved, they should afterwards join with the Irish" (*View*, 108). Sections of both the *View* (19–20, 106–108) and Book V (Canto xii) are devoted to defending Lord Grey's behavior in this incident. In Book VI, the projection of the same actions onto the Brigants purges and justifies the English. It may also suggest an intertextual anxiety—bridging the final books of *The Faerie Queene*, the *View*, and Virgil's Eclogue I—about the source and necessity of imperial dislocation, and the ability of displacement itself to be displaced.

Book VI's pastoral interlude ends with Calidore's courteous bestowal of the stolen goods on his rival Coridon:

> This doen, into those theevish dens he went,
>> And thence did all the spoyles and threasures take,
>> Which they from many long had robd and rent,
>> But fortune now the victors meed did make;
>> Of which the best he did his love betake;
>> And also all those flockes, which they before
>> Had reft from *Meliboe* and from his make,
>> He did them all to *Coridon* restore.
> So drove them all away, and his love with him bore.
>
> (VI.xi.51)

The Brigants' robbery leads ultimately to the consolidation of the pastoral lands, Meliboee's Stoic view of fortune within becomes for Calidore the right to ownership by providentially underwritten conquest, as in defenses of colonialism as a form of just war: "But fortune now the victors meed did make." The passage represents claims to property which are at once recent and legitimate. Here and elsewhere, the knight of courtesy's civil arbitrations end in the kinds of distributive acts performed by Artegall. In Book V's early episodes, Artegall confirms the redistribution of property in judgements which at once preserve social order and authorize certain kinds of innovation. To the Giant he defends the divine economy of displacement, in which nothing is lost, simply relocated:

> Ne is the earth the lesse, or loseth ought,
> For whatsoever from one place doth fall,
> Is with the tide unto an other brought:
> For there is nothing lost, that may be found, if sought.
>
> (V.ii.39)

Artegall resolves the difference between Amidas and Bracidas, their property redistributed by the sea, through reference to the sea's "imperiall might":

> For what the mighty Sea hath once possest,
> And plucked quite from all possessors hand,
> Whether by rage of waves, that never rest,
> Or else by wracke, that wretches hath distrest,
> He may dispose by his imperiall might,
> As thing at randon left, to whom he list.
>
> (V.iv.19)

In all three passages, a force (fortune, the sea) associated with providential will authorizes change within the natural order. Spenser legitimates the economic structure through the traditional conservative argument, "what is, should be," yet frees it from the accompanying reliance on precedent, "what is, has always been." This vision of conservative revolution mirrors the project of the *View*, an Elizabethan defense of that Elizabethan anathema, innovation.[36]

David Baker has argued persuasively that the *View* was censored not because it "subversively" undermines the Elizabethan spectacle of horror, but because it counsels for laws more absolute and innovative than those already in place: Spenser "does not expose the brutal rigor of English policy; he reveals that policy as less rigorous than its adherents would want to think."[37] John Guillory has described a similar kind of conservative revolution in Spenser's relation to literary authority:

> The hypothesis emerging here is that this world, in its very presentness, contains sources of power that are newly made, whose authority derives from a vertical descent of a higher power.[38]

In the "restoration" of lands to Coridon, pastoral, mythically the original, most primitive form of poetry, concludes in the creation of a new dwelling. Eclogue I had commenced Latin pastoral with an at once celebratory and anatomizing vision of a world-historical innovation. In *The Faerie Queene*, the inaugural Latin poem of the mythically oldest genre is used to represent distantly, through a muted web of allusions, elisions and transpositions, a new colonial program. In both content and form, Spenser's revisions of Eclogue I promote "conservative innovation": *The Faerie Queene* preserves and rehabilitates a potentially subversive text by placing it in the service of an absolutist project, which is itself suspiciously innovative in relation to Tudor policy. Spenser's pastoral defends dispossession by effacing the project of defense and by displacing displacement. Book VI, quite unlike Book V, never becomes explicitly an apology for policy; rather, such an apology only exists between Spenser's poem and Eclogue I, in the subdued form of tactful and tactical renovations. Thus Spenser's mode of poetic imitation innovates conservatively, while his poem represents and recommends conservative innovation through scenarios of restoration and return.

As the conclusion to Meliboee's dispossession, this consolidation of property in the hands of Coridon stands in the same place as Eclogue I's image of hospitality. As in Virgil's poem, a final scene of home-making resolves the poem's mounting tension. *The Faerie Queene*, however, uses Eclogue I's story of exile to define and defend English home-making in Ireland. The poem achieves this feat of pastoral apology by splitting the Virgilian single central power into two forces of right and wrong: the heroic Calidore serving Gloriana against the vicious Brigants. It effectively "oulaws" the Irish-like Brigants by replacing them at the dangerous borders of the pastoral world— the borders crossed by Meliboeus in Virgil's poem—and by projecting unto them the violence of Lord Grey and his men.

As in the pastoral of return, this revision restages Virgil's painful structural contrast as a diachronic tale of problem followed by resolution. Whereas, in Panofsky's words, Virgil's twilight conclusion resolves dissonance in a "vespertinal mixture of sadness and tranquillity," that is, in an image which suspends rather than dissolves the opposition it reconciles,

Spenser uses a narrative of theft and restoration to close down conflict and efface contradiction.[39] Thus repossession (Virgil's Tityrus) and dispossession (Virgil's Meliboeus) no longer stand as simultaneous effects of the same central power. Instead, restoration follows dispossession, each due to different agencies. In the process, Virgil's eclogue of exile becomes a defense of colonization, which appears as restorative resettling rather than usurping displacement.

4. "THE WHILES": "ARGUMENTS" AND CONCLUSIONS

There is one moment, however, in which Eclogue I's difficult suspension of opposing fortunes returns in Book VI. The Argument to Canto X aligns two unlike events:

> *Calidore sees the Graces daunce,*
> *To Colins melody:*
> *The whiles his Pastorell is led*
> *Into captivity.*

These two episodes, Calidore's vision on Mount Acidale and the capture of Pastorella, are not concurrent in the narrative, despite their coordination in the Argument by the phrase "the whiles."[40] What "argument," then, is being made about the relation between the dispossession of the shepherds and Calidore's vision? Here, I suggest, the poem momentarily restores Virgil's structural contrast between exile and preservation, at the expense of *The Faerie Queene*'s own sequence.

The vision on Mount Acidale places itself in the tradition of Virgil's Eclogue IV, the "parve puer" poem important to the tradition of pastoral panegyrics swelling courtly shepherds' pipes with higher songs ("paulo maiora canamus"). In Virgil, Eclogue IV isolates the contended pastoral of Tityrus from its dialogue with Meliboeus and brings it into fruition as a pastoral poetry of heroic praise. In the reception of Virgilian pastoral, Eclogue IV sometimes appears as the celebratory imperial counterpart to Eclogue I's more dissonant pastoral of war and exile; when alluded to in elliptical fashion, the two poems can harden into the brittle emblems of opposing positions.[41]

One example of this emblematic opposition is the Argument to Canto X. The vision on Mount Acidale clearly alludes to Spenser's April Eclogue, falling fourth in the *Shepheardes Calender*, and back still further to its prototype in Virgil.[42] Mount Acidale presses geographically and stylistically out of pastoral into a higher, inspired epideictic form. The capture of Pastorella, on the other hand, shares in the dispossession of Meliboee and the other shepherds, enunciated in the tradition of Eclogue I. The shepherdess' name, presented in the Argument in the shortened form "Pastorell," implies that the pastoral genre, in its intertextual historicity, is itself at stake in the events aligned by "the whiles." More specifically, in the medieval French *bergerie* tradition (from which Spenser borrowed the title *Shepheardes Calender*), "pastourelle" designated the complaint of a shepherdess abandoned by a ravishing knight whose principles of courtly love did not extend to commoners. These laments may be socially and sexually inflected versions of Eclogue I, insofar as they dwell on exclusion, "desertion," and structural disparity within the parameters of pastoral.[43] Thus the Argument to Canto X subtly counterposes and interlocks exile and empire, exclusion and inclusion, Eclogue I and Eclogue IV. In the process, the two positions of Eclogue I, combined and then temporalized in Spenser's various pastorals of return, appear once more in suspended opposition, upsetting the proper narrative sequence of the two episodes announced by the Argument.

It is in Canto X, of course, that Colin Clout, Spenser's familiar autobiographical mask, reappears, sharpening the sense of the poet's personal presence in the pastoral interlude. The scene on Mount Acidale stages itself simultaneously as a public praise of the queen in the concisely invoked tradition of Eclogue IV, and as a private, self-reflexive poetic moment.[44] The shepherd-poet stands at once in the center of power and off in a self-made world; his Orphic song both calls up and is called to the vision of the Graces: "She made me often pipe and now to pipe apace" (VI.x.27). The vision's fragility stems from its fantastic mental construction—as vulnerable as Meliboee's Stoic home-making—and from the peremptory will of sovereignty offended by improper desire. The Graces as a purely aesthetic creation may be the poet's consolation in the wake of their devastating disappearance as an emblem of power: the "aesthetic" may appear as such in the difference between this vision and its prototype in the "Aprill" eclogue. In the Mount Acidale scene, Spenser draws most heavily on the tradition of pastoral as an elevated, isolated, private world of literary self-reflection and self-confection. Here, Spenser's created "home" is not "Ireland" or "distance from the court" so much as poetry itself, a *locus amoenus* established as both compensation for and critique of the public world. Yet this poetic home-making occurs beneath the banner of Canto X's Argument. Transforming desert into idyll, the poet's banishment becomes his self-made poetic home, "the whiles" Pastorell is led away.

Virgil's Eclogue I, whose imitations bridge Spenser's *oeuvre*, from the *Shepheardes Calender* to *Colin Clouts Come Home Again* to Book VI of *The Faerie Queene*, helped frame his political career in pastoral terms, while also conceptualizing Spenser's poetic production in relation to political and domestic economies of desire and displacement. The story of return narrated by Meliboee recommends a pastoral labor of accommodation; his tale complements the explicitly (if poetically) autobiographical journey in *Colin Clouts Come Home Again*, where Ireland appears as both "home" and "exile." Meliboee's later fate at the hands of the Brigants functions in a second revision of Eclogue I, now in the service of pastoralizing the Irish politics of Book V and the *View*. Articulated across several works through techniques of narrative, poetic imitation, and pastoral autobiography, this model of Spenser's "life" as exile from England and home-maker in Ireland should help reconcile the opposing images of Spenser as alienated poet and as successful professional. Yet my reading of Spenser's life, like any other, is necessarily as much an effect of the literary conventions the poet received, transformed, and transmitted as it is an accurate portrayal of his actual life experiences. Moreover, it is only one of several possible autobiographical frames in and for Spenser's *oeuvre*—as in the related narratives of Ovidian elegiac exile, or the Virgilian poetic career.[45]

More broadly, this analysis should reinforce contemporary understandings of pastoral—for example, in the work of Louis Montrose and Annabel Patterson—as always containing an historical dimension, whether through negative self-definition, suspension, marginalization, or direct engagement.[46] Eclogue I, not only in its Spenserian imitations, but also in its reappearance in works by Shakespeare, Marvell, Wordsworth or Goethe, exemplifies the "historicity" of pastoral.[47] I invoke historicity in the obvious sense of reflecting and reflecting upon the conditions of its period, but also in a second, hermeneutic sense of a living discourse constituted through such intertextual processes as imitation, revision, interpretation, translation and transmission.[48] Pastoral is historical: it is "about" history, it "reflects" history, and it "is" a history—a history of motifs, names, concerns, and paradigmatic examples. The conventionality of pastoral, rather than drawing the line between the histories of the world and of literature, is precisely what makes possible pastoral's determination of and by historical conditions. Furthermore, generic criticism need not be doomed to the intrinsically conservative scenario of literary genre as a series of internally limited repetitions which serve only to confirm the prototypes of the tradition, nor to the related organic narrative of a genre's inevitable decline into fragmentation, parody and death. Generic repetition can unsettle as well as confirm assumptions, intentions and rules, as in the *unheimich* returns of Eclogue I. So too the "death" of a genre may be best represented through the relentless mechanical repetitions of the Freudian death drive rather than in the organic metaphors inherited from the founding text of generic criticism, the *Poetics*.

In the pastoral interlude of Book VI, the new clarity of the poet's voice as he makes a home away from court coincides with the eruption of violence within pastoral. If poetry is finally the home which Spenser creates for himself, it is an abode built with costs to others. In Book VI, the Virgilian structure recurs through the differences between the Spenserian poem and its subtext, and more directly in the Argument to Canto X, which in a muted emblematic form coordinates the pastorals of exile and empire. In this momentary return of Virgilian dissonance, *The Faerie Queene* figures forth the *unheimlich* contradictions and displacements implicit in the pastoral foundations of the Spenserian home.

University of California, Irvine

NOTES

I would like to thank Jonathan Goldberg, Mary Jane Lupton, Richard Mallette, Lawrence Manley, David Mikic, Terence Murphy, Mark Rasmussen, and Kenneth Reinhard for criticism and encouragement. The Spenser Society gave this essay a forum at the 1987 MLA Convention. Finally, without John Guillory's Yale graduate seminar on pastoral, this essay could never have been conceived.

1. For the first view, see Alexander C. Judson, *The Life of Edmund Spenser*, Vol. XI of Edmund Spenser, *Works: A Variorum Edition*, ed. E. A. Greenlaw, *et al.* (Baltimore, Md.: Johns Hopkins University Press, 1945; 1981), 156 and *passim*; and Rosemond Tuve, " 'Spenserus'," in *Essays in English Literature from the Renaissance to the Victorian Age, presented to A.S.P. Woodhouse*, ed. Millar Maclure and F. W. Wyatt (Toronto: University of Toronto Press, 1964), pp. 3–25. For the opposing view, see Muriel Bradbrook, "No Room at the Top: Spenser's Pursuit of Fame," in *Elizabethan Poetry*, Stratford upon Avon Studies 2 (New York: St. Martin's Press, 1960), pp. 91–109; and Thomas R. Edwards, "The Shepherd and the Commisar," in *Imagination and Power: A Study of Poetry on Public Themes* (New York: Oxford University Press, 1971), pp. 47–82. My own view is closest to Nancy Jo Hoffman's in *Spenser's Pastorals: "The Shepheardes Calender" and "Colin Clout"* (Baltimore, Md.: Johns Hopkins University Press, 1977), pp. 123–125.

2. Annabel Patterson, "Vergil's *Eclogues*: Images of Change," in *Roman Images*, ed. Annabel Patterson (Baltimore, Md.: Johns Hopkins University Press, 1982), p. 163. Her perceptions in this essay are expanded in her book *Pastoral and Ideology: Virgil to Valery* (Berkeley: University of California Press, 1988).

3. Patterson, p. 167.

4. *Eclogues*, trans. Guy Lee (Hardmondsworth: Penguin, 1984). Other references will be made by line number only in the body of the text.

5. Erwin Panofsky, "*Et in Arcadia Ego*: Poussin and the Elegiac Tradition," in *Meaning in the Visual Arts*, (1955; Chicago, Ill.: University of Chicago Press, 1982), p. 301. For twilight closings, see Virgil VI and X. Every eclogue in the *Shepheardes Calender* except "Julye" and "October" ends this way. Paul Alpers writes on Eclogue I: "The poem does not, in any simple sense, express his nostalgia; rather, it contains an anatomy of nostalgia." In "What is Pastoral?" *Critical Inquiry*, 8 (1982), 453.

6. Tityrus' freedom is specifically located in the erotic transition from one enslaving love irresponsible with respect to property, to another love associated with his present happiness: "For (yes, I will confess), while Galatea held me, / There was no hope of liberty nor thought of thrift" (30–33).

7. To borrow Freud's term in his essay "Der Untergang des Ödipuskomplexes" (the passing or dissolution of the Oedipus Complex), the twilight conclusion of Eclogue I is an *Untergang*: a resolution, a dissolution, an historical decline, and a setting of the sun.

8. Paul Alpers, *Virgil, Singer of the Eclogues* (Berkeley: University of California Press, 1979), p. 65. Laurence Lerner comments on suspension in his gloss of lines 75–76, in *The Uses of Nostalgia: Studies in Pastoral Poetry* (New York: Schocken Books, 1972), p. 41.

9. An English example of this "pastoral of return" is Barnaby Googe's "Eglogia Tertia," in *English Pastoral Poetry,* ed. Frank Kermode (London: Harrap, 1952). Neo-Latin examples include Enrique Cayado's 1495 poem on the French invasion of Italy, in William Grant, *Neo Latin-Literature and the Pastoral* (Chapel Hill: University of North Carolina Press, 1965), pp. 352–335; and Boiardo, Eclogues I and IV (1482). Italian examples include the scene of return in Tasso's *Aminta* (Act I), imitated again in Guarini's *Il Pastor Fido* (1580–4), V:1. David Shore discusses the relation between the *Aminta* sequence and *Colin Clout Comes Home Again* in *Spenser and the Poetics of Pastoral: A Study of the World of Colin Clout* (Montreal: McGill-McQueen's University Press, 1985), pp. 117–123.

10. This and all subsequent citations from Spenser's poetry are from *Poetical Works,* ed. J. C. Smith and E. de Selincourt (London: Oxford University Press, 1912; 1970).

11. Margaret W. Ferguson, "The Rhetoric of Exile in Du Bellay and his Precursors" (Yale dissertation, 1974), pp. 38–41.

12. *Cf.* Virgil: "maioresque cadunt altis de montibus umbrae" (83).

13. Hoffman, pp. 133–134.

14. Hoffman writes that the model of pastoral return "is, however, only partial, for embedded in the model and ultimately undercutting it is a second poem, which consists of Spenser's unsuccessful attempts to absorb into the happy formula his personal experience and the contingencies of an individual moment" (p. 126).

15. Hoffman, p. 121.

16. Hoffman, p. 133.

17. See *Colin Clout*'s dedication to Raleigh, in *Works,* p. 536.

18. Judson, pp. 84–127.

19. Hoffman, p. 123.

20. Judson, p. 128.

21. Cited in Judson, pp. 111–112. Bryskett published his book, *A Discourse of Civill Life,* in the memory of "Arthur late Lord Grey of Wilton," whom he eulogizes by citing Virgil's Eclogue I: "that honorable personage, *qui nobis haec otia fecit*" (London: Edward Blount, 1606; in facsimile, Amsterdam: Da Capo Press, 1971), pp. B, A.

22. For example, the wasting of Arlo Hill in the "Mutabilitie Cantos" gives etiology of Irish barbarism relevant to the themes of this essay.

23. Steven G. Ellis, *Tudor Ireland: Crown, Community and the Conflict of Cultures 1470–1603* (London: Longman, 1985), pp. 291–296.

24. Compare similar programs of "surrender and regrant" and "composition." For an extensive study of earlier Elizabethan colonization in Munster and Ulster, see Nicholas B. Canny, *The Elizabethan Conquest of Ireland: A Pattern Established 1565–76* (New York: Barnes and Noble, 1976). For Spenserian political puns on "plantation," see Ronald B. Bond, "Supplantation in the Elizabethan Court: The Theme of Spenser's February Eclogue," *Spenser Studies* II, ed. Patrick Cullen and Thomas P. Roche, Jr. (Pittsburgh, Pa.: University of Pittsburgh Press, 1981), pp. 55–65.

25. *A View of the Present State of Ireland,* ed. W. L. Renwick (Oxford: Clarendon Press, 1970), 150. Further quotations from this work will be cited by page number only in the body of the text. On theories of law in the *View,*

see David Baker, " 'Some Quirk, Some Subtle Evasion': Legal Subversion in Spenser's *A View of the Present State of Ireland,"* in *Spenser Studies* VI, ed. Patrick Cullen and Thomas P. Roche, Jr. (New York: AMS Press, 1987), pp. 147–163.

26. Spenser's emphasis on the stablizing effects of English domesticity echoes arguments for legal reform made by other New English administrators. For example, in 1590, Sir John Perrot recommended surrender and regrant as a program which "must breed quietness, obedience and profit. Love to their children will make them fearful to offend the laws, and desirous to build houses, purchase lands, and grow wealthy." May 10, 1590, *Calendar of the Carew Manuscripts,* Vol. 3 (London: Longman, Green, and Co., 1869), pp. 27–28. On surveying in England, see D. M. Palliser, *The Age of Elizabeth: England under the Later Tudors 1547–1603* (London: Longman, 1983), p. 199. Judson remarks on Spenser's possible participation in the surveying of Kilcolman and other Munster lands, p. 118.

27. David Beers Quinn, *The Elizabethans and the Irish* (Washington, D.C. and Ithaca, N.Y.: Folger Library and Cornell University Press, 1966), p. 132.

28. David Quinn, for example, cites it in a chapter of *The Elizabethans and the Irish* entitled "Horror Story" (pp. 132–133).

29. Judson, p. 125.

30. For the first view, see for example Michael O'Connell, *Mirror and Veil: The Historical Dimension of Spenser's "Faerie Queene"* (Chapel Hill: University of North Carolina Press, 1977), p. 160. For the second, see Donald Cheney, *Spenser's Image of Nature: Wild Man and Shepherd in "The Faerie Queene"* (New Haven, Conn.: Yale University Press, 1966), pp. 176–196.

31. O'Connell notes the connection, p. 175.

32. Spenser writes on the palatines, areas of jurisdiction fairly free from central control," . . . so to have a County Palatine is in effect but to have a privilege to spoil the enemy's borders enjoining . . . so as it being situate in the very lap of all the land, is made now a border, which how inconvenient it is let every man judge." (*View,* p. 30)

33. The enclosure debate has raged from the sixteenth century to the present. The crucial twentieth century figures include R. H. Tawney, *The Agrarian Problem in the Sixteenth Century* (1912; rpt. New York: Harper Row, 1967), which argued for the role of enclosures in the breakdown of feudalism and the rise of capitalism and its values. His most vocal critic is E. Kerridge, *Agrarian Problems in the Sixteenth Century and After* (London: Allen and Unwin, 1969), which downplays enclosure and insists on the immemorial acquisitiveness of English farmers. In recent years, the debate has shifted from large questions of epochal change and human nature to regional studies focusing on demography and on the suitability of particular geographies for certain crops. See H. P. R. Finberg, general editor, *The Agrarian History of England and Wales* (London: Cambridge, 1967—). Important to my argument is simply the fact that enclosure was linked by Tudor observers to increasing vagrancy (for example, Thomas More and William Harrison).

34. The Proem to Book V alternates between just men cropping a once virtuous garden gone to seed, and the conquest of "All th'East untam'd" (V.i.1–2). In the *View,* Irenus similarly shifts between an antiquarian appreciation of Irish antiquities and an insistence on the nation's inherent bestiality.

35. On the "outlawing" of Ireland, see Canny, pp. 115–136; on Spenser's role, p. 132.

36. *Cf.* Ellis on Elizabeth's "innate conservatism" concerning Ireland, and Spenser's arguments that "the moral imperatives of the particular situation necessitated innovation" (p. 291).

37. Baker, p. 152.

38. John Guillory, *Poetic Authority: Spenser, Milton, and Literary History* (New York: Columbia University Press, 1983), p. 33.

39. Panofsky, p. 300.

40. A. C. Hamilton notes the disparity and comments, "since the two events are not concurrent in the narrative, the term [the whiles] may imply that Calidore's vision and its vanishing correspond to Pastorella's seizure by the Brigands." In *The Faerie Queene*, ed. Hamilton (London: Longman, 1977), p. 688.

41. Examples include Enrique Cayado's 1496 poem, and Boiardo, Eclogues I and IV, cited above, Note 9. Marvell's "Upon Appleton House" and his "Mower Poems" are much more complex examples.

42. On the "Aprill Eclogue" as a type of Virgil's Eclogue IV, see O'Connell, pp. 5–9.

43. On the *pastourelle* genre, see Helen Cooper, *Pastoral: Medieval into Renaissance* (Ipswich: D. S. Brewer, 1977), pp. 58–63. She discusses Spenser and the *bergerie* tradition, pp. 152–161. A founding text for the *pastourelle* is Andreas Capellanus' chapter, "The Love of Peasants": "And if you should, by some chance, fall in love with some of their women, be careful to puff them up with lots of praise and then, when you find a convenient place, do not hesitate to take what you seek and to embrace them by force." In *The Art of Courtly Love*, trans. John Jay Parry (New York: Columbia University Press, 1941), I.xi; p. 150. Two English (and post-Spenserian) examples are Marvell's "The Nymph Complaining on the Death of her Fawn" and Hardy's *Tess of the d'Urbervilles*. In *The Faerie Queene*, the rape lamented in the *pastourelle* tradition socially inflects the Proserpina myth underlying Pastorella's cave captivity.

44. The private self-reflectiveness of this moment is stressed by O'Connell, pp. 181–182, and Thomas Cain, *Praise in "The Faerie Queene"* (Lincoln: University of Nebraska Press, 1978), pp. 156–161.

45. On Spenser and Ovidian exile see Tuve; on Spenser and the Virgilian career, see Richard Helgerson, "The Elizabethan Laureate: Self-Presentation and the Literary System," *ELH*, 46 (1979), 193–220.

46. See Louis Montrose's " 'Of Gentlemen and Shepherds': The Politics of Elizabethan Pastoral Form," *ELH*, 50 (1983), 451–459; and " 'The perfecte paterne of a Poete': The Poetics of Courtship in *The Shepheardes Calender*," *Texas Studies in Language and Literature*, 21 (1979), 34–66. This view of pastoral has, of course, strong roots in older criticism, for example, in Empson's much quoted statement that "the essential trick of the old pastoral" is "a beautiful relation between rich and poor," in *Some Versions of Pastoral*, (1936; rpt. New York: New Directions, 1968) p. 11.

47. For example, Shakespeare's *As You Like It*, Marvell's "The Mower to the Gloworms," Wordsworth's "Michael," and the Baucis and Philemon episode in Goethe's *Faust: Part II* (Act V).

48. *Cf.* Hans-Georg Gadamer's notion of *Wirkungsgeschichte* or "effective history," developed in *Truth and Method* (1960; rpt. New York: Crossroad, 1975).

MICHAEL TRATNER

"The thing S. Paule ment by . . . the courteousness that he spake of": Religious Sources for Book VI of *The Faerie Queene*

I N 1579, LAURENCE Tomson, the editor of the Geneva Bible, published a collection of English translations of John Calvin's sermons. In a sermon on I Timothy discussing what is necessary to create a Christian community here on earth, Calvin seems to refer to "courtesy" as a religious virtue:

> God hath so assembled vs together, knowe wee that it is to this end, that hee may make vs his heires, that we may haue one spirit to gouerne vs, one faith, one redeemer, one baptisme: for vnder this worde *Benefite,* all this is comprehended. Therefore when wee haue this, let vs learne to esteeme Gods graces, to the ende they may bring vs to all courtesie.[1]

The last sentence of this passage suggests that "esteeming Gods graces," a religious act, is the essence of being courteous. Such a definition fits the climactic pastoral vision in Book VI of Spenser's *Faerie Queene* remarkably well. In Canto x, the hero of courtesy, Calidore, sees a hundred naked maidens dancing in one large and one small circle around a single young maiden, all to the piping of Colin Clout. Colin explains that the maidens in the circles are all divine creatures, the Three Graces in the smaller one surrounded by hundreds of lesser "graces," all gathered in a ritual of placing a crown upon the young mortal woman in the center because she is so wonderful that she no longer seems a mere earthly "creature" but a "goddesse graced / With heauenly gifts from heuen first enraced [implanted]" (VI.x.25).[2] Spenser, too, joins in the general esteeming with a canto of eulogy to the maiden. Further, he tries to bring the reader as well to esteem the graces "enraced" in the maiden and to esteem the hundred Graces making up the whole scene: he directs the reader to look into the skies, to see and esteem the circle of stars that are the Pleiades, the "Crowne, which Ariadne wore," which serves as a physical image of both the divine creatures dancing in the meadow and the heavenly graces that can bedeck a young girl. If the vision in Canto x serves the same function that the climactic visions in the other books of *The Faerie Queene* do, namely to reveal to the hero and the reader the essential nature of the virtue of the book, then it makes sense to say that Spenser is allegorically showing that what a person needs in order to reach "all courtesy" is to "learne to esteeme Gods graces."

But the lesson is not easy to learn: Calidore twice makes a mistake in "reading" the scene, and his errors point to a distinction between proper and improper ways to esteem God's graces, a distinction that ties the scene even closer to Calvin's views. First, he tries to enter the dance, causing the entire scene to magically disappear, and Colin to break his pipe. Second, Calidore decides to abandon his life and stay with Colin in hopes of seeing the divine maidens again. Calidore seems to believe that esteeming God's graces means devoting one's life to the pursuit of revelations. His error becomes apparent as he waits: he does not find himself continually enchanted with the image of the Graces: instead, his feelings for an earthly maiden he left behind, Pastorella, become painfully intense, and drive him like a poisoned dart away from Colin back to her. I suggest that this return to his love is part of what this scene is teaching him. The ritual Calidore saw was not the honoring of the Graces directly, teaching him to seek divine visions, but rather the honoring of divine graces as they appear on earth, "enraced" within a young girl. To be courteous, he has to learn that those graces that he glimpsed in purely divine form can be seen inside humans. Calvin makes the same point, in another sermon, on Ephesians 4:32, translated by Arthur Golding in 1577. Speaking of those who are selected by God's grace to be members of the community of the faithful, Calvin says,

> In them God hath ingraued his image new agein which was as good as defaced by Adams sinne. Then sith it is so, let us learne too be gentle and courteous one too another.[3]

Calidore has to learn to esteem the image of God engraved inside those around him, and inside himself, if he is to be fully courteous.

To recognize the graces within humans is to distinguish between two kinds of properties, natural and divine, that can coexist in a person. Spenser beautifully distinguishes these two properties by using throughout Book VI imagery of "heauenly seedes" that are "Planted in earth" (VI.Proem.3). Calidore has to learn to see what is "enraced" or implanted in humans, and not to mistake these seeds for natural growths. It might seem paradoxical to use such "natural" imagery as seeds for what is not natural, but such imagery is quite common in sixteenth-century religious writings, and other writers connect it to courtesy explicitly. Consider, for example, a tract by the prominent Elizabethan theologian, William Perkins,[4] entitled "A Graine of Musterd-seed: or, the least measure of grace that is, or can be effectuall to salvation." Perkins argues that God implants only tiny seeds of grace inside those who are saved, and Christians have to act certain ways in order that the "gifts of God . . . grow up and increase as the Graine Musterd-seed to a great tree, and beare fruite answerably." Perkins lists eighteen "rules of direction" by which a Christian can "quicken and revive the seeds and beginnings of grace." The first seventeen are unsurprising suggestions: examine one's conscience, try to think about God all the time, etc. But the eighteenth rule states:

> Despise not civill honestie: good conscience and good manners must goe together . . . bee curteous and gentle to all, good and bad . . . use meat, drink and apparell in that manner and measure, that they may further godlinesse; and may bee as it were signes in which thou maiest expresse the hidden grace of thy heart.[5]

Perkins may seem to be discussing polite behavior and proper dressing in terms similar to those in secular texts, but he makes the same connection between courtesy and graces implanted inside the human heart that Calvin does. Perkins's comments suggest a religious meaning to Spenser's line in the Proem that virtue is "not in outward shows, but inward thoughts defynd" (VI.Proem.5). Inward thoughts turn the mind to the "hidden grace" of the heart for guidance in such outward shows as eating, drinking, and dressing.

Putting Perkins's tract and the two quotes from Calvin together with some Elizabethan Protestant theology, we can derive a coherent sixteenth-century religious conception of courtesy. Courtesy, according to Calvin, characterizes the behavior of Christians in an ideal community. Elizabethan Protestants, following Calvin, believed that the human will is utterly corrupt, so humans cannot on their own treat each other courteously; relying on human judgment, humans would disdain to have anything to do with each other because each person can see that all others are worthless sinners. To have a community at all, God must take control and cause humans to have proper relationships. God does this through his "graces," essentially parts of God placed inside sinful humans, images of God "ingraved" inside them that can direct their lives and even completely structure a community. These graces provide a seed, a potential for courtesy which grows if humans let it, if they quit trying to follow their own judgment and rely instead on the new images of God inside them. The peculiar logic involved can be seen in the quote from the sermon on I Timothy, where Calvin says that if Christians esteem God's graces, those graces "may bring vs to all courtesie." If God selects a group of people to be his "heires," to be part of the community of the faithful, all the members of that group then need do is have the proper attitude, properly esteem God's graces in others and in themselves, and then those graces take over and bring the whole community to a perfectly courteous state. To be courteous a Christian must look past the human qualities, past the sinful flesh of those around him, to see in them heavenly seeds of grace, and then provide a proper environment in which such seeds grow, namely, an environment of persons esteeming each other's graces.

As I will try to show, this religious interpretation of courtesy fits most of the tales in Book VI very well. But at this point, it may seem as if I am drawing large conclusions from rather slender evidence: it would be difficult to show that Spenser actually read Tomson's translations of Calvin's sermons or Perkins's tract. It does seem quite likely that Spenser knew these English Calvinists: they were involved in the Leicester circle that Spenser was part of in the 1570s and 80s. Tomson even served as envoy for Sir Francis Walsingham, one of the noblemen to whom Spenser wrote a dedicatory sonnet. Spenser certainly heard Perkins preach, since Perkins was at Cambridge when Spenser was a student. Anthea Hume even argues that the entire *Faerie Queene* is a presentation of ways of developing seeds of grace according to Perkins's scheme.[6] But Spenser did not need to read these particular texts to learn of courtesy as a religious virtue: numerous Elizabethan theologians use the term, and they are following a tradition that comes straight from the Bible. In the Geneva Bible, the one Spenser most likely used, the word is important enough to merit an entry in the "Table of principall things that are conteyned in the Bible."[7] The entry says, "Courteousness, required of all Christians, Eph. 4:32, I Corinth. 13:4." Ephesians 4:32 reads, "Be ye courteous one to another, and tenderhearted, freely forgiving one another, even as God for Christes sake, freely forgave you."[8] In almost every other sixteenth-century English Bible, in the Tyndale, Coverdale, Great and Bishops' Bibles, the word "courteous" appears in this passage. All these Bibles—except Geneva Bibles printed after 1557—also mention "courteous" in I Corinthians 13:4, either saying "Love sufreth long, and is courteous," or "Charity sufreth long, and is courteous." Geneva Bibles after 1557 render this as "love . . . is bountifull," though the Table still lists I Corinthians as a passage on courteousness.[9] The King James version has the word "kinde" in both passages instead of "courteous," which may explain why these passages have escaped notice by Spenser critics. There is a third verse that contains an injunction to be courteous in all the early English Bibles and even in the King James: 1 Peter 3:8, which reads,

Finally, be ye all of one minde: one suffre with another: love as brethren: be pitiful: be courteous. Not rendring evil for evil, neither rebuke for rebuke: but contrariwise blesse, knowing that ye are thereunto called, that ye shulde be heires of blessing.

Spenser was certainly aware of these uses of the word "courtesy." He may have had one or more of these biblical passages in mind when he wrote Book VI. The monster of discourtesy, the Blatant Beast, with its thousand mouths that spit slanderous statements at everyone, seems the allegorical representation of just what Ephesians says courtesy counters, if we read 4:32 as a continuation of 4:31:

4:31 Let all bitterness, and angre, and wrath, crying and evil speaking be put away from you, with all maliciousness. 4:32 be ye courteous, . . .

Similarly, I Corinthians 13:4 names vices that recur throughout Book VI. After saying "love is courteous," it goes on, "loue enuyeth not: loue doth not boast it self, swelleth not, Disdaineth not. it seketh not her owne things: is not prouoked to anger, thinketh not euil." Disdain and Envy are the two hags who call forth the Blatant Beast in Book VI, and represent the two basic ways discourteous characters in Book VI act—either the characters deny anyone is of any value (Mirabella, the Blatant Beast) or they become greedy and envious and try to take what seem valuable in others (the Cannibals, the Brigants, Sir Crudor). Spenser alludes directly to I Corinthians 13 in the Proem of Book VI, when he writes that men of his day see, "but in a glas, yet is that glass so gay that it can blynd," recalling the passage in I Corinthians 13:12 about seeing "in a glasse, darkely." I Corinthians 13:4 makes courtesy an essential part of the basic theological virtue of *caritas,* that mixture of love and charity which is often referred to in Protestant writings as the basis of the bonds that hold the community of the faithful, the church, together. The other two quotes also suggest courtesy is connected to the divine love that unites Christians. Ephesians 4:32 leads directly into Ephesians 5, which reads, "Bee yee therefore folowers of God, as deere children and walke in Loue [*caritas*], even as Christ loued us." In a sermon translated by on Ephesians 4:32 and 5:1–2 (translated by Arthur Golding), Calvin says that "the whole summe of this Lesson" is to "bring us too charitie [*caritas*], and maynteyne us in it." The connection of courtesy to *caritas* might explain the positioning of the Three Graces in the climactic vision: two "froward" and one "foreward." As Edgar Wind says, in the Renaissance this arrangement iconographically represented the three theological virtues, faith, hope, and *caritas;* the one facing opposite to the other two is *caritas,* because it is distinguished in I Corinthians 13:13 as "the chiefest of these" three virtues.[10]

The words "courtesy" is used to translate suggest further

dimensions to the sixteenth-century religious meaning of the term. In I Corinthians and Ephesians, the word that is translated as "courteous" is *benigna*, while in 1 Peter 3:8, which seems quite similar in intent, it is *humiles* (perhaps the different Latin explains why 1 Peter 3:8 is overlooked in the Table of the Geneva Bible, and why the King James retains "courtesy" in 1 Peter). In the English versions of Calvin's sermons, "courtesy" and "courteous" translate such words as *gracieux, gracieuseté, humains, humanité*, and *benin*. That forms of the word "courtesy" could be used to translate such diverse terms suggests that "courtesy" had several quite broad meanings in the sixteenth century. Even the *O.E.D.* recognizes that "courtesy" could mean "benevolence" or "goodness" in general in the 1500s; Tomson's sentence about esteeming God's graces is used in the *O.E.D.* as one of the sample quotes for this definition.[11]

We might think that "courtesy" is being used in its secular meaning when it translates terms such as *gracieuseté* or *humanité*. These French words do have non-religious uses, just as "courtesy" does, and these non-religious uses might seem rather similar to the religious ones: all these terms describe behavior that makes a community harmonious. But in religious contexts, this behavior has quite a different origin than in non-religious ones: humans can be harmonious only because of God's grace, not because of any natural human abilities. Calvin says that when he exhorts Christians to be *"gracieux,"* he is urging something that is "very hard, yea and utterly repugnant too man's nature, and which cannot bee brought too passe except God woork in that behalf."[12] It is only through actual recognition of God's mercy (his Grace), through having "an eye too Gods behaving of himselfe towardes us" (in other words, through revealed religion) that Christians can become *"gracieux,"* or, in the English Calvinists' translations, "courteous." Calvin seems to be playing on the secular and theological uses of "grace" in French: he seems to be suggesting that the suffix in *"gracieux"* be interpreted literally, making *"gracieux"* mean "full of Grace" rather than "pleasing." Such word play in Calvin, and the connection between courtesy and divine Grace in Perkins and in the English translations of Calvin make it plausible to see theological connotations in Spenser's frequent use in Book VI of every possible form of the word "grace"; further, Calvin's usage shows that the praise of a person for his "courtesy," his "graciousness" or even his "humanity" by sixteenth-century writers such as Spenser does not necessarily imply respect for human nature. Calvin actually seems more willing than his English translators to use words such as "humanity": "all courtesie," which Tomson says esteeming God's graces leads to, is "*toute humanité*" in Calvin's original French; for people in a community to be fully human, and not beasts, is for Calvin clear evidence of God's grace.

The biblical passages mentioning courtesy show quite clearly that the virtue involves much more than mere politeness: to be courteous is to imitate the forgiveness of Christ. Forgiving may seem rather unconnected to the esteeming of persons that Tomson's translation of Calvin describes as courteous behavior, but it is not hard to see the continuity: forgiving and esteeming are both ways of overlooking the obvious human sins in everyone, responding instead to those images of God inside some persons, and therefore accepting those persons into the community. Forgiving is the first step in forming a courteous community: accepting sinners, esteeming those who have nothing else to esteem except the sign that God has decided not to condemn them, the mark that they too are contained in the bonds of *caritas*. As Calvin says in the sermon on Ephesians 4:32:

> Let us learne to bee gentle and courteous one too another, and not too bee so churlish as too separate ourselves from the common aray and company of other men. This is the thing that S. Paule ment by the gentlenesse or courtesie that he spake of. When we see any despyzed person . . . nother hath he any thing to bee esteemed for . . . If wee have any droppe of pitie, too keepe us from rejecting them that are alyed untoo us . . . wee shall not fayle too bee gentle and courteous towardes our neighbours in all caces and at all tymes . . . [13]

Those who have do not have "any thing to be esteemed for" but are "alyed unto us" are those in whom seeds of grace lie dormant. Such persons have the potential to have faith but do not realize it, and so remain outside the community of the faithful. Pitying them is essentially an act of recognizing and esteeming the seeds of goodness inside them and so causes the first growth of those seeds, awakens God's image engraved within them and leads them to recognize their connection to the community of the faithful. Forgiving or pity thus gathers together sinners to start a courteous community.

Once a community is gathered together, the second step in developing its courtesy is providing all the members roles in the community. God directs this use by providing each person, along with the essential grace of faith, additional common graces that are the source of talents and resources which contribute to the community. To have a harmonious community, these good qualities must be seen not as human possessions, but as divine gifts, as *God's* property, and hence as the property of God's representative on earth, of the Chruch. As Calvin writes,

> Hath one man a good witte? an other strength and might? an other learning? an other in office and dignitie? let euerie one of them thinke, that God will bee served and honoured by suche meanes, this it is y [that] ought to stirre us uppe to make the graces of God auaileble. Whosoeuer is negligent in this case shall be taken for a Church robber, bicause he hath prophaned that that God had appointed to so noble and excellent an vse. . . . for that that God gaue mee was not for my selfe that I might burie it, the fruit of it is common.[14]

By devoting all his talents and resources to the Church, to the religious community, each person feeds all the others in the community by sharing with them the "fruit" that grows from the seeds of grace within him. As Calvin writes, "God hath not made vs every man for him self, but will haue vs given one to another . . . in al courtesie."[15] Some give to society by being kings and some by being strong workers, and all must accept their roles, which are dictated by God. Calvin can thus agree with Spenser that courteous Christians must "beare them selues aright to all of each degree" (VI.ii.1), but Calvin provides a reason for respecting degree, even if persons in high position are sinners: "Difference of degrees proceedeth not from this, that one is better than another: but this is, because it pleaseth God to give preeminence vnto some, whom he will also haue honored."[16] Honoring a king requires overlooking that king's sins and is just as much a charitable act as accepting a lowly beggar as a brother in the faith—in both cases, one is treating a person better than he deserves and doing so just because God has done so. One should separate the esteeming of the qualities God has given people and the judging of the persons in whom those qualities reside: admirable qualities should be regarded as, in Spenser's image, stars crowning earthly brows, unalterable by human hands, shining on and benefitting everyone in the community.

Book VI is organized to show the two steps involved in esteeming graces: the first seven cantos and half of the eighth consist of tales of reforming and rescuing lost souls, tales in which knights and religious hermits and even the God of love recognize the seed of grace in despised persons, in savages and sinners, and thus bring them into the community of the faithful; then, in Canto viii, stanza 31, Spenser turns to showing three simplified communities (the Cannibals, the shepherds, and the Brigants), contrasting the ways they keep growing and share in the graces of admirable persons who accidentally end up among them. Finally, in Canto xii, Spenser turns to a society much like Elizabethan England, to reveal the application of what he has allegorically shown in the earlier tales. Calidore's tale, running throughout the book, shows the essential difference between a secular or humanistic notion of courtesy and one based on Protestant concepts: Calidore is transformed from a person trying to make himself courteous into a person driven, rather against his will, to do what God intends him to do.

Before turning to a closer analysis of the religious basis of the tales in Book VI, I must comment on the question of Spenser's religion. Usually this question is phrased as whether he is a Puritan or an Anglican. Most critics have come down on the Anglican side, though a few have argued for Spenser's Puritanism.[17] English Calvinism tends to be associated with Puritanism, and thus if I contend that Book VI is quite close to Calvinist texts (as I do), I might seem to be joining the minority arguing for Spenser's Puritanism. However, the specific tenets of Calvinism that arise in discussions of courtesy—essentially, those involved in the Reformed theology of grace centered on the concept of predestination—were accepted quite firmly by all fervent Protestants of Spenser's time; as Nicholas Tyacke puts it, "Calvinist predestinarian teaching . . . was a crucial common assumption, shared by a majority of the hierarchy and virtually all its nonconformist opponents, during the Elizabethan and Jacobean periods."[18] Calvin's explications of "the thing S. Paule

ment by . . . the courteousness that he spake of" simply would
not have been controversial to sixtcenth-century English Protestants, though they may may seem so to some modern
scholars.[19] Thus, the texts I have discovered cannot help us
decide whether Spenser was a Puritan or not. But these texts do
shed light on Spenser's religion: they help us define a distinctive
Elizabethan Protestant conception of courtesy, one based on the
predestinarian theology of grace, and they help us see that this
theology underlies Book VI.

Previous critics, working just from Spenser's text, have suggested religious interpretations of Book VI, but they have always had a problem explaining why Spenser would use what all
scholars have hitherto assumed is a secular term to name a
virtue with religious dimensions. These critics have developed
some ingenious explanations: Humphrey Tonkin presents a
case the Spenser is reviving a broad medieval conception of
courtesy that had been lost by the sixteenth century[20]; Richard
Neuse argues that Spenser is presenting a dark vision of the
emptiness of courtesy and even of most morality in Renaissance
England[21]; other critics simply assume that Spenser is creating
his own meaning for the term.[22] No one has noticed that the
word "courtesy" appears in Calvin's writings or in the Bible,
possibly because it is readily apparent only in sixteenth-century
English translations of these texts; the word rarely appears in
later, more familiar versions. The religious references to courtesy that I have found should at least raise some questions about
what is accepted as the obvious meaning of the word in the
sixteenth century. Moreover, these references fit Book VI in
such detailed ways that they provide straightforward sources—
well-known sixteenth-century English texts that discuss "courtesy" directly as an important religious virtue—for a term that
has previously seemed either unworthy of being in the company of "holiness" and "justice" or idiosyncratically redefined
by Spenser.

FORMING A CHRISTIAN COMMUNITY

When read against the background of the religious uses of the
word "courtesy," Book VI appears permeated with Protestant
themes. In the first part of the book, the first seven and a half
cantos, Spenser shows the intial steps in the formation of the

ideal religious community. Protestantism prescribes an essential
role that mercy plays in allowing people to live together at all,
and it is this role that Spenser shows in the two parallel tales
(those of Sir Crudor and Mirabella) which begin and end the
first part. Since all men are worthless sinners, a person needs to
be merciful and to receive mercy to escape isolation, to stop
himself from treating others as they deserve—with utter disdain—and to keep from being treated equally badly. A
courteous community depends on mercy: each person,
recognizing God's graces in others and in himself, should overrule his own correct judgments and treat others as close kin, as
allied to him by bonds of *caritas*, simply because he sees God has
done so. Sir Crudor and Mirabella refuse to accept anyone as
close kin: they refuse to marry. Calvin, in the sermon on
Ephesians 4:32, describes what Mirabella and Sir Crudor need
to learn to reconcile themselves to being bound to others in a
community:

> To bee Gods children, we must loue one another . . . And
> how is that possible to bee: . . . wee haue infinite causes
> too put us away, and to cut us of from all company. And
> surely if euery man let himselfe looce, Charitie shall neuer
> take place, but bee banished farre from us. What is too bee
> doone then: Wee must first rid away all scornfulnesse and
> pryde . . . every man brydle himself and subdew his owne
> affections. But this cannot bee doone, except wee bee
> gentle, and kynd harted, namely bycause wee bee . . . knit
> together with an unseparable bond. Yit would not all this
> suffize, untyll wee haue learned too knowe our owne
> infirmities, and that therefore wee have neede of this bond
> too hold us fast togither . . . Now if common courtesie
> ought too move us too succour such as are in necessitie: it
> ought also too bee of force too reconcyle us.[23]

Spenser puts Sir Crudor and Mirabella through just what Calvin recommends: they are brought to see their own infirmities
by being condemned to what they deserve (death?), thus reduc-
ing them to begging for mercy. Then they are made aware of
their need for the bonds they rejected by being granted mercy
on the condition that they accept the roles in society God has
assigned them: Sir Crudor must marry the woman he scorned;

Mirabella must repair as many loves as she destroyed, a new role given her directly by a "God of loue," Cupid (VI.viii.19).

When Sir Crudor is granted mercy, he is also given advice by Calidore, the knight who defeats him. Calidore tells him to learn "him selfe first to subdew," then mentions that "All flesh is frayle" and concludes, "Who will not mercie vnto others shew / How can he mercy euer hope to haue?" (VI.i.42). Calidore is telling Sir Crudor to stop trusting himself and his flesh, and trust instead that which is not flesh or self, namely, his graces. The graces will not make him perfect, but will make him merciful and will bring him mercy when he sins, both from God and from humans. Calidore's act of granting mercy is itself, a way of recognizing that Sir Crudor has in him more than his sins; Calidore is esteeming hidden, dormant graces in the recreant knight and thus bringing those graces to life.

It may not seem as if Calidore is invoking divine graces in his speech or his actions, but Spenser, by showing the effect of Calidore's acts on Sir Crudor's lady, shows that Calidore is essentially eliciting God's help. Upon seeing Calidore grant mercy, Briana is "ouercome with infinite affect / For his exceeding courtesie, that pearst / Her stubborne hart with inward deepe effect," so that she is "wondrously now chaung'd" (VI.i.45–46). The words "infinite" and "wondrously" suggest that it is divine grace engraving a new image of God on her heart, not mere human action, that is changing her.

Sir Crudor and Mirabella remain isolated because of proud disdain; in another tale, that of the Salvage, Spenser shows a person who lives alone simply because he has never had contact with courteous Christians: the Salvage was abandoned as a baby. His tale shows that God's action, not training or knowledge, directs people to their roles in society, and that God does so by instilling pity in the hearts of men. The Salvage, born of noble blood, has the graces in him to be a knight, but wanders in the woods living as an animal. He has had so little human contact that he does not even know how to speak, yet when he meets others who are graced—a beautiful maiden in distress and a courteous knight—he suddenly feels "compassion" even though "neuer till this houre / Did [he] taste of pittie, ne neither gentlesse knew" (VI.iv.2). Moved by pity, he immediately knows the proper ways to act: he rescues the maiden, puts on armor he finds lying about, and ends up leaving the woods as squire to the knight. He is not taught how to act; meeting courteous persons just brings alive his graces and those graces direct him to his predestined role in the community.

Although the Salvage's tale does not involve the direct granting of mercy to a condemned sinner, it shows the merciful effects of courtesy. Courtesy brings into the community all those whom God has graced even though they may seem to deserve to be condemned or treated as animals. Further, courtesy can, by eliciting divine aid to awaken dormant graces in isolated sinners and savages, transform them into noble Christians. Book VI is full of such transformations, all miraculously brought about by courtesy: a child of unknown lineage, rescued from a bear, becomes, appropriately enough, Sir Bruin's son, fulfilling a mysterious divine prophecy; Tristram, another wild man like the Salvage, overcomes the fear of human wickedness which had made him shun human company since childhood and accepts a role as a squire, on his way to being a prince; and Pastorella, a rustic maiden, discovers she is a princess. These tales carry further the imagery of transplanted seeds introduced in the Proem; the abandoned babies and lost children are themselves seeds planted in lowly environments. As Sir Calepine says about the bear child, these persons all seem to have been "sowen / Here by the Gods, and fed with heauenly sap" (VI.iv.36). That so many characters spend time wandering or living in the woods does not show that Spenser is concerned with persons discovering some natural part of themselves; rather, the scenes in the woods always show the discovery of something unusual, something that does not belong in the natural environment, something that suddenly comes alive upon contact with a person who is courteously following the faith. Spenser is using nature imagery similar to that in John 15:4, where Christ says,

> as the branch can not beare fruite of itself, except it abide in the vine, no more can ye, except ye abide in me. I am the vine; ye are the branches: he that abideth in me, and I in him, the same bringeth forth muche frute: for without me ye can do nothing.

In Spenser's tales, finding and feeding human branches in the woods always has the effect of rather magically grafting them onto the vine, the community of Christians, whence they begin to bear fruit. Spenser thus shows that courtesy involves searching for wonderful, divine qualities hidden in the "natural" environment of the human body. Once recognized and cultivated (esteemed), these qualities transform the natural man into an image of God, and transplant him to the community of the faithful, and ultimately to heaven. Courteous actions bring those God has selected out of nature and into a heavenly community, just as the Graces in the vision in Canto x transplant a maiden out of the pastoral world directly into heaven.

Not all persons can be brought into the community of the faithful, because not all have in them seeds of grace to be cultivated. Before courtesy can operate, another virtue, another way of treating people—rigorous justice—is needed to clear away those sinners who cannot respond to courtesy. The development of the courteous community thus begins in Book V. Removing sinners, usually by condemning them to death, is the main task of Book V, performed largely by Talus, who is described in images that suggest that he is preparing society for the cultivation of the "heavenly seeds" that are introduced in Book VI. Talus's only weapon is an iron flail, with which he "thresht out falshood" (V.i.12), killing sinners and strewing their bodies about "like scattred chaffe" (V.xi.47) or "fruitles seede" (V.vii.31). His threshing supposedly separates those "seeds" which cannot grow from those that can. But Talus's killing seems to have no limits: both Artegall (V.xi.65 and xii.8) and Britomart (V.vii.36) have to restrain him, "else he sure had left not one aliue" (V.vii.36). They do not hold him back because he is killing good men by error, but "for very ruth," in horror at the "slaughtred carkasses" he is piling up (V.vii.36); Talus's justice seems to them a "cruell deed" (V.xi.65). In other words, they stop him because they pity those sinners he is killing. Talus never limits his own slaughter because he deals with humans rigorously; he represents that stern justice that could, if given free rein, condemn all men. Being made of iron, he is not fully allied to humans, so he never feels the pity that counters strict justice. His threshing works to separate the worst sinners from the rest of mankind only when he is held in check by the compassion felt by his human masters. Pity determines which men live and which die, not recognition of virtue; after justice combats sin, those left alive are not good men devoid of sins, but sinners who have been saved by human grace, which is the agent of divine grace.

Once Talus has done his job and has been restrained, once the threshing has removed those lacking any seed of grace, justice alone is no longer an adequate basis for human society. In fact, to complete the task of building the ideal community, most of the effects of justice have to be undone. Justice has revealed what all men deserve—utter condemnation—but men have to stop condemning and to begin accepting each other courteously. Courtesy is a necessary addition and counter to justice, as Spenser shows by intertwining the end of Book V and the beginning of Book VI.[24] The monster of Book VI, the Blatant Beast, symbol of evil speaking, is brought into Book V by two Hags, Envy and Detraction, specifically to attack the knight of justice, Artegall (V.xii.37). The Hags and the Beast scream curses at Artegall, and even throw a snake that bites him, yet he simply rides by, even restraining Talus from attacking them. Spenser implies that justice cannot stop the Beast's slander, or at least that slander is not an appropriate foe for justice. The Beast's slander must consist of more than lies and libelous statements, for courts of justice were appropriate places to counter such kinds of slander in Elizabethan England. But the Beast does not need to lie, because, as Calvin says, "The perfectest man that is hath yit some infirmitie insomuch that if men should deale altoogither rigorously with him, he should bee disdeyned, yea and as good as utterly disgraced and defaced."[25] In a rigorously just society, every man would hear a thousand voices telling him he was deserving of disgrace. Carried to an extreme, justice calls forth the Blatant Beast.

The only answer to the rigorous justice that would condemn all is Una's answer to Redcrosse in Book I, when he is about to kill himself because he feels that even a knight of holiness deserves to die: "Where iustice growes, there growes eke greater grace" (I.ix.53). Only the active recognition of God's grace, only undeserved and unjust courtesy, can stop the "slander" to which justice leads. Thus the knight of justice needs the knight of courtesy to counter what justice has created, and Artegall enters Book VI to tell Calidore where to find the Blatant Beast (VI.i.9).[26]

One form of God's grace does appear in Book V: mercy, in the figure of Mercilla. Although Mercilla's prominent role shows mercy in relation to justice, the way Spenser writes about mercy and the way Mercilla acts suggest that mercy is introduced into Book V for much the same reason the Blatant Beast is—to set a limit on justice and to point to what is beyond justice, what will be taken up in Book VI.[27] Spenser begins his discussion of mercy by questioning whether "this heavenly thing . . . be of Iustice part / Or drawne forth from her by divine extreate" (V.x.1). He does not answer the question, saying only "This well I wote, that sure she is as great," and then describing mercy as an alternative, a complement to justice, rather than as a part:

> For if that Vertue be of so great might,
> Which from iust verdict will for nothing start,
> But to preserue inuiolated right,
> Oft spilles the principall, to saue the part;
> So much more then is that of powre and art,
> That seekes to saue the subject of her skill,
> Yet neuer doth from doome of right depart;
> As it is greater prayse to saue, then spill,
> And better to reforme, then to cut off the ill.
>
> (V.x.2)

After such high praise, we fully expect Mercilla to perform the miracle of reforming and saving someone. But if to be merciful is to go beyond strict justice, it is also to go beyond Book V: nobody in this book grants mercy directly. When Duessa is on trial, Arthur pities and seeks to pardon her, but he is restrained by Zele and ultimately by Artegall, who with "constant firme intent, / For zeale of Iustice was against her bent. / So was she guiltie deemed of them all" (V.ix.49). Arthur's pity seems an error in judgment (and he eventually repents his "former fancies ruth"—V.ix.49), but it shows what Artegall lacks: the ability to overthrow judgment and be ruled by mercy. Mercilla's judgment mediates between Arthur and Artegall: her tearful condemnation of Duessa represents the border between justice and mercy, and hence between justice and courtesy. Artegall can just reach that border: he knows mercy only as that which stops him (or Talus) from acting, not as a way of acting in itself. Pity causes him to leave a group of sinners alone, not to join with them in a courteous community. He cannot achieve the greater praise of saving and reforming men, and so he has to leave *Irena* "ere he could reforme it thoroughly" (V.xii.27). He has done all he can by removing the worst sinners; reforming those who are left requires the transforming power of courtesy. Book VI takes up where Book V leaves off: in Canto i, Calidore meets Artegall, says to him, "Where ye ended haue, now I begin," (VI.i.6) and, in striking contrast to the judgment of Duessa, proceeds directly to grant mercy to Sir Crudor, reforming and saving the recreant knight and his lady Briana. Spenser seems to have dropped Mercilla into Book V as a foretaste of what would be developed in Book VI. Spenser even uses the Book VI imagery of things bred in heaven and transplanted to earth to describe Mercilla in Book V: "In th'Almighties euerlasting seat / She first was bred, and borne of heauenly race; / From thence pour'd down on men, by influence of grace" (V.x.1). Mercy is a seed of divine grace planted in ground cleared by justice, a seed that blossoms into courtesy.

KEEPING THE GRACES OF A COMMUNITY GROWING

Courtesy's first task, as shown in the first seven cantos of Book VI, is mercifully to bring together the collection of sinners God has selected to form the community of the faithful. After the community is formed, courtesy can shift from trying to elicit the first growth of the seeds of grace in people to nurturing and sharing in the fruit that grows from those seeds of grace. Spenser defines the way a community should react to the graces of those God sends to join it by contrasting the ways three different communities find and share the "fruits of grace" that nourish them. The shepherds are the properly courteous community. They know how to grow fruit for the community from the graces of any who enter their community. They do so be giving spiritual (as well as physical) food; Spenser describes Calidore as being "fed" through his "greedy eare," his "greedy fancy" and his "hungry eye" by Meliboe's wisdom, Colin's vision and the beauties of pastoral life and of Pastorella (VI.ix.26 and VI.x.30). We see the results of the shepherds'

giving to strangers in Pastorella, whom they have raised from
an abandoned baby to a beautiful maiden. The shepherds not
only feed and raise young girls who enter their village (such as
Pastorella), they are willing to give away, to God, the most
wonderful young woman among them (as occurs in the vision
in Canto x). They know they lose nothing by such an act,
because all that they have to give is given to them by God. As
Melibee says,

> The little that I haue, growes dayly more
> Without my care, but onely to attend it;
>
> . . .
>
> What haue I, but to praise th'Almighty, that doth send it?
>
> (VI.ix.21)

Courtesy in the shepherds' community creates a circle of ever-
increasing graces: each person gives all he has to the others in
the community of the faithful; in return, God feeds and increases the graces of the whole community, increasing what
each person has to give away. Colin's interpretation of the circle
of Graces suggests the same idea: "that good should from vs
goe, then come in greater store" (VI.x.24). Courtesy consists of
the passing of ever-increasing divine gifts in ever-widening
circles.

The discourteous communities in Book VI, the Brigants and
the Cannibals, cannot understand the logic of the circulation of
gifts. They do not see how they can benefit from anything that
is possessed by someone else, so they hoard their graces and try
to acquire the graces they see in others. Adapting a phrase of
William Nestrick's, we can say that they mistakenly treat what
is good, what only God gives, as if it were "goods," physical
properties that can be transferred, bought, sold, or stolen.[28] In
contrast to the shepherds, they are described as those who
consume rather than nourish, plant, or grow. The Cannibals
feed on "the labours of poore men," the Brigants on "spoile and
booty"; neither group ever learn to "driue / The painefull
plough, or cattel for to breed" (VI.viii.35; VI.x.39). Because the
Brigants and Cannibals do not know how to keep anything
growing, they do not understand how they can share in the fruit
that could grow from one seed. They actually have to phys-

ically divide and consume whatever "goods" are in their community, including all that is "good" in humans. When the Brigants capture Pastorella, at first they plan to share in her wondrous value by imprisoning and selling her body and dividing the profits. But Pastorella seems so wonderfully valuable a "food" that each wants her for himself, so they begin fighting among themselves like "hungry dogs ymet / About some carcase" (VI.xi.17). The word "carcase" reveals much about what they see as valuable; like the Cannibals, they are aware only of the flesh, not of the inner grace from which beauty grows.

The Cannibals, though they may seem even more extreme "consumers" than the Brigants, actually have more understanding of God's graces, and are saved from killing each other by their religion. But Spenser uses the Cannibals to show how religious truths are corrupted when interpreted by the "natural man": the Cannibals recognize that "by grace of God" Serena was "sent" to them, that she carries within her divine graces that essentially are parts of God, and that they should share in the fruits of those graces (VI.viii.38). But since they cannot actually conceive of a non-material part of a human, they end up enacting a grotesque parody of the courteous honoring of the divine within humans: they believe that they can extract the divine seed within her, her "guiltlesse bloud," "present" it to God as his share, and then make a "common feast" of the leftover, of her "dainty flesh" (VI.viii.38).

By esteeming only the outer, physical results of grace, not its inner, immaterial seed, both communities simply destroy the graces they seek to acquire. The Brigants may not plan to kill Pastorella, as the Cannibals would, but just putting her into captivity causes her beauty to fade "Like to a flowre, that feeles no heate of sunne. / Which may her feeble leaues with comfort glade" (VI.x.44). The Brigants do not realize that what seems so wonderfully valuable in Pastorella, her beauty, requires a courteous environment, requires proper esteem, to exist at all.

The Brigants and Cannibals, terrible as they are, are not as bad as the ultimate monster of discourtesy, the Blatant Beast. They destroy graces inadvertently, while trying to incorporate them into their own lives. The Beast, in contrast, does not attempt to take in anything because it does not value anything; it does not recognize graces at all. It directly seeks to cause flesh to rot, using its thousand mouths not to eat graces but to spit poison that ruins them. By the logic of the Prostestant conception of courtesy, all that is necessary to ruin graces is to stop humans from recognizing them; this is what the beast does—it infects those it bites with its own view that graces do not exist. As Spenser says, those who are bitten suffer from no physical disease, though their flesh rots, but rather by a "ranckling inward" that can be cured only by a change of attitude (VI.vi.5). Those bitten need to undergo a process of re-establishing contact with the divine realm, a process Spenser represents as a journey to the border between human and divine realms. The two who are bitten in the book, Serena and Timias, wander out of society into the woods until they meet a Hermit, a man who has withdrawn from "all this worlds incombraunce" to live in a chapel, to be as close as possible to spiritual realms (VI.v.37). The Hermit realizes that their "inner parts" must be "disciplinde . . . / To rule the stubborne rage of passion blinde" (VI.vi.5). He tells them how to cure themselves: "First learne your outward sences to refraine / From things, that stirre up fraile affection (VI.vi.7); . . . restraine youre will, / Subdue desire and bridle loose delight" (VI.vi. 14—very close to Calvin's advice quoted earlier, that each man must "brydle himself and subdew his own affections"). In other words, if they are to have sound minds and bodies, they must learn to be guided by their graces, by that inside them that is not part of their desires and affections, not part of their human wills.

CALIDORE'S TALE

The Hermit's advice embodies the paradox of grace: to become good, a person must stop trying to be good and let God make him so. To become courteous, each person must esteem his own graces, letting them grow until they overrule his will and direct him to the role God intends for him to fulfill in the community. Spenser, in the tale of Calidore, dramatizes the difference between being ruled by the best of wills and being ruled by God's graces. This tale shows the essential difference between secular and Protestant conceptions of courtesy: Calidore is transformed from a person trying hard to make himself courteous by following his natural virtue into a person driven by internal forces, rather against his will, to do what God intends him to do.

For most of Book VI, Calidore seems able to recognize other people's graces, but not his own. Whenever he sees others who have been graced, he esteems them so highly that he simply abandons whatever he is doing and tries to become like them. When he sees a knight courting a lady, he joins them; when he sees the peace of the shepherds' lives and the beauty they have raised in Pastorella, he strips off his armor to become a shepherd; and when he is ravished by a vision called up by Colin's piping, he gives up shepherding to live with Colin. Calidore mistakenly believes that human actions are the source of what is good in human lives. But as Calvin writes, a Christian must "let God be knowen to be the authur of all goodnes and let all praise be given to him and thus shal not his graces bee dispised."[29] Calidore, by trying to be the author of his own goodness, and by praising other humans, not God, for showing him how to be good, is essentially despising God's graces.

Calidore's inability to recognize God's role in his own life—or in anyone else's—is hinted at when he is first introduced in Canto i. He describes himself as pursuing "an endless trace, withouten guyde, / Or good direction" (VI.i.6). He does not realize that God is guiding him and does not trust that God has provided him with what is necessary to finish his quest. In Canto ix he states his problem explicitly in terms of divine Grace: he says to Meliboe, in admiration of the shepherds' lives, and especially of the beautiful woman who lives with them, "I . . . wish th' heaven's so much had graced mee / As graunt me liue in like condition. / O that my fortunes might transposed bee" (VI.ix.29). Meliboe tells him that all men have been graced by the heavens as much as "each can most aptly vse" (VI.ix.29) and that all Calidore needs to do to "fortunize" his life is to esteem whatever he has been graced with. But Calidore cannot hear this advice and tries to become the shepherd that he thinks Pastorella will love.

Calidore begins the process of winning Pastorella well enough; he quickly sows the "seeds / Of perfect loue" (VI.ix.45). But he has trouble getting those seeds to grow; Spenser says that it is a "long time dearely bought" before Calidore can reap the "fruite of ioy and blisse" (VI.ix.45). The logic of Protestant courtesy explains why Calidore cannot win

Pastorella: having abandoned his own graces, he has nothing to give her to feed those seeds of love. He cannot even feed himself, and thus is "hungry" and "greedy" when he first arrives at the village. He cannot offer the fruit of his graces, but only the products of his previous training, the products of human society—his skills and his money. These are not enough to allow Pastorella to distinguish him from Coridon, a shepherd who pursues her and simply imitates everything Calidore does. Coridon's actions reveal what Calidore is doing wrong: both of them are imitators, trying to become something other than what God has made them.

Calidore just does not know how to react when he sees graces stripped of the particular forms they take at court; he has never looked through the human world at the divinity behind it. Even Meliboe's good advice cannot get him to look beyond the physical realm. But in the climactic scene of Book VI, he finally comes face to face with the core of the Protestant conception of courtesy in the form of a direct vision of the connection of the heavens and earth, the vision of the circle of dancing Graces crowning a young maiden and turning her into another divine being for the way she has developed her "heavenly gifts." But since these Graces are, as Spenser tells us, the original source of all "gifts of grace," they are only reaping the full growth of what they implanted in the maid in the first place, completing a circle of grace (VI.x.15). At first, Calidore is so entranced by this vision that he, as usual, tries to join the dance, causing the vision to disappear. He believes that Colin can bring the vision back, but Colin says, "None can them bring in place / But whom they of them selues list so to grace" (VI.x.20). The vision and Colin's comments show Calidore how he should esteem Pastorella—as someone placed on earth by God, worthy of being regarded as divine, whose graces will only be shared with him if God lists to direct the two of them to love each other.

The vision's direct effect on Calidore is that he simply stops pursuing Pastorella, preferring to wait for divine maidens rather than pursuing real ones. But while he waits, a "restlesse paine" that Pastorella has "bred" inside him grows so strong that it becomes a "poysnous pointe deepe fixed in his hart" and drives him back to her, against his will (VI.x.31). These two seemingly contradictory changes in Calidore—giving up Pastorella and then being driven back to her—are actually parts of the same process: he is changing from a lover of worldly beauty to a lover of divine beauty, from being ruled by his own will and reason to being ruled by his graces. His corrupt will was pursuing Pastorella's body, and stops doing so, while at the same time his graces are taking over and leading him to the divine beauty in her that he could not see before. His heart is pierced, as Briana's was, suggesting that he is being reformed as she was, that a new image of God is being engraved on his heart to direct his actions.

Calidore's reaction to the vision is similar to Redcrosse's reaction the the sight of New Jerusalem. Both knights return to the world, to their loves, and eventually to their unfinished quests with a sense of regret. A paradox of being granted a vision of heavenly grace, of the true value of every thing in this world, is that it makes the world seem less worthwhile. Calidore leaves Colin "like as the wounded Whale to shore flies from the maine" (VI.x.31), like a creature not clearly aware of where it is going, just driven along, waiting for the escape of death. He is moved by his painful love much as Arthur is driven by a secret, "fresh bleeding wound" of love, that "with forced fury" moves Arthur on his quests (I.ix.7). Such wounds represent the ways God moves men in their predestined paths, divine love pushing them internally, replacing their "fraile affections" that are so easily led astray by the outward senses.

In the episode after Calidore leaves Colin, Spenser provides many indications that Calidore's new, painful love is not a base passion but is rather the mechanism by which his graces are taking control of his life. His love causes him to act like a knight again, to fly to Pastorella's rescue when she is attacked by a tiger, though he has none of his armor or weapons. His defeating the tiger with only a shepherd's crook shows that God is working through him, that God's graces make him a courteous knight, not his armor, his skill, or his effort. This act of fighting with no thought for himself indicates that he has a new kind of esteem for Pastorella, as Spenser shows by contrasting Calidore's actions with those of Coridon, who also has a chance to fight the tiger, but runs away because "his life he steemed dearer than his frend" (VI.x.35). Spenser's use of the word "frend" in this context makes reference to John 15:13, "Greater love hath no man, when any man bestoweth his life for his friends."

Spenser thus suggests that Calidore is being moved by a divine love like Christ's, a love that is self-less in the sense that it derives not from the self but from the source of divine love within humans, from God's graces. By esteeming Pastorella as dearer than his own life, Calidore finally causes those seeds of love he had sown earlier to grow, and he soon reaps the "timely frute" of love (VI.x.38). As soon as he wins her love (in the very next stanza), "fortune," or rather divine will, sweeps both of them out of the woods, returning them to their predestined roles: Pastorella is magically reunited with her original royal parents, and Calidore resumes his quest. Spenser says that Calidore follows the Blatant Beast "with restlesse paine" (VI.xii.22), suggesting that Calidore is being moved on his quest by an inner force similar to the one that moved him with "restlesse paine" from Colin back to Pastorella (VI.x.31). But Calidore seems to have stopped resisting that force, finally aware that his own judgment has led him astray, "Asham'd to thinke, how he that enterprize, / The which the Faery Queene had long afore / Bequeath'd to him, forslacked had so sore" (VI.xii.12). He accepts the role in life bequeathed him from higher authority, accepts being led by his graces, and they guide him well—he quickly finds the tracks that eluded him in the first half of Book VI, and completes his quest without further digression, defeating the Beast as easily as muzzling a dog.

The final battle between Calidore and the Beast is fought in "the sacred Church," which the Blatant Beast has defiled by the "theft" of "all goodness" from the "Clergy" and by the speaking of "blasphemy" from the altar (VI.xii.23–25). The Beast has destroyed the basic tenet of Protestantism, the revelation of God's grace, which Calidore, having been granted a revelation himself, can restore. Spenser thus indicates that the revealed church is the ultimate guarantor of civility, because without it, men cannot recognize and esteem God's graces, cannot overcome the hunger and greediness they naturally feel when they see graces in others, nor the disdain they feel when they see sins. Through revelation, though, humans can rather magically achieve a form of society that is utterly against their depraved nature.

Calidore found the revelation he needed while he was in the pastoral village, while he was morally truant from his duties to God and to his society.[30] Spenser thus shows that Calidore had to abandon his quest, his social role, and even his morality to grow to being fully virtuous and able to complete his quest. The strange wandering plots of Cantos ix and x, and the multiple disgressions of the whole of Book VI, are designed to make it very clear that it is entirely a fortuitous accident that Calidore finds what he needs, that he in no way wins the revelation that he stumbles upon, nor does he particularly deserve it. Spenser has created a plot that represents the granting of something to someone with no regard to his deserts or his efforts, a plot representing an act of Grace. Like Briana and Mirabella, Calidore is changed inwardly at precisely the moment he is most culpable. The paradoxes of the plot parallel the paradoxes of Grace, that that which is unmerited and even misused is also essential.[31]

In many ways Spenser emphasizes the basic tenet of Calvinist theology that each person's reward in this world and in the next has been decided before he was born. In this book, losing one's way and wandering in the woods are simply routes to one's predestined end. Spenser shows that a belief in predestination need not produce a morose and hopeless vision of life. Elizabethan Protestants, following Calvin, believed that the culmination of Christianity on earth would be a city populated by the elect, all treating each other courteously. Such persons in such a place should experience a constant interplay between divine and human realms, a circling of honors and gifts passed in both directions. Spenser may end Book VI on a note of doubt that such a city will ever be permanently established, but the climactic vision of the book, the dance of the maidens and the Graces, is a version of this sixteenth-century Protestant dream.

Palo Alto, California

NOTES

1. John Calvin, *Sermons on St. Paul's Epistles to Timothy and Titus*, translated by Laurence Tomson (London: George Bishop, 1579), p. 557.
2. All quoted passages of *The Faerie Queene* are from Edmund Spenser, *The Faerie Queene*, ed. Thomas P. Roche, Jr. (New York: Penguin Books, 1978).
3. Calvin, *Sermons on St. Paul's Epistle to the Ephesians*, translated by Arthur Golding (London: Lucas Harrison and George Bishop, 1577), folio 235.
4. Dewey Wallace, in *Puritans and Predestination: Grace in English Theology,*

1525–1695 (Chapel Hill: The University of North Carolina Press, 1982), p. 55, describes Perkins as "one of the most important of the spiritual writers as well as an English theologian of European reputation."

5. William Perkins, "A Graine of Musterd-seed: or, the least measure of grace that is, or can be effectuall to salvation." (London: John Legatt, 1635—a reprint of a tract first distributed in the 1590s), p. 644.

6. Anthea Hume, *Edmund Spenser: Protestant Poet* (Cambridge: Cambridge University Press, 1984), p. 67.

7. For a discussion of the Bibles Spenser probably used, see Naseeb Shaheen, *Biblical References in "The Faerie Queene"* (Memphis, Tenn.: Memphis State University Press, 1976).

8. All biblical passages, unless otherwise noted, are taken from the *New Testament*, translated by Laurence Tomson (Geneva: Rowland Hall, 1560).

9. For detailed comparison of the way I Corinthians 13:4 reads in the various early English Bibles, see Charles Butterworth, *The Literary Lineage of the King James Bible 1340–1611* (Philadelphia: University of Pennsylvania Press, 1941), pp. 337–353.

10. Edgar Wind, *Pagan Mysteries in the Renaissance*, second edition (New York: W. W. Norton, 1969), p. 28ff.

11. *The Oxford English Dictionary*, Vol. II (Oxford: The Clarendon Press, 1961), p. 1094.

12. Calvin, *Sermons on St. Paul's Epistle to the Ephesians*, folio 237.

13. Calvin, *Sermons on St. Paul's Epistle to the Ephesians*, folios 235–237.

14. Calvin, *Sermons on St. Pauls' Epistles to Timothy and Titus*, p. 422.

15. *Ibid.*, p. 595.

16. Calvin, *Sermons of M. John Calvine upon the X. Commandmentes of the Lause*, translated by Iohn Harmar (London: Iohn Harison, 1579), folio 55.

17. For representative opinions in this debate, see Virgil Whitaker, *The Religious Basis of Spenser's Thought* (Stanford, Calif.: Stanford University Press, 1950), pp. 7–10, 19–21; William Nelson, *The Poetry of Edmund Spenser* (New York: Columbia University Press, 1963), p. 23; Peter Bayley, *Edmund Spenser: Prince of Poets* (London: Hutchinson, 1971), p. 52; Rosemund Tuve, *Allegorical Imagery* (Princeton, N. J.: Princeton University Press, 1966), p. 418n; James Boulger, *The Calvinist Temper in English Poetry*, (The Hague: Mouton Publishers, 1980), p. 150ff.; Hume, pp. 3–5; and especially John N. King, "Was Spenser a Puritan?" in *Spenser Studies* VI, ed. Patrick Cullen and Thomas P. Roche, Jr. (New York: AMS Press, 1985), 1–31.

18. Nicholas Tyacke, "Puritanism, Arminianism, and Counter-Revolution," in *The Origins of the English Civil War*, ed. by Conrad Russell (London: Macmillan, 1973), p. 128. Tyacke is quoted with approval by Dewey Wallace in *Puritans and Predestination* (p. 29). John N. King similarly speaks of "a formal consensus on the predestinarian theology of grace" during Queen Elizabeth's reign in "Was Spenser a Puritan?" (p. 4).

19. Calvin, *Sermons on St. Paul's Epistles to the Ephesians*, folio 235.

20. Humphrey Tonkin, "Courtesy Redefined," Chapter ix in *Spenser's Courteous Pastoral: Book VI of "The Faerie Queene"* (Oxford: Clarendon Press, 1972), pp. 258–280.

21. Richard Neuse, "Book VI as Conclusion to *The Faerie Queene*," *ELH*, 35 (1968), 329–353

22. For example, Kathleen Williams writes, in *Spenser's World of Glass: A Reading of "The Faerie Queene"* (Berkeley: University of California Press, 1966), pp. 201–202, "each of the virtues [in Spenser's six books] can be defined only by its legend, and one need not read far to realize that Spenser's courtesy has little enough to do with courtesy books but much to do with nature, providence, love, death and the generous exchanges of compassion and mutual respect among men."

23. Calvin, *Sermons on St. Paul's Epistle to the Ephesians*, folio 236.

24. Ronald Horton discusses the intertwining of Books V and VI in great detail in *The Unity of "The Faerie Queene"* (Athens: The University of Georgia Press, 1978), pp. 76–99 and 112–123. Several other critics have argued that Books V and VI form a complementary pair. See Maurice Evans, *Spenser's Anatomy of Heroism: A Commentary on "The Faerie Queene"* (Cambridge: Cambridge University Press, 1970), p. 209ff.; P. C. Bayley, "Order, Grace and Courtesy in Spenser's World," in *Patterns of Love and Courtesy: Essays in Memory of C. S. Lewis*, ed. John Lawlor (Evanston, Ill.: Northwestern University Press, 1966), pp. 182–189: Williams, pp. 192–195.

25. Calvin, *Sermons on St. Paul's Epistle to the Ephesians,* folio 236.

26. Maurice Evans, in *Spenser's Anatomy of Heroism*, makes a similar point: "Courtesy is designed to combat the range of evils which justice itself in part breeds but is powerless to quell" (p. 209).

27. Ronald Horton, in *The Unity of "The Faerie Queene,"* also sees the Mercilla episode as preparation for Book VI: "In complementing absolute justice with mercy, Spenser has prepared for his complementing of justice with courtesy, for one of the meanings of courtesy in contradistinction to justice is that of mercy as opposed to severity" (p. 119).

28. William Nestrick, "The Virtuous and Gentle Discipline of Gentlemen and Poets," in *Spenser: A Collection of Critical Essays*, ed. by Harry Berger, Jr. (Englewood-Cliffs, N. J.: Prentice-Hall, Inc., 1968), p. 141.

29. Calvin, *Sermons on St. Paul's Epistles to Timothy and Titus*, p. 423.

30. For discussions of the paradox of Calidore's being rewarded for his truancy, see Tonkin, p. 172; and Daniel Javitch, *Poetry and Courtliness in Renaissance England* (Princeton, N. J.: Princeton University Press, 1978), p. 147.

31. For a discussion of the paradoxes of Grace and their connection to Book VI, see James Nohrnberg, *The Analogy of "The Faerie Queene"* (Princeton, N. J.: Princeton University Press, 1976), pp. 698ff.

KENNETH BORRIS

"Diuelish Ceremonies": Allegorical Satire of Protestant Extremism in *The Faerie Queene* VI. viii. 31–51

A FTER DELECTABLE Serena becomes lost in a wilderness, rests, and falls asleep, "lasciuious" Savages discover her, and plan to sacrifice her to their deity, then eat "her dainty flesh" (VI. viii. 31–44).[1] But intrepid Sir Calepine arrives in the nick of time, disrupting their "diuelish ceremonies" and putting them to flight (VI. viii. 45–51). This sensational episode has often been discussed as a literalistic moral comment on perverted love, and more ingeniously by Donald Cheney as a self-reflexive study of abused Petrarchan metaphors.[2] But really it deals far more with, as he puts it, how ". . . the religious impulse can be perverted and made an expression of man's bestiality."[3] Though previous commentators have given very little consideration to abuse of religion in the episode, that is indeed the central issue: the story of Serena and the Savages has a theologico-ecclesiastical context thoroughly developed in both diction and imagery. As James Nohrnberg's more recent work points out, this episode should certainly be investigated for allegorized religious satire.[4] Allegory and such satire appear through most of Spenser's oeuvre, and the Savages story explicitly deals with and comments on "religion" (VI. viii. 43).

Although Nohrnberg's brief discussion of the episode claims that it satirizes Roman Catholicism, thorough examination of textual details establishes that the target is instead the Puritans and similar Separatists in particular, and the radical Reformation in general. For the anti-Catholicism of Book I to be thus superseded in the Legend of Courtesy, published six years later in 1596, is not surprising, but topically up to date. By 1593, the government and many adherents of the Church of England found Protestant extremists more threatening than Roman Catholics; controversy over Martin Marprelate's satires favouring Puritanism had recently erupted; and anti-Puritan satire was becoming very fashionable.[5] Certainly the episode has moral implications about perversion of love, as previous critics have noted; but this study attends to its further, hitherto unexplored allegorical treatment of contemporary Protestant religious tensions. Spenser handles this subject, we find, in a way befitting the Elizabethan view of satire as an interpretively "dark" genre, and also his conception of Courtesy. Indeed, he associates Courtesy's antagonist the Blatant Beast with religious controversy, so that such material is certainly relevant to Courtesy as presented in Book VI (VI.xii.23–25).

Before considering the satiric allegory, we must briefly establish some practical terms of reference for the complex Elizabethan religious scene. In the 1590s, the important Protestant radicals in England were the Puritans and the similar but more extreme Separatists of the Brownist and Barrowist kind.[6] Both groups severely criticized organizational and liturgical aspects of the Church of England from much the same standpoint; but, whereas Puritans conceded that the English church was at least potentially acceptable, Separatists abandoned it altogether.[7] This distinction between them was not very meaningful to the Puritans' opponents, who suspected Puritans of being nascent or disguised Separatists, and condemned Puritans also as "schismatics" and "sectaries."[8] English controversialists opposed to radical Protestant religious groups tended to lump them together polemically as vicious, ignorant, unstable, and rebellious malcontents. Satirists like Thomas Nashe and even serious religious writers like John Whitgift and Richard Bancroft, who were successive Archbishops of Canterbury, associated Puritans not only with Separatists but also with the ancient Donatists, medieval Cathars, and notorious continental Anabaptists of Münster.[9]

In assessing the Savages episode for satire of radical Protestants, it would thus be wrong to distinguish absolutely between at least the main Puritan and Separatist groups, as if one were the target to the exclusion of the other. Religious polemics of the period and satire and allegory themselves tend to have a free-ranging, very general focus that invalidates exclusive or minute distinctions. For convenience, then, those who accepted the English ecclesiastical *status quo* in most respects will be pragmatically termed "Anglican" in this study henceforth; those who desired substantial further reform to purge away vestiges of Roman Catholic usage and make the English church conform to norms that they perceived in Scripture will be grouped together as "Puritans" in a broad sense including the "impatient Puritans," as a leading ecclesiastical historian calls the Separatists.[10] They will only be referred to as such where more precise definition seems genuinely useful. It should be taken for granted that the episode's direct anti-Puritan satire applies more broadly to all those whom Anglicans would have tended to consider sectarian or non-conforming Protestants. The episode satirizes fundamental doctrines and attitudes shared by both Puritans and Separatists, attacking both as a threat to the established church and indirectly attacking Protestant extremism as a general threat.

THE SAVAGES AS MOCK PURITANS

The cannibalistic "saluage nation" that torments Serena lives in a "wylde" place on thievish "spoile" gained through "stealth," serving its "owne necessities with others need" by seizing "the labours of poore men" and neighbours rather than constructively practising "any trade" (VI. viii.35). The Savages' selfish, stealthy barbarism reflects stereotypical Puritan traits often described in analogous ways: ignorance, secrecy, plotting, animosity toward culture, learning, and universities, and avaricious, uncharitable usage of others.[11] Anti-Puritans perceived them as subversive, fault-finding, hypocritical perfectionists or "precisians" who practised upon the common people for monetary and other gains. The Savages' exploitation of neighbours and "poore men," even to the extent of devouring them (VI. viii.36), likewise satirizes Puritans as flouters of the Christian principle "love thy neighbour." Spenser's portrait of the barbaric and impure Savages extravagantly mocks the Puritans' sense of themselves as a holier or purer people, dismissing it as wanton hypocrisy.

Marston's explicit denigration of Puritans in the second satire
of his *Certaine Satyres* immediately clarifies Spenser's allegory:

> . . . with his bait of purity
> He bit me sore in deepest vsury.
> No Iew, no Turke, would vse a Christian
> So inhumanely as this Puritan.
> *Diomedes* Iades were not so bestiall
> As this seeming-saint, vile Canniball.
> Take heede ô world, take heede aduisedly
> Of these same damned Anthropophagy.
> I had rather be within a Harpies clawes
> Then trust my selfe in their deuouring iawes.
> Who all confusion to the world would bring
> Vnder the forme of their new discipline.[12]

For Marston the typical Puritan is an uncharitable hypocrite
who would reduce civilization to "all confusion" and, like
Spenser, Marston uses barbaric cannibalism as a metaphoric
means of emphasis. Both implicitly associate Puritans with the
"workers of iniquitie" who "eat vp" God's people (Ps. 14:4,
53:4),[13] or with inhuman uncharity amounting to such
"monstrous cruelty gainst course of kynde" (VI.viii.36). Since
the Savages "deuoure" those brought to them "by errour" also
(VI.viii.36), Spenser may further imply that Puritan doctrine
consumes its adherents' and converts' humanity.

The Savages' thievery is not only a satiric inversion of charity, but satirizes Puritans' supposed heresy, hypocrisy, or ava-
rice. As in the parable of the good shepherd, in which "false
prophetes" are represented as "theeues" (John 10:8 and Geneva
gloss), thievery was a standard metaphor for the nature of
heresy, and it had just been extensively exploited in the anti-
Marprelate tracts against the Puritan programme.[14] In current
Christian usage, "thief" could also refer to a religious hypocrite
who seeks gain from others' losses with seeming piety, much as
the Savages prey upon those "brought by . . . wreckfull wynde"
(VI.viii. 36).[15] Since Puritan extremists wished to eliminate
church livings and university endowments, Bancroft discusses
them as the "new theeues" who "vnder . . . shewe of religion"
would "deuoure Christes patrimony," typifying them as hypo-
critically plundering heretics.[16]

Not surprisingly, then, these "theeues" (VI.viii.43) are associated with "errour" from the outset (VI.viii.36), and demonstrate a propensity to err theologically as soon as they discover Serena. Spenser produces scathing dramatic irony by first revealing that the Savages find Serena merely "by fortune blynde," and then informing us that the Savages accredit this to "heauenly grace" (VI.viii.36–37). They too readily invoke a special providence that furthers their aims, absurdly identifying God's purposes with their own. Puritans were often rebuked for sanctimony of this order; Spenser's characterization of them elsewhere as "that vngracious crew which faines demurest grace" closely approximates the satire here.[17] The Savages' subsequent resolve to sacrifice Serena "Vnto their God" "since by grace of God she there was sent" further sharpens the satire (VI.viii.38). Over-confidence in interpreting God's will can have unfortunate consequences, Spenser implies, as Richard Hooker warns about Protestant extremism in his Preface to the *Laws of Ecclesiastical Polity*: " . . . false opinions, touching the will of God to have things done, are wont to bring forth mighty and violent practices. . . ."[18]

After finding Serena, the Savages engage in a travesty of ecclesiastical deliberation, and it satirizes the Puritan pro-gramme for reformed church government, which was a main issue in the controversy between Anglicans and Puritans. The Savages jointly consider various nasty fates for Serena, but finally determine with "one consent" to sacrifice her, then "feed" on her "flesh" (VI.viii.37–38). Their procedure for religious decision-making, which crucially depends on lay opinion and "consent," satirizes Puritan doctrines of collective religious consultation and increased lay authority. Anglicans, on the other hand, were committed to regal and episcopal authority in church affairs, and rejected Puritan proposals for ecclesiastical re-organization as an irresponsible recourse to "mere popularity" that would jeopardize the order of the English church.[19] In deciding what to do with Serena, the Savages' popular assembly can only devise horrific alternatives; Spenser acidly comments that their "best aduizement was of bad" (VI.viii.38). Some Savages subsequently plan to rape Serena, much as Puritans were often said to be secretly or otherwise "lasciuious," so that the membership seems utterly unfit to exercise religious authority. However, the Savages' Priest intervenes to maintain Serena's purity for the imminent sacrifice. With sardonic verbal irony the narrator comments that "religion held euen theeues in measure": the Savages' religious order is such that it saves Serena from rape only to murder and serve her for dinner. Clearly, the Savages lack any kind of responsible guidance in religious government, such as the Anglican episcopal hierarchy claimed to provide the laity; the Savages' proto-Puritan notions of ecclesiastical organization create a bizarre religious debacle.

Aside from organizational matters, the forms of religious observance and ritual were the other main area of contention between Puritans and Anglicans in Spenser's time, and the Savages' ceremonies satirically reflect the Puritan position. They conduct alfresco religious rites with an altar "Of few greene turfes," and an *ad hoc* liturgy of "the peoples voyce/ Confused," presumably as their spirit moves them (VI.viii.44–46). Theirs is very much a folk movement as was the Puritans' and especially the Separatists', and so remote from sixteenth-century "papist" norms that the satiric allegory obviously relates to the opposite end of the ecclesiastical spectrum, and cannot reasonably apply to Roman Catholicism. The case against the episode being anti-Catholic satire can rest on this point alone, though numerous others could also be emphasized in this regard. The Savages' liturgical practices satirize Puritan emphases on simplicity and spontaneity of worship, and various details have pointed significance.

The whole ceremony takes place in a "little groue," and English Bibles of the period translate a Hebrew term referring to a goddess or idol as "grove," so that the word had strong associations of idolatrous apostasy in religious applications.[20] Those who "go a whoring" after false gods in Canaan, for example, are said to place their "idoles" in "groues" that should be obliterated (Exod. 34: 12–15 and Geneva gloss). Spenser's choice of venue for the Savages' service satirically links Puritan worship with reprehensible dereliction of the true faith. The grove is also apt for the satire because Puritans were notorious for gathering in unauthorized assemblies or conventicles, sometimes in such places.[21]

Within the grove the Savages make preparations for their religious service that are very perfunctory, as conservative Anglicans perceived Puritan arrangements:

Of few greene turfes an altar soone they fayned,
And deckt it all with flowres, which they nigh hand obtayned.
(VI.viii.44)

Somewhat more than a few turfs would be in order, presumably; "greene" may imply insufficient development here.[22]
That the altar is "fayned," playing on the senses "fashioned"
and "counterfeited," suggests hypocrisy; a genuine altar could
contrastingly signify piety.[23] Obtaining flowers "nigh hand,"
the Savages do not trouble to go further afield to cull the best.
Their general lack of effort may well imply that Puritan simplicity of worship, which excluded permanent accessories like
stone altars and all aesthetic, precious adornments, amounts to
laxity and disrespect. This whole devotional project seems
ephemeral, just as the turfs make an insubstantial altar, and
flowers often signified evanescence.

The Savages' subsequent ceremonies amount to pan-
demonium, implicitly mocking Puritans' more spontaneous
modes of worship and the reputedly erratic, uneducated character of the membership:

Then gan the bagpypes and the hornes to shrill,
And shrieke aloud, that with the peoples voyce
Confused, did the ayre with terror fill,
And made the wood to tremble at the noyce:
The whyles she wayld, the more they did reioyce.
(VI.viii.46)

Spenser comparably refers to Puritans elsewhere as "our late
[i.e., recent] too nice foles" who "saie that theare is nothinge in
the semelye forme and Comelye order of the Churche."[24] The
Savages' unseemly religious chaos mocks Puritan opposition to
set liturgical forms and ceremonial features that Anglicans considered essential for orderly worship. Like Nashe in The Vnfortvnate Traveller, Anglicans worried that Protestant extremists'
more free approach to religious observance was a scandalous
breach of decorum that would precipitate more general dis-
orders.[25] The satire involves allusions to the well-known
Pauline dictum that those lacking charity are "as sounding
brasse" (1 Cor. 13:1); and also, since Serena is to be sacrificed,
the votaries of Moloch who made a cacophany during human

sacrifices to conceal the victims' screams.[26] The Savages' use of "bagpipes," typical instruments of the sixteenth-century English countryside, satirically links Puritans with simple-minded rusticity, as was common in anti-Puritan satire, and perhaps symbolically with the carnal appetites.[27] The phrase "The peoples voyce / Confused" implies doctrinal confusion, punning on "judgement of the people" as a sense of "voyce."[28] Opponents of Puritans often likewise accused them of creating or threatening social and ecclesiastical disorder, as in Marston's attack, and that is the satiric point of the Savages' chaotic rite.

The role of the Savages' Priest itself satirizes the Puritan leadership. While suggesting arrogance, his self-coronation, in which he "doth compose" himself "a garland" "Of finest flowres" (VI.viii.39), may ironically mock the Puritan emphasis on sermon composition, because garnering flowers for a garland was a standard metaphor for literary composition, and it was applied to sermons.[29] Whitgift claims that heavy Puritan preaching requirements rushed their preachers into producing inferior work.[30] Likewise, this Priest composes his garland only just before he is to officiate; "finest" would be verbal irony. The related "holy fire" that he prepares here is probably an ironic metaphor for the Puritan zeal or fanaticism notorious to Anglicans. The Priest's further "full busie care" to "wash" "His bloudy vessels" (VI.viii.39) characterizes him as a "precisian" of sorts, and ironically recalls God's rejection of blood sacrifice in Isaiah: "What haue I to do with the multitude of your sacrifices . . . ? . . . And when you shal stretch out your hands, I wil hide mine eyes from you: and thogh ye make manie prayers, I wil not heare: *for* your hands are ful of blood. Wash you, make you cleane: . . . cease to do euil" (Isa. 1:11–16). The Savages' Priest is implicated in blood too, but attends not to cleansing his hands, which familiarly signified purification or innocence, but rather to cleansing mere appurtenances of ritual. The biblical context condemns hypocrisy, and that is very much to the purpose of an anti-Puritan satirist. The Priest's cleansing of sacrificial vessels is an outward show only, without any relation to inner purity, much as Puritans were accused of being perversely obsessed with the nature of liturgical arrangements at the expense of spiritual substance.

Spenser further satirizes the Puritan priesthood when, as the Savages set Serena before the altar, their Priest approaches

with "naked armes" "and murdrous knife well whet," mutter-
ing "a certaine secret charme, / With other diuelish ceremonies"
(VI.viii.45). What vestments were appropriate for the priesthood was a main point of controversy between Anglicans and
Puritans; that this Priest has "naked armes" seems a *reductio ad
absurdum* of Puritan insistence on simplicity of ecclesiastical
vesture. Anglican authorities prescribed "a comely surplice
with sleeves" as the properly decorous and respectful garb for a
priest celebrating Holy Communion.[31] Puritans objected that
the surplice was a papist abomination, and its sleeves volup-
tuously expansive; the Savages' Priest presides over this unholy
communion with no sleeves at all.[32] His impulse to *"mutter"* a
"secret charme" (emphasis mine) may mock the reputedly
secretive nature of Puritanism, or imply that Puritan doctrine is
contentiously conceived, subversive mumbo-jumbo. In any
case the Priest's wielding of the whetted, murderous knife over
Serena well expresses the unconscionably divisive spirit of
Puritanism as Anglicans saw it; in this context, the epithet
"diuelish" describing his ceremonies is probably a macaronic
pun on *divellere* (Lat.; "to rend asunder, divide forcibly"), just as
the ritual would climax with Serena's dismemberment. Her
plight figures forth the jeopardy of English ecclesiastical unity;
the Anglican anti-Puritan tracts, whether satiric or theological,
frequently claim that the Church of England, sometimes in a
semi-personified aspect, is torn asunder by Puritanism.[33]

SERENA AS THE ENGLISH CHURCH

As the object of the Savages' divisive purposes, Serena corresponds in part to the Church of England itself. Various aspects
of Serena's portrayal confirm this allegory by figuratively align-
ing her with Solomon's betrothed in the Song of Songs, who
was commonly understood to represent the Church; with Una;
and with Truth. The Savages are to Serena rather as Sansloy is
to Una; they contrast significantly with Una's Satyres. However, Serena does not merely duplicate Una, for Serena's role
implies considerably more ecclesiastical criticism than her counterpart's in Book I. Moreover, whereas Una is purely singular
as the Church and Truth were supposed to be unitary, Spenser
emphasizes how Serena is threatened by bloody division to

condemn radical Protestantism as a sectarian, socially disruptive threat to the existence of the English church.

The Savages first "spoile" Serena "of her iewels deare" and "all her rich array" (VI.viii.41), and this denuding of Serena associates the Puritan impulse to impose plain simplicity on the Church of England with gross and disrespectful breach of legitimate decorum. Separatists, for example, were extreme in their advocacy of abolishing ecclesiastical music, ceremony, liturgy, and property.[34] Again we see that the episode attacks Protestant extremism rather than "papist" practices; because divestment of rich attributes is clearly negative here, Roman Catholicism cannot be the satiric target of the episode. Herbert's "The British Church," Donne's "Satire III," and his sonnet "Show me deare Christ, thy spouse, so bright and cleare" comparably epitomize the Puritan church as a woman improperly plain, denuded, or dishevelled; for Herbert, as for Spenser here, the Church of England is like a woman fitly dressed, occupying a decorous mean between "Romish" frippery and Genevan undress.

As Nohrnberg observes, Serena's exposure contrasts with Duessa's in the corresponding canto of Book I (I.viii.46–49);[35] but the contrast becomes more intelligible from our present perspective. Duessa's ugliness allegorically corresponds to falsity, and Serena's beauty to Truth, as with Una. Una's knights find that Duessa laid bare is loathsome, as an analogy for exposure of religious "falshood" (I.viii.49); conversely, the Savages find that Serena's splendid array only veils yet more marvellous beauty. This implicitly mocks Puritan extremists, who believed that the Church of England was a "great whore" or "painted harlot" like Duessa, whose inner ugliness they could readily strip bare as in biblical prophecy.[36] Ironically, Serena's true lineaments are yet more glorious than outward appearance suggests; and the Savages' action against her reveals their own concupiscent impurity as would-be rapists (VI.viii.41–43). Their role as wanton unveilers of beauty contrasts with that of Una's knights, like Sansloy's behaviour. Having "snatcht" away Una's veil, Sansloy facing revelation can only conceive ways of subjecting it to "his pleasures vilde" (I.vi. 3–5); having torn away Serena's clothes, the Savages gaze at "daintie parts" "which mote not be *prophan'd* of common eyes," as Spenser significantly states, only to devise "beastly pleasure" (VI.viii.43; emphasis mine). As Nohrnberg states about Sansloy, the allegory here "implies that fanaticism, like the attempt to seize the ark or penetrate the Temple, is a kind of rape of the truth."[37] This scene relates Puritanism to travesty of spiritual love, wanton abuse of Scripture and theology, and concupiscence, which was often described in terms of sexual lust. "Each" Savage's jealousy of the rest here allegorically implies prideful desire to monopolize Truth or revelation.

Whereas the Savages are anything but pure, naked Serena seems "all faire" and without "spot" like Solomon's spouse (Song. Sol. 4:7). Spenser catachrestically inventories Serena's "daintie parts" as in the blazons of contemporary love poetry (VI.viii.42); but the development recalls passages of the Song,[38] which Spenser translated according to Ponsonby's preface to *Complaints*, and to which Spenser knowledgeably alludes in, for example, *Epithalamion*, and his description of Belphoebe in Book II. Serena's "bellie white and clere" rears itself "like an Altar"; the bride's is like "an *heape* of wheat compassed about with lilies" (Song. Sol. 7:2; emphasis mine). That Serena's "goodly thighes" have "glorie" "Like a triumphall Arch" on which "The spoiles of Princes hang'd, which were in battel won," more obviously parallels the Song's comparison of the bride's neck to "the towre of Dauid buylt for defense: a thousand shields hang therein, *and* all the targates of the strong men" (Song. Sol. 4:4).

Spenser does not associate Serena with Solomon's bride simply to express her fundamental purity. The allusion points to Serena's ecclesiastical significance because the bride was commonly held to body forth the Church.[39] The bride and denuded Serena even undergo similar difficulties, for the bride is "founde," "smote," and "wounded" by men who strip off her "vaile" (Song. Sol. 5:7). Following age-old precedent, the Geneva gloss interprets the bride's plight as the torment inflicted on the Church by "false teachers," and that is the general religious meaning of Serena's predicament.

Spenser's handling of the allusion further implies that the Church ultimately triumphs. Description of Serena's thighs as a triumphal Arch hung with princes' spoils wittily combines scriptural and classical traditions to emphasize victorious "glorie." To celebrate a major military victory, the ancient Romans hung the *porta triumphalis* with spoils won in battle;

and Roman triumphal monuments characteristically feature
sculptured trophies. Spenser's simile allegorically depicts the
Church in a monumental aspect attesting to success in difficult
spiritual battles, against false doctrine, for example, so that the
satire is counterbalanced by an optimistic perspective on ultimate ecclesiastical destiny.[40]

Contrary to modern expectations, such a reading of this
naked lady would not have seemed inappropriate in Spenser's
time. Partly on the precedent of the Song of Solomon, it was
not unusual for women, naked or otherwise, to bear ecclesiastical meanings in poetry; nudity was an attribute of Truth and
could express purity, as here; and sexual love often figured
spiritual love.[41] An account of Belphoebe's legs similar to that
of Serena's likewise expresses spiritual purity:

> Like two faire marble pillours they were seene,
> Which doe the temple of the Gods support,
> Whom all the people decke with girlands greene,
> And honour in their festiuall resort . . .
>
> (II.iii.28)

The phrase "marble pillours" alludes to the Song, relating Belphoebe to Christ (5:15); her pure body is God's "temple" as
biblically prescribed (1 Cor. 6:19). Serena's physique is sacro-
sanct too; even her "bellie" is "like an Altar." The context
expresses her inner purity, as with Belphoebe, and also Serena's
ecclesiastical significance. The passage has sexual appeal and
implications apt to the fable of the distressed maiden molested
by primitives, but also wittily befits the satiric allegory, in
which Serena's physical allure makes her a provocative epitome
of what is spiritually desirable. Donne comparably mixes
eroticism and religion in concluding his sonnet "Show me deare
Christ": the womanly Church is "most trew, and pleasing" to
God "When she'is embrac'd and open to most men."[42]

An additional, broader analogy involving Serena further
attests to her ecclesiastical meaning in the episode. Both Una
and Serena are remarkable beauties discovered by a rustic rabble
that respond to them in a thoroughly religious manner. Analogous ecclesiastically resonant similes about lost sheep are applied to both when threatened in these contexts (I.vi.10;
VI.viii.36). But Serena's reception by this "saluage nation"

(VI.viii.35) satirically travesties Una's by the Satyrs' "*saluage nation*" (I.vi.arg.; also I.vi.11). When Sansloy sexually molests Una, the Satyrs' "rablement" appears, whereupon he flees (I.vi.5–8). At first Una fears them; but they naturally "worship" her in their naive way, and celebrate her advent with "semblance glad" (I.vi.9–13). Likewise, the Savages instantly respond to Serena with a religious "gladful glee" (VI.viii.37); but their celebrations in her honour involve lust like Sansloy's and cannibalistic devotions. Whereas the Satyrs "present" Una "vnto their God" as a social introduction (I.vi.15–16), the Savages "present" Serena "Vnto their God" as a blood sacrifice (VI.viii.38). Reverently "astonied" at Una's unveiled "beautie," the Satyrs "fall . . . flat" before her, or dance joyous "as birdes" (I.vi.9–16); but the Savages tear off Serena's clothes, ogle her beauteous body, "vpstart," and "flocke" "like . . . flies" (VI.viii.40–43). The Satyrs kindly endeavour to allay Una's initial fear (I.vi.9–11); but the Savages "reioyce" in Serena's terror (VI.viii.46). The Savages are, in effect, the Satyrs run amok, gone perverse, or driven by the impulses of Sansloy.

The broad relationship between the Satyrs and Savages episodes has a twofold application to the satiric allegory. The Satyrs themselves basically express a reverence and rudimentary spiritual aptitude deemed inherent in human nature even without nurture, just as they are simple folk who respond to Una with spontaneous joy. As the Savages travesty Una's Satyrs, so Spenser satirically implies that Puritanism involves not only simple-minded ignorance but downright perversion of natural reverence toward the Church and religion. The presence of the Salvage Man in Book VI implicitly rebukes the Savages and all that they represent, for he innately responds to Serena with "gentle vsage" (VI.vi.10–11, v.1–10). Second, Serena herself is allegorically a counterpart of Una in this episode. Indeed, as with Una earlier, ecclesiastical motifs of Solomon's bride and even those of Truth and of the Woman Clothed with the Sun are associated with Serena.[43] Tormented "Where none is nigh to heare, that will her rew" (VI.viii.40), Serena figuratively corresponds to forsaken Truth, like Una when distressed or abandoned; and also, we will find, to Truth as Time's Daughter at the end of the episode. The paradoxical theme of errant Truth, in which Truth wanders, expressing implication in some error, also applies to Serena as to Una; Serena only falls into the

Savages' hands through wandering (VI.viii.31–35). Moreover, Serena's flight into the wilderness that introduces the episode and her exile and torment there recall the well-known, similar predicament of the sun-clad Woman in Revelation: an *ecclesia* figure whose tribulations were related to the trials and testing of the Church and of Truth (Rev. 12).

Having noted Serena's ecclesiastical role and basic correspondence with Una here, we can now consider certain significant differences in Spenser's portrayal of these characters that reveal Serena's individuality as an allegorical creation. Whereas Una is emphatically indivisible as her name implies, Serena is not so priveleged by definition, and threatened with imminent dismemberment. Ecclesiastical satire in this episode is not just one-sided, for Serena's conduct is less favourable than Una's, implying that the English church bears some responsibility for divisions among its members.

That the Savages scheme to carve up Serena allegorically identifies Puritans with dangerous ecclesiastical division, just as their opponents labelled them destructive schismatics. According to a biblically-derived metaphor that was in very common use, the Church is like one human body uniting various different bodily members into a corporate entity of harmonious, complementary parts.[44] Modifying this anthropomorphic concept of Church unity, Spenser satirizes Protestant radicals here as cannibalistic butchers who would dismember that body, so to speak, and thereby fatten their cause. Such polemical variations of the biblical concept were stock-in-trade for anti-sectarian controversy, though Spenser's version here is extraordinarily witty and subtle.[45]

The curiously thorough nature of the Savages' divisive scheme indeed implies such ulteriority of poetic purpose. When the Savages strip Serena as a prelude to their religious butchery, they even "teare" "all her rich array" "in peeces," "And of the pray each one a part doth beare" (VI.viii.41). The tearing asunder of garments was a traditional metaphor for ecclesiastical schism that apologists for the English church had used against dissenting Protestants. This sartorial trope derives from John 19:23–24, in which the soldiers at the Crucifixion divide up Christ's robes but not his seamless coat; ecclesiastical unity came to be associated with whole clothing, and divisions with clothing torn apart.[46] Spenser renders this metaphor in terms of

Serena, so that it is integral to the romantic narrative, as befits complex allegory, but still has an allegorically ecclesiastical application. Swift likewise handles this metaphoric convention creatively in *A Tale of a Tub*, which expresses Christian religious history through a fable of garments; Jack, the representative of Protestant radicalism, tears up his coat as an analogue for the consequences of excessive zeal to reform Christianity.[47] Here, each Savage takes a different "part" of Serena's garments for himself, implying that radical Protestants divide or exploit the English church merely for petty greed or ambition or, as Nashe complains in *Pierce Penilesse*, to gratify individual eccentricities: " . . . we diuide Christs garment amongst vs in so many peeces, and of the vesture of saluation make some of vs Babies and apes coats, others straight trusses and Diuells breeches. . . . "[48]

Moreover, the Savages' intended sacrifice of Serena would travesty eucharistic Communion in a way that specifically satirizes ecclesiastical divisions:

Vnto their God they would her sacrifize,
Whose share, her guiltlesse bloud they would present,
But of her dainty flesh they did deuize
To make a common feast, and feed with gurmandize.
(VI.viii.38)

Especially Anglicans emphasized that Holy Communion celebrates Christian unity by incorporating partakers of the sacrament into Christ's body, as in the eucharistic liturgy of the Book of Common Prayer:

. . . God, we most heartily thank thee, for that thou dost vouchsafe to feed us . . . with the spiritual food of the most precious body and blood of thy Son . . . : and dost assure us thereby of thy favour and goodness toward us, and that we be very members incorporate in thy mystical body, which is the blessed company of all faithful people . . .: we now most humbly beseech thee, O heavenly Father, so to assist us with thy grace, that we may continue in that holy fellowship, and do all such good works as thou hast prepared for us. . . . [49]

The Savages' perversely consecrated "common feast" would be an antithetical collation of discrete "morsels" (VI.viii.39) destroying Serena's bodily whole, and "common" in the ironic senses "mean, vulgar" and "polluted, unholy" as well as "shared."[50] Their sacrificial rite of division, which is the central feature of the episode, is an absolute travesty of Anglican Holy Communion with its emphasis on religious unity for the greater good of all.

Spenser's spectacle of the Savages plotting and preparing their sacrificial butchery is very telling, then, as theological satire. Whatever those whom the Savages body forth think of their own religious intentions and beliefs, their enterprise wholly opposes the Christian spirit, Spenser implies, because it violates Christian unity in Christ. By contrast with the Anglican view of the eucharist, Puritans understood it as "the holy banquet of God's elect"; the satiric allegory devastatingly inverts the Puritans' own estimation of themselves as a Christian fellowship, by implying that their sectarianism makes the English church itself their unholy feast, thus tearing apart and consuming, in effect, the corporate union of its members.[51]

Una, of course, never faces such a ghastly fate; Serena figures forth the Church of England as acutely threatened by Protestant sectarian division. Her behaviour appropriately expresses how the English church contributes to its predicament, so that Serena's portrayal implies more ecclesiastical criticism than Una's. Serena only finds herself at the Savages' mercy because, having wandered in the wilderness like wayward Truth, she decides "to rest" there, oblivious to potential perils: ". . . in *Morpheus* bosome safe she lay, / Fearlesse of ought that mote her peace molest . . ." (VI.viii.34). For Spenser, "*Morpheus*" is virtually a byword for complacency and negligence; "drowned deepe / In drowsie fit" "of nothing he takes keepe" (I.i.40), and Serena is likewise "drowned in the depth of sleepe" (VI.viii.36).[52] On account of broad biblical precedent, sleep often expressed spiritual laxity and insensibility in religious contexts. Serena at last awakes only to find that concupiscent, religiously perverse Savages are free to have their way with her; allegorically, the general complacency of the English church has left it so vulnerable to Protestant sectaries that even vigilance and reform can hardly amend the situation.[53] Serena's comparison here to "a sheepe astray" further implies that the ecclesiastical situation urgently requires dedicated pastoral care, so to speak, and the help of a good shepherd.[54] Serena's name itself is almost derisive in this context, for it has connotations of complacent tranquility ironically incommensurate with her plight here.

However, this critique of the Church of England does not evince any serious or new disaffection, for Spenser had long criticized it in more stringent, explicit ways.[55] Shortcomings of the English church concerned many committed Anglicans, partly because any perceived deficiencies strengthened Protestant extremists' popular appeal. That is clearly Spenser's position in this episode, since we are encouraged to sympathize strongly with Serena against the outrageous Savages, and her characterization has many favourable features, such as her affinities with Solomon's bride. Moreover, Spenser handles Serena's rescue in a way that ascribes substantial importance to the exercise of right reason in ecclesiastical affairs, and that view was conservatively Anglican.

Sir Calepine and the Light of Nature

The knight who saves Serena from the Savages at last is significantly the namesake of Calepine the lexicographer, whose dictionary was an essential compendium of learning, and thus something of an epitome of rational discipline. Moreover, "Calepine" itself can imply καλλι ("beautiful") and ἐπιγῶ, ("thinking") here, so that it may well involve tribute to learning and intellect in that way also.[56] Serena's dependence on Calepine's intervention indicates that the threat of Protestant extremism must be dispelled by the energetic activity of those possessing the wisdom and knowledge that Anglicans claimed the radicals lacked, and thus able to correct or expose their errors, and care for the English church appropriately.

There is a basic opposition in the episode between, on the one hand, the barbaric, impassioned Savages and, on the other, Sir Calepine the representative of cultivated, enlightened civility. While this antithesis reflects the general involvement of civilized values in Courtesy, it applies pointedly to the theological situation. What enables Calepine to save Serena is an expressively illuminated perception of the Savages' proceeding against her:

There by th'vncertaine glims of starry night,
And by the twinkling of their sacred fire,
He mote perceiue a litle dawning sight
Of all, which there was doing in that quire. . . .

(VI. viii. 48)

Thus Calepine "thrusts into the thickest throng" and prevents
the sacrifice, "euen as" the Priest's knife "adowne descends"
(VI. viii. 49). Calepine's saving comprehension of the situation
literally depends on starlight; it symbolizes right reason here as
a "sacred" force of enlightenment capable of apt ecclesiastical
use, perhaps in conjunction with illuminating grace. Stars could
comparably signify intellectual exploration, the soul, and
God.[57] Hooker, the contemporary theologian who most fully
articulated the religious role of reason for the English church,
likewise praises the "'star of reason and learning,'" maintaining
that God "hath sent out these lights whereof we are capable,
even as so many sparkles resembling the bright fountain from
which they rise"; by them we "learn in many things what the
will of God is."[58] However "vncertaine" or imperfectly possessed, such human mental illumination provides a "litle dawning sight," as it were, without which all that Serena stands for
would be lost (VI. viii. 48). Not only the word "sacred" attests
to the theological aspect of the context, but also "quire," which
bears its religious meanings ironically here.

   This allegorical application of right reason accords with Anglican emphases of the time. Whereas Puritans considered
Scripture a general code for religion and life to be followed
according to their understanding of its precepts, Anglicans limited scriptural authority to theological doctrine and essentials of
worship, thus making more room for reason and human authority in religious matters.[59] Hooker, for example, complains
of Protestant extremism that "the 'star of reason and learning'
. . . , beginneth no otherwise to be thought of than if it were an
unlucky comet"; "as if the way to be ripe in faith were to be raw
in wit and judgement; as if Reason were an enemy unto
Religion."[60] The way that Calepine intervenes in conjunction
with the image of partial but "sacred" illumination expresses
how rational capacities or "light of nature," in the once-
common phrase, have a limited but nevertheless crucial and
legitimate role in religious affairs.

Human limitations are further acknowledged by some criticism implicit in Calepine's role, as with Serena's. That he sleeps while, unknown to him, Serena's life is being threatened implies some negligence (VI.viii.47), and Anglican controversial works comparably rebuked complacency on the part of those capable of defending the English church intellectually and otherwise.[61] Though Calepine at last reassumes his arms and, allegorically, moral armament or "the whole armour of God" (Eph. 6:11) on Serena's behalf, Spenser rather critically ascribes Calepine's intervention not to his own vigilance or capacities but to mere "chaunce" and "fortune" (VI.viii.46). However, his arrival is presented as such a perfect coincidence as to seem serendipitously providential; presumably Spenser avoids claiming special grace outright here in pointed contrast with the Savages and stereotypical Puritan (VI.viii.37–38). In a subtle, aptly enigmatic and challenging manner, divine grace may be seen to supplement human capacities in Serena's deliverance and, allegorically, in that of the English church.

Calepine's antagonists the Savages contrastingly relate to the intellectual darkness of the passions and the Cimmerians. Unruly elements of society were often figuratively identified with the passions in contemporary literature, and portrayal of the passions as a rabble or "saluage nation" like the Savages (VI.viii.35) was an allegorical convention that Spenser uses, for instance, in the Alma episode (II.ix.13–17; II.xi.1).[62] Religious radicals were commonly charged with being deluded or taken over by their passions, and that is the allegorical implication here.[63] Those bodied forth by the Savages generally share in a night of the mind, in effect, which is reflected by the episode's temporal setting of the "euening" and "night" (VI.viii.36, 48): often figuratively the time of "error blind" in *The Faerie Queene* (III.iv.55–60).[64] Making "nightly rode / Into their neighbours borders" (VI.viii.35), the Savages seem wholly nocturnal; they even perform their ghoulish rites at "Euentyde," "the time ordayned / for such a dismall deed" as Serena's sacrifice (VI.viii.44). A related aspect of the satire is that the Savages have Cimmerian traits such as nightly thievery, habituation to darkness, cannibalism, and the practice of human sacrifice. The Cimmerians, a heavily mythologized historical people, were proverbial types of "monstrous Error" and that "hellish horrour, Ignorance" because they supposedly lived in perpetual darkness.[65] Because Puritans were closely associated

with moroseness, it is not inappropriate that, in Homeric tradition, the Cimmerians inhabited "a certain gloomy region
in the neighbourhood of Hades."[66] The Savages, dwelling in
a darkness which is figuratively that of the benighted mind,
are countered by Calepine as an allegorical agent of enlightened
intellect.

The epistemological aspect of the religious satire is further
expressed by the Savages' sacrificial procedure. That the specific
form of their rite is perversely scriptural implicitly mocks Puritan claims to possess genuine religious knowledge through
ostensibly strict construction of Scripture.[67] Serena's sacrifice
would precisely conform to Old Testament injunctions concerning that of livestock. The Hebrews are forbidden to consume blood (Deut. 12:23); for sacrificial offerings, the blood
must be dedicated to God and the flesh eaten (Deut. 12:27). The
Savages likewise intend to present "their God" Serena's "
bloud," then eat "her dainty flesh" (VI. viii.38). Because the
Savages' rite is strictly Hebraic in form yet involves human
sacrifice, the satire implies that Puritans practise a bizarrely
undisciplined kind of adherence to the scriptural letter, of which
Anglican controversialists often accused them.[68] If biblical for-
mulas and prescriptions are implemented without wisdom or
forbearance, Spenser indicates, not heavenly but barbaric consequences can follow. In effect, the situation portrays Puritans
as sacrificers of the English church to their eccentric perception
of Scripture; they are allegorically shown to make that church a
further sacrifice to a vengefully conceived god of quasi-Levitical
rigour, whereas Christ claimed to do away with the need for
sacrifices "once for all" with his "one offring" (Heb. 10:14).

The allegory counters perceived religious excess or savagery
with Calepine's kind of rational discipline apparently augmented by grace. His violent dispersal of the Savages befits the
chivalric vehicle of the poem (VI. viii.49), but expresses more
civilized amendment, just as Spenser's practical statements
about resolution of religious tensions are indeed mild: religion
should not be "impressed . . . with terrour and sharpe penalties
as now is the mannour, but rather deliuered and intymated with
mildenes and gentlenes."[69]

The conclusion appropriately places the ecclesiastical situation in terms of Christian doctrine about the extent to which
Truth can be known in this world. The action resolves into a

quite static scene open to an emblematic kind of reading, yet
clearly derived from Ariosto's amusing treatment of naked
Olympia's ashamed response to Orlando when he saves her
from becoming a sacrifice to Proteus and the Sea-Orc in the
Orlando furioso, Canto Eleven. As often before in *The Faerie
Queene*, Spenser conceitfully reconstructs light Ariostan materials through adjustments in detail, focus, and allusive reference
so that they become profoundly allegorical. Unlike Olympia,
bound to a tree in daylight, naked Serena sits by the altar
obscured by darkness. Armoured Calepine endeavours to comfort her; but again unlike Olympia, Serena remains absolutely
mute and withdrawn. So, whereas Orlando perceives the pro-
spective victim's identity readily on approaching, along with
her physical attractions, Calepine can perceive little of Serena,
and does not even realize that he has now found his true love,
for whom he has long searched (VI.iv.40, VI.viii.46–47):

> . . . all that night to him vnknowen she past.
> But day, that doth discouer bad and good,
> Ensewing, made her knowen to him at last:
> The end whereof Ile keepe vntill another cast.
>
> (VI.viii.51)

Here Spenser adapts the once-familiar iconography of *Veritas
Filia Temporis*, naked Truth appearing to the day,[70] to end the
story in a way befitting the religious allegory. Truth, bodied
forth as a nude maiden, was shown being led by Time from a
dark place into daylight, thus overcoming Calumny, Hypocrisy, and other oppressors. Likewise, the passing of time brings
day that will reveal naked Serena, obscured by night, to her true
devotee Calepine. In sixteenth-century religious applications, as
here, the allegory of Truth as Time's Daughter implied that
Truth is presently veiled in darkness so that falsehood besets
this life, but will be revealed in full on the last day.

Spenser's phrasing as well as imagery alludes to this concept.
Night is a traditional metaphor for the insufficiency of human
awareness that implicates everyone in error, as at III.iv.55–60;
and the approach of "day" here figuratively corresponds to the
coming of the Day of Judgement when full revelation biblically
occurs. Then, there will be "one perpetuall Day for the Righteous,"[71] for " . . . the Lord . . . wil lighten things that are hid in

darknes, and make the counsels of the hearts manifest . . . " (1
Cor. 4:5). Spenser significantly describes the coming "day" here
as one that will make things "knowen . . . *at last*" and "*discouer
bad and good*" (VI.viii.51, emphasis mine), so that it can function
effectively as a figurative counterpart for the last "day" of
revelation. The way in which Serena will be fully "knowen" "at
last" when "day" comes, dispelling night, expresses how the
Church and Truth too will be fully revealed "at last," dispelling
all darkness of human ignorance and error. In orthodox Christian doctrine, the Church is largely "vnknowen" (VI.viii.51)
during this life;[72] that is what gives scope for religious contentions such as the allegory deals with, so that this conclusion
is consummately apt for the allegorical subject.

The episode thus ends with a scene especially rich in implication: dealing with a naked lady and her lover, it has an archly
human aspect, and yet hovers on the brink of an anagogical
revelation. Serena seems dishearteningly distant from Calepine
insofar as he does not know he has regained her; yet she is with
him, naked, and only veiled from him by passing darkness. Our
quizzical sense of this literal situation, at once plangent and
comic, further applies to the allegory. From a theological viewpoint Calepine's state here rather optimistically displays the
human relation to spiritual realities in this world. Epistemological near-darkness obscures what is most spiritually desirable,
which thus seems dishearteningly inaccessible even though
actually present, palpably real, and due to be revealed in the
fullness of time.[73] The allegorical implications are very close to
Arthur's complaint about the darkness of the mortal state and
the ultimate coming of "day" which will reveal divine "Truth"
(III.iv.55–60).

In any case, Calepine must remain for the time being "in
heaùie armes" yearning for Serena's presence of which he is
ignorant (VI.viii.46–51); but his unfulfilled and thus active condition, through which Serena possesses the protection that she
requires, is the one which heralds the ultimate knowledge of
"day" when Serena will stand fully revealed, clothed only, as it
were, with the sun (VI.viii.51). The final scene of their story
significantly contrasts with their initial tryst, the complacent
idyllicism of which is all too vulnerable to disruption
(VI.iii.20). Donne is not far from Spenser here in questioning
whether Christ's spouse the Church "Dwells . . . with us," or if

"like adventuring knights" we must "First travaile . . . to seeke" her "and then make love"; and also in emphasizing that those who would reach religious "Truth" must strive to reach and then abide with her.[74] The ending of the Serena-Calepine story effectively rounds off the episode's exploration of Church affairs by constituting a profound epitome of the conditions of human religious knowledge.

Courtesy and the Satiric Allegory

Though we now conceive courtesy as a matter of etiquette pertaining to a secular social context, the religious implications of the Savages episode befit Courtesy as presented in Book VI, and as it was often conceived in the Middle Ages and Renaissance. Although Jonson's identification of the Blatant Beast with Puritans is too narrow, it rightly implies that what Spenser presents as antagonistic to the Courtesy of Book VI includes religious views and disputes like those associated with the Protestant extremists, and also establishes that Spenser's Legend of Courtesy was open to at least semi-religious interpretation in his own day.[75] Besides being understood as a general code of polite behaviour related to etiquette, affability, and humanity, courtesy could be seen to have theological implications relating to Christian charity, humility, pity, mercy, and salvation. This view is reflected in various medieval writings both English and continental, including Chaucer and Langland, so that we can even find courtesy attributed pre-eminently to Christ and God the Father, and heaven portrayed as the realm of perfect courtesy.[76] The affinities of courtesy with love, and that part of Christian charity which consists in love of neighbours, made it susceptible to religious application by writers for whom that was congenial. Jonson's perspective reflects this conception of courtesy and social conduct that had quite wide medieval currency and continued to have some force in the Renaissance.[77]

In Book VI, Spenser presents Courtesy as a very broad, socially-oriented virtue, that yet has strongly developed theological implications reflecting Christian views of courtesy. The nature of Spenser's Courtesy is still controversial, for most criticism finds it purely secular though somehow comprehensive too; but recent critics increasingly acknowledge the book's theological aspect, and the finding of this study help confirm the legitimacy of that.[78] Calidore's expulsion of the Beast from "the sacred Church" itself (VI.xii.23–25) is a most clear indication that the quest of Courtesy impinges on spiritual goals. Courtesy can do so insofar as it is involved in actions that can be considered external manifestations of Christian spirituality,[79] and also by counteracting fractious ecclesiastical tendencies, which greatly concerned many. When the Church disintegrates into bitterly acrimonious factions, even common courtesy, as distinct from Spenser's, may be seen to have considerable spiritual significance. Not unlike the *Pearl*-poet, Spenser finds this social virtue applicable not to society in a secular sense only, but rather as it further involves the Church as the society of Christians with God and each other.

The Savages episode allegorically amplifies this aspect of Book VI that surfaces at the end (VI.xii.23–25). Spenser's Courtesy includes the "friendly offices that bynde" society into a creative whole (VI.x.23; VI.i.1); Protestant extremists were considered the main threat to English social and spiritual order in the 1590s, and the religious tensions among Protestants eventually issued in the civil war. Moreover, Puritans were roundly blamed for the vicious tone of Protestant religious controversy:

In that they, like "vipers," with slanderous reports sting men privily, they be not the generation of Christ, but of Christ's adversary, howsoever otherwise they seem to be godly and zealous: for Christ doth will them "to love their enemies, to pray for them that curse them . . . ;" so far would he have them from backbiting and slandering of . . . such as profess the name of Christ with them.[80]

The impulses of courtesy counter such alleged attitudes of Puritans, and their reputed failings like hatred, pride, and lack of charity in a general sense. For example, courtesy had long been opposed to pride, or accredited with the power to subdue it, and linked with humility; heresy and schismatic movements stem partly from pride according to theological tradition and, for Anglicans, Puritanism did too.[81] Likewise, when the Priest prepares to sacrifice Serena for the divisive feast travestying Communion, he does so high-handedly, as it were, by raising his knife "aloft" in a gesture implying self-righteous arrogance, just as height often does in Spenser's writings.[82] The satire here plays off the Anglican liturgy of Communion, which contrarily stipulates that partakers do not trust in their "own righteousness," and kneel to signify their humility.[83] The religious content of the episode befits various aspects of courtesy as it could be conceived in Spenser's time, applying its powers and nature to amendment of religious contentions.

Besides attacking Puritan doctrines and stereotypical traits and, by extension, other nonconforming Protestant groups of the period, the satiric allegory applies more generally to the nature of appropriate religious commitment. Whether Spenser's religious affinities can best be described as Puritan or Anglican has been often disputed; but, whatever his earlier sympathies, Spenser totally rejects Puritanism and the whole radical Reformation in Book VI. When the Blatant Beast attacks "the sacred Church," Spenser finds "Images" "goodly" and monastic vows "holy," in full conservative reaction against felt Protestant excesses (VI.xi.24–25). The Beast's befouling of "Altars" and robbery of "the Chancell" further evidence Spenser's religious conservatism, because Puritans objected to altars and chancels, and even to favourable use of the term "altar."[84] The Savages episode, with its high valuation of intellect and mockery of ecclesiastical simplicity, Puritan modes of spirituality, and strict construction of Scripture, constitutes a general critique of Christian options that is given particular focus in the contemporary situation of the English church. The implicit attitudinal criticisms of Serena, Calepine, and the Savages contribute significantly to this aspect of the satire. Most of all, the allegory warns how religiosity can make a travesty of religion: the Savages are certainly pious, but carry piety to inhuman extremes.

Whatever may be thought of its religious perspectives, the Savages episode is not repellently dreary, sour, or heavy-handed, unlike most works of the period that engage in religious controversy. The satire, involving cannibalism and human sacrifice, is extravagant in some senses; but the treatment is brisk, deft, and urbane enough to remain engagingly witty. The fantastic hyperbole of the satire involves such intellectual and literary energy and élan that there is little if any sense of mere vilification, or "saluagesse sans finesse." The episode displays Dryden's rightly favoured value in satire of the fine "stroke that separates the head from the body, and leaves it standing in its place," instead of "slovenly" butchering the satiric target, as the Savages would deal with Serena.[85]

Spenser mainly achieves this effect by using complex allegory to express the satire in an unobtrusive manner, so that the meaning is richly conveyed through a story that is entertaining and memorable in its own right.[86] This sustains humourous appeal, preventing the satire from becoming crabbed, grating, narrow, or homiletic. Instead, Spenser demonstrates imaginative ability to produce thoughtful laughter through effective, blackly comic expression of the serious issues at stake, which are thoroughly probed, but by entertainingly indirect means. Our experience of the provocative story is caught up with its significance; the images continually inform, leaven, and amplify our sense of the allegorical implications, which in turn sharpen and deepen our appreciation of the story's features. This study has necessarily been confined to exposition of the anti-Puritan satire. But in many ways the Savages episode seems the uniquely successful Anglican riposte to Martin Marprelate's current satires favouring Puritanism,[87] and indeed one of the finer religious satires in English. Though highly reticent, Spenser's satire here could not display to such an extent the economy, apparent ease, verve, and fluid mobility of satire at best, if more obviously presented. Its subtlety may further reflect Spenser's sensitivity to matters of religious decorum, or unwillingness to become personally embroiled in controversy or charges of abusive excess in religious criticism.[88]

However, the satiric allegory would certainly have been much more accessible in Spenser's time than it is now, because even his less well-informed readers would have been far more attuned to its biblical, ecclesiastical, and other idioms than we are today. For example, the images of stripped and torn clothing in this explicitly religious context could well have seemed interpretive give-aways to readers like Nashe, who used them himself for satire, or Hooker. Moreover, it was a generic expectation that satire would be expressed in a covert, interpretively challenging manner as Spenser does here, and this assumption might well have made literate Elizabethans more sensitive or open to that kind of material than we tend to be today.[89]

Nevertheless, the Savages episode is an exceptionally subtle allegory by any standard, and that accords with the nature of

Book VI itself. As allegory is more complex and problematic in this book of *The Faerie Queene*, so the literal dimension of Book VI is more self-sufficient, and appears less allegorically resonant. Hence the narrative has tended to preoccupy critical attention to the detriment of our understanding of the allegory; some even claim that Book VI has little allegorical potential.[90] But the images and language of the Savages episode display profound mastery of narrative as a vehicle for allegory, because Spenser economically achieves remarkable density of allegorical reference without compromising the integrity of the literal sense, as naive or simple allegory does, in the least. The narrative itself sustains and rewards attention, and yet also intriguingly conveys allegorical and other kinds of significance relating to civility, Courtesy, sexual behaviour, and religious affairs in both topical and timeless senses. While Spenser's previous works contain such writing also, it is most sustained in Book VI, in which there is much material of this depth and quality that would highly repay thorough investigation, and yet still remains relatively unexplored by comparison with the initial books of *The Faerie Queene*.

McGill University   ·

Notes

1. *The Works of Edmund Spenser: A Variorum Edition,* ed. Edwin Greenlaw *et al.*, 11 vols. (Baltimore, Md: Johns Hopkins University Press, 1932–57), Vol. VI. All subsequent Spenser citations are from this edition, hereafter cited as *Variorum*. For all works cited, orthography is rendered as in the editions used, except that contractions and abbreviations are silently expanded.

I am indebted to Alastair Fowler for discussion of an early version of this study, but take full responsibility for its conclusions and present form. Completion was assisted by a Senior Fellowship at the Centre for Reformation and Renaissance Studies at Victoria University in the University of Toronto.

2. *Spenser's Image of Nature: Wild Man and Shepherd in "The Faerie Queene,"* Yale Studies in English, Vol. 161 (New Haven, Conn.: Yale University Press, 1966), pp. 103–116. One of the more provocative moral accounts is Harry Berger, Jr., "A Secret Discipline: *The Faerie Queene,* Book VI", in *Form and Convention in the Poetry of Edmund Spenser: Selected Papers from the English Institute,* ed. William Nelson (New York: Columbia University Press, 1961), pp. 53–60. Waldo F. McNeir canvasses all extant source attributions and rightly finds them both tenuous and interpretively fruitless ("The Sacrifice of Serena: *The Faerie Queene,* VI.viii. 31–51," *Festschrift für Edgar Mertner,* ed.

Bernhard Fabian and Ulrich Suerbaum [Munich: Wilhelm Fink, 1969], pp. 117–156). As James Nohrnberg argues, Spenser tends to reconstruct romance materials for allegorical purposes (*The Analogy of "The Faerie Queene"* [Princeton, N.J.: Princeton University Press, 1976]). However, McNeir unconvincingly claims that the Savages represent "the Irish Celts" and their priest is "a Druid" (p. 143). Cannibalism and human sacrifice are the Savages' most substantial connections with Celts, and McNeir admits that neither practice is particularly Celtic (p. 141). The Savages, having no distinctively Irish characteristics like mantles and glibs, contrast with the Irish in Spenser's *A Vewe of the Present State of Irelande, Variorum,* X, 97–131.

3. Cheney, p. 116.

4. Nohrnberg, pp. 712–716.

5. William P. Holden, *Anti-Puritan Satire, 1572–1642* (1954; rpt. Hamden, Conn.: Archon, 1968); see also J. E. Neale, *Elizabeth I and Her Parliaments, 1584–1601,* Vol. II of *Elizabeth I and Her Parliaments* (London: Jonathan Cape, 1957), pp. 296–297.

6. By that time, the Anabaptists and Family of Love had become insignificant. Essential guides to the general Elizabethan religious scene are Horton Davies, *From Cranmer to Hooker, 1534–1603,* Vol. I of *Worship and Theology in England* (Princeton, N.J.: Princeton University Press, 1970); and Peter Milward, *Religious Controversies of the Elizabethan Age: A Survey of Printed Sources* (Lincoln, Neb.: University of Nebraska Press, 1977). See further Marshall M. Knappen, *Tudor Puritanism: A Chapter in the History of Idealism* (1939; rpt. Gloucester, Mass.: Peter Smith, 1963); Patrick Collinson, *The Elizabethan Puritan Movement* (London: Jonathan Cape, 1967); B. R. White, *The English Separatist Tradition: From the Marian Martyrs to the Pilgrim Fathers,* Oxford Theological Monographs (Oxford: Clarendon Press, 1971); and Michael R. Watts, *From the Reformation to the French Revolution,* Vol. I of *The Dissenters* (Oxford: Clarendon Press, 1978).

7. See, *e.g.,* Davies, pp. 325–327.

8. For application of such terms to Puritans, see, *e.g.,* Thomas Cooper, *An Admonition to the People of England,* ed. Edward Arber, The English Scholar's Library, No. 15 (Birmingham, 1882), pp. 94–98, 175–179; John Whitgift, *The Defence of the Answer to the Admonition, Against the Reply of Thomas Cartwright,* in *The Works of John Whitgift,* ed. Rev. John Ayre, Parker Society, Vols. 46–48 (Cambridge, 1851), I, 4–7, 77, 170, II, 60, III, 4; Richard Bancroft, *A Svrvay of the Pretended Holy Discipline,* The English Experience, No. 428 (London, 1593); facsim. rpt. New York: Da Capo Press, 1972), pp. 311, 363, 427; and his *Davngerovs Positions and Proceedings,* The English Experience, No. 427 (London, 1593; facsim. rpt. New York: Da Capo Press, 1972), pp. 121, 127, 183.

9. *Cf.* Whitgift, in *Works,* I, 23, 46, 51, 55, 57, 76–139; Bancroft, *Svrvay,* pp. 316, 360, 427; Thomas Nashe, *The Retvrne of Pasqvill,* in *The Works of Thomas Nashe,* ed. Ronald B. McKerrow, corr. F. P. Wilson, 5 vols. (Oxford: Basil Blackwell, 1958), I, 74–79, 85, 94; *The Vnfortvnate Traveller,* in *Works,* II, 232–239; and *An Almond for a Parrat* (doubtfully Nashe's), in *Works,* III, 366–367.

10. Davies, p. 44. My terminological usage reflects discussions in Davies, Knappen, pp. 487–493, and Virgil K. Whitaker, *The Religious Basis of Spenser's*

Thought, still unsurpassed in its field (1950; rpt. New York: Gordian, 1966), pp. 8–9).

11. See, *e.g.*, Nashe, *The Anatomie of Absvrditie*, in *Works*, I, 20–23; *Retvrne of Pasqvill*, in *Works*, I, 73, 78, 84–85; *The First Parte of Pasqvils Apologie*, in *Works*, I, 131; *Christs Teares over Ierusalem*, in *Works*, II, 117–118; *Vnfortvnate Traveller*, in *Works*, II, 234–235; *Almond* (doubtfully Nashe's), in *Works*, III, 350–351, 359, 372; Cooper, pp. 27–30; Bancroft, *Davngerovs Positions*, pp. 3, 44, 133, 183; *Svrvay*, pp. 154, 206, 345, 399; and Whitgift, in *Works*, I, 33, 141, II, 422, 495, III, 1, 6, 511. See further Holden, pp. 40–42; and Clarence M. Webster, "Swift's *Tale of a Tub* Compared with Earlier Satires of the Puritans," *PMLA*, 47 (1932), 171–176.

12. *The Poems of John Marston*, ed. Arnold Davenport (Liverpool: Liverpool University Press, 1961), p. 74, ll. 71–82.

13. *The Geneva Bible*, introd. Lloyd E. Berry (Geneva, 1560; facsim. rpt. Madison: University of Wisconsin Press, 1969), from which all subsequent biblical citations derive. Spenser's writings evince most familiarity with this version (Naseeb Shaheen, *Biblical References in "The Faerie Queene"* [Memphis, Tenn.: Memphis State University Press, 1977], Ch. 3).

14. In Thomas Wilson's *A Christian Dictionarie*, *e.g.*, a figurative sense of "Theefe" is "A Seducer, which by corrupt glosses, and false interpretations, steales from the Church of God the true meaning and doctrine of the Scripture; so spoyling soules, as theeues spoyle mens bodies" (3rd ed. [London, 1622], STC 25788, *s.v.* "Theefe" 3, sig. 2V5ᵃ). This metaphor was often used for abusive purposes or mockery in religious controversy. For Puritans as thieves in various senses, see Whitgift, in *Works*, III, 395; Nashe, *Retvrne of Pasqvill*, in *Works*, I, 73, 93; *Pasqvils Apologie*, in *Works*, I, 109, 114; *Christs Teares*, in *Works*, II, 117–118; and *Vnfortvnate Traveller*, in *Works*, II, 238.

15. See, *e.g.*, Wilson, *s.v.* "Theefe" 4, sig. 2V5ᵃ.

16. *Svrvay*, Ch. 21; quoting p. 248.

17. VII.vii.35; see Holden, p. 91, and Whitaker, p. 69. That context refers to exerting "force contrary to . . . face," and thus turns to indict Puritan hypocrisy.

18. Pref., viii.6; in *The Works of . . . Richard Hooker*, ed. Rev. John Keble, 6th ed., 3 vols. (Oxford, 1874), I. 182.

19. See, *e.g.*, Bancroft, *Davngerovs Positions*, pp. 44, 121; *Svrvay*, passim; and Whitgift, in *Works*, II, 280, 398, III, 211–273.

20. *O. E. D. s.v.* "grove" sb. 2a.

21. *Cf.* this episode with the arrest of about 56 Separatists at a religious service in a wood near London in 1593 (White, pp. 94–95); likewise, Calepine interrupts the Savages' rite and forcibly disciplines them. See further Bancroft, *Davngerovs Positions*, p. 66; Whitgift, in *Works*, I, 102–108; and Nashe, *Anatomie*, in *Works*, I, 22.

22. *Cf. O. E. D. s.v.* "green" A adj. II 8a (figurative).

23. *O. E. D. s.v.* "feign" v. I. 1, II 10: on altar symbolism, see, *e.g.*, Valeriano Bolzani, *Hieroglyphica*, ed. Stephen Orgel, The Renaissance and the Gods, 17 (Lyons, 1602; facsim. rpt. New York: Garland, 1976), pp. 526–527.

24. *Vewe*, *Variorum*, X, 223.

25. For comparison of Anglican, Puritan, and Separatist worship, see Davies, Chs. 5–9. Separatist services reportedly involved a spokesman extemporizing

while the congregation groaned, sobbed, or sighed. *Cf.* Nashe, *Vnfortvnate Traveller*, in *Works*, II, 232–241.

26. See, *e.g.*, 2 Kings 23:10 and Geneva gloss, and Jeremiah 19:4–7. Sir John Harington comparably mocks Separatists in his *A New Discourse of a Stale Subject, Called the Metamorphosis of Ajax*, ed. Elizabeth Story Donno (London: Routledge and Kegan Paul, 1962), pp. 149–152.

27. See *O. E. D. s.v.* "bagpipe" sb. 1, and Edward A. Block, "Chaucer's Millers and Their Bagpipes," *Speculum*, 29 (1954), 239–243. The Savages' bagpipes do not imply a Celtic context, despite the *Variorum* editor (VI, 234). *Cf.* Nashe, *Retvrne of Pasqvill*, in *Works*, I, 90: preachers favourable to Puritanism are "fitte to preach vppon . . . Bagpipes," for " . . . they are so full of ventositie. . . . "

28. *O. E. D. s.v.* "voice" sb. I 3.

29. For the classical background, see Thomas G. Rosenmeyer, *The Green Cabinet: Theocritus and the European Pastoral Lyric* (Berkeley: University of California Press, 1969), p. 269. *Cf.* Nashe, *Retvrne of Pasqvill*, in *Works*, I, 83, 88.

30. In *Works*, III, 1–2, 6, 38. For Anglican mockery of Puritan preaching, see, *e.g.*, Nashe, *Retvrne of Pasqvill*, in *Works*, I, 73, 84–87, 90; *Vnfortvnate Traveller*, in *Works*, II, 234; and Whitgift, in *Works*, II, 75, III, 340.

31. Archbishop Parker's "Advertisements" of 1566, in Henry Gee and William John Hardy, comps., *Documents Illustrative of English Church History* (London: Macmillan, 1910), p. 471.

32. *Cf.* the Puritan Anthony Gilby's indictment of "The great wide sleeued gowne commaunded to the Ministers, and the charge to weare those sleeues vpon the armes" as "Grosse pointes of poperie" still remaining in the English church (*A Pleasavnt Dialogve* [London, 1581], STC 11888, sig. M3ᵃ). In John Lyly's *Pappe with an Hatchet*, an anti-Marprelate tract against Puritanism, a Puritan sympathizer remarks that "a good honest Minister, with a cloake hauing sleeues" is "a knaue"; those favouring Puritanism have "a sleeuelesse conscience, and thinke it no good doctrine, which is not preached with the cloak cast ouer each shoulder like a rippier" (in *The Complete Works of John Lyly*, ed. R. Warwick Bond [Oxford: Clarendon Press, 1902], III, 405). See further J. H. Primus, *The Vestments Controversy: An Historical Study of the Earliest Tensions within the Church of England in the Reigns of Edward VI and Elizabeth* (Kampen, Neth.: J. H. Kok, 1960).

33. See, *e.g.*, Cooper, pp. 96, 98; Whitgift, in *Works*, I, 9, 170, II, 60, 471, III, 4, 9; Nashe, *Pasqvils Apologie*, in *Works*, I, 132; and *Vnfortvnate Traveller*, in *Works*, II, 235.

34. Henry Barrow, a leading Separatist, even advocated destruction of all English buildings ever used for Roman Catholic worship (*A Brief Discoverie of the False Church*, in *The Writings of Henry Barrow, 1587–1590*, ed. Leland H. Carlson, Elizabethan Nonconformist Texts, Vol. 3 [London: George Allen and Unwin, 1962], pp. 468, 478).

35. Nohrnberg, pp. 713–716.

36. Isaiah 3:17–24; Revelation 17:16, 18:2–24. *Cf.* Barrow, p. 671.

37. Nohrnberg, p. 208.

38. First noted by Israel Baroway, "The Imagery of Spenser and the *Song of Songs*," *Journal of English and Germanic Philology*, 33 (1934), 35–36. However, from the standpoint of this present study, we can fully account for the presence and function of the allusion, which has not hitherto been possible.

39. As in *e.g.*, the prefatory argument for the Song in the Geneva Bible. See further Stanley Stewart, *The Enclosed Garden: The Tradition and the Image in Seventeenth-Century Poetry* (Madison: University of Wisconsin Press, 1966); George L. Scheper, "Reformation Attitudes toward Allegory and the Song of Songs," *PMLA*, 89 (1974), 551–562; and John N. King, "The Godly Woman in Elizabethan Iconography," *Renaissance Quarterly*, 38 (1985), 41–84.

40. *Cf.* the concepts of the Church Triumphant and Church Militant; thus the Church was quite commonly conceived in a triumphal or martial aspect. In the allegorized Song, *e.g.*, the bride in her role as the Church is "terrible as an armie with banners" and finds peace in Christ's eyes when she is "a walle" and her "breastes *are* as towres" (6:9, 8:10). *Cf.* Nashe's anti-Puritan martial account of the English church in *Retvrne of Pasqvill*, *Works*, I, 90–91.

41. See Scheper passim, and Stewart likewise; on nudity, purity, and Truth, see Erwin Panofsky, *Studies in Iconology: Humanistic Themes in the Art of the Renaissance* (New York: Oxford University Press, 1939), pp 155–157.

42. *The Divine Poems,* ed. Helen Gardner, 2nd ed. (Oxford: Clarendon Press, 1978), p. 15.

43. On these motifs and Una, see Nohrnberg, pp. 207–215, and John Erskine Hankins, *Source and Meaning in Spenser's Allegory: A Study of "The Faerie Queene"* (Oxford: Clarendon Press, 1971), pp. 207–215; for their Elizabethan currency, see King, *passim*.

44. As, *e.g.*, 1 Corinthians 12:12–31, Ephesians 1:22–23, 4:15–16; see further Leonard Barkan, *Nature's Work of Art: The Human Body as Image of the World* (New Haven, Conn.: Yale University Press, 1975), Index, *s.v.* "Christianity: and the Church."

45. *Cf.* Hooker's appeal to Puritans in *Laws*, Pref., ix. 3, in *Works*, I, 194: "Far more comfort it were for us . . . to be joined with you in bands of indissoluble love and amity, to live as if our persons being many our souls were but one, rather than in such dismembered sort to spend our few and wretched days in . . . wearisome contentions. . . . " See further Nashe, *Pasqvils Apologie*, in *Works*, I, 132; Cooper, p. 98; Whitgift, in *Works*, I, 9, 386, II, 426, 471, 546 (in some cases quoting Cartwright); and Bancroft, *Svrvay*, pp. 97, 123, 148, 222–223.

46. See Davies, p. 29; and Angus Fletcher, *Allegory: Theory of a Symbolic Mode* (Ithaca, N. Y.: Cornell University Press, 1964), p. 110, n. 62. Thus Nashe's anti-Marprelate tract of 1590, *Pasqvils Apologie*, exclaims against Protestant extremists that ". . . the garment of Christ is torne in peeces . . . " (*Works*, I, 114), as *Almond,* doubtfully attributed to Nashe, does also (*Works*, III, 346). *Cf.* Sir John Harington, "Of Christs cote," in *The Letters and Epigrams of Sir John Harington,* ed. Norman Egbert McClure (Philadelphia: University of Pennsylvania Press, 1930), pp. 308–309.

47. See Phillip Harth, *Swift and Anglican Rationalism: The Religious Background of "A Tale of A Tub"* (Chicago, Ill.: University of Chicago Press, 1961), pp. 13–19; and Elias J. Chiasson, "Swift's Clothes Philosophy in the *Tale* and Hooker's Concept of Law," *Studies in Philology*, 59 (1962), 64–82.

48. *Works,* I, 172.

49. An alternate prayer for reading after distribution of the eucharist; in *Liturgical Services: Liturgies and Occasional Forms of Prayer Set Forth in the Reign of Queen Elizabeth*, ed. Rev. William Keatinge Clay, Parker Society, Vol. 30 (Cambridge, 1847), pp. 195–196. See further Davies, pp. 63, 284.

50. Cf. *O. E. D. s.v.* "common" adj. II 14, II 15, and I 1, respectively.
51. Quoting Davies, p. 284. *Cf.* Whitgift mocking Thomas Cartwright, a leading Puritan, for ostensibly conceiving the eucharist in "gross imagination" as "an earthly and terrestrial supper" (*Works*, III, 91); and Marston satirizing Puritans for celebrating the eucharist "As slouenly, as carelesse Courtiers slup / Their mutton gruell" (*The Scourge of Villanie*, ii. 92–96; *Poems*, p. 109). Furthermore, even theologians used cannibalism for satiric purposes relating to the eucharist, as Nohrnberg shows (pp. 712–713), so that such an interpretive line for the Savages episode is reasonable by sixteenth-century standards. (However, Nohrnberg further asserts mistakenly that, because the doctrine of the Real Presence was sometimes satirized as cannibalism, the Savages episode is specifically anti-papist. Since Lutherans and many Anglicans shared that doctrine, the satire could not be narrowly anti-papist even if it were aimed at the Real Presence as Nohrnberg claims. Nor can we accept his related claim that the Savages' rite refers to Roman Catholic reservation of the cup. The Savages' Priest would partake only of "dainty flesh" (VI.viii.38), whereas the Catholic priesthood consumed both eucharistic Blood and Flesh. The Savages' travesty of communion does not satirize Roman Catholicism, but rather Protestant extremists' disruption of English ecclesiastical unity, which Holy Communion epitomized for Anglicans.)
52. That Serena is "in *Morpheus* bosome" further plays wittily on biblical phraseology. Christ was said to be "in the bosome of the Father," meaning " . . . he is most deare, and straictly ioyned to his Father . . . " (John 1:18 and Geneva gloss); the phrase "in Abraham's bosom" referred to being in a heavenly state (Luke 16:22 and Geneva glosses). But the Church of England, Spenser implies, is merely in that of Morpheus. See further Wilson, *s.v.* "In the bosome of the Father" and "Abrahams bosome," sigs. E5[b]–E6[a].
53. *Cf.* the sleep and waking of the lion in *Mother Hubberds Tale*, which has analogous political implications (11. 951–1384); waking commonly figured vigilant activity (*e.g.*, *O. E. D. s.v.* "wake" v. I 4b).
54. *Cf.* the parables of the good shepherd (John 10:1–18) and lost sheep (Matthew 18:11–14); pastoral images and themes were often used for ecclesiastical comment, reflecting such usage in the Bible. See Helen Cooper, *Pastoral: Mediaeval into Renaissance* (Totowa, N. J.: Rowman and Littlefield, 1977), Index, *s.v.* "Good Shepherd," "priest as shepherd," and "ecclesiastical comment." In Spenser's "July" eclogue, *e.g.*, the need for ecclesiastical care and vigilance is pastorally expressed by the injunction that shepherds must be "well eyed, as *Argus* was," rather than complacent or sleepy (11. 153–154).
55. For a compact summary, see Holden, pp. 86–93.
56. Alastair Fowler pointed out the relevance of these implications of "Calepine" to my account of Calepine's role in this episode; cf. also ἐπίνοια, "thought."
57. See, *e.g.*, Valeriano, pp. 475–478.
58. *Laws*, III.viii.4, III.viii.9, and I.viii.3, respectively: in *Works*, I, 365, 370, 227.
59. Davies, pp. 51–56. On the relation of this to Spenser and anti-Puritan satire, see Whitaker, pp. 35–41, 53–54, 68–70; and Holden, pp. 24–25, 40.
60. *Laws*, III.viii.4; in *Works*, I, 365–366.
61. *Cf.* Nashe, *Christs Teares*, in *Works*, II, 122–129.
62. The figurative association between social troublemakers and the passions

themselves originates from Plato's *Republic*, Bk. IX; see further Barkan, Ch. 2. The passions are depicted as a savage rabble in, *e.g.*, Ariosto's *Orlando furioso*, Tasso's *Gerusalemme liberata*, and Palingenio's *Zodiacus Vitae*.
63. See, *e.g.*, Hooker, *Laws*, Pref., iii. 10–14; in *Works*, I, 150–155.
64. The association of night with error, obtuseness, and ignorance is a metaphoric convention of both secular and religious Renaissance writings, with many classical and biblical precedents.
65. *The Teares of the Muses*, ll. 253–266; likewise Thomas Cooper, *Dictionarium Historicum*, in *Thesaurus Linguae Romanae et Britannicae*, English Linguistics 1500–1800, No. 200 (1565; facsim. rpt. Menston, U.K.: Scolar, 1969), *s.v.* "Cimmerii." This was a humanist commonplace used satirically by Erasmus, Du Bartas, Du Bellay, Marston, and others, and so Spenser could well afford to use it subtly here. For Cimmerian practices of nightly thieving and barbaric plundering of adjacent countries analogous to the Savages' activities (VI.viii.35–36), see Robert Estienne, *Thesaurus Linguae Latinae*, I (Basel, 1740), *s.v.* "Cimmerii"; Diodorus Siculus, *e.g.*, further associates them with cannibalism and human sacrifice (*Library of History*, V. 32). Moreover, the Savages gather around Serena when she is "in *Morpheus* bosome" (VI.viii.34–35); Ovid locates Morpheus and the House of Sleep in the Cimmerians' country (*Metamorphoses*, XI. 592–632); and Spenser would have known this passage well because it is the main source for his House of Sleep (I.i.39–41). DeWitt T. Starnes and Ernest William Talbert argue for Spenser's familiarity with Estienne on the Cimmerians in *Classical Myth and Legend in Renaissance Dictionaries: A Study of Renaissance Dictionaries in Their Relation to the Classical Learning of Contemporary English Writers* (Chapel Hill: University of North Carolina Press, 1955), pp. 76–77; see further Henry Gibbons Lotspeich, *Classical Mythology in the Poetry of Edmund Spenser* (1932; rpt. New York: Octagon, 1965), p. 47.
66. As Strabo, *The Geography*, tr. Horace Leonard Jones, I (New York: G. P. Putnam's Sons, 1917), I.2.9 (p. 75).
67. McNeir usefully canvasses Celtic and other sacrificial practices (pp. 127–128, 137–143); but they are clearly dissimilar to the Savages', which Spenser took from the Bible. The pseudo-biblical nature of their rite helps confirm the allegorically Christian focus of the episode.
68. For anti-Puritan accusations of wresting Scripture, doctrinal legalism, over-emphasis of the Old Testament, and reviving "the Synagogue," see Thomas Cooper, pp. 124–126; Whitgift, in *Works*, I, 58–61; and Bancroft, *Svrvay*, pp. 83–87, 162–164, 190, 396–416.
69. *Vewe*, *Variorum*, X, 221.
70. See Fritz Saxl, "Veritas Filia Temporis," in *Philosophy and History: Essays Presented to Ernst Cassirer*, ed. Raymond Klibansky and H. J. Paton (Oxford: Clarendon Press, 1936), pp. 197–222; Donald Gordon, "'Veritas Filia Temporis': Hadrianus Junius and Geoffrey Whitney," *Journal of the Warburg and Courtauld Institutes*, 3 (1940), 228–240; Arthur Henkel and Albrecht Schöne, eds., *Emblemata: Handbuch zur Sinnbildkunst des XVI. und XVII. Jahrhunderts* (Stuttgart: J. B. Metzlersche, 1967), cols. 1816–17; and Guy de Tervarent, *Attributs et symboles dans l'art profane, 1450–1600: Dictionnaire d'un langage perdu*, Travaux d'Humanisme et Renaissance, 29 (Geneva: E. Droz, 1958), cols. 165–167.
71. Wilson, *s.v.* "Day of the Lord . . . ," 2, sig. I8ᵃ; see further Isaiah 59:9, 60:19–20, and I Corinthians 3:13 and Revelation 22:5 with Geneva glosses.

72. See, *e.g.*, Jean Calvin, *The Institution of Christian Religion*, tr. Thomas Norton (London, 1599), STC 4423, IV.1.2–7.
73. *Cf.* Calvin, III.25.1: "because we hope for those things which appeare not," " . . . our life is hidden with Christ in God, and . . . when he which is our life shall appeare, then shall we also appeare with him in glorie. . . . Heere we neede a singular patience, that we be not wearied and either turne backe our course or forsake our standing. . . . [W]ee seeme to followe the blessednesse hidden from vs, as it were a fleeing shadowe" (tr. Thomas Norton).
74. "Show me deare Christ," in *Divine Poems*, p. 15: and "Satyre III," in *The Satires, Epigrams and Verse Letters*, ed. W. Milgate (Oxford: Clarendon Press, 1967), p. 13, ll. 79–92.
75. *Conversations with Drummond*, in *The Man and his Work*, Vols. I–II of *Ben Jonson*, ed. C. H. Herford and Percy and Evelyn Simpson, 11 vols. (Oxford: Clarendon Press, 1925–52), I, 137. The *Conversations* consist of Drummond's jottings reporting Jonson's comments, so that the remark about the Beast may well be Drummond's short-hand version of Jonson's more full or apt formulation.
76. See D. S. Brewer, "Courtesy and the *Gawain*-Poet," in *Patterns of Love and Courtesy: Essays in Memory of C. S. Lewis*, ed. John Lawlor (London: Edward Arnold, 1966), pp. 54–85; W. O. Evans, "'Cortaysye' in Middle English," *Mediaeval Studies*, 29 (1967), 143–157; Sr. Anna Maria Reynolds, "'Courtesy' and 'Homeliness' in the *Revelations* of Julian of Norwich," *Fourteenth-Century English Mystics Newsletter*, 5, No. 2 (1979), 12–20; J. Stephen Russell, "*Pearl's* 'Courtesy,' " *Renascence*, 35 (1983), 183–195; and *M.E.D. s.v.* "courteisie," sb. 4, "courteisnesse," sb., and "courteis" adj., sb., 2a and 4a.
77. See my "Courtesy" in the forthcoming *Spenser Encyclopedia;* for comprehensive discussion and documentation, see my "A Commentary on Book Six of *The Faerie Queene*," Diss. Edinburgh University 1985, pp. 19–35. An Elizabethan courtesy book explicitly associating courtesy with Christian charity and salvation is George Pettie and Bartholmew Young, tr., *The Civile Conversation*, by Stephano Guazzo, introd. Sir Edward Sullivan, The Tudor Translations, Second Series, 7, 2 vols. (New York: Alfred Knopf, 1925), I, 228. In doing so, Pettie chooses to clarify what is contextually implicit in Guazzo (see Borris, "A Commentary," p. 34).
78. For this trend, see especially Alexander Corbin Judson, "Spenser's Theory of Courtesy," *PMLA*, 47 (1932), 135–136; Thomas P. Roche, Jr., *The Kindly Flame; A Study of the Third and Fourth Books of Spenser's "The Faerie Queene"* (Princeton, N. J.: Princeton University Press, 1964), p. 200; P. C. Bayley, "Order, Grace and Courtesy in Spenser's World," in *Patterns of Love and Courtesy: Essays in Memory of C. S. Lewis*, ed. John Lawlor (London: Edward Arnold, 1966), pp. 178–202; Kathleen Williams, *Spenser's World of Glass: A Reading of "The Faerie Queene"* (Berkeley: University of California Press, 1966), Ch. 6; and Maurice Evans, *Spenser's Anatomy of Heroism: A Commentary on "The Faerie Queene"* (Cambridge: Cambridge University Press, 1970), Ch. 10. Moreover, various scholarly studies of the Graces in Book VI, such as Nohrnberg's, Humphrey Tonkin's, Gerald Snare's, and Lila Geller's, interpret them in a semi-theological manner; since the Graces episode is central for Spenser's conception of Courtesy by all accounts, that kind of approach should not be inapplicable to at least some other parts of Book VI.

79. In the Geneva and Bishops' Bibles, for example, "courteous" is used for translating the injunctions of 1 Pet. 3:8–9, and Luther comments that these verses are a detailed analysis of the way in which " . . . we should love one another." They are "the sum and substance of the kind of outward life" that Christians "should lead"; "a true Christian life" has just such "external manifestations" (Sermons on the First Epistle of St. Peter, tr. Martin H. Bertram, Vol. XXX of Luther's Works, ed. Jaroslav Pelikan and Walter A. Hansen [St. Louis, Mo.: Concordia, 1967], pp. 93–94, 99). Elizabethan biblical translators apparently understood courtesy in a way commensurate with the high significance of this Petrine admonition.

80. Whitgift, in Works, I, 56; see further Bancroft, Svrvay, p. 421.

81. On the opposition of pride and courtesy, see Borris, "A Commentary," pp. 26–34; Arthur fights Disdain, a form of pride, in Book VI. On pride and Puritanism, see, e.g., Bancroft, Svrvay, pp. 124, 149, 415, 463.

82. The "July" eclogue, e.g., turns on a topographically expressed contrast between elevated pride and lowly humility. Orgoglio is a giant; Disdain stands on "tiptoes hie" (VI.vii.42).

83. Book of Common Prayer, in Liturgical Services, pp. 193–195.

84. Puritans advocated elimination of the chancel as an area of special distinction within churches (the eastern, most sacred part, primarily the clergy's preserve, where communion was usually celebrated). Moreover, controversies raged over the proper form and function of altars. That Spenser singles out "Altars" and "the Chancell" for emotionally fraught desecration evinces conservative Anglican sympathies: for Puritans, neither were legitimate features of "the sacred Church" anyway. See Davies, pp. 363–365; Whitaker, pp. 24, 27; and G. W. O. Addleshaw and Frederick Etchells, The Architectural Setting of Anglican Worship (London: Faber, 1948), pp. 25–27, 30–34, 40, 118.

85. A Discourse Concerning the Original and Progress of Satire, in Essays of John Dryden, ed. W. P. Ker (Oxford: Clarendon Press, 1926), II, 93.

86. On the use of allegory in conjunction with satire, see Ellen Douglass Leyburn, Satiric Allegory: Mirror of Man, Yale Studies in English, Vol. 130 (New Haven, Conn.: Yale University Press, 1956).

87. On the general failure of the anti-Martinist tracts to satirize Puritanism and promote the Anglican position effectively, see Holden, p. 51.

88. On these considerations for Elizabethan satirists, see Raymond A. Anselment, "Betwixt Jest and Earnest": Marprelate, Milton, Marvell, Swift, and the Decorum of Religious Ridicule (Toronto: University of Toronto Press, 1979), Chs. 1–3.

89. See Arnold Stein, "Donne's Obscurity and the Elizabethan Tradition," ELH, 13 (1946), 104–118; Alvin Kernan, The Cankered Muse: Satire of the English Renaissance, Yale Studies in English, Vol. 142 (New Haven, Conn.: Yale University Press, 1959), pp. 60–61, 97–98; and K. W. Gransden, ed., Tudor Verse Satire (London: Athlone Press, 1970), pp. 20–22.

90. For further discussion of Book VI in these respects, see A. C. Hamilton, ed., The Faerie Queene, Longman's Annotated English Poets (New York: Longman, 1977), pp. 621–623: " . . . Book VI is part of a whole which is a 'continued Allegory, or darke conceit', and different only in that its complex allegory is especially fine and subtle."

PATRICK CHENEY

The Old Poet Presents Himself:
Prothalamion as a
Defense of Spenser's Career

*H*OW ARE we to understand Spenser at the end of his career? To
what end came the "new Poete" so enthusiastically celebrated
by "E. K." in *The Shepheardes Calender*?[1] How successful, finally, was the confident, aspiring poet of *The Faerie Queene*—the
self-proclaimed heir of Chaucer and England's Virgil—in enacting the ideals of his own humanist poetics? Did the barking dog
"Envie" so feared in "To His Booke," the prefatory poem to
The Shepheardes Calender, and still dominant in Books V and VI
of *The Faerie Queene* as the Blatant Beast, silence the poet
himself? In sum, at the end of his career, how did the *old* poet
present himself?

According to David L. Miller, "it has become a commonplace of Spenser criticism that the poet's attitude toward
the historical world changes in his late work. There the central
value of Spenser's religious idealism . . . seems held in a far
more tentative and self-conscious way. And the central premise
of his idealized vocation, the humanist faith in literature as a
mode of persuasion, is repeatedly questioned."[2] For Miller, as
for most critics, the final books of *The Faerie Queene* (1596),
together with other late poetry—*Colin Clouts Come Home
Againe* (1595), *The Mutabilitie Cantos* (1595), and *Fowre Hymnes*
(1596)—strongly suggest that Spenser "abandons the quest" of
using his humanist poetics "to fashion a gentleman or noble
person in vertuous and gentle discipline" (*Letter to Ralegh*).[3]

As final evidence of Spenser's disillusionment, recent historical critics often cite his last published poem, "*Prothalamion* or a
Spousall Verse," written in the fall of 1596—as the title page
informs us—to "honour" the "double marriage" of Elizabeth
and Katherine Somerset to Henry Gilford and William Peter.[4]

According to Thomas H. Cain, "In *Prothalamion* . . . disillusionment with his role is especially poignant. . . . nostalgia, complaint, and sense of loss so insinuate themselves as almost to overwhelm the expected strain of celebration"; thus the memorable refrain—"Sweete Themmes runne softly, till I ende my song"—is "shot through with swansong," and the poem as a whole anticipates the "withdrawal from the Orphic role of national poet . . . completed by the escapism ending the *Mutabilitie* cantos."[5] Similarly, Richard Helgerson believes that the poem "casts a valedictory glance back over his career . . . with the regretful air of a man who would still join in the affairs of the great world if the great world would have him. When he says that 'some brave muse may sing' the glories of the new champion, Essex, it is hard to tell whether he is putting himself definitively out of contention or bidding for the job. But in the refrain . . . we hear the sound of an ending, an impending withdrawal from the public world that this poem still celebrates."[6]

While acknowledging Spenser's sense of frustration in *Prothalamion*, I want to suggest that we need to look more carefully at his treatment of that frustration. Significantly, in Stanza 1 he opens by presenting himself precisely as recent historical critics describe him: overcome with "sullein care, / Through discontent of [his] long fruitlesse stay / In Princes Court," he withdraws to the "shoare of silver streaming Themmes" (ll. 5–11). Suddenly, however, in Stanzas 2–7 he "chance[s] to espy" (l. 20) an idealized vision—in the form of an elaborate flower ceremony—which later he acknowledges to be a source of "joye" (l. 142): a "Flocke of Nymphes" gather "flowers" in their "wicker basket[s]" (ll. 20–26), strew the flowers on "two Swannes of goodly hewe" (l. 37) who sail down the Thames, then crown the swans with "Garlands" (l. 83), while "one" of the Nymphs sings a "Lay" of wedded love (l. 87) to honor the swans. Then, almost as suddenly as the swans appeared, in Stanzas 8–10 the idealized vision seems to metamorphose into historical reality: the procession enters "mery London" (l. 127), prompting the poet to recall the city as his "kyndly Nurse" and the "house of auncient fame" from which he takes his "name" (ll. 128–131), to review the history of the Temple at the Inns of Court and his lost patronage with Leicester, to praise Essex for his victory over Spain, and to witness Essex uniting "Two gentle Knights" (l. 169) with what earlier appeared as "Two faire . . . Birds" (l. 39) but now appear as "two faire Brides" (l. 176).

This peculiar narrative movement—from autobiographical images of pastoral retreat to allegorical images of idealized nature to realistic images of history and politics—looks very much like an enactment of the humanist idealism that informs Spenser's earlier poetry—an idealism in which human beings overcome disillusioned withdrawal into pastoral *otium* through an idealized artistic vision that motivates ethical action in society. Accordingly, I want to argue that *Prothalamion* shows Spenser at the end of his career engaging precisely in his earlier humanist idealism. Specifically, the peculiar narrative movement dramatizes the humanist ideal that *The Faerie Queene* promotes, the very ideal which Miller himself states but believes Spenser abandons: "the withdrawal into vision prepares for a return to history through poetry as a motive for virtuous action" ("Spenser's Vocation," p. 217).

The relation between *Prothalamion* and *The Faerie Queene* is indeed intimate. In 1715, the poem's first commentator, John Hughes, hinted at this relation by criticizing the "Spousall Verse" for transgressing an "essential property" of allegory adhered to by *The Faerie Queene*—the property that the allegory "be every where consistent with it self":

> Most of the allegories in the *Fairy Queen* are agreeable to this rule; but in [*Prothalamion*] the author has manifestly transgress'd it. . . . the two brides are figur'd by two beautiful swans sailing down the River Thames. The allegory breaks before the reader is prepar'd for it; and we see [the "birdes"], at their landing, in their true shapes [as "brides"], without knowing how this sudden change is effected. If this had been only a simile, the poet might have dropp'd it at pleasure; but as it is an allegory, he ought to have made it of a piece, or to have invented some probable means of coming out of it.[7]

Hughes assumes that *Prothalamion* is an allegory comparable to *The Faerie Queene*. Although his criticism implies that the "Spousall Verse" is a failed allegory, and the national epic a successful one, we might consider an alternative: that the transgression is both a clue for interpreting *Prothalamion* and a tacit directive to relate it to *The Faerie Queene*. Indeed, as critics have shown, the "Spousall Verse" shares enough features with the national epic to occupy a unique position in Spenser's minor poetry: pictorial techniques, the relation between sentence and stanza, and diction.[8] One other similarity seems striking: both poems use the first-person narrator to present an allegory of love having national significance. As yet, no one has examined the relation between the two poems to suggest that in *Prothalamion* Spenser participates in (rather than abandons) the humanist idealism informing *The Faerie Queene*.

In addition to the poem's narrative movement, its allusions to classical myth suggest that Spenser participates in his earlier idealism. Critics have long recognized allusions to Spenser's own poetry (*The Shepheardes Calender*, *The Ruines of Time*, *Epithalamion*, *The Faerie Queene*) and to numerous sources inspiring this poetry: English river poetry (Camden, Leland, Vallans), medieval dream vision (Chaucer, Langland), and classical poetry, especially epic and lyric (Virgil and Ovid, Horace and Catullus).[9] As yet, however, no one has shown how these allusions form a carefully integrated strategy of imitation that supports the national ideal of Spenserian poetics in *The Faerie Queene*.

By attending to *Prothalamion*'s narrative movement and strategy of imitation, we can see more than an occasional poet passively celebrating a double marriage or lamenting his own private woes: at the end of his career, a major poet steps back to offer a defense of allegorical love poetry in the national epic itself, and in so doing manages to offer an *apologia* for the humanist tradition inspiring his poetry. *Prothalamion* emerges as a defense of the poet's career.

I

The poem's peculiar narrative movement has long been a source of criticism, and it seems possible that recent views about the role of the poem in Spenser's career result from misunderstanding of that movement. For instance, C. S. Lewis feared that "perfect unity has [not] been achieved": "The references to Spenser's own discontents, to the history of the Temple, and to the achievements of Essex, interesting as they are in themselves, do not seem to have been made to contribute much to the total effect."[10] Harry Berger summarizes the problem thus: "in a poem of ten stanzas nominally celebrating [a] double marriage, . . . why are two stanzas devoted to the poet's own life and troubles, and a third to some patron-seeking praise of Essex?" While Berger himself and Alastair Fowler each detect unity (albeit on different grounds), both join Lewis in ignoring the poem's narrative movement or structure; instead they discuss the poem's dichotomy of "realism" in Stanzas 1 and 8–10 and "allegory" in Stanzas 2–7.[11]

I propose to concentrate on the poem's three-part structure: Stanza 1, which presents the poet's withdrawal from "Princes Court"; Stanzas 2–7, which presents his espial of the flower ceremony; and Stanzas 8–10, which present his return to "London." While any interpretation needs to establish the relation among these parts, to do so presents problems, because the transition between Parts 1 and 2 is as troubling as the more commonly criticized transition between Parts 2 and 3. What, that is, does the poet's dissatisfaction with the world of public politics in Stanza 1 have to do with the private world of the swan-brides' procession in Stanzas 2–7? Narratively, the poet's career problems have nothing to do with the swans' marriage. In fact, the poet's public vision of others appears to *intrude* into his own private troubles. Correspondingly, when he watches the procession enter London, *he* intrudes autobiography and national ceremony into *their* procession. Again, what does his life have to do with theirs? Each transition creates confusion.

The effect of the confusion, however, should be familiar to readers of *The Faerie Queene*: we wonder how the parts relate. The transition from Part 1 to Part 2 establishes a dichotomy between the poet's public career and the ladies' private marriage; the transition from Part 2 to Part 3 establishes a dichotomy between the poet's seemingly private vision and their public marriage. We seem to have two sets of problems: that of the poet, who moves from a public to a private to a public world; and that of the ladies, who move from a private to a public world. The dichotomies that seem so disjointed here, however, are precisely central to *The Faerie Queene*.

Specifically, the poem's three parts trace the threefold poetic process that informs allegorical writing in the national epic: 1)

the poet becomes disillusioned with the actual world; 2) he
retreats to an idealized world, where he miraculously envisions
allegorical ideals; and 3) he returns to the actual world transformed to perform virtuous action.[12] The poetic process has
three corresponding parts for the reader: he or she 1) becomes
disillusioned with the actual world; 2) retreats to the idealized
world of poetry; and 3) returns to the actual world transformed
to perform virtuous action.

In tracing the poetic process, Spenser may be defending himself against the charge that Elizabethan readers like Burleigh
were making against his poetry: "poemes" are "vaine . . .
weedes" feeding merely "fancie," not a "discipl[ine]" of "vertue" leading to wise social action (IV.Pr.1; see also VI.xii.41 and
the Dedicatory Sonnet to Burleigh in the 1590 edition)—*dulce
non utile*. For such readers, evidently, Spenser is a pleasing
magician, an escapist from reality, and his idealized *Faerie
Queene* is a magical means by which he and his reader escape to
a world of dream, independent of the world of affairs.[13]
According to Helgerson, "As his work on *The Faerie Queene*
drew toward a close, the poet, who years before [in a Latin
verse epistle printed in a letter to Harvey] had complained that
'the gods made me the gift of delight but not of the useful,'
found those two Horatian poles of his literary identity once
again pulling apart" (p. 96). In *Prothalamion*, I believe, Spenser
formally acknowledges this *pull* in order to resist the pressure.
Even if other late poetry shows him frustrated with politics by
emphasizing his Orphic withdrawal, the "Spousall Verse" acknowledges these frustrations to announce his Orphic return.
Rather than passively reflecting his dejection at the end of his
career, *Prothalamion* is what Louis Adrian Montrose would call a
" 'primary activity' in its own right"[14]: privately, the poem
reinvigorates Spenser's Orphic spirit; publicly, it demonstrates
his national value to Essex, the Somersets, and Elizabeth. Quite
literally the poem is a "Spousall Verse." While lines such as
those in the refrain do have the elegiac tone noted by recent
historical critics, we need to be careful not to turn a betrothal
poem into a funeral elegy. Rather, we need to seek phrasing that
accounts precisely for the tension between the elegiac tone
emerging in parts of the poem and the humanist idealism informing the poem as a whole.

II

In Part 1 (Stanza 1), Spenser presents himself precisely *escaping* from "Princes Court"; he meets his reader's objection by portraying the poet as a dreamer whose imaginative art *seems* to lack cultural utility:

> When I whom sullein care,
> Through discontent of my long fruitlesse stay
> In Princes Court, and expectation vayne
> Of idle hopes, which still doe fly away,
> Like empty shaddowes, did aflict my brayne,
> Walkt forth to ease my payne
> Along the shoare of silver streaming Themmes. . . .
>
> (ll. 5–11)

Frustrated at "Princes Court" by an "expectation" that proves "vayne," a "hope" that proves "idle," and aiming to "ease [his] payne," he walks down to the "rutty Bancke" of the Thames, which is "hemme[d]" by a "meade" painted with "variable flowers" and adorned with "daintie gemmes" (ll. 12–14). Significantly, the motivation for this walk into seeming Nature is "ease"—that "nourse of sin" in the pageant of the Seven Deadly Sins (I.iv.18).[15]

Yet, by portraying himself in this way, Spenser presents the first stage of the poetic process—the origin of his desire to "fashion" virtuous readers: his necessary retreat from the disillusioning actual world. While he does not mention the specific cause of the "payne" motivating his retreat, critics believe that it resulted from his failure to win preferment for *The Faerie Queene*.[16] The significance of this point has been overlooked: *Prothalamion* was motivated by Spenser's concern over his national epic. Thus, to open *Prothalamion* he shows himself inverting the idealism of *The Faerie Queene*. Whereas he "expect[ed]" to transform his idealistic "hopes" into reward, he sees his "idle hopes . . . fly away, / Like empty shaddowes." In effect, he inverts the experience of Arthur in his dream of Gloriana (I.ix.5–13): the poet's hopes become "idle," his vision of glory an "empty shaddow." Rather than his dream inspiring him to find the incarnate form of the ideal, as with Arthur, actuality interferes with his dream. Evidently, the visionary idealism from his national epic fails to sustain him during this new affliction: he cannot enact his own humanist poetics.

However, in Part 2 (Stanzas 2–7) he "chance[s] to espy" an elaborate flower cermony: a "Flocke of Nymphes" (l. 20) are "in a Meadow, by the Rivers side," gathering "flowers" in their "wicker basket[s]" (ll. 19–26). The mention of "Nymphes" and the language of dream vision ("I chanced to espy") indicate that "the world this vision evokes is not natural" (Wine, p. 44), while the mention of the Nymphs' "greenish locks" (l. 22), as Berger points out (p. 511), alerts us to the poet's entry into or creation of an ideal, allegorical world. Miraculously, the poet's escape from court leads to imaginative effort, showing that, as Sidney says in *The New Arcadia*, "ease" is "the nurse of poetry."[17]

Most critics agree that the poem "describes . . . a water-fete that in all likelihood actually took place" (Fowler, p. 59; see the *Variorum Edition*, pp. 662–664). If so, Spenser presents the second stage of the poetic process: the poet converts fact into fiction—the equivalent in *The Faerie Queene* of converting London into Cleopolis. Hence, the catalogue of flowers in Stanza 2 (ll. 30–34) functions like the catalogue of trees in the Wood of Error (I.i.8–9), except that here the allegorized flowers ("The virgin Lillie, and the Primrose trew" [l. 33]) reveal that the poet has escaped from a world of error to enter a garden of allegorical forms.[18]

Accordingly, Spenser uses causal language ("With that") to introduce the two swans. As the pun on "Somers-heat" in l. 67 reveals, the two swans figure the Somerset sisters. In realizing this, we can see the poet completing the second stage: although withdrawing from "Princes Court" in frustration, he imaginatively molds individual court members—the Somerset sisters—into allegorical ideals he hopes the sisters will "aread."

Hence, in this second part the Nymphs perform actions for the swan-sisters *like* the process of writing allegory. Fowler notes that "Much of the poem goes in flower gathering and flower arrangement," even though "these operations are not now attended to very carefully" (p. 61). He identifies the garlands the Nymphs make as "poems," their baskets as "stanzas," the basket twigs as "lines," the "Lay" as an "aspect" of *Prothalamion* itself (pp. 64–65), and concludes: "It would be surprising if all this representation of garland-making did not give some clue to *Prothalamion*'s formal structure" (p. 66). He anticipates a salient point: in the flower ceremony, Spenser allegorizes the process of allegorical creation. We see the making of an allegorical image, created out of the garden of allegorical forms.[19]

Spenser's use of the swan image suggests a self-reflexive allegory. According to Rosemary Freeman, "The swan was often used by emblem writers as the symbol of the poet"; seemingly perplexed, she adds, "But in *Prothalamion* the swans symbolize marriage in general, and the two brides for whose wedding the poem was written in particular" (p. 104; see Prager, p. 117). While usefully reminding us of the link between the swan and the poet, perhaps Freeman brushes the link aside too quickly in attending to Spenser's literal use of the symbol. Although the swans are clearly not symbols of the poet alone, neither are they merely symbols of the brides in their state of marriage; rather, they are symbols of the juncture between the two—of the poet's power to "fashion" the other in the shape of the self. As such, the swans are *symbols of the poet's creation*—a quite literal *insignia poetarum*. In the swan allegory, Spenser figures the fashioning process underlying his poetics.

Thus the vehicle for the swans' appearance, the river, becomes a figure for the poet's inspiration, as the refrain hints: "Sweet Themmes runne softly, till I end my Song." The poet who has left court for the river "chaunce[s] to espy" the very process of poetic creation he has become "sullein" about. Significantly, though, by recalling *The Faerie Queene* we can interpret this key event: chance signals the working of grace.[20] The poet receives grace because, however frustrated, he retains his faith, revealed in the causal link between the refrain and the swans' arrival: "Sweete Themmes runne softly, till I end my Song. / With that, I saw two Swannes" (ll. 36–37). Through grace grounded in faith, he recovers his role as divine poet: he transforms the sisters into swans to reverse the failed idealism that made his "idle hopes" "fly away." In doing so, he envisions his own allegory at work.

Just as the Nymphs' actions allegorize the poetic process by which idealized allegorical images are created, so the creations themselves, the swan-brides, act out the allegorical quest—a water voyage down the Thames. Thus a parallel exists not merely between the poet and the Nymphs, but, as Berger notes, between the poet and the swan-brides: Spenser's "description of the brides emphasizes the same tendencies and implies the same problems" (p. 514; see Fowler, p. 80, and Wine, p. 42). Berger finds a clue to the brides' problem in the often-noted ambiguity of the refrain: "In the phrase, 'Against the Brydale day,' *against* may mean *in preparation for, looking forward to* or *in avoidance of, hoping to fend off;* 'which is not long' may mean the bridal day is not far off, but also, it is a very short day" (p. 513). According to Berger, the brides have "their own version of the escape impulse" (p. 514): they are *secretly* unwilling to marry (see "Loves dislike" at l. 99). He refers to the "feminine love psychology" in Books III and IV of *The Faerie Queene*, "especially in the treatment of Belphoebe and Amoret, in his portrayal of the virgin's natural *daunger* as well as her natural fear and desire of erotic possession" (p. 514). The swan-brides are in danger of mirroring the poet's mood in Stanza 1: pressure from the reality of marriage threatens to transform their dream of marriage into an "empty shaddow." They, too, seem in danger of inverting the visionary idealism of *The Faerie Queene*. Berger's reference to Belphoebe and Amoret is not coincidental: as these sisters are conceived through the Sun "Upon a *Sommers* . . . day" (III.vi.6), so the Somerset sisters are "bred of *Somers* heat." The details suggest that Spenser evokes *The Faerie Queene* to motivate Elizabeth and Katherine to "aread" Belphoebe and Amoret well.

Berger's reading helps explain Spenser's allegorical method in this part of the poem: Spenser refers or alludes to myths which, in the context of a betrothal poem, often arrest the reader's attention. Such a strategy of imitation reveals that here the poet furthers the humanist aims from his earlier work, including *The Faerie Queene*. In Stanza 3, for example, he refers to Leda's rape by the swan, Jove. Literally, Spenser uses the myth in an elaborate *ploce* to praise the *whiteness* or purity of the swans: Jove is not as white as they, "Yet Leda was they say as white as he, / Yet not so white as these, nor nothing neare; / So purely white they were" (ll. 44–46). According to the editors of *The Explicator*, "Spenser successfully conveys an impression of the godlike passion represented in the espousal."[21] While this reading is consistent with the surface of the text, it overlooks the tragic resonance the myth inescapably evokes. Such resonance emerges clearly in Spenser's most memorable use of the Leda myth—on the tapestries of Busyrane's Castle (III.xi.32), which hint precisely at Amoret's problem with "daunger." According to Berger, "Since the divine rape may project both sides of the threat to feminine self-control—wish-fulfillment as well as nightmare force—its appearance in *Prothalamion*, even though relatively circumspect, disturbs the bland surface of celebration" (p. 515). Whereas the editors of *The Explicator* deny the tragic resonance, Berger prepares us to identify its significance. The myth, within the framework of the swans' quest, works allegorically: read literally, it inspires virtuous behavior through its praise; read figuratively, it warns against "daunger."

In Stanza 4, in presenting the Nymphs' "amazed" sight of the two swans, Spenser may be using a Virgilian myth in a similar way:

> they stood amazed still,
> Their wondring eyes to fill,
> Them seem'd they never saw a sight so fayre,
> Of Fowles so lovely, that they sure did deeme
> Them heavenly borne, or to be that same payre
> Which through the Skie draw Venus silver Teeme,
> For sure they did not seeme
> To be begot of any earthly Seede,
> But rather Angels or of Angels breede.
>
> (ll. 58–66)

For the image of Venus and her swans, critics usually refer to Horace's *Odes* (IV.1) or Ovid's *Metamorphoses* (X.717–718).[22] Neither of these poems, however, treats the question, so central to Spenser's passage, of whether Venus is a goddess or a real woman. To find a Venus/swan passage that treats this question, we may turn to a passage in the *Aeneid*—and one which Spenser draws on in *The Faerie Queene*: Aeneas' sight of his mother, Venus in disguise as a mortal: "by what name should I call thee, O maiden? for thy face is not mortal nor has thy voice a human ring: O goddess surely!"[23] In the *Aeneid*, this event functions as a revelation, for Venus reveals to Aeneas the location of his shipwrecked landing (Carthage) and prophesies his reunion with his lost ships: "I bring thee tidings of thy comrades restored. . . . Lo! yonder twelve swans in exultant line, which the

bird of Jove . . . was scattering . . . ; now in long array they
seem . . . to be settling in their places" (ll. 390–396). When
Venus turns away, Aeneas recognizes his mother, and although
he complains of her mysterious behavior, he benefits from her
powers on his voyage to the New Troy.

Like Aeneas before his mother, Spenser's Nymphs are daz-
zled by their sight of the swans' beauty, which they believe
comes from heaven. On the surface of the text, they turn out to
be mistaken: "Yet were they bred of Somers-heat they say, / In
sweetest Season, when each Flower and weede / The earth did
fresh aray, / So fresh they seem'd as day" (ll. 67–70). The swans
only "seem" to be "of Angels breede"; in fact, they are mortals,
the Somerset sisters, bred on "earth" and subject to withering
just as "Flowers" are. Yet the text shows a further complication:
the impregnating force is "Somers-heat"—the sun itself, the
divine force of creation (Apollo is the god of poets). Significantly, Spenser twice uses the Virgilian myth in the Belphoebe story
(II.iii.33 and III.v.35): like Belphoebe (and Amoret), the Somerset sisters are incarnations of heavenly light (literally, of heat).
In short, Spenser may evoke the Virgilian myth to suggest the
divine nature of the brides' beauty, to remind them of the
mortality of their physical beauty, and to alert them to the
proper use of their powers, service towards a national destiny—
an idea confirmed by the end of the poem, when the swan-
brides sail into Troynovant.

In Stanza 5, Spenser uses two additional Ovidian myths in
similarly allegorical ways: the myth of Daphne and Apollo, and
the myth of Orpheus and Eurydice. The Nymphs, we learn,
throw "Great store of Flowers" from their baskets onto the
"goodly Birds," strewing "all the Waves" (ll. 74–77),

> That like old Peneus Waters they did seeme,
> When downe along by pleasant Tempes shore
> Scattred with Flowres, through Thessaly they streeme,
> That they appeare through Lillies plenteous store,
> Like a Brydes Chamber flore.
>
> (ll. 78–82)

Berger notes the "sense of loss, of pain and passage . . . press-
[ing] into the bridal vision" here: "time, change and death lace
the fluid landscape. . . . lilies symbolise virginity and death, cut

lilies symbolise marriage as a death to virginity, and [thus], marriage is merely one of the steps to death" (p. 517). The idea of "scattred . . . Flowers," of "stream[ing]," and the haunting anatomical suggestion of "Brydes Chamber flore" support this meaning.

Spenser's association of the Thames with the Peneus may recall more than the often-cited ode of Catullus (64.278–288; see the *Variorum Edition*, p. 499, and Maclean, p. 547, n. 4). Tempe is the site of two events central to *Prothalamion*: possession by the "daunger" of love and the triumph of poetry over time and death. Tempe is dedicated to Apollo, the god of poetry and the lover of Daphne. According to Ovid, Daphne was the daughter of Peneus but "She hat[ed] as a haynous crime the bond of bridely bed."[24] When Apollo chased her, she prayed to her father and turned into a laurel tree; thereafter, Apollo crowned poets and heroes with the garland of the laurel. Like Daphne, the swan-brides seem to fear marriage, but several verbal echoes suggest that Spenser actually had the Ovidian myth in mind. Spenser's "Lillies" recall Daphne's "lillie armes" (l. 604); the "Scattred" flowers recall Daphne's "scattred haire" (l. 664); and Spenser's flowers that "streame" may recall Daphne's "golden haire" that "did wave . . . behind hir backe" (ll. 643–644).[25] Moreover, insofar as Spenser's Nymphs figure the poet, it seems significant that immediately following the Peneus reference they "two Garlands bound" and crowned the "snowie Foreheads" of the two swans (ll. 83–86). In the Nymphs' crowning of the swans, Spenser allegorically figures the poet's crowning of heroines through poetry—further inspiration for completing their water quest. In effect, he self-reflexively alludes to his own "laureate" role. Hence, he may use the myth, in part to suggest the danger emerging when ladies fear wedded love, and in part to reveal the poet's role in triumphing over this problem through his art.

Like Daphne, Eurydice was from Tempe, and Orpheus was the son and student of Apollo. According to Ovid, after Orpheus lost Eurydice a "second tyme" (X.64), he "did utterly eschew / The womankynd" (ll. 88–89). After his own death, his lyre continued to sound and his head to sing as they floated down the Hebrus (XI.1 ff.), while his spirit descended to Hades where "He found his wyfe Eurydicee" (l. 70). Spenser's "Brydes" accompanied by "Nymphes" recall Eurydice, "the

Bryde" that "did rome / Abrode accompanyde with a trayne of Nymphes too bring her home" (X.7–8), while Spenser's Nymphs "thr[owing]" flowers on the Brides vaguely recollect the Maenads "throw[ing] their Thyrses greene" at Orpheus while he is dying (XI.29–30), and the imagery of streaming and scattering recalls those "Nymphes of brookes and woods" who appear at the bard's death—"uppon theyr streames [they] did sayle / With scattred heare" (ll. 51–52). Finally, Spenser's Nymphs who scatter the Flowers so that "through Thessaly they streame" recall Orpheus' dismemberment, especially if, as Fowler suggests, the flowers are poetic flowers. As with the Daphne myth, Spenser may evoke the Orpheus myth to acknowledge possible problems in marriage, to encourage the sisters to overcome their fear, and to assert the poet's powers to transcend time and death.[26]

Despite these echoes, critics overlook the Orpheus allusion in the Peneus river passage. In *Virgils Gnat*, however, the poet addresses "Peneus" during an Orpheus passage (ll. 177–184). Indeed, *Prothalamion* seems permeated by the Orphic myth. Later, in the reference to the "Lee" "Making his streame run slow" (ll. 115–118), Fowler notes an "allusion to Orpheus' slowing of the Peneus" (p. 74). But this whole passage (ll. 109–118) seems indebted to Ovid's myth as well. Spenser's song that resounds a "gentle Eccho from the neighbour ground" (l. 112) recalls Orpheus' song to which "bothe the banks in moorning wyse made answer too the same" (XI.57). Spenser's Lee that "lackt a tong" (l. 116) recalls the head of Orpheus with its "livelesse toong" making "A certeine lamentable noyse" (ll. 55–56). Moreover, Spenser's catalogue of flowers (Stanza 2) may be indebted to Ovid's catalogue of trees in the Orpheus myth (X.93 ff.), often cited as the source for Spenser's catalogue in the Wood of Error (see Hamilton, ed. n. I.i.8:1–4, p. 32). And Spenser's refrain is, as Cain says, an "Orphic incantation charming the river" (p. 46). These Orphic allusions suggest that Spenser in *Prothalamion* asserts the Orphic role from his earlier poetry, especially *The Faerie Queene*.[27]

In the "Lay" of Stanza 6, Spenser further clarifies his Orphic role. Cain calls the Hymn to Venus in Book IV, Canto x, of *The Faerie Queene* (44–47), sung by an anonymous "one," an Orphic hymn (p. 37). In doing so, he prepares us to identify the role of the "Lay" (also sung by an anonymous "one" [l. 87]) for the swan-brides. If Berger is right about the brides' problem, as well as about their success in solving the problem, we may wonder *how* they solve it: if they fear marriage at the beginning but accept it at the end, how do they change? The song, I suggest, may be the ⁻ource; it serves as the visionary core of their quest, the moment of epiphany—in Britomart's quest, the equivalent of Merlin's prophecy (III.iii.24–50). The song thus becomes what we might call an Orphic hymn adjusted to the prothalamic circumstance. The two parts of the traditional Orphic hymn reappear in the two parts of the "Lay": ll. 91–93, which invoke the "Gentle Birdes" as "the worlds faire ornament, / And heavens glorie," correspond to the Orphic invocation to the deity, while ll. 94–108, which pray for "Joy" and "Peace" in the forthcoming marriage, correspond to the Orphic prayer.[28] Through Spenser's brilliant design, the refrain of the poem as a whole functions as the specific conclusion of the "Lay"; thus what Cain says of the former we can say of the latter: it is an "Orphic incantation charming the river." As an adjusted Orphic hymn, the "Lay" magically aims to protect the brides from their fear of marriage and to teach them the value of marriage in society.[29]

The prayer in the "Lay" also confirms the ambiguities and ambivalences already noted: "let" Venus and Cupid "remove / All Loves dislike, and friendships faultie guile" (ll. 96–99). Here the "daunger" becomes explicit, and the singer uses her powers of love to triumph over fear and hate. As verbal echoes reveal, the song captures the essence of chaste married love, not merely in *Epithalamion*, but also in Books III–IV of *The Faerie Queene*.[30] As in the Garden of Adonis, Spenser hopes that Venus and Cupid will live in harmony in the brides' lives—"faire Venus, that is Queene of love, / With her heart-quelling Sonne upon you smile" (ll. 96–97). As an adjusted Orphic Hymn, the "Lay" defends heroic love and directs the reader—the Somerset sisters, the larger Elizabethan audience, and even the general reader—to the role *Prothalamion* plays in his or her life.

In Part 2, then, the poet completes the second stage of the poetic process. Through faith augmented by grace, he sees a vision in which poetry (the "Lay") transforms valuable members of "Princes Court" (the swan-brides). In seeing the swans' progress, the poet sees the success of his own poetry; he sees his own value as a poet within society.

Hence, in Part 3 (Stanzas 8–10), he sees the procession enter "mery London," prompting him to recall the city as "my most kyndly Nurse, / That to me gave this Lifes first native sourse" (ll. 127–129), and to refer to the "house of auncient fame" from which he takes his "name" (ll. 130–131). In the narrative, the autobiography is arresting, for it literally "breaks" the allegorical vision of the swans' progress. But, as commentators note, the poet's reference to his own life returns us to the beginning of the poem. While the structural design creates unity, the interruption reminds us that the poem is about the place of allegorical love poetry in Spenser's life—ultimately in the reader's. The references to Spenser's birth and name alert us to a symbolic process of identity resembling Redcrosse's experience atop the Mount of Contemplation, where the knight learns of his birth and name (I.x.61–67).

Spenser shows himself amidst this process when he presents the swans' progress passing the Temple (ll. 132–136). The short history of the Temple, in which the "Templer Knights" "decayd through pride" only to be replaced by "the studious Lawyers" (ll. 134–136), indicates more than the obvious cultural change from a chivalric to a business or legal ideal (Berger, p. 519, Fowler, p. 79); it also indicates the poetic movement from timeless allegorical vision to current actuality. History becomes Spenser's way of dramatizing that movement.

Significantly, however, the poet's own reentry into actuality creates a final temptation to despair, for "Next" to the Temple "standes a stately place," formerly Leicester House, "Where oft I gayned giftes and goodly grace / Of that great Lord, which therein wont to dwell, / Whose want too well now feeles my freendless case" (ll. 137–140). As in Stanza 1, the poet's own quest is threatened by his "freendles case." Suddenly, however, he remembers decorum: "Ah here fits not well / Olde woes but joyes to tell" (ll. 141–142). By remembering his own poetic principles, he overcomes "Olde woes" with new "joyes." Rather than interrupting the narrative, the Temple/Leicester House passage dramatizes the poet's successful reentry into time; as with the "Lay" in the brides' quest, his own poetry, as he says in the Proem to Book VI, "strength to [him] supplies, and chears [his] dulled spright" (1). As such, the passage is a microcosm of the pattern in the poem as a whole: feeling the pressure of "woe," the poet triumphs over it through inspiration from his own poetry.

His recovery prepares for Stanza 9, his sight of the "noble Peer, / Great Englands glory and the Worlds wide wonder" (ll. 145–146): Essex, by freeing his "country" from "forraine harmes," "ring[s]" "great Elisaes glorious name" (ll. 156–157). Cain says that the "basic mythological figures underlying *The Faerie Queene* . . . are Hercules and Orpheus, . . . the archetypes of the hero and the artist" (p. 39; *cf.* p. 24). If Spenser does allude to Orpheus earlier, then the association of Essex with "Hercules" in l. 148 alerts us to a critical similarity between *Prothalamion* and the national epic: the Orphic poet celebrates the Herculean heroism inspired by Elizabeth's glory, "Which some brave muse may sing / To ages following" (ll. 159–160).

While the identity of the "brave muse" may be controversial, it inescapably evokes Spenser and his *Faerie Queene*.[31] According to Michael O'Connell, in Book I Spenser's association of Mount Sinai and Mount Olivet with Parnassus (x.53–54) "means that poetry too achieves a prophetic function" (p. 44). The "brave muse" passage may hint at poetry's "prophetic function." If so, the lines are self-reflexive in more than the obvious way: they prophesy Elizabeth's glory and they prophesy the poet of *The Faerie Queene* to be the prophet; they identify Spenser as England's prophetic poet by prophesying future books of *The Faerie Queene*. As such, the action of *Prothalamion* originates in concern over *The Faerie Queene*, moves to a vision analogous to it, and concludes with a tactful prophecy of future books in the national epic itself.

But, if in the "brave muse" passage Spenser does identify his own prophetic function, does his prophecy reach eternity (as he hints in Book I)? Usefully, Fowler finds recurrent imagery of stellification: in addition to the brides' association with Venus and her swans (= Cygnus) and with Cynthia (ll. 121–122), the grooms' association with the Gemini (ll. 173–174), and Essex's association with Hesperus (l. 164), he finds traces of all twelve of the zodiacal signs (pp. 66–73). In Book VI of *The Faerie Queene*, during the Mount Acidale episode, Spenser likens the beauty of Colin's Dance of the Graces to "the Crowne, which Ariadne wore": "Being now placed in the firmament, . . . is unto the starres an ornament, / Which round about her move in order excellent" (x.13). This principle of stellification or transcendence is consistent with the ending of *Epithalamion*, with its prophecy of the newlyweds' creation of children who are destined to "inherit" the "heavenly tabernacles" (l. 422), with the ending of *Fowre Hymnes,* with its espial of "that soveraine light, / From whose pure beams al perfect beauty springs" (ll. 295–296), and with the ending of *The Mutabilitie Cantos,* with its vision of "all" resting "eternally / With Him that is the God of Sabbaoth hight" (viii.2). But in *Prothalamion* Spenser may intend to reverse the principle of stellification or transcendence to approximate a principle of incarnation: divine power takes up residence on earth; the stellar imagery works down, rather than up. Although Spenser associates the Somerset sisters with Venus, with Cynthia, and with "Angels," he does so to emphasize the divine origin and nature of very real women. Similarly, although he associates Essex with Hesperus, he does so to emphasize the divine origin and nature of a very real man. The principle of incarnation emerging from the stellar imagery reinforces the movement back into the historical world and may aim to show how history partakes of eternity.[32]

Accordingly, in Stanza 10 Essex "*Descend*[s] to the Rivers open vewing" (l. 166; emphasis added) "Like radiant Hesper" bathing his "golden hayre / In th'Ocean billowes" (ll. 164–165) in order to unite "Two gentle Knights" (l. 169) with "two faire Brides" (l. 176). Essex's "descent" recalls Arthur's role as a figure of grace when reuniting Redcrosse and Una in Book I (Cantos vii–viii). Spenser seems careful to associate Essex with the Prince in other ways: he likens both to Hesperus (I.vii.30 and l. 164) and to Hercules (I.vii.17 and l. 148). He calls Essex that "Faire branch of Honor, flower of Chevalrie" (l. 150), an echo of Arthur, that "Faire braunch of noblesse, flowre of chevalrie" (I.viii.26). And he says that Essex performs heroic deeds that sound "great Elisaes *glorious* name" (l. 157; emphasis added), an echo of Arthur, who heroically searches for Gloriana.[33]

Evidently, Spenser identifies Essex with Arthur because he aims to remind the great Lord of his ideal form—a reminder necessary because of Essex's propensity for pride—concealed in the meaning of "those high Towers" (l. 163) from which he steps, as Fowler notes (pp. 82–83). Like Arthur, the "noble Peer" (l. 145) is on an allegorical quest, fraught with its own danger. Importantly, however, Essex is a real man associated with an allegorical hero; Arthur, an allegorical hero figuring a real man (Essex). The reversal of the allegorical method in *The Faerie Queene,* along with that noted by Hughes, in which the "birdes" become "brides," signals the end of the swan allegory.

In the third part of the poem, then, Spenser may be introducing a "probable means of coming out of [the allegory]." The allegorical swans' entry into a real London and their transformation from "birdes" into "brides" is Spenser's way of dramatizing the effect of allegory on their lives: they experience the poet's allegorical vision, they literally live through one of his allegorical quests, then they "come out of it." Their experience with the poet's allegory of love transforms them so that they unite happily with the grooms. In this light, the Cynthia simile ending Stanza 7, in which the swan-brides surpass "all the foule" who have arrived, "as Cynthia doth shend / The lesser starres" (ll. 121–122), may serve as a transitional device between the second and third parts. Critics usually see here a reference to Elizabeth (see, *e.g.,* Norton, "Tradition," p. 238, Woodward, pp. 42–43, Auberlen, p. 99), but they do not ask why Spenser would associate the swan-brides with their sovereign—especially at this point. In *The Faerie Queene*, a female who reads the allegory carefully would imitate Elizabeth's virtues, since, as Spenser often tells us, several of his heroines—Gloriana, Britomart, Belphoebe—imitate the Queen's virtues. The Cynthia reference allegorically reveals that the swan-brides have successfully read the Spenserian allegory of their own quest: they have fully *imitated* their sovereign. Only when the brides imitate "Cynthia" can they transform vision into action; at precisely this point the allegory breaks and the "birdes" enter London as "brides."

Similarly, the poet's own transformation of allegorical vision (the swans' progress) into actuality (London) is Spenser's way of dramatizing the effect of allegory on his own life. Like the brides, he lives through an allegory of love, is transformed by it, and "comes out of it," thus recovering from his earlier dejection by reenvisioning Elizabeth's glory.

Finally, Essex experiences the transformation as well, for he is its narrative agent. By uniting the swan-brides with the "gentle Knights," he demonstrates his imitation of Arthur; only then do the allegorical "birdes" transform into real "brides."

Stanzas 8–10 thus use imagery of history and politics to figure a world beyond allegory. They show what happens when readers read allegory carefully: the poet, the brides, and Essex all serve Elizabeth, the source of their glory. Spenser transgresses the allegorical method of *The Faerie Queene* to figure the effect of allegory on poet and readers. The "realism" of the final stanzas *is* inconsistent with the earlier "allegory" because Spenser presents a "meta-allegory" in order to defend the process by which the poet directs the reader's responsible action. By innovatively figuring a defense of allegorical love poetry, the "Spousall Verse" takes poetry one step further than the national epic. In this sense *Prothalamion* is a defense of allegorical love poetry in *The Faerie Queene*—and thereby of Spenser's career as a whole.[34]

III

While Spenserians often see *The Mutabilitie Cantos* as the coda of Spenser's career, *Prothalamion* functions as a coda of an equally powerful kind. *Mutabilitie* moves from time to "the pillours of Eternity" (VII.viii.2); *Prothalamion*, from eternity to the pillars of time. According to Montrose, "To make poetry a vehicle of transcendence is tacitly to acknowledge its ethical and political impotence" (" 'The perfect paterne,' " p. 54). In *Prothalamion*, Spenser's "imaginative transformation" of "birdes" into "brides" reverses what Montrose calls Spenser's "escapist" tendency (p. 54) by assimilating vision to history in order to defend the ethical and political potency of allegory in *The Faerie Queene*. Whereas most recent historicists argue that Spenser at the end of his career "comes home to the pastoral, the personal, and the amorous" (Helgerson, p. 97), I believe that Spenser in *Prothalamion* follows this arc only to close the circle: through grace augmented by faith, he comes home, not to Colin's pastoral Ireland, but to his own civic "London," overcoming his escape into *otium* by assimilating pastoral to epic, the personal to the public. The poem's three-part structure—withdrawal, vision, and history—dramatizes the ideal *The Faerie Queene* promotes, an ideal confirmed by the elaborate strategy of imitation linking the poem with earlier poetry—both his own and that in the Western tradition. Spenser may have had trouble following this ideal, but *Prothalamion* shows he had not abandoned the quest. Although his life would presumably follow the pattern outlined by the hermit Contemplation to Redcrosse—when "high emongst all knights [thou] hast hong thy shield, / Thenceforth the suit of earthly conquest shonne" (I.x.60; see Helgerson, p. 99 and n. 54)—*Prothalamion* indicates that the poet's time, like the knight's, had not yet come. What Lawrence Manley says about *The Faerie Queene* I apply to *Prothalamion*—"a triumphant act of Orphic reconstruction, a recreation of a city that will stand against the flow of time" (p. 210). Spenser qualifies as a "brave muse" because he confronts what he fears most, mutability, through what he most believes, the power of his Orphic poetry to triumph over time for the benefit of culture: "Sweet Themmes runne softly, till I end my Song." The refrain captures all of Spenser's fears yet all of his hopes: his fear that the source of his inspiration will run dry; his hope that it will not. Yet the refrain does more than balance fear and hope to create tension between the two; it transcends the balance, precisely expressing the pattern of the poem as a whole: surging fear calmed by anchored hope, haunting despair thrilled by piercing faith, greedy hate fulfilled by priceless love. In the refrain, I do not hear "the sound of an ending, an impending withdrawal from the public world," but rather Herculean resistance to that ending, Orphic incantation against that withdrawal. As M. L. Wine reminds us, "Themmes" puns on *tempus,* suggesting that the river is "associated in the poet's mind with time and mutability," the forces that destroy "human beauty and dignity" (p. 43 and n. 9), but that here "the poet has triumphed over 'sweete *Themmes*' " (p. 45; see Fowler, p. 80). More than a gift for the Somerset sisters, the "Spousall Verse" is a gift for an entire culture. Assimilating private vision to national history, *Prothalamion* reveals how Spenser helps his reader complete the quest for Gloriana.[35]

The Pennsylvania State University

NOTES

1. Dedicatory Epistle to *The Shepheardes Calender*, ll. 6, 19, and 170–171, in *The Poetical Works of Edmund Spenser*, ed. J. C. Smith and Ernest De Sélincourt (Oxford: Clarendon, 1909–1910). All quotations from Spenser's poetry are from this edition; the archaic i-j and u-v are modernized, as are other obsolete typographical conventions, such as the italicizing of names and places. The main title of my essay derives from the title of Richard Helgerson's Spenser chapter in *Self-Crowned Laureates: Spenser, Jonson, Milton and the Literary System* (Berkeley, Los Angeles, and London: University of California Press, 1983): "The New Poet Presents Himself" (pp. 55–100).

2. Miller, "Spenser's Vocation, Spenser's Career," *ELH,* 50 (1983), 215–216.
3. In his edition of *The Faerie Queene* (London and New York: Longman, 1977), A. C. Hamilton traces the "commonplace" to Harry Berger, Jr., "A Secret Discipline: *The Faerie Queene,* Book VI," in *Form and Convention in the Poetry of Edmund Spenser,* Selected Papers from the English Institute, ed. William Nelson (New York and London: Columbia University Press, 1961), p. 41; and to Richard Neuse, "Book VI as Conclusion to *The Faerie Queene,*" *ELH,* 35 (1968), 331, rpt. in *Essential Articles for the Study of Edmund Spenser,* ed. A. C. Hamilton (Hamden, Conn.: Archon-Shoe String, 1972), pp. 366–388. Subsequent critics contributing to the "commonplace" include the following: Isabel G. MacCaffrey, *Spenser's Allegory: The Anatomy of Imagination* (Princeton, N. J.: Princeton University Press, 1976) (see p. 422); Michael O'Connell, *Mirror and Veil: The Historical Dimension of Spenser's "Faerie Queene"* (Chapel Hill: University of North Carolina Press, 1977) (see pp. 163 and 188); Thomas H. Cain, *Praise in "The Faerie Queene"* (Lincoln and London: University of Nebraska Press, 1978) (see p. 184); Helgerson, *Self-Crowned Laureates* (see p. 91); Louis Adrian Montrose, " 'The perfect paterne of a Poete': The Poetics of Courtship in *The Shepheardes Calender,*" *Texas Studies in Literature and Language,* 21 (1979) (see pp. 63–64); and Miller, "Abandoning the Quest," *ELH,* 46 (1979) (see p. 188).
4. The betrothal evidently occurred in September 1596, and the marriage was celebrated on November 8. We do not know the circumstances surrounding the poem's composition—whether the Earl of Worcester (the brides' father) or Essex (Spenser's patron) commissioned it or whether Spenser wrote it on his own. On the date and composition, see *The Works of Edmund Spenser: A Variorum Edition,* ed. E. Greenlaw, C. G. Osgood, F. M. Padelford, and R. Heffner, 10 vols. (Baltimore, Md.: Johns Hopkins University Press, 1932–1949), VIII, 662–666. While critics believe *Prothalamion* to be the last poem Spenser published, Russell J. Meyer, " 'Fixt in heauens hight': Spenser, Astronomy, and the Date of the *Cantos of Mutabilitie,*" *Spenser Studies IV,* ed. Patrick Cullen and Thomas P. Roche, Jr. (New York: AMS, 1984), pp. 115–129, implies that it may also have been the last poem Spenser wrote, since astronomical evidence suggests a date shortly after April 1595 for *The Mutabilitie Cantos*—well before the November 8, 1596 marriage of the Somerset sisters and the September betrothal. Alastair Fowler, "Spenser's *Prothalamion,*" in *Conceitful Thought: The Interpretation of English Renaissance Poems* (Edinburgh: Edinburgh University Press, 1975), says that "Essex's engagements, and correspondence . . . limit the probable date to 7–29 Sept." (p. 60, n. 3).
5. Cain, "Spenser and the Renaissance Orpheus," *University of Toronto Quarterly,* 41 (1971), 46. Future quotations from Cain will be from this article.
6. Helgerson, *Self-Crowned Laureates,* p. 88. Miller, "Spenser's Vocation," notes that "Spenser tempers the dominant motive of celebration still more openly in *Prothalamion,* where accidents of the historical world intrude directly and the poet seems uncertain whether to exclude them" (p. 219), and he quotes Helgerson on the sound of withdrawal emerging from the refrain (p. 221). This recent historical view is consistent with the view held earlier in the century. Sir Sidney Lee, *Great Englishmen of the Sixteenth Century* (London: Archibald Constable, 1904), called *Prothalamion* "Spenser's fit farewell to his Muse" (p. 187, rpt. in the *Variorum Edition,* p. 496). S. E. Winbolt, *Spenser and*

His Poetry (London: G. G. Harrap, 1912), labled the poem "a swan-song in another sense" (p. 140, rpt. in the *Variorum Edition*, p. 661). And B. E. C. Davis, *Edmund Spenser: A Critical Study* (London: Russell & Russell, 1933), called the "Spousall Verse" a "proud and glowing eulogy of a Londoner to his native city, Cleopolis, the fair and venerable home of civility" (p. 53, rpt. in the *Variorum Edition*, p. 662). For past critics as for present, the terms for evaluating *Prothalamion* remain consistent: it is a "farewell," a "eulogy," a "swan-song," a "valediction," a "withdrawal." However, for a recently dissenting historical voice, see Lawrence Manley, "Spenser and the City: The Minor Poems," *Modern Language Quarterly*, 43 (1982), 203–227, rpt. in *Modern Critical Views: Edmund Spenser*, ed. Harold Bloom (New York, New Haven, and Philadelphia: Chelsea House, 1986), pp. 207–209.

7. Hughes, *The Works of Mr. Edmund Spenser* (London, 1715), I: xlviii–ix, rpt. in the *Variorum Edition*, p. 666.

8. On pictorial techniques, see John Bender, *Spenser and Literary Pictorialism* (Princeton, N. J.: Princeton University Press, 1972): "in no other minor poem does Spenser employ the pictorial techniques [that] he does in *The Faerie Queene*" (p. 175); his comparison is anticipated by Rosemary Freeman, *English Emblem Books* (London: Chatto & Windus, 1948), pp. 104–105. On the relation between sentence and stanza, see Paul J. Alpers, *The Poetry of "The Faerie Queene"* (Princeton, N. J.: Princeton University Press, 1967): in both *Prothalamion* and *The Faerie Queene* "the formal requirements of line and stanza carry the sentence, whose structure has little or no independent force" (p. 77). On diction, see Vere L. Rubel, *Poetic Diction in the English Renaissance from Skelton through Spenser* (New York: Modern Language Association of America, 1941): "the language in [*Prothalamion*] is somewhat more conscious" than in the other late verse, except *Epithalamion,* and the distinctive words exemplify those Spenser "had used so plentifully in *The Shepheardes Calender* and *The Faerie Queene* [so] that he appeared to be using a language peculiar to himself" (p. 264, rpt. in the *Variorum Edition*, p. 676). Moreover, according to W. B. C. Watkins, *Shakespeare and Spenser* (Princeton, N. J.: Princeton University Press, 1950), the first line of *Prothalamion's* refrain has its genesis in a line from *The Faerie Queene* (p. 221): "That we may us reserve both fresh and strong, / Against the Turneiment which is not long" (IV.iv.12). Similarly, according to Daniel H. Woodward, "Spenser's 'Prothalamion,' " *ELH*, 29 (1962), the second line of the refrain has its genesis also in *The Faerie Queene* (p. 45, n. 25): "[The tide] Drives backe the current of his kindly course, / And makes it seem to have some other source" (IV.iii.27).

9. For these and other sources, see the *Variorum Edition*, pp. 495–505 and 667–673; and Dan S. Norton, "The Tradition of Prothalamia," in *English Studies in Honor of James Southall Wilson,* University of Virginia Studies (Charlottesville, 1951), IV: 223–241.

10. Lewis, *English Literature in the Sixteenth Century, Excluding Drama* (Oxford: Clarendon Press, 1954), p. 373.

11. Berger, "Spenser's *Prothalamion*: An Interpretation," *Essays in Criticism,* 15 (1965), 363–379, rpt. in *Essential Articles*, ed. Hamilton, p. 509. Berger explains the dichotomy of allegory and realism by emphasizing Spenser's psychological process when mastering inner experience to perform his role as poet (pp. 509–523); nonetheless, like Lewis, he remains "uneasy" over Spenser's "praise of Essex," because it is "so conventionally hyperbolic and so

234 SPENSER STUDIES

blatant a piece of patron-seeking": "the poet as man must . . . compromise his purity and be realistic in order to survive" (p. 520). Fowler, "Spenser's *Prothalamion*," explains the dichotomy by emphasizing the generic expectations Spenser follows when converting "occasion" into "poetry" (pp. 59–86); he objects to Berger's "modern stance that . . . dwells on its element of personal complaint, and treats its compliments as ironic or cynical or wryly practical—or anything, but sincere" (p. 61), yet eventually he follows Berger in describing the complaint as "resolved through the distancing process of poetic mediation and 'the inward mastery of experience' [Berger, p. 521]" (p. 84). Thus, even though Berger and Fowler argue for unity, each hints at interpretive dissatisfaction. Other critics who treat or refer to the question of unity include J. Norton Smith, "Spenser's Prothalamion: A New Genre," *Review of English Studies*, N.S. 10 (1959), 173–178; M. L. Wine, "Spenser's 'Sweete *Themmes*': Of Time and the River," *Studies in English Literature*, 2 (1962), 111–117, rpt. in *Spenser: A Collection of Critical Essays*, ed. Harry Berger, Jr. (Englewood Cliffs, N. J.: Prentice-Hall, 1968), pp. 40–46; Woodward, "Spenser's 'Prothalamion,' " pp. 34–46; Carolyn Prager, "Emblem and Motion in Spenser's *Prothalamion*," *Studies in Iconology*, 2 (1976), 114–120; Sandra R. Patterson, "Spenser's *Prothalamion* and the Catullan Epithalamic Tradition," *Comitatus*, 10 (1979–80), 97–106; and Eckhard Auberlen, "Spenser's 'Olde Woes' and the Epithalamic Convention," in *The Commonwealth of Wit: The Writer's Image and His Strategies of Self-Representation in Elizabethan Literature* (Tübingen: Gunter Narr, 1984), pp. 93–106.

12. Spenser hints at this process in the *Letter to Ralegh* and amplifies on it in the Proems to the six books of *The Faerie Queene*. This is essentially the process Sidney articulates in *The Defence of Poesie*. As Sidney knew, poetry needed to be defended as more than narcissistic delight and private instruction. However, in *Prothalamion* Spenser uniquely grounds the poetic process in the poet's disillusionment with the actual world.

13. While this charge is present in the sixteenth century, it becomes rampant by the nineteenth. It surfaces as early as 1598 when Everard Guilpin, in *Skialetheia*, notes that "Some blame deep Spenser" for writing a "masterpiece of cunning" (in Paul J. Alpers, ed., *Edmund Spenser: A Critical Anthology* [Harmondsworth: Penguin, 1979], p. 52). For Warton (*Observations on "The Faerie Queene" of Spenser* [1754], in Alpers, p. 103), for Wordsworth (Dedication to *The White Doe of Rylstone* [1815], in Alpers, p. 125]), and for Coleridge (from notes for lectures on Spenser [1818], in Alpers, p. 144), Spenser is a great "enchanter" who "waves his wand of enchantment," as Hazlitt says, "and at once embodies airy beings, and throws a delicious veil over all actual objects" (from *Lectures on the English Poets* [1818], in Alpers, p. 131). See also Leigh Hunt, "A New Gallery of Pictures" (1833), in *The Prince of Poets: Essays on Edmund Spenser*, ed. John R. Elliott, Jr. (New York: New York University Press, and London: University of London Press, 1968), for a passage on the poet's withdrawal that could be inspired by the opening of *Prothalamion* (p. 16). In an essay inaugurating modern Spenser studies, Edward Dowden, "Spenser, the Poet and Teacher," in *The Prince of Poets*, ed. Elliott (pp. 49–65), tries to refute precisely this view of the poet's art: "Shall we say . . . that Spenser is . . . the creator of illusions, the enchanter of the Elizabethan age . . . ?" If men of affairs like Ralegh, Drake, Bacon, and Hooker were reforming society, "where was Spenser? Was he forgetful of England, forgetful of earth,

THE OLD POET PRESENTS HIMSELF

lulled and lying in some bower of fantasy" (p. 49)? Dowden's answer, of course, is "no": Spenser entered and created his magical world, not to escape from contemporary affairs, but to reform them. While recent historical critics join Dowden in reading Spenser's poetry more sensitively than did the Romantics, they seem to overlook their usual rejection of Romantic readings by arguing for a Romantic Spenser at the end of his career and by seeing *Prothalamion* as evidence for their argument.

14. Montrose, "Of Gentlemen and Shepherds: The Politics of Elizabethan Pastoral Form," *ELH*, 50 (1983), 419. Montrose, speaking about pastoral, takes the term "primary activity" from Raymond Williams, citing *Culture* (London: Fontana, 1981), p. 13, and *Marxism and Literature* (New York: Oxford University Press, 1977), p. 133.

15. The poet's walk is consistent with the "escapism" noted by Richard Neuse in Book VI, with its "repeated motif of retirement from court to a greener world" ("Book VI as Conclusion," p. 371). On escapism in *Prothalamion*, see Berger, "Spenser's *Prothalamion*," pp. 514–517.

16. See, for example, Alexander C. Judson, *The Life of Edmund Spenser* (Baltimore, Md.: Johns Hopkins University Press, 1945), pp. 190–191.

17. Sidney, *The New Arcadia*, Book I, p. 24, l. 26, in *Sir Philip Sidney: The Countess of Pembroke's Arcadia (The New Arcadia)*, ed. Victor Skretkowicz (Oxford: Clarendon Press, 1987).

18. Essentially, he walks among "the flowers of poetry" in "Apollo's garden" (Sidney, *An Apologie for Poetrie*, in *Elizabethan Critical Essays*, ed. G. Gregory Smith, 2 vols. [London: Oxford University Press, 1904], I, 105).

19. Critics recurringly associate features of *Prothalamion* with the poet and his poetry without providing a comprehensive framework. Although Fowler makes the identification of flower gathering with poetry, he does not extend the identification. Later, he finds an "unmistakable self-reference in the . . . account [in Stanza 7] of how the Lee . . . lackt a tongue" (p. 74), and he finds a pun on "posies" (l. 34)—a variant of "poesy" (*O.E.D.*, p. 65, n. 21). Berger, "Spenser's *Prothalamion*," associates the "gentle spirit" of l. 3 with "the slowing spell of imagination" (p. 514). Woodward ("Spenser's 'Prothalamion',") notes "the fertility imagery" associated with the Nymphs (p. 37), even though he does not associate that fertility with poetic creation. And William Elford Rogers, "Proserpina in the *Prothalamion*," *American Notes and Queries*, 15 (1977), interprets Spenser's well-recognized allusion to the Proserpina myth of Ovid as "an allegory of generation" (p. 134), but he does not associate that allegory with poetic generation. Once we read the poem in light of Spenser's poetics, we can more satisfactorily interpret the evocative opening quatrain, in which "Sweete breathing Zephyrus did softly play / A gentle spirit, that lightly did delay / Hot Titans beames" (ll. 2–4): the elements of air and light evoke a kind of groundplot for poetic inspiration. According to Berger, "Spenser's *Prothalamion*," "The periphrases of the opening quatrain suggest the *locus amoenus* which is an artificial and mental rather than a natural 'place' " (p. 513).

20. Although Spenser does not explicitly link chance with grace here, elsewhere in his poetry he does. In Book I of *The Faerie Queene*, for instance, he uses the language of pagan philosophy (chance, fortune, necessity) to indicate the working of grace—an idea he clarifies during Redcrosse's fall to the dragon: "It chaunst (eternall God that chaunce did guide) . . ." (xi.45). See also III.vii.27: "It fortuned (high God did so ordaine)."

21. Editors of *The Explicator*, 1 (1942), art. 36, rpt. in the *Variorum Edition*, p. 667. Fowler, "Spenser's *Prothalamion*," would agree: the "swan incident occasioned by Leda's purity might signify . . . no more than the supernaturality of the union" (p. 81).

22. See, for example, the *Variorum Edition*, p. 498; and Hugh Maclean, ed. *Edmund Spenser's Poetry*, 2nd ed. (1968; New York and London: Norton, 1982), p. 546, n. 2.

23. *Aeneid*, I.327–328, in *Virgil*, trans. H. Rushton Fairclough, The Loeb Classical Library, 2 vols. (Cambridge, Mass.: Harvard University Press, and London: William Heinemann, 1956) I; although critics overlook this Virgilian allusion, they find others: see, *e.g.*, Fowler, "Spenser's *Prothalamion*," pp. 74 and 83.

24. Ovid, *Metamorphoses*, I.585, tr. Arthur Golding (1567), in *Shakespeare's Ovid*, ed. W. H. D. Rouse (New York: Norton, 1966). Berger, "Spenser's *Prothalamion*," refers briefly to the myth (pp. 516–517), as does Patterson, "Spenser's *Prothalamion* and the Catullan Epithalamic Tradition," p. 100, and Rogers, "Proserpina in the *Prothalamion*," p. 131, but none of these critics examines the myth's function. Fowler, "Spenser's *Prothalamion*," refers to Spenser's use of "myths of rough sexual capture" (p. 62).

25. In l. 40, Spenser mentions another part of the Peneus/Tempe/Thessaly landscape, Mount Pindus, indicating his debt to Ovid, whose myth concludes: "There is a lande in Thessalie enclosed on every syde / With woodie hilles, that Timpe hight, through mid whereof doth glide / Peneus gushing full of froth from foote of Pindus hye. / Which with his headlong falling downe doth cast up violently, / A mistie steame lyke flakes of smoke, besprinckling all about / The toppes of trees . . ." (ll. 701–706). All four places—Thessaly, Tempe, the Peneus River, and Mount Pindus—reappear in Spenser's poem, linked with the action of falling and of besprinkling.

26. Cain, "Spenser and the Renaissance Orpheus," cites Boccaccio on Orpheus' death as the triumph over time (pp. 26–27); Patricia Vicari, "The Triumph of Art, the Triumph of Death: Orpheus in Spenser and Milton," in *Orpheus: The Metamorphoses of a Myth*, ed. John Warden (Toronto, Buffalo, and London: University of Toronto Press, 1982), cites *The Ruines of Time* for Spenser's own use of the myth in this way (pp. 211–213).

27. In *The Ruines of Time*, Spenser envisons Sidney's harp swimming "adowne the Lee" (l. 603), which prompts him to refer to Orpheus' death (ll. 607–608); the phrase "adowne the Lee" recurs in *Prothalamion* (l. 115). Cain, "Spenser and the Renaissance Orpheus," says, in another context, that "the woods-resounding formula . . . always betokens the Orpheus archetype" (p. 29). The commendatory verse to *The Faerie Queene* by "R. S." is revealing: "Fayre Thamis streame, that from Ludds stately towne, / Runst paying tribute to the Ocean seas, / Let all thy Nymphes and Syrens of renowne / Be silent, whyle this Bryttane Orpheus playes: / Nere thy sweet bankes, there lives that sacred crowne, / Whose hand strowes Palme and never-dying bayes, / Let all at once, with thy soft murmuring sowne / Present her with this worthy Poets prayes." In effect, Spenser in *Prothalamion* enacts the role of Orphic poet assigned to him by "R. S." *Cf.* Manley, "Spenser and the City," pp. 209–210, and William Elford Rogers, "The Carmina of Horace in Prothalamion," *American Notes and Queries*, 15 (1977), 149 (Rogers also points out the link between Mount Pindus and Orpheus in Horace, *Odes*, I.12: 6–8

[p. 148]). Two other recent articles on the Orpheus myth in Spenser overlook the Orphic details I identify: Harry Berger, Jr., "Orpheus, Pan, and the Poetics of Misogyny: Spenser's Critique of Pastoral Love and Art," *ELH*, 50 (1983), 27–60; and Joseph Loewenstein, "Echo's Ring: Orpheus and Spenser's Career," *English Literary Renaissance*, 16 (1986), 287–302.

28. For helping me see that the "Lay" is not a formal Orphic hymn but an adjusted one, I am grateful to Professor Cain. The singer, rather than addressing the gods, as in an Orphic hymn, addresses the brides; nonetheless, the praise of Venus and Cupid (ll. 96–100) is consistent with the Orphic tenor of the song.

29. Berger, "Spenser's *Prothalamion*," notes that the "Lay" "dramatically opposes the daunger that keeps the brides from seizing the day" (p. 518), and he sees the song as a "mask or mouthpiece" through which "Spenser addresses the brides" (p. 518). We need to ask, how does the "Lay" function? why is it sung for the swan-brides? what is its effect? Clearly, the "Lay" has a rhetorical purpose within the narrative; it does what poetry does: it transforms the audience's active life.

30. The reference to "blisful bower" (l. 93) evokes Belphoebe's "bowre of blis" in Book III (v.35), while the actual phrasing appears at III.vi.11 (referring to Venus' "blisfull bowre"). Similarly, the phrase "Loves dislike and friendships faultie guile" evokes the central virtues of Books III and IV. Essentially, the vocabulary of the song is the vocabulary of the middle books.

31. Dan S. Norton, "Queen Elizabeth's 'Brydale Day'," *Modern Language Quarterly*, 5 (1944), assumes that the muse is Spenser's (p. 152); Cain, "Spenser and the Renaissance Orpheus," disagrees (p. 46). Fowler, "Spenser's *Prothalamion*," comments: "whether the 'brave Muse [who] may sing / To ages following' of Elizabeth's name and Essex's exploits is himself or not, his poetry will in any case outlast them all. Here as elsewhere Spenser fronts posterity more confidently than any previous English poet" (p. 80). Norton explains the clumsy conclusion of this stanza as a reference to Accession Day, and says that ll. 156–162 express "a mystical paradox which [Spenser] had developed allegorically in *The Faerie Queene* [in the union of both Britomart/Artegall and Arthur/Gloriana—the paradox of Elizabeth as the virgin bride of England] and which is a part of his countrymen's conception of their virgin sovereign" (p. 154).

32. Commenting on Spenser's use of Revelation in Book I, O'Connell, *Mirror and Veil*, shows an analogous technique: "By gesturing toward events in the recent past through the medium of allusion to the book of Revelation, [Spenser] suggests that Britain's history has itself become a partaking of sacred myth. . . . Elizabethan Englishmen should sense the ways in which their own age and nation have shared in those sacred, transcendent patterns" (p. 43).

33. Professor A. Kent Hieatt has kindly alerted me to the Dedicatory Sonnet to Essex published with the 1590 edition of *The Faerie Queene*: "when my Muse . . . / With bolder wing shall dare alofte to sty / To the last praises of this Faery Queene, / Then shall it make more famous memory / Of thine Heroicke parts" (ll. 7–12). Professor Hieatt suggests that the sonnet offers additional evidence for thinking that Spenser's celebration of Essex in *Prothalamion* continues the poet's original frame of mind in *The Faerie Queene*, because the sonnet celebrates Essex in terms analogous to those in the "Spousall Verse." On the Arthur/Essex connection, see Isabel E. Rathborne,

The Meaning of Spenser's Fairyland (New York: Columbia University Press, 1937), pp. 235 ff.; and Merritt Y. Hughes, "The Arthurs of The Faerie Queene," Etudes Anglaises, 6, (1953), 195–196.

34. I gratefully borrow the term "meta-allegory" from Professor Gordon Teskey (in his response to my paper, "Prothalamion and The Faerie Queene: Spenser's 'Spousall Verse' as a Defense of Allegorical Love Poetry," during the 22nd International Congress on Medieval Studies, Western Michigan University, Kalamazoo, Michigan, May 9, 1987).

35. For perceptively reading earlier drafts of this paper, I extend special thanks to Professor Mark A. Heberle, to Professor P. J. Klemp, and to Professor John W. Moore, Jr. I wish also to thank Ms. Michelle Marie Schlak for working with me on Prothalamion in her Senior Honors Thesis, "Fashioning Self and Society: Structure and Career Vision in Edmund Spenser's Prothalamion" (University Park, Pa.: Pennsylvania State University, 1987); and Professor Jeff Walker for suggesting that I open this paper with the "commonplace" of Spenser's "disillusionment." Finally, I wish to express my gratitude to Professor Anne Lake Prescott for her encouragement from nearly the beginning of this project and for thoroughly reviewing the paper at the end of it.

S. K. HENINGER, JR.

Spenser and Sidney at Leicester House

A LEGEND persists that Sidney was a solicitous patron early in Spenser's career and that he had a direct and decisive effect upon Spenser's writing. This legend, which Spenser actively encouraged,[1] is as old as the commendatory verses printed with the first installment of *The Faerie Queene* in 1590. In that clutch of gratulatory material, a substantial poem signed with the initials W. L. claims that Spenser owes a considerable debt to Sidney. The second stanza reads as follows:

> When *Spencer* saw the fame was spredd so large,
> Through Faery land of their renowned Queene:
> Loth that his Muse should take so great a charge,
> As in such haughty matter to be seene,
> To seeme a shepeheard then he made his choice,
> But *Sydney* heard him sing, and knew his voice.

The implications are clear. Spenser hesitated to attempt so audacious a task as praise of Elizabeth and preferred to continue in the lowly vein of pastoral. But Sidney became aware of his poetical talent and urged him to write *The Faerie Queene.*

If Spenser had any personal interaction with Sidney, it must have taken place between the early months of 1579, when Spenser entered Leicester's employ, and July 1580, when Spenser left London for Ireland in the employ of Lord Grey de Wilton. By the time Spenser returned to London with Sir Walter Ralegh in 1590, Sidney had been dead for over three years; and Sidney, despite his father's involvement in Ireland, never visited that rebellious country. We know very little about Spenser's service with Leicester, however, and fundamental quesions remain. What were Spenser's duties in Leicester's household, and how might he have been occupied during this crucial period of approximately a year and a half? What was his proximity to the seat of power in England, and what was his relationship to those in power? The evidence is scanty, and much doubtful speculation has been based upon it. Most particularly, what is the likelihood of a personal relationship between Spenser and Sidney; and, if the two young poets were acquainted, what might the nature of that relationship have been?

To sketch quickly Spenser's life in the immediately preceding years, he had gone down from Cambridge perhaps as early as the autumn 1574, and for a long while drops completely out of the biographer's sight. It has been assumed that he spent at least some of those years in the north of England, though there is no evidence for this other than inferences from *The Shepheardes Calender*,[2] and no particular place in the north has been suggested with any plausibility. In any case, so goes the accepted biography, Spenser came south during 1578. At some time during that year he accepted employment with John Young, the former master of Pembroke, Spenser's college at Cambridge, who in March 1578 had been installed as bishop of Rochester and at that time had taken up residence at Bromley in Kent. The fact of Spenser's employment by Bishop Young rests upon a single piece of external evidence: an inscription in a book which belonged to Gabriel Harvey. On the title page of Jerome Turler's *The Traveiler* (1575) Harvey has scribbled a note indicating that the book was given him by Spenser: *ex dono Edmundi Spenserii, Episcopi Roffensis Secretarii*, accompanied by the date 1578.[3] So it is reasonable to conclude that in 1578 Spenser was employed by John Young, Episcopus Roffensis. And this assumption is confirmed by internal evidence in *The Shepheardes Calender*, specifically by the tale of Roffy and his dog Lowder embedded in the September eclogue. I am less than convinced, though, that Spenser was actually the bishop's private secretary. Given Harvey's propensity to exaggerate, it is advisable to weigh this chance notation prudently. If Spenser were merely in Young's household, Harvey was capable of inflating any appointment, no matter how menial, to the important post of personal secretary.

At the least, though, it is safe to say that by the end of 1578 Spenser was living in Kent, ten miles outside London, and that for some months he was employed by John Young, who as a protegé of Edmund Grindal, Archbishop of Canterbury, held the highly political post of bishop of Rochester. But exactly what Spenser did for the bishop cannot be determined. As A. C. Judson asks rhetorically in the biographical volume of the Spenser *Variorum* (which, incidentally, has been little emended since it was published over forty years ago): "Did he aid the bishop with his correspondence? Did he serve as tutor to Susan Watts [Young's stepdaughter]? Did he enjoy alike the beautiful rolling country of Kent and the proximity of Bromley to both court and city? Did the ecclesiastical problems that had disturbed the calm of Cambridge acquire even a deeper significance when viewed over the shoulder of a bishop?"[4] Judson concludes: "No categorical answer, it appears, may be given to any of these questions." And I would add that we must not allow the formulation of these questions to take on the certainty of answers. The truth of the matter is that we really do not know how Spenser spent his time in Kent or with whom he spent it.

Nor do we know when Spenser moved to London to take up service with Leicester, or what circumstances prompted that move. According to a letter that Harvey copied into his letter-book, Spenser was in London by mid-summer 1579,[5] but he could have made the move at any time during the preceding six months. A more cogent question is what Spenser was expected to do in Leicester's employ. The glib assumption has been that he became Leicester's secretary, but there is no firm evidence to support that assumption, and much circumstantial fact would suggest otherwise. Apart from Spenser's poems, the only evidence we have for Spenser's biography during the time he might have served Leicester is the putative correspondence between Spenser and Harvey published in June 1580. The reliability of that evidence, however, is seriously impugned. Judson is candid about the scantiness of real evidence and the doubtfulness of what we do have:

> The documents which give us a glimpse of this *annus mirabilis*, aside from *Mother Hubberds Tale*, which appears to belong in part to this time, are chiefly letters, written by Harvey and Spenser to each other. One of these seems unfortunately not to be a genuine missive, and even the others may have been altered for publication.

(54)

When we look into the reasons for publishing this correspondence, we understand Judson's caution.

In April 1580 the post of Public Orator at Cambridge was being vacated, and Harvey began actively to seek the appointment. Virginia F. Stern in her biography of Harvey reconstructs the whole affair.[6] Harvey wrote to Burleigh, Chancellor of the University, asking for his support; and indeed Burleigh complied with a letter to the Cambridge authorities. But to no avail. Harvey had already generated insuperable opposition within the University. Although the post was not filled until the following March, almost a year later, Harvey succeeded only in damaging his future prospects. It seems probable, however, that Harvey published his correspondence with Spenser as part of his campaign to secure the office of Public Orator. Therefore the letters were engineered, if not originally contrived, to bolster Harvey's importance by taking advantage of Spenser's position in London and by exploiting the success of The Shepheardes Calender. Very little in the letters can be taken at face value. In all fairness to Harvey, judging from the deference paid to him as Hobbinol, it would seem that Spenser was a willing accomplice in furthering his friend's academic career. The scheme was so transparent, though, and the letters so offensive to certain personalities at Cambridge and in London that the project backfired and lessened Harvey's chances for any University appointment.[7] Given Harvey's ulterior purpose in publishing these letters, we must take their contents in large part as puffery. I am not the first, of course, to question the dependability of the Spenser-Harvey correspondence; as Eleanor Rosenberg bluntly states in her authoritative study of Leicester's patronage, "Some scholars regard it as bogus."[8]

The sort of vain speculation this correspondence can lead to is well exemplified by yesteryear's scholarly war over the Areopagus. Was there or was there not a coterie of poetry lovers meeting in Leicester House and presided over by Spenser and Sidney, as these letters indicate? No one any longer puts much stock in the notion of such a group, and it is now clear that the whole thing was persiflage between two Cambridge cronies. At most, Spenser was aware of certain poetical activities involving Sidney and Edward Dyer. But the probability of a "senate" of literary theorists meeting on any sort of regular basis and bringing Spenser into contact with other practicing poets now seems far-fetched. A legend from the past.

Moreover, the other so-called facts of Spenser's service with Leicester similarly disappear. Judson jumps to a momentous conclusion: "However the connection was formed, there can be no doubt that Spenser for a time served Leicester and was on a friendly footing with Sidney, Dyer, and [Daniel] Rogers, frequented Leicester House, and had the entrée of the court" (59). But he bases these conclusions upon the Spenser-Harvey correspondence. We can be reasonably certain that Spenser enjoyed employment of some sort with Leicester, but the nature of that employment is wholly unknown. The easy comment that he was Leicester's secretary is unwarranted. We have no idea what Spenser was expected to do or how he spent his time. There is no evidence that he was entrusted with letter-writing or with any other confidential duties.[9] In contrast, the career of Arthur Atey, who became Leicester's secretary in late summer 1580, is well documented (Rosenberg 150 [n. 61]). We cannot be sure even that Spenser "frequented Leicester House," although one of his letters that Harvey printed is addressed from there.

An ancillary question inquires into the circumstances surrounding Spenser's exit from Leicester's service and his going to Ireland in the retinue of Lord Grey de Wilton.[10] Beginning with Edwin A. Greenlaw,[11] it has been generally assumed that the political content of *The Shepheardes Calender* and "Mother Hubberds Tale" produced an angry reaction (from unspecified quarters) and that Leicester shipped off Spenser as a rebuke for his presumptuousness. The dedicatory verse that Spenser prefixed to "Virgil's Gnat," addressing the work to the "late deceased" Leicester, supports this surmise. But again, the evidence is far from complete and should not be over-interpreted. Such a reading makes Spenser a too-important player in Leicester's game. More plausible, and perhaps not mutually exclusive, Spenser received his post in Ireland upon the recommendation of Sir Henry Sidney, Philip's father, who had immediately preceded Lord Grey as Lord Deputy of Ireland. Arthur Collins in his long adulatory account of Sir Henry notes: "His immediate Successor [as Lord Deputy] was *Arthur* Lord *Grey* of *Wilton,* who requested his Opinion in what Manner he should act to serve his Queen and Country"[12]; and later historians have accepted this statement of Henry Sidney's legacy in Ireland.[13] So if Lord Grey engaged Spenser upon Sir Henry's advice, the appointment in Ireland may have been an advancement for Spenser, not a reprimand.[14] In either case, Henry Sidney was acquainted with Spenser, even if Philip was not. Again, however, the conditions of Spenser's departure for Ireland in July 1580 can be speculated about, but nothing certain can be concluded.

Equally questionable is Judson's assertion that Spenser "was on a friendly footing with Sidney, Dyer, and Rogers." Judson was led to this conclusion by references to Sidney and Dyer in the Spenser-Harvey correspondence. According to that publication, Spenser wrote to Harvey: "They have me, I thanke them, in some use of familiarity" (*Poetical Works*, 635). But such a comment goes beyond boasting. It rings of presumption, and even more probably of pretention—and most probably of pretense. It is a bold claim to impress the world; but its lack of basis in fact, coupled with similar indiscretions in the correspondence, had a negative effect upon Spenser's career as well as upon that of Harvey. It is difficult for the modern mind to appreciate the difference in rank between Sidney and Spenser. Sidney was the godson of King Philip of Spain and the Duchess of Northumberland, the nephew and heir to both Leicester and Warwick, and the beneficiary of several years' travel on the Continent visiting the political and intellectual centers of Europe. In contrast, Spenser could at best claim distant kinship to a northern family of some social standing, and because of straitened means had never left the shores of England. Sidney was assured of a glorious future; Spenser was struggling for recognition, even a livelihood. There was also an unbridgeable disparity between the social rank of Spenser and that of Dyer, a gentleman in his own right as well as a long-standing and trusted friend of the Dudley family. At most, Sidney or Dyer may have been aware of Spenser's presence in London, and perhaps on occasion one or the other engaged him in conversation. But the likelihood of intimacy with either of them is remote, and certainly undocumented. The difference in social degree and the press of business ruled out long discussions about poetry.

Finally, Judson's statement that Spenser "had the entrée of the court" now seems ludicrous. If he ever gained access to the court, it would have been as Leicester's underling, and no one would have paid him much attention. Spenser may have been at the center of power in England for a brief period in 1579–80, but there is no evidence that he had any influence whatsoever in the exercise of that power. As Rosenberg notes, the letters in the Spenser-Harvey correspondence attributed to Spenser are full of optimism. In her words, "Airy references to his seeing the Queen, to the 'Areopagus,' to frequent visits to court, give an impression of great busyness and prosperity. He is so well placed that he hopes for important preferment for himself and intends to use his influence on his friend's behalf" (331). But those hopes came to nothing and, of course, have no substance, based as they were in Harvey's schemes.

From various sources—not only the Spenser-Harvey correspondence, but also the incidental material published with *The Shepheardes Calender* and the headpiece by William Ponsonby published before the *Complaints* volume in 1591—we are led to believe that Spenser at this time was working on a large number of pieces and indeed had a great many ready for publication. So we may assume that he had been left alone to read his books and write his poetry. Suspiciously, however, none of the dozen or so titles mentioned actually exist in fact, unless we take the marriage of the Thames and Medway in Book 4 of *The Faerie Queene* to be a later incarnation of a poem referred to as *Epithalamion Thamesis*. All of the others have vanished without a trace. And in my role as doubting Thomas, I question whether they ever did exist. I am not willing to accept evidence from the writings of Spenser and his friends without relentless scrutiny, because all of these young men were on the make. They were ambitious to a fault and were fully trained in the language arts as a means of furthering a political career.

The only evidence from this period that we have yet to examine derives from publication of *The Shepheardes Calender* in the waning weeks of 1579. This work is flamboyantly addressed to Sidney by an obtrusive dedication on the title page itself: "To the noble and vertuous Gentleman most worthy of all titles both of learning and chevalrie M. Philip Sidney." Remembering the marriage negotiations between Elizabeth and the duc d'Anjou which had gone on for almost a year, we rightly ask: Wasn't *The Shepheardes Calender* part of Leicester's effort to oppose the Anjou match, and doesn't this evidence show Spenser hobnobbing with the great and participating in power politics? Perhaps, but only perhaps. William A. Ringler, Jr., has shown that Spenser first intended to dedicate *The Shepheardes Calender* to Leicester, and then rather at the last minute changed his mind and addressed it to Sidney instead.[15]

This shift in strategy—considering one patron, and then seeking approval from another—reveals indecisiveness at the least, and more probably exposes Spenser in the act of figuring how to get the surest reward from his literary efforts. To me it suggests an outsider trying to get in, rather than an insider carrying out secret orders from a party leader.

Well, then, how about Sidney's mentioning *The Shepheardes Calender* in his *Defence of Poesie*? Sidney praises Spenser as one of only four English poets who have written anything worthwhile. Isn't this testimony of their friendship? First, we must note that Sidney's praise of *The Shepheardes Calender* is tepid at best. It "hath much poetry in his eclogues, indeed worthy the reading," Sidney says, then adds problematically, "if I be not deceived."[16] Second, Sidney does not mention Spenser by name. Some might argue that Sidney omits Spenser's name in keeping with an attempt at secrecy about authorship, since Spenser modestly signed the work "Immeritô" and didn't reveal his true identity anywhere in the volume. But it is equally plausible that Sidney did not know the name of the author of *The Shepheardes Calender*. Although Sidney's writings are extensive, there is no other indication that he was aware of Spenser or any of his works.

Elsewhere I have shown that the typographical layout of *The Shepheardes Calender* pointedly replicates Francesco Sansovino's illustrated edition of Sannazaro's *Arcadia* printed at Venice in 1571, and I argue that Harvey contrived this allusion to Sannazaro in order to secure the patronage of Sidney, who by 1579 had already made known his literary preferences by a self-conscious imitation of Sannazaro's pastoral.[17] Following the stratagem of Gascoigne, who had adopted the sham initials G. T. as ghost editor of his own volume of *Hundreth Sundrie Flowres* (1573), Harvey adopted the initials E. K. and in effect appropriated his friend's calendar of eclogues to further his own career. The point was to attract Sidney's attention in the hope that he would sponsor a literary coterie similar to the Neapolitan Academy presided over by Pontano and Sannazaro—indeed, to fulfill the wishing expressed in the Spenser-Harvey correspondence by talk of an Areopagus. The decision to dedicate *The Shepheardes Calender* to Sidney instead of Leicester then becomes part of this maneuvering. In this scenario, Harvey played his frequent role of exploiting his talented friends and addressed Spenser's poem to Sidney with effusive announcements of Hobbinol's identity while suppressing the identity of Colin Clout. Although Sidney saw a text of *The Shepheardes Calender*, probably in manuscript before its publication, he was unacquainted with its author.

In fine, I am afraid we must give up our cherished legends that Spenser was private secretary to the magnificent earl of Leicester and that he played a significant role in the power brokerage of Elizabethan England as one of Leicester's agents.[18] We must also forego the attractive notion that he was a familiar of Philip Sidney. Actually, there is no indisputable evidence that the two poets ever met.

And that brings us back to the quotation from the commendatory verse signed by W. L. and appended to *The Faerie Queene* in 1590. Doesn't this contemporary comment prove that Sidney had an intentional hand in Spenser's career? As a matter of fact, no. We cannot determine for sure who "W. L." might have been; but for lack of a better candidate, he is usually identified as William Lisle, in 1590 a twenty-year-old scholar at Cambridge who spent most of his adult life working on Anglo-Saxon manuscripts. If this identification is correct, "W. L." would have been about ten when Sidney supposedly turned Spenser away from pastoral trivia and directed him toward the heroic praise of Elizabeth. Whoever "W. L." may have been, what we have, of course, is a latter-day Gabriel Harvey, another university man trying to make his way in the world by exercising his wits and pleasing the powerful. I doubt if the truth was in him; certainly, he was not recording personal knowledge to inform posterity. And so this report of patronage between Sidney and Spenser also dissolves into legend. The result, in fact, is a legend twice compounded: the already legendary Astrophel is evoked to enhance the reputation of an expatriate poet seeking the legendary post of Elizabeth's laureate.

University of North Carolina, Chapel Hill

NOTES

1. See the dedicatory headpiece to "The Ruines of Time" as well as the envoy at the end, the dedicatory sonnet addressed to the Countess of Pembroke

appended to *The Faerie Queene*, and the lines devoted to Sidney in *Colin Clouts Come Home Againe* (448–451). Spenser also composed the elegy "Astrophel," though this memorial came so long after Sidney's death (nine years) that it required an apology. Furthermore, the tone of the elegy is remarkably impersonal—the curious identification of Stella as Sidney's wife, in fact, makes me wonder what Spenser knew about the more intimate details of Sidney's life, or at least what he was willing to comment upon in public.

2. *Cf.* E. K.'s gloss on "June" 18.

3. Turler, *The Traveiler*, intro. Denver Ewing Baughan (Gainesville, Fla.: Scholars' Facsimiles, 1951).

4. *The Life of Edmund Spenser* (Baltimore, Md.: Johns Hopkins University Press, 1945), p. 49.

5. *Letter-Book of Gabriel Harvey*, ed. Edward John Long Scott. Camden Society, NS 33 (Westminister, 1884), p. 64.

6. *Gabriel Harvey: His Life, Marginalia and Library* (Oxford: Clarendon Press, 1979), pp. 53 ff.

7. See G. C. Moore Smith, *Gabriel Harvey's Marginalia* (Stratford-upon-Avon: Shakespeare Head Press, 1913), pp. 31–41.

8. *Leicester: Patron of Letters* (New York: Columbia University Press, 1955), p. 329 (n. 19).

9. A post-script to a letter in the Spenser-Harvey correspondence dated 5 October 1579 implies that Spenser was soon to be sent abroad by "my Lorde" (*i.e.*, Leicester); see *The Poetical Works of Edmund Spenser*, ed. J. C. Smith and E. De Selincourt (London: Oxford University Press, 1912), p. 638. This trip never took place, however, and I attribute the statement to the badinage then passing between the two friends. Harvey was publicly embarrassed by a similar expectation of foreign service on Leicester's behalf (Rosenberg, pp. 324–326).

10. Recently historians of political thought have shown considerable interest in Spenser's Irish experience, largely through reexamining *A View of the Present State of Ireland*: see Nicholas Canny, "Edmund Spenser and the Development of an Anglo-Irish Identity," *Yearbook of English Studies*, 13 (1983), 1–19; Ciaran Brady, "Spenser's Irish Crisis: Humanism and Experience in the 1590s," *Past and Present*, 111 (May 1986), 17–49; and Canny, "Edmund Spenser as Political Theorist: A Comment on 'Spenser's Irish Crisis: Humanism and Experience in the 1590s,'" forthcoming. See also, though with caution, Richard Berleth, *The Twilight Lords: An Irish Chronicle* (New York: Knopf, 1978) *passim*. But no new light has been thrown upon the circumstances of Spenser's going to Ireland in the first place.

11. "Spenser and the Earl of Leicester," *PMLA*, 25 (1910), 535–561.

12. *Letters and Memorials of State, in the Reigns of Queen Mary, Queen Elizabeth, King James, King Charles the First, Part of the Reign of King Charles the Second, and Oliver's Usurpation*, 2 vols. (London, 1746), 1, 92.

13. Canny asserts, "Lord Grey de Wilton . . . was advised in everything by [Henry] Sidney" (*The Elizabethan Conquest of Ireland: A Pattern Established 1565–76* [New York: Harper, 1976] 159). Pauline Henley says confidently, though without additional evidence, "Sir Henry Sidney, who was a friend of Lord Grey's, would have recommended him for the post, as the poet was certainly a protegé of the statesman's son, Sir Philip Sidney" (*Spenser in Ireland* [Dublin and Cork: Cork University Press, 1928], p. 17).

Given the current interest in how Irish affairs affected Spenser's thinking and in how the Irish experience shaped colonial attitudes in the settlement of America, we should be more clear about the role of the Sidney family in the governance of Ireland. Sir Henry's service in Ireland dates back to May 1556, during the reign of Mary. When Sir Thomas Radcliffe, Lord Fitzwalter (Sir Henry's brother-in-law, and later earl of Sussex) took up his duties as Lord Deputy, Henry Sidney accompanied him as Vice-Treasurer (Richard Bagwell, *Ireland Under the Tudors*, 3 vols. [London, 1885–90], 1, 397; Canny, *Conquest of Ireland*, p. 34). Already Lord President of Wales, Henry Sidney was appointed Lord Deputy of Ireland in May 1565 (Canny, *Conquest of Ireland*, p. 44). Lord Grey was considered for appointment in Ireland as early as 1571 (Bagwell, 2, 207), but he did not actually go to Ireland until he was named Lord Deputy in July 1580. He was uncertain of how to proceed and sought the advice of Henry Sidney (*DNB*, "Arthur Grey," 613b). In 1582 Henry Sidney was approached with an invitation to return to the governing of Ireland, and he was agreeable to the appointment provided certain conditions were met, including "that Philip would accompany him thither, and bear the office after he had resigned it" (*DNB*, "Henry Sidney," 216a).

14. According to Brady, Spenser saw the appointment as a step toward realizing his political aspirations: "Like most of his contemporaries he regarded his appointments not as ends in themselves but as means towards personal advancement in other spheres through the acquisition of land, capital or merely favour" (p. 17).

15. "Spenser, Shakespeare, Honor, and Worship," *Renaissance News*, 14 (1961), 159–161.

16. *Miscellaneous Prose of Sir Philip Sidney*, ed. Katherine Duncan-Jones and Jan van Dorsten (Oxford: Clarendon Press, 1973), p. 112.

17. "The Typographical Layout of Spenser's *Shepheardes Calender*," *Word and Visual Imagination: Studies in the Interaction of English Literature and the Visual Arts*, ed. Karl Josef Höltgen, Peter M. Daly, and Wolfgang Lottes (Erlangen: Universitätsbibliothek, 1988) forthcoming.

18. Spenser did not make a noteworthy appearance at court until he was brought back to London from Ireland by Ralegh in 1589–90. At that point, under Ralegh's protection and with publication of *The Faerie Queene*, his career began a new phase. But even so, we should not exaggerate his importance in English politics. As Brady comments about the end of Spenser's career: "The recognition and advancement which he had looked for on the publication of the first instalment of the *Faerie Queene* had failed to materialize. After a fruitless sojourn in England in 1589–90 he returned to Ireland in the spring of 1591 with a small pension but without the honoured place at court for which he had yearned, and . . . he expressed his disillusionment with public life in *Colin Clouts Come Home Againe* and in the bitter additions which he made to his earlier satire *Mother Hubberds Tale*" (pp. 41–42).

ROGER KUIN

The Gaps and the Whites: Indeterminacy and Undecideability in the Sonnet Sequences of Sidney, Spenser, and Shakespeare

"L'armature intellectuelle du
poème, se dissimule et—a lieu—tient dans l'espace qui isole les
strophes et
parmi le blanc du papier; significatif silence qu'il
n'est pas moins beau de composer que les
vers."

(Mallarmé, *Le Livre*)

1

When the bed first answered back, Astrophil wondered if he was going mad. Then he remembered that he had merely lost his Reason, and with a sigh of relief gave it his full attention. From beyond the window, the highway muttered. A dog's bark and the cheep of a sparrow chimed in. With a malign whisper, Cupid spoke to him from the saddle. A friend's voice (was it old Languet again?) shouted to make itself heard. A coach rattled by, its curtains possibly drawn. And behind it all, the unceasing murmur of the Muse. Not for the first time, Astrophil reflected curiously upon the space he was trapped in. He had tried to raise (Edmund) in the next volume; but (Edmund), who was himself but not a name, pretended to be in Ireland and courtship. Two tomes away, *Will*, ambiguously triangulating, could not hear: which was probably just as well.

251

2

The trouble with *this* space was that it would not let him think his body. Yet every time he was lifted from the shelf, he felt new eyes completing him. Within a week, sometimes a day, his hair went from brown to blond to black, his frame from sturdy to slender, his features from grave to aquiline to fresh. Only his Desire came furiously erect for every reader; and his usually formless ears were doomed to hear Stella's refusal repeated time after painful time. He felt old and very tired. But his Maker, in his questionable wisdom, had given him not only no determination but no end. No state funeral for Astrophil; and (he kept coming back to this, obsessively) no *shape*, even. He existed, he knew, in parts, and damned few of those. Sometimes he felt, whitely, like one enormous Gap.

3

If you are here, with what I will have written, you will understand the story of the Harvard psychologist who was discovered, as his students filed into the lecture hall, flat on the table, eyes tight shut, three-piece suit carefully arranged. Uncertainly, they sat down; the worried buzz grew louder. After five interminable minutes he jumped up, smiled briskly, and said: "Now you know what we mean by *role expectation*."

4

The only way to begin an article on gaps in the sonnet sequences is by dis-concerting. For the gaps, like the beginnings of articles, normally go unnoticed.[1] To write *about* them without writing *in* them is a task fraught with hazard. Yet it is, in a sense, the essence of criticism which, being at all times a gloss, invariably occupies the white around and between the (poetic) texts. The danger of writing a gloss about the gaps is that there is no *space* for such a metatext, except to write across the text itself. This essay, then, is a *crossing* of the text(s)—like an old-fashioned cheque or an eighteenth-century letter—in order to save the white: to *save space*. We (you and I: indeterminate through each other's gaps) will cross them together. Not as

Virgil and Dante crossed the nether world, for no matter how pleasurable or terrifying the distractions, the *end* was always in view. Rather as a noncombatant might have crossed No–Man's–Land—or, if you prefer, a deserter. A deserter crosses at the same human peril as an innocent; but in addition, he knows his going a transgression, and although the intention of his destination is firm, he has no clear idea (or fore-conceit) of what he will find upon his arrival.

5

We will cross the texts also in their seeming purpose. To be written, to be printed, is to make your mark: to be present, to impinge, to instruct, to delight, to move. Exploring gaps, we will cross these meanings, these I-mean-to-says. We will listen to the texts, but not to what they want to say. Rather, to what they say in spite of themselves, what they cannot help saying; and, most disconcertingly, to what they appear not to say at all. Our examination and the texts will be—and guiltlessly—at *cross-purposes*.

6

Finally we may find, at the end of *our* text, that we have *crossed over*. The text is first a ptyx,[2] then a Styx. Exploring the gaps of the first, can we fail to find the second? Three sequences of love-sonnets cannot fail to engage us in our death (which physic did except). Crossing the ab-ject to study its gaps is to subvert[3] (every parallel between) the text and our lives: it is doing what comes naturally *in order* to cross over the immortality of art *in order* to reach, through the little death, the Big One. To *plunge into* the gaps of three texts that de-scribe love in short spurts is to accomplish the *erosis*[4] of the texts. It is one way to reach Bataille's "sovereignty" of (self-) abandonment in the face of Death.[5]

7

First we must agree on a choice of no–man's–lands. I propose a short Taxonomy of Gaps (which will later have to be destroyed). In so doing, I refer to other, theoretical, texts. Not to place them in the margins of the sonnet sequences, which would defeat my purpose; but to cross the sequences with them (first). This pre-liminary crossing will *produce* our own, which will thus wear openly its status as a *hybrid*.

8

The first in our taxonomy—as my numbers 1 and 2, above, will have suggested—is what we may call Ingarden's Gap. Such gaps are what the Polish philosopher referred to as *Un-bestimmtheitsstellen*, translated by Grabowicz[6] as "spots of indeterminacy" and by Iser[7] as "gaps of indeterminacy".[8] Ingarden's Gap is not a physical but an intellectual phenomenon. In the context of his analysis, it belongs to the Stratum of Represented Objects, and is what distinguishes *any* object represented in language from the corresponding (or any) "real" object. A real object is absolutely determined; while, no matter how exhaustive the description, an object represented in language will invariably present gaps of (in-)determinacy. These allow/force the reader to, in part, complete the "picture"; in fact his doing so is habitual and largely unconscious. Ingarden's Gap on one level is very simply grasped, and may seem trivial; yet on another it is of the greatest importance. In Ingarden's work, it helps to define the manner of a literary work's being, and the nature and range of its mimetic activity. For the present study, it is a useful gap with which to begin: both the most intellectually remote and the most embedded in subsequent theoretical concerns, it allows the beginning of subversion by way of apparent application.

9

The second is Iser's Gap.[9] This is essentially an extension of Ingarden's, effected by transfer from the Stratum of Represented Objects to that of Schematized Aspects (Ingarden) or Schematized Views (Iser).[10] This transfer is, concomitantly, also one from the paradigmatic to the syntagmatic dimension: Iser's Gap lies between the differing *Ansichten* of, for example, two plots of a narrative, successively actualized in alternating chapters. Two further points of Iser's Gap are relevant. The first is worked out in his discussion of the nineteenth-century serial novel, where syntagmatically-realized indeterminacy not only is associated with the process of text production but also creates, via continuous interaction with readers, a feedback effect. The second is demonstrated via a study of *Ulysses*, and shows that the multiplying of *Ansichten*, a device which in Ingarden's sense would reduce indeterminacy, in fact increases it by increasing the number of (Iser's) Gaps. To put it more theoretically: a consideration of textual time (the sequential nature of language/writing) undermines the effectiveness of the device which reduces paradigmatic indeterminacy by allowing it to increase syntagmatic indeterminacy. It is this transfer from model to movement, and the implications it raises, that makes Iser's Gap particularly relevant to the sonnet *sequences*.

10

More complex still is Derrida's Gap.[11] This spills over from the conceptual to the physical: in fact, in keeping with Derrida's project of the deconstruction of metaphysics via *écriture*, it intimately associates the two. One effect of the Derridean deconstruction is to make this kind of taxonomy virtually impossible, and his Gap almost impossible to describe. It is, as a gap, not only a gap but a *space*; as a space, also a *white*; as a white, because of a French polysemy that must be unfolded in English, additionally a *blank*. This, however, is by no means the end of its de-scriptions. Derrida's Gap is also the slash (/) that both joins and separates its flanking elements; it is the *limen,* the threshold, that marks a barrier *and* invites one to cross it; it is the *hymen,* the membrane that protects a space yet covers an opening into it; it is the space between the two texts of *Glas*.[12] It is, finally, the fold, the *brisure* (both break and joint), in and through which two texts are folded over on to each other and, as Derrida puts it, re-mark each other.[13] Within the present taxonomy (which, as remarked, it subverts), we may note that it not only effects a transfer from the purely conceptual to a conceptuality that embraces the physical, and potentially includes both the paradigmatic and the syntagmatic dimensions, but that it also allows (forces) us to extend indeterminacy to *undecideability*, which implies (as we shall see below) an added dimension of *active process*.

11

(At this point Derrida, characteristically, impels a digression. His Gap derives almost entirely from the consideration of nineteenth- and twentieth-century texts: Mallarmé and Genet and Sollers—who transform even earlier texts such as Plato and Hegel by the touch of his application. A necessary effect of his deconstruction is to make us question the applicability of not only his but *all* indeterminacy to early texts. In the case of Ingarden's Gap this problem is covered by Derrida's discussion of Husserl[14]; further applications involve the still-unfinished debate concerning the validity of structuralism. This, however, is not the place to pursue it. I propose, therefore, to remind ourselves of its existence and subsequently to continue the interrogation of our subject. In the case of the sonnet sequences, our enterprise is thus a *crossing* of the texts; yet we may find that they allow, or even invite, such a crossing to an unusual degree.)

12

The final element in our taxonomy is what I was tempted to call the Obvious, but have renamed the White, Gap. Its appearance is that of purely physical space: the space between (and, to a certain extent, the space around) the individual sonnets[15] of a sequence. In most versions, both MS. and printed, of sonnet sequences,[16] the sonnets are not printed as single texts per page. The White Gap, then, is a fairly small area of unprinted paper left between texts, usually filled with the number of the following sonnet. The layout also involves sonnets running over from the end of one page to the beginning of the next; in which case the respective lower and upper margins are given the role of what might be called a *self-denying* gap or space. Our evaluation of the White Gap's potential for more than a physical interpretation will be closely related to its differentiation from other, physically similar, gaps between a) the stanzas of a long poem, and b) the independent poems in an anthology or Miscellany. I propose to defer this differentiation until the final stages of my application; but I am prepared to state here my conviction that the White Gap is both physical and conceptual—that it is, in short, a gap of *Unbestimmtheit*.

13

"Now let me take some rest," sighed *Will*, temporarily between sonnets and driven (as so often) to quote his mentor Astrophil. He always seemed to be *between* things: between Friend and Lady, between Reason and Passion, between a name and an organ. *His* Maker (who was himself) had placed him there, for reasons he was tired of guessing at. Astrophil, for ever worrying about his shape, was no help; and he bitterly resented (Edmund), who claimed, with God's help, to have solved all the problems. Placed *between*, he was prevented from using the space between sonnets to rest; it hummed and echoed with the disseminating activity of his ambiguities. His bonds might be determinate: his texts were not.

14

Between the Taxonomy[17] and its placing-at-risk in a series of applications, an interim reflection may not be out of place. Since our four kinds of gap—or white—clearly span a wide range of signification, from philosophical indeterminacy to blank paper, we may begin to ask ourselves what they have in common. The first answer, I think, must be that they are all, in one way or another, *negativities*. They are each a negative space, a hollow, a *creux*[18]: but a *creux* in which things (can) happen. They are the negative face of the text (the "entre"/"antre", the cave: the con-cave?); they are the locus of *every* text's undecideability, and to an extraordinary degree that of the sonnet sequences.' Undecideability here may be defined as indeterminacy plus a dynamic of urgency; or indetermination plus overdetermination. The locus—or rather the loci, for there are many—of undecideability thus create(s) in the reader that tension which draws him into the text, which motivates him; and they provide, moreover, the liminary spaces through which he constructs his entrance into the text. Of all "early texts," I submit, it is the sonnet sequences which most inescapably activate these undecideabilities.

15

To begin, then, let us apply Ingarden's Gap to *Astrophil and Stella*; and let us at once tackle Iser's objection about trivialities by starting with represented *objects*. To some extent, of course, he is right. The fact that you, as a reader, unthinkingly assign a breed and a colour to Stella's dog (59) is of major importance neither for your interpretation of the text nor for the practice of reader-response criticism. Similarly, the hangings of Astrophil's bed (98), the breed of his horse (49), and the topography and destination of the highway (84) are, in more senses than Ingarden's, neither here nor there. Their indeterminacy, however, is of value only when it is brought together with both their referential unimportance and their textual prominence. For they are indeterminate not only to us but *to Sidney as well*. They furnish the pseudo-specificity on to which the concerns of both Astrophil and the reader may be projected; as such they are an innocent meeting-place for the object of the text and that of text-production.

16

This innocence of the indeterminately represented object is, however, soon left behind. As an example of the next stage of Ingarden's Gap, let us examine an object that appears in sonnet 105:

> Unhappie sight, and hath she vanisht by
> So neere, in so good time, so free a place?
> *Dead glasse,* doost thou thy object so imbrace,
> As what my hart still sees thou canst not spie?

The brief and foolish critical history of "Dead glasse"[19] (does it "mean" the mind's eye?) is of no importance. That any object designated "glasse" may have properties of transparency or reflectivity, either of which may be activated, helps us a little farther along, but not much. That the modern reader may associate it with the "miroir sans tain" topos so lovingly analyzed by Riffaterre[20] brings us closer still, but the aporia remains. And even common sense, which will consider "sight" the antecedent of both "dead glasse" and "thou," leaves an irreducible residue of discomfort. What, then, is happening here? It is perhaps best explained by saying that Ingarden's Gap is beginning to *come alive*. The indeterminacy that was of philosophical importance only in relation to Stella's dog has, in "dead glasse," been heightened to aporia. It has become *active*: and it has done so, in this case, by contaminating the most reliable of a text's features, its lexicality. Ingarden's Gap, in other words, has produced its indeterminacy, but this indeterminacy is one that the reader is prevented from (satisfactorily) completing. The result is an itch that must be scratched but will not go away.[21] Within the Stratum of Represented Objects, the reader is confronted with an *Unbestimmtheitsstelle* which, from being philosophical, has become textual, and thus inescapable. Not being given a decideable meaning, he is driven to *make* sense: and thus, to participate.

17

(A possible objection prompts me to a brief digression on indeterminacy and metaphor. Does—it might be asked—Ingarden's Gap properly apply to a trope such as "dead glasse"? Without tackling in too much detail a question of which the relevance goes well beyond the sonnet sequences—the relation of indeterminacy and rhetoric will need much of what Derrida would call "patient and rigorous work"[22]—I would suggest that it does so in a particular way. On the one hand, metaphor can be characterized as an indirect way partially to cancel or complete Ingarden's Gap. It does so by *triangulation*: providing another object, in a separate space, which points at the same essence, it locates that essence at the crossing of the two imaginary lines. On the other hand, the metaphor does not *fully* complete the Gap and thus control the reader's decoding: for at the heart of all the major tropes lies a further gap, which we might call Ricoeur's Gap[23] and which is epitomized by his citation of the Majorcan story-tellers' formulaic exordium "Aixo era y no era" (this was, and was not). Each of the four Great Tropes—metaphor, metonymy, synecdoche, and irony—consists of two poles in an indeterminate relation.)

18

Ingarden's Gap operates in a more complex way when the Represented Objects are human features. In this regard (and in few texts is it more of a *regard* than in the sonnet sequences) we should distinguish between two separate functions: those pertaining to the subject (the narrator, the Poet/Lover, the "self") and those involving the object (the beloved, the Other). About the former, little is said, perhaps because the whole sequence is an internalization of his[24] features: the closest we are allowed to come is *Will*'s age in the *Sonnets,* externalized in lines and wrinkles (63). The Other's features, on the other hand, are given considerably more attention. Counting only those mentions that appear descriptive, Stella's lips are shown in six poems, her hair in five, her eyes in four, her cheeks in three, her teeth in two, and her forehead, skin, and hands each in one. All these descriptions—and this is a first sign that something is amiss—pertain to color: Stella, the reader learns, is a lady with red lips, blonde hair, dark eyes, red and white cheeks, and white teeth, skin, and hands. When we remember that every one of these attributes is a commonplace of European love-poetry, we realize that Ingarden's Gap remains thoroughly unfilled.

19

In fact, what is happening in these blason-derived "descriptive" passages is an important variant of metaphor as described in no. 17, above. Oscillating between metaphor and simile, these descriptions about (around) the Other, instead of maintaining the indeterminacy of Ingarden's Gap (or partially completing it), create what we might call a *false determinacy.* Where a normally active metaphor or simile attempts partially to fill the Gap by triangulation, the blason "compare" (which, as Shakespeare asserts, is *inherently* "false"—*Sonnets* 130:14) has the effect of *widening* Ingarden's Gap. It does so by using the normal triangulation pattern as a *feint*, while in fact pointing the reader to a conventional signified we may call the Beloved, or the Lady, to whom the signified "Stella" is thus implied to stand in a synecdochal, or exemplary, relation. Let me try to make this clearer in two diagrams. Both contain the standard levels of signifier (S^r), signified (S^d) and referent (R)[25]. The first shows the establishing of the Object by standard metaphoric triangulation (via the MR, or Metaphoric Reference) as well as by direct reference (DR); the second shows the procedure in the case of the blason reference (MR/B).

Level   *I*   *II*

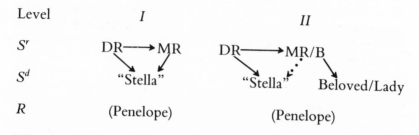

The effect of thus establishing the object (the Other) as a synecdochal and exemplary part of a coded conventional whole is to deflect the apparent metaphoric completion of Ingarden's Gap, to increase the indeterminacy of the signified, and thus to weaken the relation between signified and referent. And the effect of *this* upon the reader is not only to reward him for knowing the code, but also to increase the adaptability of the text's Other as a target for his own projection—in a characteristically Renaissance way.

20

The relation of Ingarden's Gap to the text's mimesis of *character* presents a different range of problems. We may object to this application in principle, on the grounds that "character" seems indeterminate even in "life."[26] However, if we remember that Ingarden's "determinacy" is a *philosophical* one, this objection disappears: philosophically, a human being's character is as determinate as his/her corporeal entity. It is only the *Ansichten* of it that are more obviously indeterminate, as well as (perhaps for this reason) more hermeneutic in nature. In the text of a sonnet sequence such as *Astrophil and Stella*, Ingarden's Gaps relating to character are many, and highly active. It might be said that the narrative element in *Astrophil and Stella is* character: the unfolding of two characters and of the unstable space (the gap) between them. As such, character's indeterminacy and the text's *intermittent* attempts to complete it are a *continuing* element, which involves Ingarden's syntagmatic categories as well as his Gap: notably his concept of *Parathaltung* or "holding-in-readiness".[27] This will be further discussed below; what can be said here is that the sonnet sequence, with its emphasis on short, situational utterances and its frequent, built-in interruptions, creates a discourse that, while valorizing character, encourages a high level of Ingardenian indeterminacy in its representation.

21

The final dimension of Ingarden's Gap I shall look at is that of *identity*. Astrophil, we remember, sometimes felt like one enormous Gap, and was doomed to live on after his Maker died a hero's death. The trickiness of the relation Astrophil/Philip and Stella/Penelope is an ancient critical topos, which I do not propose to go into here. In the light of indeterminacy and the Gap we may remember that the text takes care to over-determine *both* the signified (Astrophil and Stella) *and* the referent (Philip and Penelope), not only by name but by situational references.[28] Once again, however, this apparent completing of Ingarden's Gap is a feint: for the apparent parallel of levels is continually destroyed (or rather: deconstructed) by contradictions of which any reader conversant with Philip's and Penelope's lives is (and would have been) aware. The effect of this feint is to turn the normal Ingarden's Gap of philosophical indeterminacy into what is almost a Derrida's Gap of experiential undecideability: "Aixo era y no era." The relation between the signified identities and the referential ones thus becomes, in Ricoeur's sense, *metaphoric*: an aspect that has not received the attention it deserves.

22

Having—in one, limited, aspect—crossed *Astrophil and Stella* with *Das literarische Kunstwerk*, what have we learned about its gaps? In the first place, that generically (as *a* sonnet sequence) this text not only, like all literary texts, is based on and contains Ingarden's Gap(s), but structurally exploits it/them. In the second place, that this exploitation occurs not only paradigmatically but syntagmatically and thus points ahead, via Ingarden's *Parathaltung*, to Iser's Gap. Thirdly, that on certain levels Ingarden's Gap becomes both experiential and undecideable, and thus approaches Derrida's. And fourthly, that the syntagmatic nature of the sonnet sequence as a text of modular interruptions has something to do with all this, which leads us to suspect that the White Gap may not be irrelevant. With these elaborations, Ingarden's Gap functions as one of *Astrophil and Stella*'s fundamental structural principles, an integral part of its particular (as well as its generic) code.

23

The last, careless, hand that had returned him to the shelf had placed Astrophil between *The Literary Work of Art* on one side and *Winnie-the-Pooh* on the other. Roman had been explaining him (though in rather general terms) for a long time. Cumbered with good manners, Astrophil pretended to go on listening; but not only did he keep thinking (inconclusively) of Stella, he kept falling asleep. Confusedly, he wished that he could have had a Shepard to illustrate him. Finally Roman's guttural voice was still. The silence seemed poised for a reply. "Oh, I see," said Astrophil, sadly.

24

In crossing the *Amoretti* with "Indeterminacy and the Reader's Response", it will be well to keep in mind the twofold nature of Iser's Gap. The *Ansichten*, or "views," *function* paradigmatically but are *actualized* syntagmatically: the indeterminacy, therefore, is one of both reason and (gradual) revelation; in the text's practice, of both concept and movement, of "plot" levels and of the language's progress.

25

As early as 1956, Lever[29] was troubled by what he experienced as, in Riffaterrean terms, "ungrammaticalities" in the *Amoretti*. While the concrete locus of these lay in certain sonnets' imagery, the nature of their power to disturb lay in an anomaly of tone, seen as a function of the representation of an emotion and a relationship. Subsequent criticism has largely discarded the literary-historical aspects of the argument; what remains is an early and valuable insight into what I should like here to characterize as the text's two "plots."[30] Before we apply Iser's Gap to these, they may be usefully described as follows. The two "plots" in the *Amoretti* are two kinds of love, and thus[31] two kinds of love-*poetry*. The first (the one that bothered Lever) is a traditional one, based upon the fidelity/cruelty topos which is, in this text and for its purposes, often represented in a greatly exaggerated form. The second "plot", which functions as a radical renewal of love/poetry, is that of a love made conformable to the Creator's purpose (*amor re-ligatus* and thus *religiosus*) and experienced (via the bold equation of *eros* and *agape*: see *Amoretti* 68) as a confident and cheerful mutuality. The *guerra amorosa* of this text is the war between (the memory of) the first "plot" and (the experience of) the second.

26

Iser's Gap, as the taxonomy (above, number 10) reminded us, can be the indeterminacy of (*between*) the *Ansichten* involved in multiple plots and their sequential actualization in the text. The *Amoretti's* comfortably traditional opening has the effect of lulling the reader into what we may call a security of literary competence. Throughout the early part of the text, this security is reinforced (and the "skillful reader's" competence rewarded) by the clearly-marked use of intertexts from Petrarch, Tasso, and Desportes.[32] And this security is not only a general one, but specifically generic: it maintains in the reader an awareness that the text confronting him is, in senses other than the formal, *a* sonnet sequence. He is thus (in every sense) *un*prepared for the fact that, *from time to time* (*i.e.* both sequentially and sporadically) the text troubles him with the hyperbolic indecorum of its "compare" (*e.g.* Sonnets 20, 31, 32, 37, 47, and 56). The effect of this indecorum is to unsettle the reader by "solliciting" (in the Derridean-etymological sense of "shaking") his expectations and subverting the security of his competence.

27

We may find, then, a first manifestation of Iser's Gap between the *Ansicht* presented by the early sonnets and its displacement in the "solliciting" sonnets. It is a very active gap of indeterminacy, subverting as it does the reader's sense of an understood code with an intermittent *Ansicht* not readily explicable. The reader is forced into a hermeneutic of this new "view"; and even if he reaches what I believe to be its most likely interpretation—that it is an *ironic* one—he is forced into a further hermeneutic: both of the relation between this view and that of the surrounding text, and of the *intermittency itself.* The text provides a multiple indeterminacy which the reader cannot proceed without completing, and it gives him *(as yet)* no instructions for the decoding.

28

With Sonnet 62 (the first text in the history of the love-sonnet to use, however ambiguously, the first-person-plural pronoun), the second "plot" makes its appearance; and a new version of Iser's Gap thus applies. On the one hand, the second (or "mutuality") plot functions as an instruction for decoding (completing the indeterminacy created by) the first. Yet at the same time, by adding a third *Ansicht* to the earlier two, it multiplies the Iserian indeterminacy gaps. It does so not only technically but specifically, by creating a new active indeterminacy between itself and the "solliciting" sonnets. Once again the reader, experiencing the text in its gradual unfolding, is halted and forced to *make sense*.

29

(The syntagmatic progression here invites a digression on the *Amoretti's* use of textual time and movement. In accordance with Spenser's contemporary technique in the *Faerie Queene*, there is a constant use of completion via *Parathaltung*: a deliberate indeterminacy creates an enigma, which some later actualization in the text—often much later—then "solves."[33] It is clear that this use of "suspense," in areas well beyond what is usually thought of as "narrative," is a clear example of Iser's Gap. What is equally interesting is the back-and-forth movement this forces the reader to perform. There is, in the *Amoretti* as in the *Faerie Queene*, a constant use of retroactivity which is in every sense a feature of *écriture*—of writing/reading rather than of speaking/hearing. This subverting of logocentricity in Spenser invites much further study.)

30

The *Amoretti's* second "plot" only gradually gains the upper hand. Although the indecorum of the "solliciting" sonnets has ceased, the traditional code reappears (*e.g.* Sonnets 64 and 70). The new plot, however, is so strong that it can co-opt not only the tradition but a subversion of the tradition to overdetermine it. This the reader experiences in the strongly intertextual Sonnets 63 (in which the Petrarchan lover's tempest-tossed ship gains safe harbour) and 67 (in which Tasso's "Questa fera gentil," reversing Petrarch's "Una candida cerva", is deepened to fit the second plot's re-ligio).[34] In this context, two aspects of Iser's Gap are worth noting. In the first place, the indeterminacy between *Ansichten* is maintained (though at a reduced level of both intensity and frequency) after the introduction of the second, ultimately victorious, plot. Thus the reader is not *given* this plot as a maximally determinate, "realistic" alternative: sense must continue to be *made*. Secondly, we are alerted to the indeterminacy produced by the *conversion* of an intertext.[35]

Within the Renaissance method of text production, with its enormous stress on the reader's literary competence, the conversion of an intertext is one of the chief loci of the reader's role as co-creator of the text's signification—a fact that has extensive implications for the validity of the "open work" or "indeterminacy" concept's application to early texts.

31

All, however, is not settled with the apparent victory of the "mutuality" plot. Once again the reader's (new) security is "sollicited," first by a new hyperbole and then by a series of traditional topoi *misused*. Sonnet 83 ("Let not one spark of filthy lustfull fyre") is addressed by the Poet to himself with "ungrammatical" vehemence. Iser's Gap here functions in both its synchronic (and syntagmatic) sense—the indeterminacy created by this new *Ansicht* in relation to the preceding one—and in its diachronic, intertextual one: as an echo of *Astrophil and Stella* 71 and 72 (the "Desire" sonnets). The reader is forced once again into an active role: his competence called on and his (co-) creative powers put to the test.

32

The "absence" sonnets (86–88), introduced by the "slander" text of 85, create the same indeterminacy in a different way. In 85, the poet uses a self-referential intertextuality (the Blatant Beast from the *Faerie Queene*) to create a climate of uncertainty. The final texts following this, while situationally reassuring (they and 85 mutually "explain" each other, by suggesting a situational signified), create a strongly-overdetermined Iser's Gap by their positioning with regard to both the second "plot" (which they appear to undermine) and the sequence as a whole (which they appear to conclude). It is significant that they do so, as I suggested above, by *misusing* (rather than "converting") a coded topos (most recently and influentially used in *Astrophil and Stella* 88, 89, and 106). In keeping with this text's practice, *Parathaltung* is employed. Yet here its function is reversed: for the appearance of the *Epithalamion*, rather than completing the indeterminacy of 86–88, creates it, *retroactively*. As the situational signified of the "absence" sonnets is cancelled (*aufgehoben*[36]), the enigma is created. Here Iser's Gap points toward Derrida's: the indeterminacy here produced is in fact an undecideability.

33

Perhaps the most shocking version of Iser's Gap in the *Amoretti* comes after the *indetermination* (the non-closure) of the absence-sonnets. As the reader's literary competence scrabbles amomg its intertextual memory of other sequences to create meaning, still another *Ansicht* is presented which makes a mockery of that very competence. The presence of the Anacreontics in a maximally overdetermined liminary position between the sonnets and the *Epithalamion* is a phenomenon I intend to deal with more fully elsewhere. In the present context we may see it in two ways. In the first place it functions as an extreme version of Iser's Gap. Blatantly belonging to neither "plot," the Anacreontics may be said to *incarnate* the indeterminacy between views: to be, in fact, an Iser's Gap *become text*. On the other hand, the extreme nature of their indeterminacy tempts me to see them as the *Aufhebung* of Iser's Gap. According to this view, the Anacreontics entirely subsume Iser's Gap—itself a dynamic development of Ingarden's—into the exponentially greater indeterminacy of Derrida's Gap. We should then be dealing with, not the indeterminacy of a text's progression from *Ansicht* to *Ansicht,* but a text suddenly and brutally converted to undecideability.

34

What of Iser's Gap in the *Epithalamion* itself? This triumphal Ode to the victory of the second plot and the consequent transformation of love(poetry), is very strongly overdetermined,[37] recapitulating as it does a number of the *Amoretti*'s motifs. Yet a closer look reveals a surprising proliferation of "views" (though at a much lower level of intensity). The text shifts constantly between the *Ansichten* of classical myth, Protestant Christianity, Catholic Christianity, homespun Irishness, and folkloric superstition. At each transition, technically, an "Iser's Gap" appears. What, in this case, is their effect? Most obviously, I suspect, the reader is invited to construct, via these transitional indeterminacies, his own participating sense of the marriage's totality: he becomes, as the text's co-creator, a "member of the wedding." Less intentionally, however, the gaps' effect is to maintain a level of indeterminacy at the heart of what is presented as the fulfilled totality of *experientia re-ligata*: an indeterminacy brutally exploited later by Shakespeare's *Sonnets*.[38] While such a proliferation of Iser's Gaps is, in the *Amoretti,* ordered and held in check by the regularity of a sonnet sequence's White Gaps, in the *Epithalamion* they multiply in the same way as (though to a far lesser degree than) those illustrated by Iser in his discussion of *Ulysses.*

35

Concluding our crossing of Spenser's text with Iser's, then, we may say that the dynamic and syntagmatic nature of Iser's Gap is particularly relevant to the textual practice of the *Amoretti.* It provides an unparallelled instrument for the perception and the interpretation of Spenser's characteristic preoccupation with the sequentiality of a poetic text, and with the way this can be used to actualize a multiplicity of "plots." Furthermore, it prompts us to meditate on the phenomenon of retroactivity and on the back-and-forth movement of the reader's activity, which the reader of the present essay is invited to pursue (rewardingly, I think) by applying Iser's Gap to the Shakespeare *Sonnets.*[39] Finally, it awakens us to the existence, and the possible nature, of a relation between Iser's Gap and Derrida's; and it throws further light on the importance and function of the White Gap in structuring the pattern of a sonnet sequence's indeterminacies.

36

(Edmund) was not amused. "Simple truth and mutual good will," (he) had written. And had (he) not proved it? "Good will" was God's Will, in or out of a sonnet sequence. Yet here, in the neighboring volume, was *Will: Will* who, turning to good account an accident of baptism, mockingly overturned all (his), (Edmund's), achievements. He had had the nerve to take Astrophil's perverse invitation to Reason to "leave Love to Will" as a call to deconstructive action, and had set about the task with relish. But it was (Edmund's) Love that had been left to him: and he had placed a crowbar in its every Gap. Everything that, with God's help, (Edmund) had decided and ordered, *Will* had disordered and distorted into undecideability. Was that a chuckle he heard from *SHAKE-SPEARES SONNETS* next door? A melancholy chuckle, certainly; but with a good deal of malice in it. No, (Edmund) was not amused.

37

It is almost inappropriate to try to deal with Derrida's Gap in the *Sonnets* by means of a single (meta-)text such as this. Ideally, as Derrida himself has demonstrated embryonically in *Dissemination*[40] and fully in *Glas*, this Gap should be shown. Shown in the simultaneous presentation of the text and *a* metatext, or rather of *another* text, thus *creating* Derrida's Gap and forcing the reader to experience it. "The importance of this text," says *Glas*, "lies in the air circulating between its screens."[41] In addition, it should never be forgotten that Derrida's own purpose is a philosophical, not a literary-critical, one; and that the light-hearted conversion of "deconstruction" into "deconstructionism" (especially when the results are presented in unaltered North-American-scholarly discourse) is at best an epiphenomenon. This said, let us proceed (as in a *mined* no-man's land).

38

(What I have called Derrida's Gap is, in the sense used hitherto, not a Gap at all. This fact proceeds from his inclusion of Husserl (Ingarden's mentor, as Ingarden is Iser's) in the "onto-theology" he attempts to deconstruct. Thus there can be no confident phenomenological discussion (much less use) of a paradigmatic, metaphysical, *Unbestimmtheitsstelle*. Derrida's realization that onto-theology pervades even the language we use to discuss it, and his consequent selection of writing as the locus for its (gradual and subtle) deconstruction, means that Derrida's Gap is in fact a *displacement* in and of the text's apparent determinacy. This slight subversive jarring creates (or reveals) a space of tension where elements (do not) touch. Most frequently, as I have suggested above, this tension exists as a "gap," not of indeterminacy but of undecideability.)

39

Unlike Iser's Gap, which prompted us to a sequential application in the *Amoretti*, Derrida's can and should be applied anywhere. Shakespeare's *Sonnets* lend themselves particularly well to this practice. As it allows no theoretical distinction between physical and conceptual dimensions, it is appropriate to begin with the text as printed. (The currently authoritative Booth edition,[42] by reproducing—though, as we shall see, with one important omission—the 1609 text, happily eliminates the choice between the original text vs. a modern one.) And let us go at once to the notable crux of Sonnet 126. Not fourteen lines, but twelve; and arranged in couplet rhymes. In terms of the reader's genre-expectation this is mildly surprising but in no way unsettling: "sonnets" came in various lengths and with all sorts of rhymes. The text of 126, then, cannot be said to provide any sort of unusual indeterminacy. Its uniqueness in the *Sonnets,* and its placing within their overall text, is more interesting. But what in the 1609 text our eyes are drawn to most urgently is the appearance, after line 12, of two pairs of spaced but empty parentheses in the place of a hypothetical couplet (ll.13–14★). These marks are normally given a bibliographically-dismissive interpretation,[43] and omitted in modernized editions. This solution leaves 126 as a 12-line lyric which marks a turning-point in the character-centered structure of the macrotext: from Friend to Lady. Yet if we for a moment refuse the *doxa* of the parentheses' dismissal, what do we find them to be? *The mark of an empty line.*

40

At the turning-point of the macrotext are two overdetermined adjuncts to the White Gap, two *marks* of *space*. The paradox this makes visible spreads across the text in either direction. It cannot (witness all editorial practice) be left alone: it forces an attempted solution. And this (dis)solution can only be reached by intervention, by doing violence to the text: by *removing* the marks—and *thereby* removing the space. For without such violence, the parentheses create an *absolute* indeterminacy. By marking emptiness at the core of the text, they question (they "sollicit") not only *the* text but *text*—the enterprise of writing (and, by implication, of reading). Nor do they sollicit it by erasure: there is no text that has been removed from them, nor is there any text which can be added to them. They sollicit text by undecideability: the irreducible tension between mark and emptiness, between Black and White.

41

Their paradox, I wrote, spreads across the text. In fact, the parentheses of 126 are the mark of Derrida's Gap in the *Sonnets*. Every other undecideability in the text (and there are many) finds itself re-marked here. Following the spread, let us glance, first, very briefly at 145. Ostensibly, again, this tetrameter "sonnet" is—*merely?*—another permitted variant of the paradigm. In the light of the Parentheses, however, we notice that its shorter lines create a wider margin. While discussion of margins belongs with that of the White Gap in general (see below, number 51), we may remark here that our perception of the phenomenon prompts us to look for a reason, and that neither the microtext nor its immediate context provides us with one. Derrida's Gap in this case, then, opens between margin and meaning.

42

There is another typographical crux close by. The repetition of "my sinfull earth" in line 2 of 146 is normally, again, dismissed as a printer's error: an "explanation" made the more persuasive by the fact that the repetition overloads line 2 with two syllables surplus to the metre. However, as Booth's parallel printing (pp. 124–125) clearly shows, omitting the repetition leaves line 2 "incomplete." The result is the most infuriatingly silly of in-determinacies. Of undecideabilities, for this too is Derrida's Gap: and it takes on a new dimension by appearing ("of all places") in the one sonnet that is itself a major crux of the macrotext. Not only its nature but its existence within the sonnets has been repeatedly questioned[44]; and even if it is accepted as a reference to the intertext of Sidney's palinodic "Leave me O Love," its placing in the macrotextual order can quite effectively generate Derrida's Gap all by itself.[45] We may attempt to find separate "solutions" to these two *cruces*: we cannot escape the fact that they overdetermine each other and create a gap of extreme instability for 146 to exist in.

43

Worse is to come. The significant omission in Booth's edition (even in the facsimile reproduction[46]) of the 1609 text is the *Lover's Complaint*. Once again (as with the parentheses of 126) the editorial "solution" to a case of Derrida's Gap is the violence of radical surgery. And once again the editor in question can feel free to do so because of a long-standing consensus. I intend to pursue the relation of the *Lover's Complaint* to the *Sonnets* at length in a further article; yet I cannot altogether omit discussion of it here. What makes the *Complaint* the generator of Derrida's Gap? What, we might better ask, does not? The *Sonnets* are universally recognized as a masterpiece; the *Complaint* is, equally universally, considered at best mediocre. (Via a leap of faith more usual in past than in current Shakespeare criticism, this inevitably entailed doubts as to its authenticity in the canon.) The *Sonnets*, for all their undecideabilities (usually known as "problems"), seem to create a tight and coherent world: the *Complaint* introduces (apparently) quite different characters in an unrelated situation. And so on. Yet *at the same time* there exist, in both, a woman, a young man and an older man, within an *ambiance* of faithless loving: *at the same time* the *Complaint* contains mysterious images too haunting to be ignored (the broken rings, the nun's love callously sacrificed); and *at the same time* the *Sonnets* and the *Complaint* co-exist within the same original volume, printed continuously.[47] If, then (as with the parentheses), we disallow ourselves the surgery of excision, we find that in numerous ways the *Complaint* and the *Sonnets* re-mark each other, and do so both irreducibly and undecideably. These two texts, then, relate to each other via a characteristically Derridean "fold" or "joint", and the space of their joint signification is the space (the membrane) between them.

44

The indeterminacy noticed in Astrophil's and Stella's identities vis-à-vis their referents is also, in the *Sonnets,* activated, energized, into undecideability. For the Poet, here, is *Will,* and exploits to the fullest the polysemy of this name. On one level, of course, there is *Will* in the "honest" (non-Sidneian!) sense of "(Edmund)" or "(Francesco Petrarca)", involved in the characteristic indeterminacy between Poet and poet, between *Will* and Will (Shakespeare). But the *energia* comes from the co-incidence of *Will's* centrality in the moral microcosm (between divine Reason and animal Passion, it was for Pico and others the locus of the "Dignity and Excellence of Man"), of *Will's* colloquial meaning of genitalia, *and* of its capacity to indicate the genitalia of *either* sex. Together, these co-incidences (which consistently re-mark each other) produce a field of interlocking undecideabilities so intense that it embraces, and in many ways interprets, the entire text. For this version of Derrida's Gap *cannot* be cut away. The reader is left to face it, and at all points to "decide" it. But he cannot do so. There are other important cases of Derrida's Gap in the *Sonnets*: the order of the text, for instance, which has been perceived as a "crux" ever since Benson's edition of 1640. But none illustrates the Gap more clearly than *Will.*

45

Nowhere does crossing the text with the (other?) (meta-?) text produce such an active consciousness of the gap(s) than in this case. Derrida's Gap operates, as was predicted, differently. It overdetermines the urgency of a response (a "solution") from the reader; *at the same time* it makes any determinate, or determinating, response impossible. An excellent example of this is provided by the method that underlies Booth's commentary: sensing, probably rightly, that it is (as was democracy to Churchill) the worst possible system except for all the other ones, he assembles every conceivable denotative and connotative meaning, and then leaves the reader with the sort of polysemic confusion that De Man describes in *Allegories of Reading*.[48] In other words, where Iser's Gap both urged and allowed the reader of the *Amoretti* to *make* sense, Derrida's Gap forces the reader to try, but simultaneously denies him the possibility of succeeding. The result is a sonnet sequence that develops, to a height never reached before, the form's latent power of getting under the reader's skin (and thus, we might subversively add, creating an unprecedentedly adequate mimesis of "love": the whole of the *Sonnets* is the dismembered and disseminated Body of Cupid). It does so by indissolubly associating the physical aspect of writing and of space with the conceptual, and by insisting without respite on the undecideability of its tensions.

46

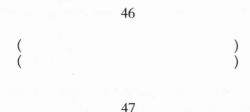

47

My final crossing is the most complex, and the most unusual. For what we must now bring ourselves to do is to cross our three texts with each other, and to cross the resultant complex with the omnipresent reality (which is not—yet—a concept) of the White Gap. The White Gap is in many ways the most difficult to deal with, because its insistently physical nature dissimulates its status as a gap of indeterminacy, as an *Unbestimmtheitsstelle*. And yet our experience with Derrida's Gap should have prepared us for perceiving it this way: I believe that I have demonstrated the extent to which its (Derrida's Gap's) association of the physical with the conceptual dimension functions, not only for Mallarmé but for an "early text" as well. There is, however, another reason for trying. The sonnet se-

quences—*all* sonnet sequences—overdetermine their undecideability at every turn. One of the few laws that can be
formulated concerning them is that nothing one can say about
them will be *completely* true (which may be one reason for the
form's complete neglect by early theorists). There is thus a case
to be made for at least investigating the White Gap.

48

The White Gap, in the first place (in all its places) is, in the most
literal sense, a *Stelle*—a *place*. And this (multiple) place is the
place of, the locus of, the sonnet sequences' indeterminacies *as
sonnet sequences*. It is, for example, the space of their *generic*
indeterminacy. The status of the sonnet microtext within the
sequence macrotext is, as we have seen, neither stanza nor
independent poem: the locus of this indeterminacy is the White
Gap, which alone decides the undecideable relation to the preceding and following (micro)texts. In this case, its presence
helps to create the conceptual dimension (of indeterminacy)
without which the genre would not be what it is.

49

Of far more importance is the White Gap's relation to the order
of the sonnet sequences. The order, we have seen, is subject to
Derrida's Gap: it is not only indeterminate but undecideable.
The crucial result of this attribute, however, is *enabled* by the
White Gap. For it, and it alone, allows and urges upon the
reader the characteristic action of (co-)creative *grouping* common to all serious readers' responses to the sonnet sequences.[49]
With the exception of the strongly-marked *volta* between the
Sonnets' Friend and Lady sections (which may itself be an echo
of the popular *In Vita* and *In Morte* division of Petrarch's text),
and the less strongly marked demarcation of the same text's
"procreation" sonnets (1–17), all groupings in our texts are
evidence of both an irresistible hermeneutic urge and the un-
convincing nature of the result. It is not, I think, too bold an
assertion to attach a semiotic significance to this fact: to state
that the urge to group hermeneutically, the ability to do so, and

the individuality of the result, are a major factor of the sonnet sequences' status as what Eco calls an "open work", in which the reader is an *essential* (as opposed to either an incidental or a perverse) co-creator of the meaning. Neither, I submit, is it unreasonable to point to the White Gap as the enabling locus of this indeterminacy.

50

A special version of the White Gap appears to be its own denial: the *text as Gap*. This we have noted in the case of the *Amoretti's* Anacreontics, and we may here point out that it is not an isolated case: Shakespeare's 126 can make a claim to this status, and Shakespeare's 153 and 154 much more so. They are texts simulating a *blanc*, and it is no coincidence that in each case they appear as the dividers between a macrotext's major sections. So far from "solving" (dissolving) the White Gap between the sonnets and the subsequent long text, these "texts-as-gap" in fact overdetermine it. They both hide and reveal *this* particular White Gap's privileged status as a major *limen/hymen,* both threshold and membrane, *simultaneously* separating and joining the textual spaces on either side of it in an undecideable relation. As, in fact, the *Stelle* of the text's major *Unbestimmtheit.*

51

The most apparently far-fetched form of the White Gap is the *margin.* This does not seem like a gap of indeterminacy, and certainly not relevant in any special way to the sonnet sequences. After all, it is common to all texts, and in the form in which we meet it in the sequences it is common at least to most lyric texts. What, then, is its claim to the status of a White Gap (of indeterminacy)? Such a status is, in this case, determined by the text's *other* indeterminacies, and by two of them in particular. The normal White Gap, first: the gap between microtexts, highly active as it is in a sonnet sequence, *spills over* into, contaminates, the margins in its significance as in its physical presence. The reader, in other words, is sensitized by the normal White Gap into re-marking the physical page's other *blancs.*

The second factor valorizing the margin as a White Gap is the characteristically undecideable relation between a sonnet sequence text and the referential "world." This relation, symbolized by the (non-)identity between Astrophil and Philip, is unique to the genre (though the *Faerie Queene*, not surprisingly, comes close). The margin, where the reader's hand touches the book, is always the interface between text and world. In a medieval text, it is often filled ("illuminated") with the scribe's, or the illuminator's, frequently irrelevant figures: the world, in a very particular and *physical* way, invades the text. In the text of a sonnet sequence (whether manuscript or printed), the margin is "blank" *(blanc)*. As it is in other sixteenth-century lyrical texts: but because the text itself of a sonnet sequence has already established its relation to the "world" as an undecideable one, the White Gap of the margin becomes the invisible space where this particular undecideable tension *happens*.

52

We have crossed No-Man's-Land, you and I; and it is time to look around us, to take stock. I propose a brief meditation on theory and practice. In the progression from Ingarden via Iser to Derrida we can see a gradual liberation of the concept of "indeterminacy" from the Husserlian phenomenological framework. Necessarily, in this process, the concept had to be redefined. Its first redefinition lies in its move from the Stratum of Represented Objects to that of Schematized Aspects or Views. Thus, from being a single dimension of the "transcendental" work it becomes a multiple dimension of its sequential actuality. The second major redefinition lies in Derrida's association of the physical with the conceptual dimensions, so that indeterminacy now becomes a dynamic feature revealed by the process of displacement. As such, it undergoes a change also in relation to the reader: from indeterminacy it becomes undecideability. The *Unbestimmtheitsstelle* becomes the *blanc* as a locus for the fold, the membrane. The White now becomes the *Unbestimmtheitsstelle* and, as such, the White Gap: the locus where indeterminacy as a dynamic *practice* can *take place*. The *blanc* is the reader's door into the work's indeterminacy. The reader is Lord of the Marches of the text (Derrida speaks often of the association "marque/marche/marge"): the Marches are the locus of his freedom and his activity.

53

In crossing these texts—the sonnet sequences—with these metatexts of indeterminacy we have arrived, I suggest, at the following observations. In the first place, we have found a genre of "early texts" that brilliantly embodies even the most apparently "postmodern" concepts of indeterminacy. Such a discovery necessarily effects a displacement, however small, of critical attitudes that tie "indeterminacy" too closely and restrictively to nineteenth-, and especially to twentieth-century texts. Secondly, we have found that *crossing* the texts did not inconvenience, much less invalidate, them: on the contrary, the crossing involved in interrogating their "gaps" enabled them to reveal essential elements of their character. Thirdly, the crossing, and the gap, have revealed a number of important freedoms for us as readers: the freedom of *involvement* (urgency plus undecideability); the freedom of *grouping* (a non-verbal hermeneutic); and the freedom of (from) *time* (we are no longer bound to *either* interpretation of the term "contemporary"). And, lastly, interrogating the Gaps has given us a radical means of understanding the sonnet *sequence* as a form: a means that goes beyond all previous methodologies for grasping this most elusive of literary objects.

54

Thus, in analyzing the gaps, have we dealt with the text as ptyx. One further dimension beckons: the text as Styx. In no. 6, above, I made what may have seemed the curious statement that crossing the text of the three sequences could not fail to engage us in our death. Only now are we in a position to look more closely at this claim. Crossing the texts has meant ignoring their "meaning" and examining what they do not say. As those familiar with the work of Riffaterre will recognize, this process is not unrelated to his version of literary semiotics. To adapt some of the Riffaterrean concepts, the *significance* of all love-sonnet sequences' uniquely-structured indeterminacy is their constant turning around an empty space. This space of the unsaid—and, usually, the unattained—represents sexual fulfilment: openly so in some texts (many troubadours, *Astrophil and Stella*); dissimulated, sublimated, or tamed in others (Petrarch, Spenser).

55

The treatment of sexual fulfilment as a central silence establishes *it* as a gap of indeterminacy also. At first sight this may seem odd: whether one regards it mimetically according to experience or semiotically as a matricial presence, it might seem not only determinate but overdetermined. What, then, is the nature of its indeterminacy? A clue to the answer may lie in its contemporary nickname of the "little death." Ecstatic sexual union traditionally is, or at least precedes, *the end of a (love-) story;* and the experience itself (ec-static) is lived as a loss of the (rational, social, "human") self. This loss is a loss of experience's determinate nature, as well as of the language that is its fundamental structuring material. In this case, the *specific* determinate experience subjected to the loss is, paradoxically, the plot we call "love": which is why long sequences of love-*poems* must repress it into silence, if *it* is not to silence *them.*

56

The accomplishment of this significance by the reader is what, by analogy with Peirce's "semiosis," I have called the *erosis* of the texts. As mentioned above, it can be achieved only by plunging into their gaps, which enables us then to plunge further into their central, matricial, gap. Such a plunge, though not yet a crossing *over,* is at least a departure from comfortable banks. It represents the intermediate stage of the text's becoming Styx.

57

To travel beyond this stage, we must re-ascend the brief
metaphoric chain that originally produced the "little death."
If—in the dis-illusioned Ricoeurian sense of being-like, of be-
ing-and-not-being—ecstatic sexual fulfilment "is like" the
greater Death, then the indeterminacies of love-sonnet sequences lead us to the final Indeterminacy. This is not the place
for an extended review and application of Blanchot's *L'espace
littéraire*, but its complex and challenging connections of the
"work's" mode of existence with the "space" and nature of
Death ("L'oeuvre et l'espace de la mort") strongly support the
direction of our crossing-over. Where we (may) arrive is at the
Open Sign *par excellence*: Death-as-sign is both maximally overdetermined, by its universality and its urgency, and maximally
undecideable. It is the Gap where all our gaps meet, mingle, and
are subsumed.

58

And the point of this extension? Blanchot has made it for the
writer; let us here try to do so for the reader. The crossing of the
text as Styx should once and for all rob us of all possible
detachment from it. We have each our Death to accomplish; we
cannot but accomplish our text. *Our* text: for we are here
re-minded—reminded that we are its co-creators. I, the reader
of these sequences, am also the artist; and, as such, am not
absolved from the need to *create* my death—to create *my* text.

59

Astrophil, (Edmund), and *Will* were going to end this essay for
me, allowing me to escape a final reflection on the critical text as
(meta) text. But they are silent in the face of a Death of which
they know nothing; and I am left with the (un)certainty that, on
that level, nothing is solved. Having crossed over, we are still
strangers. Having accomplished (perhaps) the gaps of our three
texts, we (you and I) have produced, and consumed or co-

produced, still another text, whose own gaps now entice and challenge us. All criticism is (or should be) "fragments of a lover's discourse." In the light of our Death, we are free to enjoy the pleasure of criticism. The pleasure of criticism is dependent on the acceptance, and the accomplishment, of indeterminacy. "The importance of *this* text is the air that circulates between its screens." *(Glas)*

York University

NOTES

1. *Cf.* R. Ingarden, *The Literary Work of Art,* tr. G. G. Grabowicz (Evanston, Ill.: Northwestern University Press, 1973) 246–254. While we are on the subject of (disconcerting) unnoticed beginnings, this is perhaps the place for a Derridean *coupe sombre.* The usual lengthy and bibliographical First Footnote is here cut away, so that the surrounding words (and especially the surrounding spaces) may seed the area thus cleared. Naturally, this affects all expectation attuned to the First Footnote's usual coding, which signifies that the author has done his homework. Ingarden is mentioned above (and below); Iser will presently appear; Derrida and Riffaterre are not far; but we should not forget *The Collected Silences of Dr. Murke,* or Roland Barthes' card file. The former reminds us that an expanse of white is neither space nor (especially) the notation of a silence; while the latter may suggest a structural principle in which gaps are not only indispensible but carry essential meaning. They both organize and disturb the economy of the text: it cannot exist without them (a sonnet sequence, as we shall see, least of all), yet every cost-conscious publisher resents their insolence. How they relate to the crucial principle of loose leaves is a question still largely unresolved.
2. See the discussion of this Mallarmé ghost-word in Michael Riffaterre, *Semiotics of Poetry* (Bloomington: Indiana University Press, 1978), pp. 16–19. It is, as Riffaterre convincingly shows, a neologism designed to act as a verbal nothing: impossibility-made-text, hence also text as impossibility.
3. This subversion, in fact, points the way to what is possibly the only remaining metaliterary "relevance" of literature: to generate in the reader a premonition of the ulfimate existential indeterminacy. *Cf.* Maurice Blanchot, *L'espace littéraire* (Paris: Gallimard, 1955), pt. 2: "L'oeuvre et l'espace de la mort".
4. I have coined this word to refer to the reader's accomplishing of a love-poem's erotic reality-as-text. *Cf.* Peirce's *semiosis,* elaborated by Riffaterre, *op.cit.,* pp. 4, 8–10. For the term "accomplishing", and the valuable concept it introduces, see Roland Barthes, "Par où commencer?" in *Essais critiques* (Paris: Seuil, 1964).

5. *Cf.* Georges Bataille, *L'expérience intérieure* (Paris: Gallimard, 1943), p. 239 and *passim*. There is a fine discussion of Bataille's "sovereignty", in relation to Hegel's "Herrschaft", in ch. IX of Derrida's *L'écriture et la différence* (Paris: Seuil, 1967).

6. *Op.cit.*, pp. 246ff.

7. W. Iser, "Indeterminacy and the Reader's Response", in *Aspects of Narrative*, ed. J. Hillis Miller (New York: Columbia University Press, 1971), p. 13n.

8. Neither is a very good translation. A *Stelle* is a place or locus, which puts Grabowicz closer to the intention than Iser, but for the unfortunate "stain" connotation of *spot*. To translate *Unbestimmtheit* by "indeterminacy" has an effect very like the translation of Freud's *Ich* and *Es* by "ego" and "id." The denotative relation cannot be faulted, but in each case the German original is a common word, connotatively linked to everyday language (*unbestimmt* normally means "vague," with etymological overtones of a lack of destination— *Bestimmung*), while the Anglo-American translation is a specialist word, connoting the jargon of a science or an academic discipline. "Places (or *loci*) of vagueness" would be a better rendering; but we are probably stuck with "indeterminacy", which in a few short years has become a battle-flag in the wars of North American literary theory.

9. I am using primarily the discussion in "Indeterminacy and the Reader's Response"; that in *Der Akt des Lesens* (Munich: Fink, 1976; tr., as The *Act of Reading*, Baltimore Md.: Johns Hopkins University Press, 1979) is in many ways a repetition of this, in the context of a more complex development pertaining primarily to narrative. The later discussion's chief relevance to the present subject lies in the new term "*Leerstellen*" (lit. "empty places"), which seems promising in view of the "white gaps" (see below, nos. 12 and 47–51); it is, however, not in this direction that Iser develops the term.

10. Iser, "Indeterminacy", p. 10. Both are translations of Ingarden's *Ansichten*. In this case, Grabowicz' "aspects" may be the more precise translation, as long as it is taken in its precise, not its colloquial, sense.

11. See especially "La double séance" in *La dissémination* (Paris: Seuil, 1972; tr., as *Dissemination*, Chicago, Ill.: University of Chicago Press, 1981).

12. Jacques Derrida, *Glas* (Paris: Galilée, 1974).

13. *La dissémination*, pp. 63, 257–317. The whole of this last section (part II of "La double séance") provides Derrida's most challenging discussion of the *blanc*, and should be studied carefully in the light of the sonnet sequences.

14. *Cf. L'écriture et al différence*, ch. V.

15. The fact that, following Petrarch's example, all three of the sequences under discussion also contain non-sonnet elements (*canzoni* or long poems), is partially dealt with below, nos. 33, 34, and 43.

16. See "Astrophil and Stella" in William A. Ringler, Jr. (ed.), *The Poems of Sir Philip Sidney* (Oxford: Clarendon Press, 1962), pp. 165–237; for early editions, see for example Jacopo Sannazaro, *Sonnetti e Canzoni* (Venice: Gioli, 1543), and *Shakespeares Sonnets* (London: Thomas Thorpe, 1609).

17. It is, of course, only a limited Taxonomy. Other Gaps could be postulated and explored: Barthes' Gap (between the five codes of *S/Z*, for example), or Riffaterre's Gap (between the levels of meaning and significance in *Semiotics of Poetry*). Their relation to the concept of indeterminacy is more

complex, though no less rewarding: the reader is encouraged to explore and, as Barthes would have said, to accomplish them.

18. I use the word here in the sense derived from the significant French phrase *un temps creux:* a space of empty or vacant time.

19. *Cf.* Ringler, *op.cit.*, p. 490, n. to 105:3.

20. In *Semiotics of Poetry*, pp. 32–39.

21. This situation to some extent resembles that of Riffaterre's "ungrammaticality" concept (*op.cit.*, p. 2 and *passim*); the difference is that, like a good structuralist/semiotocian, Riffaterre devotes much of his admirable method to making it go away.

22. Ever since Saussure's remarks on the imperative of a future semiotics, *obiter dicta* on remaining tasks and their necessary rigour have become a minor and amusing topos of French theory and criticism. It would be pedantic to give specific references here; but any reader familiar with the work of Barthes, the *Tel Quel* and Greimas schools, and Derrida, will have no trouble finding examples.

23. See *La métaphore vive* (Paris: Seuil, 1975; tr., as *The Rule of Metaphor*, Toronto: University of Toronto Press, 1978), esp. ch. 7.

24. This, upon reflection, sexist particularization should lead us to study much more carefully the semiotics of the female sonneteers' work: Louise Labé in particular repays careful analysis.

25. I am here using these terms in the following sense: the *signifier* is the word or phrase in the text; the *signified* is the object in the diegesis to which the signifier refers; while the *referent* is the external reality embodied in the object.

26. For a challenging discussion of our consciousness of our lives as a "literary" and hermeneutic one, see Paul Ricoeur, *Temps et Récit*, vol. I (Paris: Seuil, 1983), esp. ch. 3 ("Mimésis I").

27. *Cf.* Ingarden, *op.cit.*, pp. 265–268. As this involves the syntagmatic relation of the *Ansichten*, it will be further discussed in relation to Iser's Gap: see below, nos. 29 and 32.

28. The former is everywhere; for the latter, see Sonnets 30, 33, 83, and Song viii (Astrophil); and Sonnets 24, 35, 37, 78, and Song viii (Stella).

29. J. W. Lever, *The Elizabethan Love Sonnet* (London: Methuen, 1956), pp. 97–103.

30. It should be borne in mind that the term "plot", while usually applied to narrative, need not be. In a more diffuse and situational sense, the love-lyrics of Catullus, Propertius, and the troubadours all depend on implicit "plots." It is in this specifically lyrical sense that I use the word here.

31. On the narrative structure of experience in general, see Ricoeur, *Temps et Récit I*; on that of love in particular, see Julia Kristeva, *Histoires d'amour* (Paris: Denoël, 1983), p. 259 and *passim*.

32. For Petrarch, *cf.* 35, 59, 63, and (via Tasso) 67; for Tasso, *cf.* 4, 5, 13, 21, 43, 67, 72, 76, 79 and 84; for Desportes, *cf.* 15, 22, 30, 42, 50, 60, and 69.

33. There is a considerable similarity between this procedure and Barthes' "hermeneutic code" in *S/Z* (ch.X): "all those units whose function it is to articulate, in various ways, a question, its answer, and the various accidents which may either prepare the question or delay the answer; or also: to formulate a riddle and to bring about its deciphering." (*S/Z;* Paris: Seuil, 1970; p. 24).

34. *Cf.* Lever, *op.cit.*, pp. 124–125.
35. For conversion, see Riffaterre, *Semiotics*, pp. 63–80.
36. Hegel's term *Aufhebung*, implying something simultaneously cancelled and preserved, has been introduced into the lexis of literary theory and criticism by the French Hegelians and anti-Hegelians. It might be translated as "sublimation," if the popular-Freudian misuse of that term could be ignored.
37. Not only in the text itself but, via numerological techniques, in its organisation and disposition. *Cf.* A. Kent Hieatt, *Short Time's Endless Monument: The Symbolism of the Numbers in Edmund Spenser's "Epithalamion"* (New York: Columbia University Press, 1960).
38. I intend to deal more fully with the intertextual relation of these two sequences elsewhere.
39. For example, such an analysis might provide a much-needed clue to the placing of a sonnet like Shakespeare 42 within the macrotext.
40. *Cf.* the preliminary page to "La double séance" in *La dissémination*, p. 201.
41. *Glas*, p. 88.
42. *Shakespeare's Sonnets*, ed. Stephen Booth (New Haven and London: Yale University Press, 1977).
43. See Booth, p. 430n.
44. See Booth, pp. 507–517.
45. An undecideability which, in this case, awareness of the (possible) Sidneian intertext does nothing to remove; as the latter's persistent and unjustified association with *Astrophil and Stella* (definitively refuted by Ringler, *op.cit.*, pp. 423–424) shows.
46. That this represents an editorial decision on Booth's part is clear from the fact that the previous facsimile edition (Menston, Yorks.: Scolar Press, 1970) includes the *Lover's Complaint*.
47. Gathering K begins, not with the first page of the *Complaint* (K1^v), but with the final page of the *Sonnets*, comprising no. 154, the word "FINIS", and the "A" of "*A* Lover's Complaint" as catchword.
48. Paul de Man, *Allegories of Reading* (New Haven and London: Yale University Press, 1979), p. 19.
49. Almost any lengthy criticism of our three sequences will demonstrate this practice: convenient examples may be found in Ringler, pp. xlvff; Lever, pp. 115ff.; and Booth, pp. 545–546.

GREG KUCICH

The Duality of
Romantic Spenserianism

S PENSER HAS ever been a favorite among the poets, but the
Romantics loved him in an exceptional way and to an extreme
that is unique in literary history. Coleridge and Wordsworth
went by Spenserian nicknames in their youths. Southey looked
upon *The Faerie Queene* with "a religious love and veneration."
Scott, as he put it, "devoured . . . whole cantos" of *The Faerie
Queene* in boyhood and wrote Spenserian stanzas throughout
his poetic career.[1] Byron and Shelley composed their epic
visions of the nineteenth century, *Childe Harold* and *The Revolt
of Islam*, in Spenserian stanzas. Hazlitt called Spenser "the most
poetical . . . of poets." Lamb labelled him "the Poet's Poet."
And it was Keats's legendary "ramping" through *The Faerie
Queene* as an adolescent that made him become a poet, an
experience that characterizes much of the flowering of
Romanticism.[2] For the period's fertile engagement with Spenser produced some of its finest poems, like *Adonais* and *The Eve
of St. Agnes*. Yet it is the collective appearance between 1790–
1830 of the first variorum Spenser edition, multiple reprintings
of eighteenth-century Spenserian commentary, countless periodical discussions of Spenserian topics, and some one hundred
fifty recorded imitations that fully shows how thoroughly
Spenser informed and inspired Romantic literary culture.[3]
Leigh Hunt, who proudly branded himself a "Spenser-
ophilist," summarized: "The most poetical poets of the last and
present generation have all passionately admired him; and no
stanza has been so popular as the magnificent one of his invention."[4]

Few would deny Spenser's tremendous impact on Romanticism or its significance as the principal conduit through which
he has reached us from the Renaissance. Yet the complete
breadth of Romantic Spenserianism has never been satisfac-

287

288 SPENSER STUDIES

torily measured nor its full character ascertained by scholars of
Spenser's reputation and influence. There is no companion
Spenser volume to Joseph Wittreich's *The Romantics on Milton*,
for instance, which means that most of the prodigious amount
of Romantic editorial, critical, and poetic reactions to Spenser
has never been reprinted or even studied.[5] Anthologies of
Spenser's historical reception usually limit the Romantic section
to a few abridged and often-repeated commentaries.[6] The three
major studies of Spenser's developing reputation—Jewel
Wurtsbaugh's *Two Centuries of Spenserian Scholarship*, Earl Wasserman's *Elizabethan Poetry in the Eighteenth Century*, and R. M.
Cummings's Critical Heritage Spenser volume—all stop chro-
nologically before the full advent of Romanticism.[7] *The Spenser
Encyclopedia,* apparently, will not contain a separate entry surveying and assessing the Romantics' overall reaction. And despite all the recent work on poetic influence and the
Renaissance/Romantic interchange, no sustained critical study
of Romantic Spenserianism exists.[8]

The subject has actually been avoided because of a strong and
long-standing scholarly distaste for the Romantics' seemingly
perverse habit of trivializing Spenser's thought in fatuous worship of his beauty. Hazlitt's notorious advice to relish Spenser's
"sensuality" instead of "meddling" with his allegory has been
taken to epitomize this unfortunate bias. Hunt's florid hymns to
Spenser's luxury suggest even more strikingly why the Romantics' role in Spenserian history has been so widely slighted.
"Divine Poet! " Hunt characteristically exclaims of Spenser,

sitting in the midst of the endless treasures, thy luxurious
landscapes, and thy descending gods! . . . We have found
consolation in thee at times when almost everything
pained us, and when we could find it in no other poet of
thy nation, because the world into which they took us was
not equally remote. . . . in coming to thee, we have
travelled in one instant thousands of miles, and to a quarter
in which no sin of reality is heard.[9]

Such outbursts became a regular feature of Romantic
Spenserianism, and a sampling of them has been collected and

reprinted as the basis for the twentieth-century's dismissal of what Paul Alpers has called the Romantics' "tired and hackneyed view of . . . [Spenser's poetry], one that is justly outmoded because unfruitful. . . . [Its] characterization of Spenser's passivity, sensuousness and love of beauty . . . makes *The Faerie Queene* seem a monument to 'poeticalness' in a bad sense."[10] Some readers, like C. A. Patrides, have tried to defend the Romantics by showing how they established a new appreciation of Spenser's poetical craftsmanship that persists to this day.[11] But even Patrides's argument seems to acknowledge the myopia of Romanticism's Phaedria-like voyage to that beautiful Spenserian quarter "in which no sin of reality is heard." It would seem an errant quest that few modern readers would care to pursue.

Yet our perception of this voyage has been distorted all along by our exclusionist focus on a small, spectacular body of writings that constitutes only a fraction of Romantic Spenserianism. And even that fraction of commentary has been removed from its immediate context and read in a reductive manner. Scott said in reviewing Todd's variorum Spenser of 1805 that a "complete and respectable edition of Spenser's works has been long a *desideratum* in English literature."[12] We might add that a complete or at least truly representative presentation of Romantic Spenserianism, in its full range and complexity, has been long a desideratum of studies in the history of Spenser's influence. For, contrary to our stereotypical views and as Robert Gleckner and Joseph Wittreich have recently shown us in their excellent studies of Blake's visionary Spenser, the intellectual dimension of Spenser's art could profoundly inspire Romantic writing.[13] And if we consider the full sweep of the Romantics' conversation with Spenser, we may find that they were actually and fundamentally divided about Spenser's thought and his beauty. Their dualistic response is especially significant because of its close relation to their own conflicts about imaginative and realistic art—one of the major tension points in Romantic poetry. By opening up the contours of Romantic Spenserianism along these lines, we may thus gain a new understanding of Spenser's relevance for nineteenth-century poetics and a deeper appreciation of the way his legacy has been transmitted to our own age.

I

One of the more surprising truths to arise from a wide reading of Romantic Spenserian writings is the primacy accorded to Spenser's thought. It may be right to say that the Romantics felt more deeply inclined to his beauty than most of their predecessors, and that some of them were also more resistant to his theological and political orthodoxy. But most of them, even those like Coleridge who adored his luxurious style, still considered his thought the single, most important feature of his achievement. Wordsworth and Coleridge admired more than anything else in his art the visionary character of his allegory—a stunning display of "mental space," Coleridge argued, in which, Wordsworth added, the "highest" spiritual truths are manifest in a degree comparable with the writings of Milton and the Hebrew prophets.[14] Blake felt, as Joseph Wittreich has shown us, that it was Spenser's contribution to the same prophetic line in the "Sublime Allegory" of *The Faerie Queene* that made him a true poet and a fit companion to stride forward with through eternity. The psychological interiority of his epic, what Harry Berger has called its "inscape," also gave Blake an important model for his own epic psychodramas of inward regeneration. His illustration of "The Characters in Spenser's Faerie Queene," as Robert Gleckner has exhaustively demonstrated, is a sustained record of his fascination with the mental landscapes of *The Faerie Queene*.[15] For others, the political dimension of Spenser's art was most compelling. Scott was particularly interested in the "political allegory couched under . . . [Spenser's] tissue of romantic fiction,"[16] and he shaped his own longest Spenserian imitation, *The Vision of Don Roderick,* as an extended political allegory. With the Irish problem flaring up anew around the turn of the nineteenth century, the *View of the Present State of Ireland* also gained considerable attention. It was reprinted separately in 1809, and despite some objections to its harshness it received wide praise as an "excellent and profound" political treatise, one that could still provide "useful" instruction for England's management of Ireland.[17]

But above all, and this claim most radically upsets our traditional reading of Romantic Spenserianism, it was Spenser's moral teaching that struck most of the Romantics as his greatest accomplishment. Instead of killing off the eighteenth century's didactic Spenser to make room for what Keats called the "Fair plumed syren" of *The Faerie Queene*, the Romantics, especially in popular reading circles, preserved and reinforced his conservative reputation as England's great moral poet. Todd introduced him on the Variorum title page, in fact, as "The Moral Poet." And John Aikin, another influential early-nineteenth-century editor, began a biography of Spenser by claiming that his "works breathe a fervent spirit of piety and morality."[18] He was frequently classified by critics and poets as one of "the best moral writers," an "unrivalled" teacher, Wordsworth said, of "virtue and prudence."[19] Coleridge declared that "Above all, a deep moral earnestness" distinguishes his art.[20] The periodical press, in reviewing Spenserian poems, criticism, and editions for a wide reading audience, tended to stress the "moral judgment," the "moral purity," and the "monitory wisdom" of Spenser's allegory.[21] The moral glosses of eighteenth-century Spenserian commentators like Upton, Warton, and Hughes were often reprinted and made available for wide consumption throughout the Romantic period. Popular critics, such as Percival Stockdale, were recommending for study and emulation the didactic sections of eighteenth-century Spenserian imitations like Thomson's *The Castle of Indolence*.[22] And highly moralistic poems based on these models became standard fare among the era's general readership.

A juvenile Leigh Hunt, for instance, wrote a widely read didactic poem in Spenserian stanzas modeled upon Thomson's imitation and titled *The Palace of Pleasure*. Chandos Leigh, little known today but one of Romanticism's most prolific Spenserian poets, wrote a series of imitations in support of "Religion, order, law, the triple card / Of states. . . ."[23] Charles Lloyd, an occasional collaborator with Coleridge, did the same in numerous imitations with such titles as "Lines on the Death of a Friend" and "Stanzas on the Difficulty with Which, in Youth, We Bring Home to Our Habitual Consciousness, the Idea of Death." In *A Tale of Paraguay*, Southey spent over two hundred Spenserian stanzas on the comforts of orthodox religion and domestic harmony. Henry Boyd devoted three hundred to the dangers of alcoholism in *The Woodman's Tale*. And Sir James Bland Burges, in *Richard the First,* incredibly wrote nearly two thousand Spenserian stanzas about the follies of ambition.

Clearly, the Romantics were both serious and deadly dull about the moral center of their Spenserianism.

This was precisely the problem, as Hazlitt, the mature Hunt, and several of the period's more gifted writers understood it. Reforming popular misperceptions and prejudices about poetry was something of a mission to both Hunt and Hazlitt. Spenser's case must have seemed in particular need of redemption. For while the beauty of his craft had become appreciated as never before in sophisticated literary circles, most readers were being buried with Spenserian moralism. And their understandable exasperation, as Hazlitt and Hunt both argued, was the cause of a growing popular resistance to Spenser. Evidence of such a backlash was not hard to find. Periodical critics were beginning to complain about Spenser's "monstrous allegories" and the "pedantic manner" of his modern followers (R, V, 2291; I, 450). Calls for modern poets to "wash their hands" of Spenser were growing frequent (R, II, 566). One reviewer even declared that the "Spenserian school" had been quite "shut out" from "popular reading" (R, II, 566). In response to such a mounting bias, Hazlitt lamented that Spenser had become "little known to the ordinary run of English readers" because people are "afraid of the allegory, as if they thought it would bite them."[24] Hunt thought that Spenser was being "excluded" from the general readership because of fears that "he wrote a good deal of allegory."[25] To think of Spenser as "The Moral Poet," it appeared, could very well mean consigning him to the shelves. The best strategy against this tendency lay in temporarily diminishing the importance of his moralism while building up a new appreciation for the most accessible and immediately attractive qualities of his art—his stylistic graces.

Those sensational claims for his beauty over his thought were delivered in precisely this context, reflecting the immediate dynamics of Romantic literary culture more than the absolute aesthetic opinions of its leading critics. Hunt was far from unsympathetic to Spenser's "virtue and prudence," writing Spenserian stanzas against vice in his youth and completing a long Spenserian allegory on worldly vanity, The Shewe of Faire Seeming, shortly before his death. And Hazlitt was sensitive to what he called the "visionary medium" of Spenser's intellectual world.[26] When he privileged Spenser's luxury above his ideas, therefore, he was only responding to a particular situation in

which heavy-handed Spenserian moralism like Southey's was
threatening to deny Spenser a popular following. In the full
context of his argument, he thus explained:

> Mr Southey says of Spenser: "Yet not more sweet / Than
> pure was he, and not more pure than wise;" . . . The love
> of beauty, however, and not of truth, is the moving prin-
> ciple of his [Spenser's] mind. . . . some people will say that
> . . . they cannot understand . . . [him] on account of the
> allegory. . . . This is very idle. If they do not meddle with
> the allegory, the allegory will not meddle with them. . . .
> For instance, when Britomart, seated amidst the young
> warriors, lets fall her hair and discovers her sex, is it
> necessary to know the part she plays in the allegory, to
> understand the beauty of the . . . [scene]?[27]

Hunt was thinking of this specific argument and its way of
replying to the Spenserian moralists when he raised some of his
most controversial and exclusive paeans to Spenser's beauty.
For it was in response to those who "objected" to Spenser's
tedious allegory that he argued,

> as to allegory . . . in Spenser's hands it became such an
> embodiment of poetry itself, that its objectors really de-
> serve no better answer than has been given by Mr. Hazlitt,
> who asks, if they thought the allegory would "bite
> them.". . . Spenser's great characteristic is poetic luxury.
> . . . His allegory itself is but one part allegory, and nine
> parts beauty and enjoyment; sometimes an excess of flesh
> and blood. . . . Spenser is the farthest removed from the
> ordinary cares and haunts of the world of all the poets that
> ever wrote, except perhaps Ovid; and this, which is the
> reason why mere men of business and the world do not
> like him, constitutes his most bewitching charm.[28]

This is the statement of a man who had written numerous
Spenserian stanzas, in youth and old age, precisely about the
ways of the world. Instead of singling it out as further evidence
of Romanticism's blindness to Spenser's complexity, we should
therefore read it as an expression of the period's debate about
how to appreciate the full variety of his achievement.

II

That debate ultimately suggested Spenser's most significant relation to nineteenth-century poetics. For by focusing so acutely on his radical extremes—his moralism versus his sensuousness—critics like Hunt and Hazlitt came to recognize in him a duality of mind that closely matched a dominant condition of the Romantic psyche. The philosophical context of his oppositions was less important here, especially to those like Shelley who resisted his theology, than the psychological reflex in itself of his doubleness. Jack Stillinger and, more recently, Stuart Curran and Susan Wolfson have characterized one of the principal mental motions in Romantic poetry as the dynamic tension between imaginative idealism and relentless realism. Indeed, we are coming to believe, as Peter Thorslev puts it in his study of Romantic contraries, that the "doubling discourses" of this self-debate make up the central drama of Romantic poetics.[29] Keats's odes, with their ongoing swings between magical fairy lands and realms of human suffering, form the most succinct examples of such a discourse, but its contrarieties may be traced throughout the era's poetry. As some of the Romantics weighed and readjusted the balance of Spenser's dramatically different impact on moral and voluptuous readers, they began to sense within his native imagination a doubling habit of mind strikingly apposite to their own condition. They even came to suspect that, like themselves, he was torn by mixed commitments to aesthetic luxury and intellectual realism. Hence dichotomous readings of him as both a poet of thought and beauty, caught between two poles, began to shape the most sophisticated form of Romantic Spenserianism, one in which Spenser's own duality of vision directly addressed the poetics of Romantic experience.

Hazlitt, for instance, commended Spenser's profound insight into "the truth of human passion" in the same essay that announced his "love of beauty over truth."[30] Hunt approvingly quoted Wordsworth on Spenser's "highest moral truths" at the same time that he read *The Faerie Queene* luxuriously, in order "to shut myself away . . . from care and sorrow."[31] Thomas Campbell preferred "the magic of [Spenser's] . . . colouring" to the clouds of his allegory while stressing "the form and symmetry of truth" in "his moral meaning. . . ."[32] Not at all contradictory, these comments locate the part of Spenser where the Romantics, in their most insightful moments, found themselves—what Hunt called Spenser's "piquancy of contrast" and Hazlitt identified as his "splendid chiaro-scuro."[33]

This capacious dualism actually became the primary topic of the Romantics' most complex Spenserian criticism. Aikin was puzzled by Spenser's "intermingling the ideas of reality with those of fiction"—a complaint that had been frequently raised throughout the eighteenth century. But Hazlitt recognized that such doubleness constituted a breadth of vision at the heart of Spenser's genius and his relevance for the present age. "The two worlds of reality and of fiction," he thus characterized Spenser's way of seeing, "are poised on the wings of his imagination." "Nothing is more striking in Spenser," Hunt expanded, "than the astonishing variety of his pictures, and the rapidity with which he passes from one kind to another . . . an extraordinary mixture of light and darkness—of the sublime and the sordid. . . . No man, by seeing one thing exquisitely, saw further into its opposite than he did. . . . [He is] at once sacred and seductive."[34] For Hunt, Hazlitt and the more advanced readers of Spenser among their peers, such a range of vision meant that Spenser was not simply ambivalent about his morals, but that at bottom he spoke to the present as a poet of psychological complexity who looked deeply into the doubleness of all experience.

That startlingly innovative reading laid the basis for the most complex form of Romantic Spenserianism, in which Spenser's Janus-like vision helped the Romantics play out their own fundamental conflicts between realism and ideality, truth and beauty. Wordsworth's early poem in Spenserian stanzas, *The Female Vagrant*, centers in a mad woman's difficulty in separating reality from nightmarish delusions. And his more elaborate revision of the tale, titled *Guilt and Sorrow*, probes much deeper into the psychological dynamics of guilt-ridden hallucinations and the mind's struggle to recover a hold on reality. His shorter Spenserian poem, "Stanzas Written in My Pocket Copy of *The Castle of Indolence*," specifically adapts Thomson's divisions between fancy and realism to his own vacillation between a poetry of imaginative indolence and responsible action in the world. Blake's "Imitation of Spen[s]er" balances "truth's beams" against "fairy dreams," and his illustration of the characters in

The Faerie Queene reveals his deep interest in what Robert Gleckner calls the "studied contrariousness" of their mental situations.[35] Coleridge's playful imitation, "Lines in the Manner of Spenser," examines a similar conflict by juxtaposing real and ideal visions of the poet's wife—a division treated with greater elaboration in the more well-known though less obviously Spenserian lyric "The Eolian Harp."

This appreciation of Spenser's "studied contrariousness" deepened considerably as Hazlitt, Hunt, and others responded to the heavy moralism of early Romantic Spenserianism, which explains why the period's Spenserian poetry grew most sophisticated and figured most prominently in the works of the younger poets of its second generation. For them, *The Faerie Queene* presented a compelling model of mental questing that traced out the specific contours of psychological doubling essential to their own pilgrimages of the spirit. The significance of this special line of influence can be measured by the way each of the leading second-generation Romantic poets felt inspired not only to write a major Spenserian narrative but to make it reenact, in some substantial manner, the kind of "doubling discourses" now thought to be fundamentally embodied in Spenser's divided world of truth and beauty.

That reenactment entailed a basic reformulation of Spenserian allegory. It meant delving beneath the overt philosophy, the ideas, of Spenser's allegory to recover and intensify the mental doubling embedded within it. Keats, Shelley, and Byron may have resisted, even subverted at times, Spenser's orthodox theology and his conservative politics. But they ultimately forgave his conventionality, as Shelley put it in *A Defence of Poetry*, because they found so much of value beneath what Yeats called his "official morality."[36] Thus in the act of unseating him as a rigid teacher, they consistently brought out what they considered to be the deeper, more significant mental dynamic of his allegory. Put another way, they redeemed that part of the allegory which could inspire and help sustain the poetics of their own modern experience.

Keats, for instance, transformed Spenser's recurrent castle allegory to shape his own history of creative division. He was always drawn to the stunning juxtaposition of beauty and lurking danger in Spenserian castles like the House of Pride, a "piquancy of contrast" which he elaborately marked in his personal copy of *The Faerie Queene*.[37] But instead of fastening on Spenser's overt moral about vice's false temptation, he extracted from these sequences what he considered to be the deeper drama of a poet's division between imaginative beauty and intellectual realism. That Spenserian subtext inspired one of his most well-known metaphors of his own poetic maturation, the "Mansion of Many Apartments," in which he presents the "sharpening" of his poetic vision as a journey through a castle-like structure of many chambers. Like the typical Spenserian castle, Keats's mansion contains a gorgeous entry room that intoxicates with "light" and "pleasant wonders." But as the quester moves further into the mansion, just as Redcrosse travels into the inner reaches of the House of Pride, he discovers like Redcrosse a "World . . . full of Misery and Heartbreak, Pain, Sickness and oppression. . . ."[38] This voyage of discovery unlocks and elaborates what Keats found to be the deepest significance of Spenser's allegory. For it does not reveal, in any conventional sense, vice's false allure. Rather it acts out a drama of Keats's own division between the "pleasant wonders" of the imagination and the reality of worldly suffering. Such is the drama Keats recovered from the core of Spenser's allegory to help formulate his own poetic identity as a self-divided traveller through mental labyrinths.

The poetics of that Spenserian drama also helped him articulate such a voyage in lyrical form. *The Eve of St. Agnes* has often been characterized as one of the closest poetic approximations ever of Spenser's style, mainly because of its opulent sensuousness. But the poem more complexly recreates Spenser's style, as Keats understood it, in the way that it carries out another journey like Redcrosse's through an enigmatic castle. Luminous delights and "pleasant wonders" pervade the castle's outer chambers:

> At length burst in the argent revelry,
> With plume, tiara, and all rich array,
> Numerous as shadows haunting fairily,
> The brain, new-stuff'd, in youth, with triumphs gay
> Of old romance. . . .
>
> (lines 37–41)[39]

But as the narrative moves within the castle's interior, the scenery becomes, as in the Spenserian pattern, increasingly more complicated. Images of beauty—the famous "triple-arched" casement—are consistently juxtaposed to sinister details—Madeline's Philomela-like appearance as "a tongueless nightingale" and her indictment of Porphyro as a "Cruel . . . traitor." These juxtapositions, as Stillinger and many others have argued, produce an extended poetic form of the same kind of mental allegory figured in Keats's Mansion of Many Apartments. They also constitute a more elaborate version of the same Spenserian "chiaroscuro" that made *The Faerie Queene* and its castle allegory such a sustaining force in Keats's overall creative pilgrimage.

It was the duality of Spenser's mutability myth that provided a similar kind of inspiration for Byron and Shelley. Like Keats, they both read through the "official morality" of Spenser's allegory to cultivate and extend what they saw as the doubling pattern of mind at its center. The last canto of *Childe Harold* narrates a prolonged voyage through Italian ruins, during which sustained meditations on impermanence obviously recall Spenser's Mutabilitie Cantos and his *Complaints* on the differences between the world's "tickle" state and the eternal fixity of Providential design. Byron looked beyond the theological implications of that contrast, finding more significance in the way it seemed to dramatize the mind's divided inclinations toward realism and idealism, toward what he called "fairy-land" and "strong reality."[40] Such a division, recovered and expanded out of Spenser's allegory, conditions the mental drama of *Childe Harold,* canto four, one of Byron's most extensive and poignant reflections on the duality of "over-weening phantasies" and "waking Reason" (IV, 60–61).

In *The Revolt of Islam* Shelley similarly narrates a long voyage through a series of worldly ruins, during which he consistently yearns for a millennial ideal of immutable bliss. This tension of opposites develops into a specific reformulation of the Mutabilitie Cantos near the epic's conclusion, when Shelley's protagonists travel in a kind of "ever changing," "labyrinthine" procession reminiscent of Mutabilitie's ever-revolving masque of change. Where Spenser finally juxtaposes Mutabilitie's rule to God's "stedfast . . . pillours of Eternity," however, Shelley ultimately contrasts his own world of suffering to the "Temple of the Spirit," which "Survives all mortal change in lasting loveliness."[41] In that secularization, Shelley discards Spenser's theology but preserves and extends the psychological dualism that Byron was also learning to appropriate from the center of his allegory. For Shelley's new formulation of his mutability myth culminates the ongoing drama in *The Revolt of Islam* of a mind divided between imaginative idealism, in its vision of the Temple of the Spirit, and the painful facts of experience, in its sustained focus on the worst atrocities of the French Revolution. The rudiments of that drama, as Shelley saw it, lay embedded within Spenser's dynamic of heavenly joy and human suffering. Read as an allegory of the mind's debate with itself, it supplied the poetics for the modern, self-questioning pilgrimage of *The Revolt of Islam*. And transformed into an even more condensed, highly wrought drama of the mind in conflict, it helped empower the action of *Adonais*, arguably Romanticism's greatest poem in Spenserian stanzas and its most passionate contemplation of the reality of impermanence and the ideal of transcendence.

Similar tensions of realism and ideality form the basic design of many lesser works that ranked among the era's most highly regarded Spenserian poems—James Beattie's *The Minstrel*, Mary Tighe's *Psyche*, Thomas Campbell's *Gertrude of Wyoming*, John Hamilton Reynolds' *The Romance of Youth*. This pattern of conflict in the leading Romantic Spenserian works was so pervasive, and its links to Spenser so obvious, that contemporary reviewers finally characterized the poetry as a modern outgrowth of Spenser's own duality. Thus one reviewer of *Childe Harold* explained: "The genius of Spenser has stamped upon [modern adaptations of his poetry] . . . a character in which the grotesque and the sedate, the lofty and the mean, the sad and the humourous, are . . . harmoniously blended . . ." (*R*, I, 401). That Spenser should have stamped such a "character" of duality on nineteenth-century verse suggests how profoundly he helped administrate Romanticism's deepest debate about its own poetic mission.

III

Perhaps the most poignant expression of this formative impact lies in the way Spenser helped shape the mature, double-sided vision of his two greatest champions among the Romantics, Hunt and Keats, as they lived out their last days. In a recent essay for the *Keats-Shelley Journal*, I have shown how Hunt worked out his life-long divisions between aestheticism and intellectual responsibility by projecting them onto Spenser.[42] Throughout most of his long literary career Hunt felt "bound" to confer "moral benefit[s]," yet he constantly wished to abandon his tasks as a teacher-critic in order to luxuriate in the "luminous enjoyment" and "perpetual solace" of literary beauty.[43] No one he read seemed to embody this same division as much as Spenser. The "Moral Poet" always seemed engaged, as Hunt saw it, in a dramatic struggle against his own sense of intellectual obligations, repeatedly leading us toward scenes of instruction only to "turn his back upon everything real . . . however he may pretend to bear it in mind; and to give himself up to the dreams of books, of romances, of mythology, of whatsoever is remote from the prose of human affairs." Spenser resolved this conflict, Hunt argued, by combining a deep pathos for "poor human nature," expressed in the psychological drama of such "ghastly realit[ies]" as the Despair and Malbecco episodes, with a provision of solace in the luxury of his aesthetic beauty.[44] He thus appeared like the Countess of Pembroke in his own *Ruines of Time*, whose "Sorrowing [song is] tempered with deare delight"—a description that Hunt underlined in his two copies of Spenser's poetry.[45] In his last reading of *The Faerie Queene*—"I know not what-*th* reading of the book," Hunt said, "whether my fiftieth or hundreth"—he simultaneously felt struck "at home" by Spenser's sorrow and "solace[d]" by his "deare delight."[46] This powerful impression of Spenser's duality became the basis for his own final reconciliation of thought and beauty in a poetics embracing the mixture of joy and sorrow, idealism and reality, that constitutes all experience. In his last substantial poem, the Spenserian *Shewe of Faire Seeming*, written very near the end of his life, he actually pictured his ideal poet as the Countess of Pembroke from *The Ruines of Time*. Like the "sacred and seductive" Spenser, and the poet of duality that Hunt finally became, she sings a lyric of "grief" and beauty while her face interchanges "grave" and "gay" looks.

Keats, who studied Spenser with Hunt, may have reached in his last days a similar vision of poetry and experience through Spenser's way of seeing. We know that he was marking passages from Spenser for Fanny Brawne near the torturous end of his life. It now appears, as I have argued elsewhere, that portions of his last markings of *The Faerie Queene* have been recently discovered at the Keats House Library in Hampstead.[47] These markings consistently single out Spenser's many poignant depictions of the mingled joys and torments of love. If we consider the strikingly close relation of these sequences to Keats's own anguish in his divided love for Fanny, we may imagine what a strong impact their duality of temperament would have made on his thinking. One such passage, for instance, describes the confused experience of deep pain and sweetness that Timias undergoes as he awakens from his grievous injuries to witness Belphoebe's loving attendance on him: "And groaning inly deep . . . By this he had sweet life recur'd again" (3.5.34).[48] His joyful recovery, of course, becomes even more thoroughly mixed with anguish when Belphoebe deserts him. And the marginal strokes in the Keats House Spenser that emphasize his consequent self-dessication in the throes of love and grief—"consumed quight . . . like a pined ghost" (4.7.41)—suggest the reflection that Keats must have seen of his own consumptive decline in his last experience of love and alienation with Fanny. The implications here point to Spenser's substantial role in Keats's well-known developing sensitivity to the presense of Melancholy's "sovran shrine" in "the very temple of Delight." Keats was certainly intrigued by Spenser's duality in his first readings of *The Faerie Queene*, when he marked what Hunt often cited as the "chiaroscuro" of Una's unveiled face brightly shining in the "secret Shadow" of a "shady place." That same "piquancy of contrast" later helped produce the tensions of cold and warmth, romance and realism that constitute the major interest of *The Eve of St. Agnes*. And Spenser's vision may very well have inspired Keats, in the end and at the most personal level, to feel the doubleness of experience along his own pulse.

All this goes far toward explaining why Keats and so many of his contemporaries looked upon Spenser as one of the poets closest to their own hearts. Yet there was something even more special about their feeling for his duality that made him an utterly unique inspiration among their great precursors. The mighty poets of England's Renaissance tradition habitually came to them as gigantic rivals whose threatening tendency to belittle them produced what we are coming to distinguish as one of the most anxious preoccupations of their poetry. Yet Keats was not alone in recognizing that Spenser's poignant experience of self-division, recurrently worked out in the dramatic pathos of episodes like Timias' encounter with Belphoebe, made him appear strikingly mild and congenial compared to his imposing peers. Where a lofty and austere Milton, in particular, seemed to frown upon those who would dare attempt to follow him, engendering the anxiety of belatedness that overshadowed so many nineteenth-century poets, a gentler Spenser welcomed the Romantics with the benevolent gestures that Keats celebrated in his early Spenserian narrative, *Calidore*:

> Spenser! thy brows are arched, open, kind,
> And come like a clear sun-rise to my mind;
> And always does my heart with pleasure dance,
> When I think on thy noble countenance:
>   . . .
> Therefore, great bard, I not so fearfully
> Call on thy gentle spirit to hover nigh
> My daring steps . . .
>
> (lines 49–57)

With the Covering Cherub of the literary past seeming to lock the Romantics out of the grounds of poetic election, as Harold Bloom would argue,[49] the appearance of one of their illustrious forebears as a "gentle spirit" whom they could invoke "not so fearfully" must have seemed like a cherished beacon to guide them through the perilous paths of poetic revisionism.

How much that illumination meant to them may be measured by the consistency with which their discussions of Spenser's duality culminated in enthusiastic praise for his mild and beneficent character. Todd stressed the "amicable temper" and "gentle disposition" of the "tender-minded Spenser." Lamb described him as "Our elder Bard, Spenser, a gentle Name." A "soft and feeling heart" seemed to more than one reviewer the moving principle of his art. Even the rather hard-nosed Hazlitt could think affectionately of Spenser's "romantic" and "passive tenderness."[50] Wordsworth, in contrasting that "tenderness" with Milton's severity, pinpointed the tremendous appeal of such an "amicable" Spenser for a generation deeply anxious about its own domineering poetic inheritance: "in all that Milton writes, you can find the exalted being that he was . . . [in] all that Spenser writes, you can trace the gentle affectionate spirit of the man. . . ." It was that distinction, on which so much of Spenser's allure for the Romantics finally depended, that enabled Wordsworth in *The Prelude* to pause from his protracted wrestlings with Milton to welcome Spenser happily as "that gentle Bard . . . Sweet Spenser . . . I call him Brother, Englishman, and Friend!"[51] We need only consider the Oedipal pressures so often at work upon the Romantics when they looked back upon their poetic "fathers" to realize that Spenser's duality meant so much to them not only because it spoke to their own hearts but also because its message came to them in a rare spirit of fraternity.

Some may be tempted to conclude that however complexly the Romantics adapted Spenser they still distorted him in the reflection of their own image, especially in their notion of his mental ambivalence, which seems to make their response more a phenomenon of nineteenth-century poetics than a useful contribution to Spenser studies. But they may be able to teach us something about Spenser after all. For we have come today, as Paul Alpers, Leigh DeNeef, David Miller, Jonathan Goldberg, and A. Bartlett Giamatti among others have been recently arguing, to think of the tension of contraries and dualities in Spenser's poetry as one of the great unifying and energizing principles of his art.[52] The Romantics understood this very well, and they explored its implications not only in their criticism but in their most widely-ranging epic poems and their most psychologically intense lyrical works. If we read their discoveries as a significant anticipation of the ways we are now beginning to comprehend Spenser, we can certainly learn a great deal from them about the dualistic "character" of Spenserian poetics. We may even find their more controversial insights into the full depth of that "character" readjusting our own notions of the dynamic between truth and beauty in Spenser's art. And perhaps most significantly, the psychological emphases of Romantic Spenserianism can lay to rest the old claims that Spenser appeals only to the mind of a teacher or the passion of a sensualist.[53] For the Romantics, he also thought deeply into the human heart's divisions. And he bestowed his experience upon his poetic descendants with a special generosity of spirit that made him a uniquely enabling muse for a belated age. The Romantics' engagement with his sympathetic knowledge of "poor human nature" can thus deepen our appreciation of his relevance for modern poets and help clarify our understanding of his overall achievement.

University of Notre Dame

NOTES

The argument of this article is worked out more elaborately in my forthcoming book, *Keats, Shelley, and Romantic Spenserianism* (Pennsylvania State University Press).

1. Charles Mounts records the shared delight with Spenserian names and stories that helped cement the beginning friendship between Wordsworth and Coleridge. "Wordsworth's Transparent Sobriquet," *Huntington Library Quarterly*, 15 (1951), 201–203. William Haller quotes Southey's remark in *The Early Life of Robert Southey* (New York: Octagon Books, 1966), p. 264. Sir Walter Scott, *The Letters of Sir Walter Scott 1787–1807*, ed. H. J. C. Grierson, 12 vols. (London: Constable & Co., 1932–37), I, 320.

2. William Hazlitt, *Lectures on the English Poets* (London, 1818), p. 68. Lamb's term is quoted by Leigh Hunt in *Imagination and Fancy* (New York, 1845), p. 51. Hyder Edward Rollins chronicles Keats's first reactions to *The Faerie Queene* in *The Keats Circle*, 2 vols. (Cambridge, Mass.: Harvard University Press, 1965), II, 148.

3. Henry John Todd's eight-volume variorum Spenser was published in 1805. It contains a substantial amount of eighteenth-century commentary on Spenser. Thomas Warton's *Observations on the Fairy Queen of Spenser* (1754) went through new editions in 1811 and 1820. Richard Hurd's *Letters on Chivalry and Romance* (1762), containing an important chapter on Spenser, was reprinted in 1811. Many other eighteenth-century comments on Spenser reappeared in the collected editions of the Britich poets, by John Bell, John Aikin, and Alexander Chalmers for instance, that went through multiple reprintings during the Romantic period. My estimate of Romantic Spenserian poems is based upon Phillips C. Davies' check list of Spenserian poems, "A Check List of Poems, 1595 to 1833, Entirely or Partly Written in the Spenserian Stanza," *Bulletin of the New York Public Library*, 77 (1974), 314–328. All this Spenserian activity provoked a voluminous amount of periodical criticism on Spenser, his critics, and his imitators, which has never been collected or reprinted.

4. Leigh Hunt, *Leigh Hunt's Literary Criticism*, eds. Lawrence Huston Houtchens and Carolyn Washburn Houtchens (New York: Columbia University Press, 1956), p. 447. Hunt characterized himself as a "Spenser-ophilist" in a letter written near the end of his long literary career. *The Correspondence of Leigh Hunt*, ed. Thorton Hunt, 2 vols. (London, 1862), II, 264.

5. Joseph Anthony Wittreich, Jr., ed. *The Romantics on Milton* (Cleveland, Ohio: Case Western Reserve University Press, 1970).

6. See, for instance, *The Critics of Edmund Spenser*, ed. Herbert E. Cory (1911; New York: Haskell House, 1964), pp. 98–108; *Spenser's Critics: Changing Currents in Literary Taste*, ed. William R. Mueller (Syracuse: Syracuse University Press, 1959), pp. 73–81; *The Prince of Poets: Essays on Edmund Spenser*, ed. John R. Elliott (New York: New York University Press, 1968), pp. 14–17, 23–27; *Edmund Spenser*, ed. Paul J. Alpers (Harmondsworth: Penguin Books, 1969), pp. 119–152.

7. Jewel Wurtsbaugh, *Two Centuries of Spenserian Scholarship* (Baltimore, Md.: Johns Hopkins University Press, 1936); Earl Wasserman, *Elizabethan Poetry in the Eighteenth Century* (Urbana: University of Illinois Press, 1947); R. M. Cummings, ed., *The Critical Heritage: Spenser* (New York: Barnes & Noble, 1971).

8. Traugott Bohme collects a great deal of source material on Spenser's developing reputation in *Spenser's literarisches Nachleben bis zu Shelley* (Berlin: Mayer & Muller, 1911), but only a portion of his book focuses on Romantic Spenserianism and it offers little in the way of interpretation. The only other extensive studies of Romantic Spenserianism are in dissertation form. And these works either treat the subject within a broader historical perspective— David Hall Evett, "Nineteenth-Century Criticism of Spenser," Diss. Harvard University, 1965—concentrate only on the Romantics' critical responses to Spenser—Dorothy Wayne Zimmerman, "Romantic Criticism of Edmund Spenser," Diss. University of Illinois, 1957—or focus primarily on a single dimension of Spenser's impact—George Richard Pitts, "Romantic Spenserianism: 'The Faerie Queene' and the English Romantics," Diss. University of Pennsylvania, 1977.

9. Hunt, *Literary Criticism*, p. 456.

10. Alpers, *Edmund Spenser*, pp. 68–69.

11. C. A. Patrides, "The Achievement of Edmund Spenser," *Yale Review*, 69 (1980), 427–443.

12. Sir Walter Scott, "Todd's Edition of Spenser," *The Edinburgh Review*, 7 (1806), 203.

13. Robert Gleckner, *Blake and Spenser* (Baltimore: Md: Johns Hopkins University Press, 1985); Joseph Anthony Wittreich, Jr., *Visionary Poetics: Milton's Tradition and His Legacy*, (San Marino, Cal.: Huntington Library, 1979).

14. Samuel Taylor Coleridge, *The Literary Remains of Samuel Taylor Coleridge*, ed. Henry Nelson Coleridge (London, 1836), p. 94; William Wordsworth, *The Prose Works of William Wordsworth*, eds. W. J. B. Owen and Jane Worthington Smyser, 3 vols. (Oxford: Clarendon Press, 1974), III, 35.

15. Wittreich, *Visionary Poetics*, pp. 25, 42–44, 69–72; Gleckner, *Blake and Spenser*, pp. 158–262.

16. Scott, *Letters*, II, 227.

17. Anonymous, "Todd's Edition of Spenser's Works", *The Critical Review*, 7 (1806), 416.

18. John Aikin, ed., *The Works of the British Poets,* (Philadelphia, 1819), II, 8.

19. Henry Hugh Boyd, *The Woodman's Tale, after the Manner of Spenser,* (London, 1805), p. xxi; Wordsworth, *The Prose Works of William Wordsworth,* ed. Alexander B. Grosart, 3 vols, (London, 1876), I, 322.

20. Coleridge, *Literary Remains*, p. 97.

21. Anonymous, "Todd's Edition of Spenser's Works," 412; Robert Southey, "Todd's Works of Edmund Spenser," *The Annual Review*, 4 (1805), 544; Anonymous, quoted in *The Romantics Reviewed, 1793–1830: Contemporary Reviews of British Romantic Writers. Part B: Byron and Regency Society Poets*, ed. Donald Reiman, 5 vols. (New York: Garland Publishing, 1972), I, 400. Hereafter cited parenthetically as *R*.

22. Percival Stockdale, *Lectures on the Truly Eminent English Poets*, 2 vols. (London, 1807), II, 127–30.

23. Chandos Leigh, "America," in *Poems Now First Collected* (London, n.d.).

24. Hazlitt, *The Collected Works of William Hazlitt*, ed. P. P. Howe, 21 vols. (London: Dent, 1930–34), X, 73; *Lectures*, p. 74.

25. Hunt, *The Autobiography of Leigh Hunt*, ed. J. E. Morpurgo (London: The Cresset Press, 1949), p. 151; *Imagination and Fancy*, p. 49.

26. Hazlitt, *Lectures*, p. 81.

27. Hazlitt, *Lectures*, pp. 69, 74.

28. Hunt, *Imagination and Fancy*, pp. 50–51.

29. Jack Stillinger, *The Hoodwinking of Madeline and Other Essays on Keats's Poems* (Urbana: University of Illinois Press, 1971); Stuart Curran, *Poetic Form and British Romanticism* (Oxford and New York: Oxford University Press, 1986); Susan J. Wolfson, *The Questioning Presence: Wordsworth, Keats, and the Interrogative Mode in Romantic Poetry* (Ithaca, N.Y.: Cornell University Press, 1986); Peter L. Thorslev, Jr., *Romantic Contraries: Freedom Versus Destiny* (New Haven, Conn.: Yale University Press, 1984).

30. Hazlitt, *Lectures*, p. 83.

31. Hunt, "English Poetry Versus Cardinal Wiseman," *Fraser's Magazine*, 60 (1859), 754; Annotations of Todd's Spenser (Victoria & Albert Museum Library, London). Permission to quote from Hunt's annotated Spenser texts has been granted by the Trustees of the Victoria & Albert Museum Library and the University of Iowa Libraries.

32. Thomas Campbell, ed., *Specimens of the British Poets*, 7 vols. (London, 1819), I, 126–31.

33. Hunt, *Literary Criticism*, p. 442; Hazlitt, *Lectures*, p. 82.

34. Aikin, II, 13; Hazlitt, *Lectures*, p. 69; Hunt, *Literary Criticism*, pp. 427, 435, 443; "English Poetry Versus Cardinal Wiseman," 749.

35. Gleckner, p. 229.

36. W. B. Yeats, *Essays and Introductions* (New York: Macmillan, 1968), p. 369.

37. Amy Lowell records Keats's markings of *The Faerie Queene* in *John Keats*, 2 vols. (Boston: Houghton Miflin, 1925), II, 545–574. Several errors in her transcription have been corrected recently by Beth Lau, "Further Corrections to Amy Lowell's Transcriptions of Keats's Marginalia," *Keats-Shelley Journal*, 35 (1986), 30–38.

38. John Keats, *The Letters of John Keats*, ed. Hyder Edward Rollins, 2 vols. (Cambridge, Mass.: Harvard University Press, 1958), I, 280–281.

39. All citations of Keats's poetry are from *The Poems of John Keats*, ed. Jack Stillinger (London: Heinemann, 1978).

40. George Gordon, Lord Byron, *Childe Harold*, IV, 50–51. All citations of Byron's poetry are from *Byron*, ed. Jerome J. McGann (Oxford and New York: Oxford University Press, 1986).

41. Edmund Spenser, *The Faerie Queene*, ed. Thomas P. Roche, Jr. (New Haven, Conn.: Yale University Press, 1981), 8.2.3–4; P. B. Shelley, *The Revolt of Islam*, in *Shelley: Poetical Works*, ed. Thomas Hutchinson; rev. by G. M. Matthews (London: Oxford University Press, 1970), line 4782.

42. Greg Kucich, "Leigh Hunt and Romantic Spenserianism," *Keats-Shelley Journal*, 37 (1988), 110–135.

43. Hunt, *The Poetical Works of Leigh Hunt*, ed. H. S. Milford (London: Oxford University Press, 1923), p. xxvi; *Autobiography*, p. 420.

44. Hunt, *Literary Criticism*, pp. 420, 442.

45. The quotation from *The Ruines of Time* is taken from *The Poetical Works of Edmund Spenser*, eds. J. C. Smith and E. De Selincourt (1912, London: Oxford University Press, 1963), line 319. The two Spenser editions that Hunt used are the Todd Variorum at the Victoria & Albert Museum Library and George Craik's annotated collection of Spenserian passages, *Spenser and His Poetry*, 3 vols. (London, 1845), now located at the University of Iowa Library.

46. Hunt, *Correspondence*, II, 212–213.

47. Kucich, "A Lamentable Lay: Keats and the Marking of Charles Brown's Spenser Volumes," forthcoming in *The Keats-Shelley Review*.

48. The following quotations from *The Faerie Queene* are taken from the Spenser text in question at the Keats House Library, which makes up a part of John Bell's edition of the English poets (1778).

49. Harold Bloom, *The Anxiety of Influence* (London: Oxford University Press, 1973).

50. Henry John Todd, ed. *Spenser's Works*, 8 vols. (London, 1805), I, lvi, clxvi, cxxvi; Charles Lamb, *The Letters of Charles Lamb*, ed. E. V. Lucas, 3 vols. (London: J. M. Dent, 1935), I, 41; Anonymous, "Works of Edmund Spenser," *The Critical Review*, 7 (1806), 412; Hazlitt, *Works*, V, 379.

51. Wordsworth, *The Letters of William and Dorothy Wordsworth. The Later Years (1821–1828)*, ed. Ernest de Selincourt; rev. by Alan G. Hill, 5 vols. (Oxford: Clarendon Press, 1978), II, 264; *The Prelude: 1799, 1805, 1850*, eds. Jonathan Wordsworth, M. H. Abrams, and Stephen Gill (New York: Norton, 1979), III, 281–285.

52. Paul Alpers, *The Poetry of "The Faerie Queene"* (Columbia: University of Missouri Press, 1982); A. Leigh DeNeef, *Spenser and the Motives of Metaphor* (Durham, N.C.: Duke University Press, 1982); David Miller, "Spenser's Poetics: The Poem's Two Bodies," *PMLA*, 101 (1986), 170–185; Jonathan Goldberg, *Endlesse Worke: Spenser and the Structures of Discourse* (Baltimore, Md.: Johns Hopkins University Press, 1981); A. Bartlett Giamatti, *Play of Double Senses: Spenser's Faerie Queene* (Englewood Cliffs, N.J.: Prentice-Hall, 1975).

53. See Patrides, "The Achievement of Edmund Spenser."

FORUM

JOSEPH LOEWENSTEIN

A Note on the Structure of
Spenser's *Amoretti:*
Viper Thoughts

O NE of the signs of erotic debasement in Spenser's epic, one of
the greatest threats to its earnest hymeneal eroticism, is the
solipsism that imprisons the likes of Amoret and Florimell as
they react to the threatening cultural flux around them. Even
the Britomart of the Cancelled Stanzas is touched by a peculiar
isolation as she contemplates the erotic spectacle at which she
has assisted:

> Britomart halfe envying their blesse,
> Was much enpassioned in her gentle sprite,
> And to herselfe oft wisht like happinesse.
> (*FQ*, III.xii.46a)[1]

The Faerie Queene had been left hanging here at the end of Book
III when, in 1595, Spenser published his wedding volume, the
Amoretti and Epithalamion. We can hardly be surprised that the
1595 volume opens with the concerns that conlude the third
book of the epic.[2] As Book III ends, so Spenser's sonnet sequence begins, with an eroticism that expresses itself in terms of
imprisonment or bondage:

> Happy ye leaves when as those lilly hands,
> Which hold my life in their dead doing might
> Shall handle you and hold in loves soft bands,
> Like captives trembling at the victors sight.
> (*Am.*, I, 1–4)

And the next sonnet is similarly recursive, at once describing
the same curse of solipsism that afflicts Amoret, Scudamour,
and Florimell and exhorting the self to transcend its own isolation:

311

Unquiet thought, whom at the first I bred,
Of th'inward bale of my love pined hart:
And sithens have with sighes and sorrowes fed,
Till greater then my wombe thou woxen art.

(*Am.*, II, 1–4)

Neely has remarked on the prevalence, in Elizabethan sonnet sequences, of this trope, in which poetic invention is described as a gestation, and composition as a parturition.[3] But love itself, tinged as it seems to be with womb-envy, is here expressed as a poisonous and isolating internality. It is the work of both poetry and courtship to relieve the self by expelling the "unquiet thought":

Break forth at length out of the inner part,
In which thou lurkest like to vipers brood

(11. 5–6)

The poet's womb-envy has a somewhat misogynist cast, for private libido, the womb of thought, is a nest of vipers, and once expelled the serpent of privacy must be cast down:

seeke some succour both to ease my smart
And also to sustayne thy selfe with food.
But if in presence of that fayrest proud
Thou chance to come, fall lowly at her feet

(11. 7–10)

I have no wish to deny the accents of gallantry in this rhetoric of erotic submission. Nonetheless, at the level of figure, the labor of the sequence is announced as a struggle to breach the privacy of the lover, a struggle carried out within the very act of poetic utterance. The third sonnet articulates the difficulty of articulation itself:

looking still on her I stand amazed,
At wondrous sight of so celestiall hew.
So when my toung would speak her praises dew,
It stopped is with thoughts astonishment:
And when my pen would write her titles true,

It ravisht is with fancies wonderment:
Yet in my hart I then both speake and write,
The wonder that my wit cannot endite.

(*Am.* III, 7–14)

This completes the prologue to the sequence, which then embarks on that most recursive of Spenserian programs, marking time. The next poem begins, "New yeare forth looking out of Janus gate," thus recasting the *Amoretti* in the mold of the *Shepheardes Calender*. Calendrical structure is Spenser's recurrent vehicle for attempts to mediate between mutable experience and eternity, between Culture and a transcendent Nature.[4] My purpose in this note is to suggest how Spenser's amatory calendar addresses the issues raised in the "prologue" to the *Amoretti*. In effect, I shall be arguing that, in this sequence, calendrical structure seems to be a load-bearing one, a public matrix for a private experience whose very privacy threatens that experience with an implosion of the inarticulate. The calendar keeps this sequence moving, draws it out.

The reader of the volume is led from New Year's, in Sonnet 4, to Ash Wednesday, in Sonnet 22, through a Lenten sequence that culminates with an Easter poem at Sonnet 68, and on toward June 11, the feast of St. Barnabas, in the *Epithalamion*, and this passage through a calendrical program provides a structure for a courtship narrative neither burdened by privacy, nor tainted by the publicity of a debased Petrarchan discourse. Liturgical pattern thus helps to provide a teleological alternative to the designs of Busyrane, which isolate the lover, and condemn him or her to interminable and undifferentiated re-enactments of the Masque of Cupid. The extent to which the calendrical program is worked out and the degree to which that program is coordinated with the extraordinary calendrical schemata of the *Epithalamion* are the subjects of the more technical aspects of this note, but I should like to defer discussion of the technical arguments for the continuity between sonnet sequence and epithalamium until the thematic plot that unites the two is clearer.

J. W. Lever observed that the lady of this sequence is unsettlingly inconsistent: she is both a traditional "cruel fair" and a charming presence, both scornfully aloof and kindly conversant.[5] That strain of criticism intent on cozying up to the sequence tends to ignore the traditional inaccessibility of the lady or the merely mechanical praise that Spenser frequently lavishes on her, attending instead to the novel rendering of a lady's good humor, intelligence, and warmth. It is important to the sequence that both versions of the lady assert themselves, that the "cruel fair" should be jostled by someone whom we should like to think of as Elizabeth Boyle. The two conceptions of the lady are genuine rivals; the sequence engages in a struggle to discover, within the language of sonneteering, a vocabulary of praise that will bring the two into accord.

The struggle can be clearly seen in one of the most powerful sonnets of the sequence, Sonnet 67:

> Lyke as a huntsman after weary chace,
> Seeing the game from him escaped away:
> Sits downe to rest him in some shady place,
> With panting hounds beguiled of their pray.
> So after long pursuit and vaine assay,
> When I all weary had the chance forsooke,
> The gentle deare returnd the self-same way,
> Thinking to quench her thirst at the next brooke.
>
> (*Am*. LXVII, 1–8)

The achievement here roots itself in the grammar of comparison. Strictly speaking, that which is "Lyke as a hunter" is not the poem's "I," who enters the syntax by way of a temporal clause, but "the gentle deare" herself. Expectation—the pressure of cultural habit, the erotic code of patriarchy, the *topoi* of Petrarchism—engages grammar, so that huntsman, speaker, and deer, find themselves taking the softly emphatic "self-same way." Lady and lover cannot meet on equal terms, yet the poem makes as great an advance toward mutuality as can perhaps be achieved given the sexual politics that prevailed on Spenser. This encounter takes place *after* erotic predation (the frustrated hunt, perhaps, of such Actaeons as Wyatt) has been given over. The deer is still:

> Till I in hand her yet halfe trembling tooke

—and the persistent tremor is shared out syntactically between dear and speaker—

Till I in hand her yet halfe trembling tooke
And with her owne goodwill hir fyrmely tyde.
(11. 11–12)

So that the good will of the lady is not only a condition, but an instrument of what cannot honestly be described except as a kind of bondage.

The discourse of what might be called " vulgar Petrarchism" is given a scrupulous going over here, but it is not rejected out of hand. Th dear, "so goodly wonne," is nonetheless "with her owne will *beguyld*." An erotics of predation cannot be summarily dismissed—Spenser is a reformer, but not a foolhardy one—though female will is given fuller play in this sequence, by being shown capable of genuine agency, than in any male-authored sonnet sequence with which I am familiar.[6] The critical achievement is limited here, for Spenser does not wish to leave himself in the situation in which Britomart finds herself after she has destroyed the ideological apparatus of Busyrane's erotic culture:

Returning backe, those goodly roomes, which erst
She saw so rich and royally arayd,
Now vanisht utterly, and cleane subverst
She found, and all their glory quite decayd,
That sight of such a chaunge her much dismayd.
(*FQ*, III.xii.42)

No doubt Spenser suspects that even marriage would be shaky without the discourse of traditional eroticism, so that in the *Amoretti* he sets himself the difficult task of finding a redeemed use for that discourse. Redemption is short. After the sonnets of Holy Week, as the poems grow more frankly intimate, the recurrence towards an erotics of predation, of concealment, and of solipsism is palpable; the sequence reaches a nadir of cultural regression in the four Anacreontic poems. Kaske has suggested that these poems give us an example of a common Spenserian device, the use of "anticlimax as link," but this may put the case too mildly, for we are dealing with something more problematic than anticlimax in the Anacreontic poems.[7] There Cupid is said to have "fresh againe enured / His former cruelty" (*Anacr.*, 11. 75–76), restoring the embittered Petrarchist psychic world with which the sequence opened. The reversion after the son-

nets of Holy Week prepare for the determinations of the
Epithalamion, and so provoke its urgency—an urgency that I
discuss elsewhere, but which can be summarily described here
as a tense attempt to conjure the persistence of poetic voice
despite depredations as various as poverty, the fear of sexual
consummation, and the necessity of working within the cultural idiom of a Busyrane. The viper thoughts of the *Amoretti*
anticipate the anxieties of the wedding poem, where much of
the same labor of loving must be repeated.

I have spoken of the *teleology* of this volume, of a pattern of
development that bridges the two poems. So far what I have
had to say accords substantially with what Kaske has argued
about the thematic structure of the volume; I again follow her
by asserting that a chronological pattern which supports the
thematic program embraces both the poems of courtship and
the poem of the wedding. We differ on the details of that
chronology.

I began my argument by describing the first three poems of
the sequence as a prologue, one which ends with the announcement of a calendrical program in the New Year's poem, Sonnet
4. Kaske finds in Sonnet 62, "The weary years his race now
having run," a second January 1st poem, which closes out a year
of erotic frustration: she is thus enabled to make the exceedingly
powerful argument that "the symbolic year of pleasure" which
Kent Hieatt has so carefully elucidated in the *Epithalamion* com-
pensates "for the autobiographical year of pain in the *Amoretti*."
She lays much stress on the teasingly mysterious Sonnet 60,
"They that in course of heavenly spheares are skild," with its
suggestion of a complex commutability of temporal schemes:

> As Mars in three score yeares doth run his spheare.
> So, since the winged God his planet cleare,
> Began in me to move, one yeare is spent:
> The which doth longer unto me appeare,
> Than al those fourty which my life outwent.
> Then by that count, which lovers books invent,
> The spheare of Cupid fourty yeares containes.
>
> (11. 4–10)

But in order to defend this appealing reading Kaske is obliged to
reject Alexander Dunlop's association of the New Year's son-

net, Sonnet 62, with Lady Day, the canonical Lenten New Year.[8] Dunlop's chronology, which Kaske calls "the Lenten interpretation" of the *Amoretti*, unfolds neatly: if we take Sonnet 22, "This holy season fit to fast and pray," as an Ash Wednesday poem and Sonnet 68 with its grave opening—

> Most glorious Lord of lyfe that on this day,
> Didst make thy triumph over death and sin

—as an Easter poem, then we have a very simple Lenten schema, with one sonnet assigned to each day of "this holy season" and Lady Day precisely located within that particular season. Such a principle of organization would sort well with the precise numerological structure of the *Epithalamion*, and despite Kaske's strictures, this principle deserves to be entertained further. In fact, something like a poem-per-day structure actually extends beyond the confines of the Lenten calender: counting sonnets to the end of the sequence, counting stanzas through the short sequence of the Anacreontic poems, and counting trimeter lines to the line that explicitly dates the *Epithalamion* and Spenser's marriage—"With Barnaby the bright"—we reach a total of seventy-eight, the precise number of days intervening between Lady Day and the feast of St. Barnabas.

Such a decoding of structure locates the obtrusive Anacreontic poems within a teleological structure that extends from the *Amoretti* through to the *Epithalamion*, confirming this anticlimax as a true link. But "the Lenten intepretation" has rather more to recommend itself. In Hieatt's major study of the numerology of the *Epithalamion*, the late chapter devoted to the symbolic structure of the short lines begins with the admission that some numerological significance must be found for them in order to "save the appearances" within the totality of his reading. (He is not the only person to remark on the problem of the short lines: Kaske simply alleges that "no convincing numerical value is assigned to them.")[9] One virtue of extending the Lenten interpretation is that it at last uncovers a convincing numerical value for these lines: they count days. Indeed, the diminution of the unit of counting—from poem-as-day in the *Amoretti* proper to short-line-as-day within the *Epithalamion*—provides a formal analogue for some of the systems of commutability explicitly described within these poems: the "welcome Night" of the *Epithalamion* "that long days' labor dost at last defray," the numerological equivalence of day and year within the wedding poem, and the complex equivalence of forty terrestrial years to one year within "the spheare of Cupid." We begin to see the wedding volume as an attempt to mediate between a metaphysics and a phenomenology of Time.

But Kaske's critique of the Lenten interpretation articulates two problems that seem to me to demand at least provisional solution, if that interpretation is to be reasserted. First, there is the fact that Sonnet 60 announces that "since the winged God his plant cleare, / Began in me to moove, one yeere is spent": since the Amoretti begins on, or near, the January first of Sonnet 4, Kaske argues that these lines stipulate the passage of 365 days before one reaches the new year of Sonnet 62; the Lenten interpretation will thus require a convincing counter-intepretation of these lines. The Lenten interpretation must also answer to a second of Kaske's challenges: why should a poem or a sequence of poems begin with one calendrical system, in which the year begins on 1 January, and shift to a different one, in which the year starts with Lady Day?

The first problems might be solved variously—by asserting that the year that passes before Sonnet 60 need not be one that commences at the New Year's of the beginning of the sequence (as the sequence may only record the last stages in a courtship); or that a single *Cupidean* year has passed, a single period in the typical chronology of courtship, a period that does *not* correspond to the terrestrial year.[10] Either of this sorts well with the theme of the sonnet, the disparities of phase and frequency between various kinds of time. Admittedly, neither of these solutions may be asserted conclusively, but both prepare for a single solution to the second problem, the problem of calendrical shift.

We should be clear about the extent of the shift. Kaske raises the problem of a shift from a January New Year to a Lenten one, but as I have presented it, the shift is more drastic. Although the Lenten sequence offers a sonnet for each day, that pattern does not maintain between the New Year's poem and the beginning of the Lenten sequence. Only after Lent begins is a perfect calendar instituted, with each day marked by a sonnet. We can thus speak, not simply of calendrical shift, but of calendrical reform. And putting it thus begins, I think, to solve the problem that Kaske finds in the Lenten interpretation.[11]

In Sonnet 60, which immediately precedes that which celebrates Palm Sunday, Spenser suggests that the temporality of Petrarchan eroticism, the periodicity of "the spheare of Cupid" is fundamentally out of phase with the divinely ordained motion of our own planet. This temporal problem is analogous with the difficulty of adapting the discourse of acculturated eroticism for use as a hymeneal rhetoric, of finding a public language that can sanctify private eroticism. The Holy Week poems that follow mark a major achievement: they affirm a homology between the liturgical calendar and the structure of a sonnet sequence even as they achieve a concord between the conventional amatory rhetoric and the language of scrupulous piety. Thus on Palm Sunday, the lady may be a curiously popish "Idoll of my thought" (reminiscent of the "sweet Saynt" of Sonnet 22, the Ash Wednesday poem), but the poet is now capable of working *from* this private cult towards a recognition that the lady's beauty is an "image of the makers beautie." The poet's worship of "such heavenly formes" is accompanied by a sense of the lady's place within a discriminated ontological hierarchy. That pious discrimination is given its clearest and firmest statement in the Easter poem itself.[12] The first twelve lines are addressed to Christ; I give the sestet in order to show how carefully the turn to the lady in the couplet is set:

> And that thy love we weighing worthily,
> May likewise love thee for the same again:
> And for thy sake that all lyke deare didst buy,
> With love may one another entertayne.
> So let us love, deare love, lyke as we ought,
> Love is the lesson which the Lord us taught.
> (*Am.*, LXVIII, 10–14)

This poem, then, readjusts that relation of the poetics of gallantry to the poetics of devotion that two centuries of Petrarchist sonneteering had all but permanently distorted.

These sonnets, then, constitute a week of astonishing personal and poetic achievement: after the poem for Lady Day comes the anticipation of success, of a genuine teleology within courtship (LXIII); then comes perhaps the richest English imitation of the sacred eroticism of the Song of Songs (LXIV, an anticipation of the exquisite tenth stanza of the *Epithalamion*); this is followed by a meditation on female freedoms within marriage, in which Spenser (alas) inscribes the limits of his momentous feminism; the lady's acceptance of the poet's suit occurs between sonnets LXV and LXVI; then comes the delicate Christological allusion in the Good Friday poem (LXVI) when the poet asks his newly betrothed, with an awe that effaces gallantry, "Why did ye stoup unto so lowly state?" And between this and the Easter poem comes the great triumph of the sequence, "Lyke as a huntsman after weary chace," the sonnet for Holy Saturday. So I think that Kaske is correct in taking the Lady Day poem as pivotal. From the old January New Year we shift to a new New Year, the day of Mary's conception; her blessed womb replaces the bitter womb of viper thoughts.

Here is a teleology indeed. Coleridge was probably not thinking of medieval beast-lore when he composed the anti-matrimonial Ode from which I take the phrase, "viper thoughts," but how Physiologus' account of the viper might have haunted the author of *Amoretti and Epithalamion*:

> Porro femina non habet secretum locum, id est menbrum pariendi sinum, sed ut foramen acus habet. Si autem masculus habeat cum femina, effundet semen in os femine, et si biberit semen eivs, precidet femina necessaria masculi (hoc est virilia), et moritur masculus; cum autem creuerint filii eius in utero matris sue, non habens illa sinum unde pariatur, tunc filii adaperiunt latus matris suae, et exeunt occidentes matrem.

> Indeed the woman has no secret place, that is, genitals for giving birth, but has only a pinhole. If the male lies with the female and spills his seed into her mouth, and if she drinks his seed, she will cut off the male's necessaries (that is, his male organs) and he will die. When, however, the young have grown within the womb of their mother who has no genitals for giving birth, they pierce through her side, killing her in their escape.[13]

From such a nightmare of lurking thoughts—of consummation as emasculation, of suicidal procreation—Spensers amatory sequence redeems itself, its singer committing himself and his spouse to the protection of that Genius whose "secret ayde doth succour and supply, / Till they bring forth the fruitfull progeny" (*Epith.*, 11. 403–404).

The Lady Day sonnet may anticipate the blessed womb, but the vipers are not entirely left behind. The next movement of the sequence will be subtly regressive, so that the achievements of courtship and betrothal in the *Amoretti* may be given celebratory repetition in the *Epithalamion*. It is worth noting, though, how the vipers return:

> But if ye saw that which no eyes can see,
> The inward beauty of her lively spright,
> Garnisht with heavenly guifts of high degree,
> Much more then would ye wonder at that sight,
> And stand astonisht lyke to those which red
> Medusaes mazeful hed.

> (11. 185–90)

The moment of tongue-tied arrest before a virginal woman recalls the confounded privacy with which the *Amoretti* begins. Yet we must also recall that Medusa's snaky locks may be "read" on Athena's breast, worn there as a broach, the decorative emblem of threats already conquered, of powers reappropriated, of debilitating terror reconditioned as awe.

Washington University

Notes

1. I cite *The Faerie Queene* from the edition of Thomas P. Roche, Jr. (New Haven, Conn.: Yale University Press, 1981); citations from the *Amoretti* and the *Epithalamion* are taken from Richard S. Sylvester's *The Anchor Anthology of Sixteenth Century Verse* (Garden City, N.Y.: Doubleday, 1974).
2. For some more general notes on the relation between the two volumes see my "Echo's Ring: Orpheus and Spenser's Career," *English Literary Renaissance*, 16 (1986), 287–302. I believe the wedding volume to have been fully imagined as an *interruption* of *The Faerie Queene,* and that the volume anxiously insists on the unity of that literary corpus which it articulates around itself. On the unity of the wedding volume itself, see Carol Kaske, "Spenser's *Amoretti and Epithalamion* of 1595: Structure, Genre and Numerology," *En-*

glish Literary Renaissance, 8, (1978), 271–295 and Richard Neuse, "The Triumph over Hasty Accidents: A Note on the Symbolic Mode of the Epithalamion," Modern Language Review, 61 (1966), 163–174.

3. Carol Thomas Neely, "The Structure of Elizabethan Sonnet Sequences," ELH, 45 (1978), 359–389, particularly 364–367.

4. For a summary of earlier calendrical arguments about the sequence, see Kaske, "Spenser's Amoretti and Epithalamion," particularly 285–295, as well as the second part of this essay.

5. J. W. Lever, The Elizabethan Love Sonnet (London: Methuen, 1956), pp. 97–102.

6. In Chaucer, Spenser, Milton: Mythopoeic Continuities and Transformations (Montreal: McGill-Queen's University Press, 1975), pp. 110–111, A. Kent Hieatt adduces this sonnet to remark a contrast with "the figure of the deer unwilling to be held," which Spenser employs near the end of Book IV of The Faerie Queene (IV.x.55) to describe Scudamour's "conquest" of Amoret. To his remark I would wish to add that the mutual relevance of the two passages is pointed: the "mythopoeic transformation" here marks a crucial continuity of concern, a pattern in Spenser's erotic poetry.

In "Spenser's Amoretti and Epithalamion," Carol Kaske has useful things to say about the evocations of "mutuality of desire" within the sequence; see 284.

7. Kaske, 273.

8. For Dunlop's argument, see "The Unity of Spenser's Amoretti," in Silent Poetry: Essays in Numerological Analysis, ed. Alastair Fowler, (London: Routledge and Kegan Paul: 1970) pp. 153–169. Kaske concludes her arguments against Dunlop's chronology by describing it as an interpretation "of which my criticism must be wholly destructive" (p. 293).

9. Kaske, "Spenser's Amoretti and Epithalamion," 286.

It should be noted that I am treating the trimeter line, not the "short line" of Hieatt's argument, as the significant unit; that is, I am excluding the metrically discrepant line 16, "So Orpheus did for his owne bride," from the calendrical scheme. I hope that my discussion of this line in "Echo's Ring": Orpheus and Spenser's Career" makes it clear why this tetrameter line should stand outside the celebratory calendar: it is the most viperous line in Epithalamium. (Note that 1. 424, in "short position," symmetrically answers to the Orphean line, counterpoising fatality with hope, and restoring direct address to the bride, a form of address silenced since Stanza 5, when the lady was not awake to hear it).

10. In "A Numerical Key for Spenser's Amoretti and Guyon in the House of Mammon," The Year's Work in English Studies, 3 (1973), A. Kent Hieatt proposes several adjustments in Dunlop's theory, one of which entails an interesting account of Sonnet 60; see his pp. 21–22.

11. I say "begins." Much remains unexplained: my Lenten interpretation does not settle the calendrical status of the pre-Lenten sonnets, it by no means provides a full-dress interpretation of the crucial Sonnet 60, it intuits grounds for excluding the Orphean line from the calendar without fixing them, and it does not account for the 24 trimeter lines that follow on Epith. 266 ("With Barnaby the bright")—though numerology digests twenty-fours like golden sections. The case for a Lenten interpretation is, I think, strengthened, though it is undeniably incomplete.

12. Such discrimination is not, however, absent from other sonnets within the Holy Week sequence. In Sonnet 68, the poet spies "the happy shore" of his success, describing that goal as "Fayre soyle." No more pious and reverent description of a Christian bride could be formulated.

13. I cite from *Physiologus Latinus, Versio Y*, ed. Francis J. Carmody, *University of California Publications in Classical Philology*, vol. 12, no. 7 (Berkeley: University of California Press, 1941), 110, the English version is taken from *Physiologus,* trans. Michael J. Curley (Austin: University of Texas Press, 1979), p. 16. Carol Kaske suggested the potential relevance of bestiary material to my argument; I am grateful for the suggestion.

CAROL V. KASKE

Rethinking Loewenstein's "Viper Thoughts"

L OEWENSTEIN IN his note addresses two separate issues: alternatives to Petrarchism, and the symbolism of the short lines in the *Epithalamion*. (He contributes no free-standing support to the "Lenten" interpretation of the *Amoretti*, merely assumes and extends it.[1]) On the first issue, already dealt with by himself and others, he contributes some new insights and memorable formulations; on the last, his contribution is new but to me not convincing.

I find Loewenstein most illuminating on the self-reflexive theme of ways to escape from Petrarchistic solipsism and self-destructiveness in *Faerie Queene* III and IV and in the wedding volume. This subject is only tenuously connected to his main subject, the calendrical imagery of the volume. One such connection, if I understand him correctly, is that such imagery makes the sentiments public without damaging their authenticity, much as marriage, in the Spenserian view, does to love. This sounds plausible in itself, although it needs literary support, since if Spenser is correcting Petrarch, as most agree that he is, his correction cannot consist of his calendrical structure, because, as is well known, the *Canzoniere* uses calendrical structure too.[2] I agree that *Amoretti* 2 is gloomy and grotesque enough to fit Loewenstein's project begun in his article "Echo's Ring" (*English Literary Renaissance*, 16 [1986]) of discovering gloom beneath the celebratory surface of the volume; that this gloom can act as a welcome note of discord; that one source of gloom is the solipsism and self-destructiveness of the typical Petrarchan poet-lover, troped by the viper ill-equipped to bring forth her cannibalistic foetuses; and that the "breach" of this "privacy" in the act of poetic utterance is difficult and painful. I cannot agree that *Amoretti* 2 exhibits "womb-envy" and possesses "a somewhat misogynist cast." The poet, indulging

325

his taste for bizarre imagery from the bestiary (see also *Am.* 38, 53, and 71), does not hate but identifies himself with the mother viper; and he possesses a womb and achieves parturition in every sense that the terms of the metaphor require. Similarly, the womb represents privacy; the infant vipers represent not privacy, not love, but amorous thoughts, be they private or expressed; although perhaps still embarrassingly libidinous because phallic, even these are not necessarily self-poisoning and isolating but potentially curative, according to the penultimate line, once they have been expressed.

I also find both new and true Loewenstein's idea, pressed too hard in "Echo's Ring," that the *Amoretti and Epithalamion* of 1595 originally functioned for the audience as an educative entr'acte between the two instalments of *The Faerie Queene* (1590 and 1596). Given the now accepted interpretation of Amoret's and Scudamour's separation by Busirane as some sort of incompatibility more complex than mere temptation to lust (see Lewis, Roche, Williams, Hieatt, Berger, and their successors), a problem of reception remains: how did Spenser's audience interpret it, and how did Spenser intend them to interpret it, in the six years before the second instalment (1596), which contains almost all the evidence for their incompatibility (*e.g.*, IV.i and IV.x)? Loewenstein plausibly answers that the volume showed the audience incompatibilities anticipatory of Scudamour's and Amoret's in the person of the lover and his lady—chiefly bondage to various Petrarchan roles.

Spenser's *Epithalamion* is one of the few great single poems (along with the *Divine Comedy* and the Middle English *Pearl* and *Sir Gawain and the Green Knight*) exhibiting an indubitable numerological structure—its twenty-four stanzas composed of 365 long lines. And this structure is attractive: it makes the poem "a small working model of the behavior of the sun," as A. Kent Hieatt says in his announcement of it in *Short Time's Endless Monument* (1960), expressing in cosmic terms that compensation which the poet has and hopes for in human terms. Anyone who has ever put his hand to numerological criticism would welcome a strengthening of the one weak link, the explanation of one datum, its short lines, as not only a solution to a mystery but a deepening of the poem's meaning and an enrichment of its design. Loewenstein's eloquence is persuasive; how could someone be wrong who was sensitive enough to

coin a phrase like "earnest hymeneal eroticism," which captures
so well the tone of, say, *Amoretti* 8? And my interpretation of
betrothal as a newly recognized separate stage in courtship
would welcome a calendrical imitation of this period such as
Loewenstein proposes.

Nevertheless, I cannot throw up my pen and say "this is it."
Although no inquiry, least of all criticism, is completely empirical, some of us are too empirical to buy a strained interpretation just because it makes the poem "better." Loewenstein's
solution to this numerological problem is strained, first, because it has to skip one line altogether; second, because it offers
an interpretation not of all sixty-eight short lines but only of the
first forty-two of them (as he concedes); third, because it adds
apples and oranges; and fourth, because it overlaps and thus
competes with a quite different and more credible scheme.

My first and my last objections require some elaboration. In
order to obtain a total of seventy-eight and not seventy-nine
units from adding the twenty-seven sonnets, the nine stanzas,
and the forty-three short lines up to and including the dating
line 266 (which is short line forty-three, according to Hieatt's
separate numbering of short and of long lines) Loewenstein has
to exclude one of them altogether from the calendrical scheme.
He excludes "the metrically discrepant line 16 'So Orpheus did
for his owne bride.' " He cannot transfer it to the class of long
lines, as its extra syllables would indicate, because that would
raise their total to 366. A scheme that has to exclude one of its
givens is not exact enough to convince the reader. Spenser
could easily have limited himself to exactly the required forty-
two short lines if he had really had Loewenstein's scheme in
mind. In a move which he later concedes is intuitive (n. 11), he
appeals to content: "it is the most viperous line" in the
Epithalamion (n. 9). If "viperous" content disqualifies a line from
a celebratory calendar, then line 190, "Medusa's mazefull head,"
short line 31, should be the one excluded. Numerological critics
generally seem a little too ready to exclude recalcitrant data in
this way.

As to my final objection about competing schemes, Hieatt
proved that one function of the short lines was not to symbolize
anything but to divide the hour-stanzas into quarter-hours,
which become thematic when these mime the fall of night in the
course of Stanza 17. Although this interpretation is only a frill

on the main numerological scheme and thus can be rejected without rejecting it, and although the short lines vary slightly in a few stanzas, nevertheless, this correspondence is too precise to have come about by chance, and no subsequent interpretation can contradict it with impunity. But according to Loewenstein, in Stanza 15, only two stanzas earlier, the short lines do not divide hours but symbolize days. Granting the possibility of different meanings in different places, the reader could not be expected to switch meanings so quickly. Moreover, Loewenstein's interpretation of the short lines conflicts with Hieatt's main numerological scheme. Somewhere in the 365 long lines symbolizing the year, there exist seventy-eight of them which symbolize the seventy-eight days from Lady Day to St. Barnaby's Day, March 25 to June 11. If Loewenstein's interpretation is right, then these seventy-eight days get symbolized twice, once cardinally and once ordinally. In contrast, Hieatt's interpretation of the short lines does not conflict with his main scheme, since for him they are only markers.[3]

The critical establishment can always use a reminder of the possibility that further numerological patterns remain to be discovered. Until he resolves the difficulty of the extra short line, Loewenstein's main contribution will be his highlighting of Spenser's narrow escapes from Petrarchism.

NOTES

1. As I said in my article (*English Literary Renaissance*, 8 [1978]), I agree with the Lenten critics that the format gives a vague impression of a poem per day as in a diary and that there is an early reference to Lent (22) and a late reference to Easter (68)—dates which metaphorically characterize the courtship as one long Lent; but I find all attempts so far to line up others of the forty-six sonnets between 22 and 68 with specific days in Lent of 1594 contradictory of Sonnet 60 and inconsistent with the church calendar's festal Sundays, as Hieatt admits; see "A Numerical Key for Spenser's *Amoretti* and Guyon in the House of Mammon," *Yearbook of English Studies* 3 (1973), 23. Loewenstein suggests "that the year that passes before sonnet 60 need not be one that commences at the New Year's of the beginning of the sequence (as the sequence may only record the last stages in a courtship)." Similarly, in her rich article "The Thirsty Deer and the Lord of Life: Some Contexts for *Amoretti* 67–70," *Spenser Studies*, VI (1985), Anne Lake Prescott dismisses "*Am*. 60's reference to a year spent loving" as irrelevant to the calendrical scheme (p. 71, n. 21), presumably on the same grounds, that Spenser does not specify the

date on which he began loving, so that it could be before the curtain rises. To both I answer as before that a year is mimed within the calendrical references in the sequence by the gaps between two New Years (mentioned in Sonnet 4 and Sonnet 62) and between two parallel and contrasting springs (mentioned in Sonnets 19 and 70).

2. See for example Thomas P. Roche, Jr., "The Calendrical Structure of Petrarch's *Canzoniere*," *Studies in Philology*, 71 (1974), 152–172; and Chapter One, "Petrarch: Myths and Structures," pages 1–69 of *Petrarch and the English Sonnet Sequences* (New York: AMS Press, 1989).

3. To arrive at a meaning at the annual level for the cardinal number of short lines, sixty-eight, Hieatt rather apologetically throws the four seasons, the twelve months, and the fifty-two weeks together into a mixed bag (pp. 66–68); see Fowler's refutation in *Triumphal Forms: Structural Patterns in Elizabethan Poetry* (Cambridge: Cambridge University Press, 1970), p. 167). Building on Hieatt's convincing interpretation of the short lines as dividers, Alastair Fowler counts the number of the stanza fragments they demarcate (which Hieatt calls quarter-hours) and finds that it totals ninety-two, the number of days in the summer quarter (*Triumphal Forms*, pp. 166–167). Fowler also has some competing (or, as he would put it, overlapping) schemes which resemble Loewenstein's in adding sonnets, Anacreontic poems (not stanzas of poems), and lines to span the three sections of the volume—sonnets, anacreontics, and epithalamion. These schemes merit no special priority; I mention them only to show that schemes as loose as this are all too easy to construct and that we do not have to accept Loewenstein's by default.

Orion Once More:
Revisiting the Sky over Faerieland

I wish to refine the claims I made in my recent article "Orion's Flaming Head: Spenser's *Faerie Queene,* II. ii. 46 and the Feast of the Twelve Days of Christmas,"[1] (*Spenser Studies* VII). By using the Julian calendar rather than the Gregorian calendar as the basis of my calculations for interpreting Spenser's descriptions of the movement of the stars over Faerieland, I find that I can strengthen my argument for interpreting the Faerie Queene's twelve-day feast as the Feast of the Twelve Days of Christmas.

To make this point, I need to review my original argument. In last year's article I claimed that Spenser imagined Guyon's visit to Medina's castle (*FQ* II. ii. 12 ff.)[2] as occurring early in April. My argument was based on an interpretation of a comment made by the narrator at *FQ* II. ii. 46 that Guyon recounts the origin of his quest at a gathering of Medina's court; after some time has passed, we are told, the attendant company notes that "Night was far spent" because "in *Ocean* deepe / Orion . . . / His flaming head did hasten for to steepe."

My interpretation depended on determining what dates the constellation Orion sets at a time that reasonably could be considered when the "Night was far spent." Originally, I calculated that at 52 degrees north latitude (the approximate latitude of Spenser's Irish home), Orion's "flaming head" set between 10:30 p.m. and midnight between the end of the first week of April and the middle of the month, times that accord well with Spenser's description of events in the poem. When Orion sets, he notes, those listening to Guyon's tale believe the night is "far spent" so they hasten to bed and to "kindly sleepe" until "the morrow faire . . . / Disperst the shadowes of the mistie night" (*FQ* II. iii. 1).

I then used this observation as a context for interpreting Guyon's remark that he was assigned his quest by the Faerie Queene three cycles of "faire *Phœbie's*" visits to "the neather world," or three months, prior to the evening during which he tells his story to Medina and her court (*FQ* II. ii. 44). This placed the meeting between the Faerie Queene and Guyon in early January and made possible the identification of the twelve-day feast of the Faerie Queene referred to by Spenser in his Letter to Ralegh as the Feast of Christmastide, which included the "day that first doth lead the yeare around" (*FQ* II. ii. 42), identified by Guyon as the day on which he was given his quest.

Since making that argument, I realized that my calculations of star movements were based on the Gregorian calendar, which was not adopted in England until 1752 and thus was not in use when Spenser wrote *The Faerie Queene*. Elizabethans still used the Julian calendar; this is important for my argument because in comparison with the Gregorian calendar, the Julian calendar dated astronomical and seasonal phenomena as occurring ten days earlier because it was literally ten days "ahead" of the sun in its annual progress.

We know that Spenser used the Julian calendar because only according to that calendar would June 11, 1594 (St. Barnabas' Day and his wedding day) coincide with the summer solstice and make that day's special astronomical features available to him for use in structuring his *Epithalamion*.[3] If he had used the Gregorian calendar, he would not have been able to do this because on the Gregorian calendar the summer solstice, the longest day of the year, falls on June 21.

From Spenser's perspective, therefore, the movement of the stars overhead as Guyon tells Medina of the origin of his quest are slightly different than I envisioned in my original essay. The difference is in a way a small one, but in these matters one honors whatever degree of precision one can achieve. The key point is that, according to the Julian calendar, Orion's "flaming head" sets at almost exactly eleven p.m. at 52 degrees north latitude on April 1, and not on April 11, as it does according to the Gregorian calendar. Thus, according to the Julian calendar, the movement of the stars is ten days "ahead" of the same movement when computed according to the Gregorian calendar.

As a result, the celestial events described by Spenser in *FQ* II.

ii. 46 (Orion's "flaming head" setting when "Night was far spent") would, according to the Julian calendar, now fit evenings during the last week of March and the first few days of April. This shift backwards in locating the evening of Guyon's discourse is important because it allows me to be more precise at another point in my original argument; in counting backward three months before the date of Guyon's meeting with Medina, I originally interpreted Guyon's phrase "Now hath faire *Phoebe* . . . / Thrise seene the shadowes of the neather world, / Sith last I left that honorable place" (*FQ* II. ii. 44) to refer loosely to calendar months rather than strictly to lunar months (of 28 days), so as not to wind up with a date in the middle rather than the beginning of January for the "day that first doth lead the yeare around." Now, however, working backward from dates in late March or the beginning of April, I find that both lunar months and calendar months take me back to January 1, called New Year's Day in the Book of Common Prayer of 1559,[4] as the strongest candidate, in Spenser's calendrical scheme, for the day on which Gloriana gives Guyon his quest.

This recalculation of the movement of the stars as Spenser knew them thus strengthens my original argument because it locates the day that Guyon received his quest from Gloriana even more firmly within the Elizabethan Feast of Christmastide. We may now see as clearly as the evidence permits that Spenser imagined Guyon's telling Medina his tale in late March or early April, a night Guyon remembers was three months after New Year's Day, one of the twelve days of feasting during Gloriana's annual celebration of the Twelve Days of Christmas. Implicit in my argument, of course, is the premise that the sky over Faerieland was the same sky as the one Spenser observed over England and Ireland. Spenser was certainly free to imagine any sky he wanted, and may well have done so. If he did, however, the movements of Orion become arbitrary and make of Gloriana's festival an event also unconnected to any event of Elizabeth's court. But if the Orion in Guyon's sky was the Orion in Spenser's sky, then it also follows that Gloriana's annual feast was the Elizabethan Feast of Christmastide.

John N. Wall
North Carolina State University

NOTES

1. *Spenser Studies* VII, Patrick Cullen and Thomas P. Roche, Jr., eds. (New York: AMS Press, 1987), pp. 93–101.

2. Edmund Spenser, *The Faerie Queene*, ed. A. C. Hamilton. London: Longman, 1977.

3. See A. Kent Hieatt, *Short Time's Endless Monument: The Symbolism of the Numbers in Edmund Spenser's "Epithalamion"* (New York: Columbia University Press, 1960), pp. 10–15; and Alistair Fowler, *Spenser and the Numbers of Time* (New York: Barnes & Noble, 1964), pp. 170 f.

4. John Booty, ed., *The Book of Common Prayer: The Elizabethan Prayer Book* (Charlottesville: University Press of Virginia for the Folger Shakespeare Library, 1976), p. 85.

A. KENT HIEATT

The Projected Continuation
of *The Faerie Queene:*
Rome Delivered?

*T*HE FAERIE QUEENE implies that Arthur conquered Rome and was crowned emperor of the Roman Empire.[1] No edition of the poem has recognized this, yet at the time when Spenser wrote the Letter to Ralegh, and probably later, he is likely to have been meditating this exploit as his hero's masterstroke of politic (not private) virtue in the continuation of *The Faerie Queene* proferred there. The exploit would have paralleled the politic highpoints of classical and classicizing epic, not least Godfrey of Bouillon's liberation of a Jerusalem violated by infidels. While doing so, it would allegorically have lent glory to the idea of the deliverance of papistically unbelieving Rome by an army under the leadership of some likely patron (a Protestant-activist type of Arthur) so as to establish a Universal Reformed Church. Casting the poem irretrievably in this mold would have had to wait upon some resolution of the conflict between activism and caution among Spenser's patrons, but I believe he had the notion in mind up to three years before his death. Its effect on the character of the poem that we know may be important.

What Spenser surely knew about Arthur's supposed Roman conquest starts with the version of John Hardyng's fifteenth-century rhymed chronicle which was printed in 1543.[2] Before Hardyng, the English tradition initiated by Geoffrey of Monmouth had maintained that Arthur defeated the Roman imperial forces in France and sent the corpse of their leader Lucius to Rome as a novel form of the tribute which the Romans had been extorting from Britain since Julius Caesar's conquest, five hundred and more years earlier. According to this earlier claim,

Arthur was deflected from conquering Rome itself only by news of Mordred's having seized the crown in England and having ravished Guenevere.

The printed version of Hardyng's chronicle claimed instead that Arthur advanced into the Italian peninsula, entered Rome, and was crowned emperor in the Capitol shortly before 542 A.D. Only after a winter of rule there did he get the bad news from home.

Perhaps it was from Hardyng that Malory got the idea, and then filled it in. Book V of the *Morte Darthur* offers a much more extensive version of this part of the story. And of course closure is postponed: Mordred does not make his move until years later, in Book XXI, during another of Arthur's Continental campaigns.

According to both Malory and Hardying the Roman stipulation of British subjection and tribute-paying because of Julius Caesar's conquest is reversed by Arthur's claim that by rights the Romans should be subject to him. In both, Arthur terminates the tribute by paying it in the intolerable coin of enemy corpses: in Hardyng, the body of the Roman emperor Lucius, killed by Arthur in the climactic battle, is sent to Rome; in Malory, the bodies of Lucius, twenty kings, and sixty senators are packed off similarly. In both, Arthur threatens the Senate with more such tribute and adjures them never to demand tribute of Britain again and always to grant Britain the freedom which is its right. In Hardyng's Chronicle, Arthur is the only British king, after five centuries of unsuccessful British resistance to the heirs of Julius Caesar, who succeeds in casting off the yoke.

We know that Spenser was familiar with both Hardyng's Chronicle in its 1543 printed form and Malory's book, and made use of both of them in *The Faerie Queene*.[3]

While Spenser's Arthur is reading the Book of Briton Moniments, in *Faerie Queene* II.x, the narrative voice says something important in Stanza 49, just after its account of Julius Caesar's taking of Britain through help of domestic treason, and just before launching into the five centuries of valiant but ineffective British resistance to the Romans, down to Arthur's time and the termination of this book of memory in the narrative present. "*Caesar* got the victory," and:

Thenceforth this land was tributarie made
T'ambitious *Rome,* and did their rule obay,
Till *Arthur* all that reckoning defrayd;
Yet oft the Briton kings against them strongly swayd.

Presumably the third line above means "Until Arthur defrayed the reckoning according to which Britain paid tribute to Rome and obeyed its rule." By "defrayed" Spenser always means "paid," something like "paid off the tally and cleared the account."[4]

It is hard to imagine a closer match to the pseudo-history of Arthur's conquest and assumption of the imperial crown as described by Hardyng and Malory.[5] Arthur subjects the subjectors, and in particular he pays the tribute in a way which its recipients cannot endure and must terminate. Since we know that Spenser had read both these accounts, it would be very strange to suppose that he was not alluding directly to the tradition here. The note to "all that reckoning defrayd" in the most heavily annotated recent edition of *The Faerie Queene* calls out for this explanation: "evened the account either by getting revenge or by withholding 'tribute'."[6]

Immediately after this stanza Spenser embarks on the stories of those distant predecessors of Arthur (first Cymbeline, in the time of Christ) who, as he has just said, struggled powerfully against the Romans but could not attain the decisive success that Arthur gained five centuries later. In the Book of Briton Moniments, the Romans remain the chief external enemy up to the time of Arthur's immediate predecessors, although a new, serious threat—the Saxons—appears during the childhood of Arthur's father. As the chronicle story continues in Merlin's prophecy, Arthur's own career is left secret, in a tricky hiatus, but after him the Romans never reappear. Although they had already grown weaker, it is easy to believe (as in early chronicles, so here) that Britain lives under the simultaneous threat of Rome and the Saxons around Arthur's time and only then. After him the Romans drop out of Spenser's chronicle because Arthur has put the fear of God into them. Spenser has slipped in this information casually, in a short passage, as though it were to be taken for granted in a completed work, like other such traditional tidbits with which we are all acquainted: the fact, for instance, that Uther, Arthur's father, is fighting traditionally named Saxon chieftains (III.iii.5) during the course of *The Faerie Queene's* main action, and the fact that Arthur will die and Gloriana will convey not his sword but at least his shield to Faery Land-Avalon (I.vii.36).

So Spenser put Arthur as the conqueror and emperor of Rome into his fictional space. This is a new datum. I now want to make something of it, but this will be more difficult.

It is generally accepted that Arthur would have needed to perform a signal exploit if *The Faerie Queene* were ever to become what Spenser at some point intended—an epic surpassing, for instance, Ariosto's *Orlando furioso*. We generally perceive this in terms of what Spenser says in the Letter to Ralegh. The first twelve books would show Arthur's private moral virtues, as Homer, for instance, did in the person of Ulysses in the *Odyssey,* or Tasso in the person of Rinaldo in the *Jerusalem Delivered.* If all went well, a second set of books would show Arthur's politic virtues after he became king, as for instance Homer had done with Agamemnon in the *Iliad* (says Spenser), and as Tasso had done in the person of Godfrey of Bouillon.

"Politic" does not necessarily mean bellicose, but in the context of the traditional epic something esteemed by one social group is first violated or captured by another group, and then the first group rights the wrong by force under a politically qualified leader, typically seizing the second group's center of power.[7] To be politically virtuous in this context is to focus the force of the group, polis, nation effectually. Charlemagne's center, Paris, is reached and besieged by the unbelievers at the beginning of the *Orlando furioso*; at its end, Orlando, reequipped with his wits, guides the Christian armies to the capture of Biserta, the unbelievers' center of power. The Saracens take Jerusalem; a Christian army recovers it. The Greeks lose Helen; they recover her and capture Troy. The Trojans lose Troy; they reestablish themselves by war in Latium, the future Rome. The successful leader of each group displays politic virtue. Whatever our disenchantment with one or two of those politic leaders, our extant *Faerie Queene* would have had to be the *Odyssey* to a later *Iliad,* or a kind of *Enfances Artu* to a more ample *chanson de geste,* if Spenser were going to accomplish what he had in mind when he wrote that Letter to Ralegh or when he told Gabriel Harvey that he was going to overgo Ariosto.

One reason why I am prepared to espouse the notion that the conquest of Rome was to be Arthur's exploit, in the epic Spenser was thinking about while penning those lines in 1590 or earlier, is that the subject fits historical circumstances so neatly. *La Gerusalemme liberata*, which Spenser first read in the eighties, was the great Catholic epic, and it bore witness to the liberation of the Holy City from the infidels. The ardently protestant Spenser, with a need to please a nest of Protestant Activists— Leicester, Sidney with his dream of a Protestant League of Northern Europe under the leadership of Elizabeth, and Essex with his ultra-Protestant leanings and warlike ambitions— would surely have seen in an allegorical epic of Arthur's sixth-century capture of Rome the protestant answer to Tasso: Spanish power crushed and the Spanish-dominated paradigm of the secular and holy City, Rome, allegorically delivered from papistical unbelievers in the cause of a Universal Reformed Church. For such a Spenserian epic it would have been unnecessary for an English, or English-led, force to have captured Rome in Spenser's time, although just after the Armada such a dream was possible. In Book V, the allegorically rendered capture of Antwerp by Leicester as Arthur (without an army and displaying in public the private virtue of justice) has nothing to do with the way it really was. Correspondingly, the capture of Rome by Essex, or some such, as Arthur, displaying politic virtue in leading a possibly Pan-European host in some *Faerie Queene* Book XXIII, would not have needed to happen. Not what is, but what should be.

My second reason for espousing the Roman conquest as Arthur's politic exploit is that there seems to be nothing else to espouse. Although the display of the private virtues of Spenser's Arthur has little to do with Arthur's British tradition, the national Arthur of *The Faerie Queene* is framed traditionally except for his spouse. His father is Uther Pendragon fighting traditional Saxons; his death is as close to traditional Avalon as makes no matter. Almost all the British documents that Spenser knew, beginning with Geoffrey of Monmouth in the twelfth century, assign Arthur many lesser accomplishments but two main exploits: the temporary quelling of the Saxons in Britain and the fight with Rome, aborted by Mordred's treason except in Hardyng and Malory. In *The Faerie Queene*'s own chronicle record, the Romans are the great external enemy up to Arthur's

time. Beginning then, and in the time of the following genera-
tions of the Britons as recorded in Merlin's prophecy, the
Saxons are the main enemy and finally become the rulers of
England. It is only around Arthur's time that the Romans and
Saxons in tandem are the main threats. It may well be that the
Paynim king and "Briton fields with Sarazin bloud bedyde" of
I.xi.7, which have formerly been our best hints to Spenser's
ultimate plan, point to just those pagan Saxons and their
supporters.[8] For two good reasons, however, the conquest of
the Saxons could not have been an exploit of Spenser's Arthur.

The Faerie Queene's battle with them belonged in Arthur's
day to Artegall and Britomart, and would eventuate in British
defeat after their time. Like Ariosto and Tasso, Spenser assigns
a praiseworthy narrative role to an heroically loving couple
who will be the progenitors of his patron, a ruler, and whose
future, down to the present of the poet and his first readers, is
described in the narrative mode of prophecy. On the other hand
the main epic exploit in the narrative present of each of the three
most remarkable sixteenth-century heroic poems belongs respectively to Orlando, to Godfrey of Bouillon, and to Arthur,
for none of whom a pregnant future is in the contract. On the
other hand, Merlin in Faerie Queene III and the priest of the
Church of Isis in V pronounce the roles to come of Artegall and
Britomart. Their descendants will finally outlast the conquering
Saxons, Danes, and Normans, and return from their western
fastness as Tudors. Evidently Spenser found it epically decorous
to assign part of the traditional Arthur's exploits to an alter ego,
his half-brother, whose multivalent name means for our purposes here "the same as Arthur." It seems to me an elegant
solution that Arthur himself should perform the decisive half of
the traditional task—the freeing of Britain from Rome—not the
delaying action against the finally successful Saxons. Un-
traditionally, Arthur himself will not return; but Artegall is the
same as Arthur, and will return. Ergo Arthur will return.

I have now given my reasons for supposing that the conquest
of Rome was admitted into The Faerie Queene's fictional space
in the 1590 edition, with the thought, in 1590, that the Roman
conquest would be Arthur's epic exploit. But "fictional space"
conceals more than it reveals in this context. Did the Roman
caper remain in Spenser's plan right to the end of the road? Or
had he already given it up by the time of the second edition? Or
did he intentionally procrastinate until it was too late, because

he preferred to write romance and thought that he was incapable of epic? Or anyway was the allusion to the conquest only a trial balloon in the first place?

I am going to leave several aspects of this problem for another time. We all know about disenchantment with initial writing plans. Also, many of us are particularly interested in postponement of, avoidance of, and inability to achieve closure, and in the negation of the message that arises from framing it. It may be that Spenser's 1595 promise to go on stoutly beyond the completed six books of *The Faerie Queene*, and his 1596 return (three years before his death) to the traditional material of Saxon enemies, and his 1596 reference to a brave muse honoring exploits abroad upon the bridal day were all whistlings in the dark. He may have lost his way, although Ariosto's ability to move beyond more desperate circumstances than those of Books VI and VII argues the contrary. Spenser's temperament and immediate narrative tradition were not the same as Ariosto's; and maybe Ariosto attained superficial *Abschluss*, not deep closure. Of course I am not claiming that Spenser would have finished writing *The Faerie Queene*, even if he had survived into his fifties.

University of Western Ontario

NOTES

1. See my "The Passing of Arthur in Malory, Spenser, and Shakespeare: The Avoidance of Closure," in *The Passing of Arthur: New Essays in Arthurian Tradition*, ed. Christopher Baswell and William Sharpe (New York: Garland, 1988), pp. 173–192. What I now say brings some of this up-to-date.

2. Minimum guides to this chronicle and Malory's use of the same theme: E. D. Kennedy, 'Malory's use of Hardyng's Chronicle,' *Notes & Queries*, N.S. 16 (1969), 167–170; another piece by Kennedy in *Aspects of Malory*, ed. T. Takamiya and D. S. Brewer (London: Boydell and Brewer, 1981), pp. 42–48; R. H. Wilson in *Notes & Queries*, N.S. 17 (1970), 208–210; L. D. Benson, *Malory's Morte Darthur*, (Cambridge, Mass.: Harvard University Press, 1976), pp. 92–108. The late version of Hardyng (the only one claiming that Arthur conquered Rome) was printed by Grafton in 1543. Spenser used this. It is likely that Malory used this version in manuscript, but he may have been affected by other traditions: see John Withrington, "King Arthur as Emperor," *Notes & Queries*, N.S. 35 (1988), 13–15. For their help my thanks to Withrington, to James Simpson (who is editing the longer version of Hardyng), and particularly to Felicity Riddy, who is editing the Arthurian sections in versions of Hardyng, and whose paper "John Hardyng in Search of

the Grail" is enlightening. See also *Caxton's Malory: A New Edition of Sir Thomas Malory's Le Morte Darthur*, ed. James W. Spisak (Berkeley: University of California Press, 1983) (introduction in Vol. II). The editions (1557, 1578) of Malory in Spenser's lifetime contain Caxton's original material in Book V. In 1550 a brief passage in John Coke, *Debate Between the Heralds of England and France*, follows Hardyng verbally on Arthur's conquest and coronation, and other matters. The *Miroir des histoires* (before 1400) of Jehan d'Outremeuse contains the earliest description of Arthur's conquest that I know of. This appears not to relate to either Hardyng or Malory. In his interesting *Spenser's 'Fierce Warres and Faithfull Loves'* . . . (Totawa, N. J.: Barnes and Noble, 1983), Michael Leslie seems to me to be perpetuating a false idea when he says (p. 187) that in Tudor times Arthur was thought not only to have become emperor but also to have defeated the Saracens. I am unaware of an English tradition that Arthur did the latter. In the version of Malory in the Winchester Manuscript, Arthur considers, but rejects, the possibility of a crusade after he has conquered Rome. The only tradition I find for Arthur's having expelled Saracens from England is a single statement in William Lambard's *APX-AIONOMIA* (1568) that in accordance with a certain law Arthur drove out "predictus Saracenos, & inimicos" from the kingdom (Ff. 137v–138). But "Saracenos" here almost surely means no more than outsiders and unbelievers in general: the "predictus" takes us back to the article FOLCMOTE 1, where the law is intended "ad defendendum regnum contra alienigenas et contra inimicos." Thanks to Anne Prescott and Richard R. Green for help with various related matters.

3. Carrie Harper documents Spenser's use of Hardyng. Her comments are spread through the Variorum notes to Briton Moniments and Merlin's prophecy. Her points are often doubtful, but one or two are sure. Spenser's use of Malory is most obvious in the matter of Pelleas and Lamoracke in VI.xii.39. It is generally agreed to be widespread. Walther's book (see below) not surprisingly overstates the case.

4. *Cf. Epithalamion*, 315–318: "Now welcome night . . . / That long daies labour doest at last defray, / And all my cares, which cruell loue collected, / Hast sumd in one, and cancelled for aye."

5. I had believed myself to be the first to claim that Spenser drew on Malory here. In fact the datum appears in a Heidelberg dissertation of *ca.* 1896–7: Marie Walther, *Malory's Einfluss auf Spenser's Faerie Queene* (Eisleben: Kloppel, n.d.), p. 16. In this catalogue of possible influences she devotes three lines to this one. No editor of *The Faerie Queene* has noticed the point.

6. Editors did not put the two sets of matching facts together because, probably, they stopped with Harper's otherwise trustworthy 1910 survey of Spenser's chronicle history. Harper covered Hardyng's chronicle but not Malory.

7. That is why I think Spenser's Arthur would have to reach Rome, as in Hardyng and Malory, not simply defeat Lucius in France and go home as in the previous sources for the Rome episode. Failure to carry the campaign through is not a thing to ascribe to an allegorically represented patron; and Spenser gives other British kings temporary victories over the Romans without praising them for having defrayed the former reckoning.

8. As C. B. Hieatt points out, "Saracen" is a familiar medieval epithet for a pagan Saxon. *Cf.* Jehan Bodel's *Chanson des Saxons*.

THOMAS P. ROCHE, JR.

A Response to A. Kent Hieatt

[The following piece was presented at the International Congress on Medieval Studies, Kalamazoo, Michigan in May, 1988 as a response to a twenty minute paper (since revised) read by A. Kent Hieatt derived from his already published article on the subject, referred to in his footnote 1. My comments remain what they were at Kalamazoo, which should go far to justify the tone of banter that occasionally surfaces in what I consider a serious reply. Any additions to that original presentation are enclosed in brackets.]

How like Kent Hieatt to invent (in the Renaissance sense of that word) something wonderful and then to beat us all over the head for not having invented it ourselves! I find myself in total agreement with his paper as presented except for the fact that what Hieatt suggests is not what Spenser did with his poem as we have it today. That is, of course, a big proviso, but I would rather credit Hieatt's brilliant reconstruction on the basis of that one line in 11.10.49, "Till *Arthur* all that reckoning defrayd," which we all have read, and not read, for all these years, and think about the implications of that reading before going on to suggest reasons that Spenser did not, and could not, take the Hieatt route. I say this in clear recognition of the fact that Jesus agrees with Hieatt's suggestion. I refer, of course, to the Jesus of Milton's *Paradise Regained*, Book 1, lines 211–220:

I went into the Temple, there to hear
The Teachers of our Law, and to propose
What might improve my knowledge of their own;
And was admir'd by all; yet this not all
To which my Spirit aspir'd; victorious deeds
Flam'd in my heart, heroic acts; one while
To rescue *Israel* from the *Roman* yoke,
Then to subdue and quell o'er all the earth
Brute violence and proud Tyrannic pow'r
Till truth were freed and equity restor'd. . . .

343

Rescuing Israel from the Roman yoke is precisely what Hieatt is suggesting that Spenser wanted to do, and apparently Milton agreed that this was the task that Jesus saw in Book I, but which Milton would not let him do.

Hieatt must be given credit for this invention because in point of fact Malory in Book V does not make much of Arthur as Emperor of Rome, nor could he because the defeat of Rome as an international Antichrist could not occur [fully] until the Reformation. Arthur's triumph in Malory is treated merely as a by-product of his defeat of Lucius and does not portend any of the apocalyptic Protestant triumph over Roman Catholicism that Hieatt suggests. In fact, Hieatt's reading is a massive collusion with Spenser's text alone. Spenser probably did get the hint from Hardyng and Malory, but Hieatt is much closer to the truth when he cites the conquest of Jerusalem in Tasso's *Gerusalemme liberata* as a possible analogue to Spenser's intention. Spenser's elaborate reworking of Books XIV–XVI of that poem as the Bower of Bliss shows beyond any doubt that he knew Tasso's poem almost immediately after its publication in 1581. If Spenser continued through the last four books of [Tasso's] poem, which I have no doubt he did, he would have seen that the recovery of Jerusalem by Godfrey and his crusaders was not only the triumphant conclusion of Tasso's epic but also the end to which all Christians might aspire. That is, [Spenser] would have read Tasso allegorically: one thing (the earthly Jerusalem) standing for another thing (the heavenly Jerusalem) expressed through the dark but enlightening medium of words. The great power to be defeated in this world was the Antichrist represented by the Egyptian and Saracen forces for Tasso and by Roman Catholicism for Spenser, Roman Catholicism with all its political power spread in a circle round the saints of Spenser's reformed church: Scotland, with its deposed papistical queen, Mary; the Low Countries dominated by the Catholic military power of Spain; France running hot and cold between Catholicism and Protestantism; Spain itself dominating the Southern scene; and finally Ireland to the West, embattled and fretful as we find it even today. As Hieatt suggests, the conquest of Rome would be the proper triumph for Arthur.

Such a conquest makes sense of what most of us think Spenser had in mind when he began his "overgoing" of Ariosto. The *Orlando furioso* is a dynastic romance, like the *Aeneid*, in that its poetic subject is a story about the founding fathers or mothers of the ruling dynasty. Arthur's eventual marriage to Gloriana was to figure not only the union of all virtues—magnificence—with its proper reward—glory, but also the historical union of Elizabeth with the most worthy Protestant prince, and most of us still think that Spenser undoubtedly had the Earl of Leicester in mind. Leicester [himself] certainly had such intentions early in the 1580s, and if it is true that the young author of *The Shepheardes Calender* was employed in the household of Leicester as alleged [see article by S. K. Heninger, Jr. earlier in this volume], then Spenser with his epic ambitions would have been johnny-poet-on-the-spot with a poem already underway to celebrate the royal union and to challenge Ariosto. I think that Spenser wanted Leicester to be the historical identity of his fictive Arthur, but that possibility was denied him not only because the union did not take place but also because Leicester died in 1588. I further think that the death of his epic ambitions for Leicester is recorded as a muted elegy in that stanza cited by Hieatt, Book 1, Canto 7, stanza 36 [omitted in this recension]. Spenser has been describing the appearance of Arthur on his very late entry into the poem:

Ne let it seeme that credence this exceedes,
For he that made the same [Arthur's armor] was knowne right
    well
To have done much more admirable deedes.
It Merlin was, which whylome did excell
All liuing wightes in might of magicke spell:
Both shield and sword, and armour all he wrought
For this young prince, when first to armes he wrought
But when he dyde, the Faery Queene it brought
To Faerie Lond, where yet it may be seene, if sought.

                                                        (Italics mine)

Contrary to Hieatt, I think that the "it" brought to Faeryland is the whole armor of Arthur, not just the shield, but whatever is brought to Faeryland, those last two lines are most peculiar. I know of no other epic poet who almost gives the address of the museum where the armor of his hero is on display, "*if sought.*" I would like to suggest that this stanza is Spenser's epitaph for Leicester and the demise of his early plans for this poem. There would be no marriage with Gloriana. There would be no conquest of Rome.

It seems to me that Hieatt's brilliant suggestion dies with Leicester in 1588 two years before the first instalment of the poem appeared. I do not see that the conquest of Rome, as appealing as I find it, could have continued after Spenser had planned, written, and published Books IV–VI. Essex as Arthurian hero is not possible after Essex, like Leicester, aborted Spenser's dynastic plans by marrying the widow of Sir Philip Sidney, Essex himself the brother of Sidney's Stella. That is too cosy even for English literature.

I tend to agree with Northrop Frye that the scheme of private virtues to be followed by political virtues gets conflated into the six books we now have, the first three dealing with private virtues, the second three dealing with political virtues, since Holiness, Temperance, and Chastity can refer only to individuals, while Friendship, Justice, and Courtesy require at least one other participant to be operative at all. It seems to me also that the *political* peak of the poem is reached in the last four cantos of Book V, that book so much maligned by the majority of modern critics, whether seduced by C. S. Lewis's innuendo about the poisoning of Spenser's imagination through his prejudice against the Irish or because of our own inability to deal with the concept of justice without psychological adjudication. Those last four cantos are Christian prophecy, vision as strong as that on Mount Acidale. Neither really happened; neither really prevailed except in the imagination fired by the words of Spenser's poem. In those last four cantos of Book V Spenser rewrites the history of his own times as if he were writing a happy ending to the Vietnam War, not out of stupidity, not out of ignorance. It was his vision of what might have been. The ending of Book V rewrites history just as the ending of Book VI deconstructs romance. It is all Camelot for a while, as our former First Lady reminded us long ago. We tend to forget in our modern arrogance toward past history that Grantorto is something more than a glowering romance name out of the Italian, that for Spenser the triumph of Grantorto was an historical probability that might determine the success of his poem and of civilization. The triumph of Protestant propaganda during the Renaissance (who knows not that the Protestants were right?) has made us immune to the horrendous threat that Rome represented to the sixteenth-century protestants.

Most epics get written after political crises. The *Aeneid* is finished after the death of Marcellus; *Paradise Lost* only after the collapse of the Commonwealth. Modern historical events get very short shrift in the epic, and therefore Spenser's efforts to redo contemporary history should be looked on as a massive breakthrough of the imagination in the writing of epics. By the time Spenser published the second instalment of *The Faerie Queene* he knew that Elizabeth had written the end to the Tudor dynasty and that he had better seek closure outside the dynastic marriage in the manner of Ariosto. His choice was to hoist himself on the petard of Mutabilitie as the universalizing pulley of his epic venture.

My suggestions about the closure of the poem, like Hieatt's, are part of the archeology of Spenser's *Faerie Queene*. I agree with Kent that Spenser may have had Arthur's conquest of Rome in mind at some earlier stage of the poem's development. I can even imagine a marvellous scene where Grantorto, Emperor of Rome, receives into his sumptuous court the re-vived Duessa (after her muted death in Book V), the evil genius of the occasion being none other than our old friend Archima-go, and surely in a dark but lush bower adjacent would be the undead Sansjoy consorting with Ate, got up for the occasion. But none of this happened, and beyond this phantasy all is Porlockery, and we all know what that means especially at Kalamazoo.*

---

*Porlockery, a reference to the Porlock Society, the annual meeting of which is held on the occasion of the Medieval Conference at Kalamazoo, Michigan. Its primary function is the celebration of unfinished works, its patron saint is Coleridge's "visitor from Porlock," its sporadically appearing journal is *Cogito Interruptus*.

Index

Contents of Previous Volumes

VOLUME V (1984)

VOLUME VI (1985)

VOLUME VII (1987)